The Legal Base for Universities in Developing Countries

THE LEGAL
BASE FOR
UNIVERSITIES
IN DEVELOPING
COUNTRIES

----

by H. W. Hannah and Robert R. Caughey

University of Illinois Press
URBANA • CHICAGO • LONDON 1967

ACKNOWLEDGMENTS

The advisory group which gave the author wise counsel and helpful guidance in the production of *Resource Book for Rural Universities in the Developing Countries* repeated its role in the production of this book. Members of the group were Dr. Arthur D. Weber, Vice President Emeritus and Director, Office of International Activities, Kansas State University; Jack D. Gray, Director, Office of International Programs, Texas A. & M.; Dr. Kenneth L. Turk, Director, International Agricultural Development, Cornell University; Dr. A. H. Moseman, Director, Agricultural Sciences, Rockefeller Foundation; Dr. H. Brooks James, Dean of Agriculture and Life Sciences, North Carolina State University; and Raleigh Fosbrink, Assistant to the Dean of Agriculture, Purdue University. During the time the group functioned, Dr. A. H. Moseman left the Rockefeller Foundation to become Assistant Administrator for Technical Cooperation and Research in the Agency for International Development (AID).

In the Agency for International Development, Dr. Frank Parker, Deputy Director, Rural and Community Development Service, Office of Technical Cooperation and Research, again provided effective liaison, guidance, and ideas.

The work done by Dr. O. N. Liming, Chief of the Agricultural University Division for the AID mission in India, and Dr. Ralph Cummings, Field Director for the Rockefeller Foundation in India, in preparing drafts of acts and statutes and writing about policy questions in aid of the new Indian agricultural universities has been extremely helpful. Dr. Liming read the manuscript for this book in detail and made countless improvements.

The International Rural Development Office of the Association of State Universities and Land-Grant Colleges again made its facilities available for meetings of the advisory group.

The AID missions, contract team personnel, and administrative officers and staff of the countries and institutions visited by Robert Caughey were helpful and friendly.

The University of Illinois, through its Office of International Programs, University Press, Campus Office of International Projects, Legal Counsel, and Colleges of Agriculture and Veterinary Medicine, gave the writers valuable assistance.

PREFACE

Though the writers are aware that good laws alone cannot make a good university, they know that bad laws or the absence of needed authority can frustrate good men, denying them avenues they would like to take and frequently dissipating their energies on matters which seem highly important at the moment, but which could have been settled in the beginning if the right words had found their way into the law. Many important policies and procedures rest on a legal base. It is important that this base be complete, understandable, and available. State legislation creating the American land-grant universities varies greatly. Yet, certain fundamentals appear in all these varied laws. The writers have tried to find and discuss the fundamentals which should be established by legislation or university statutes for any university together with those features of the law which help commit an institution to the development aims of its country, to production of the right kind of educated manpower for agriculture, and to the solution of the problems of farmers.

All countries desire good universities. Certainly there is room for some difference of opinion about what makes them so. What a university does is more important than how it is structured. But there is a relationship and one of the prime purposes of this book is to be as forward-looking as possible and suggest legal structures which will encourage service, growth, and innovation. Also, good laws can preserve the integrity of a university and protect it so that it can play its role in society despite the political and religious pressures which sometimes develop.

In a sense this book is a sequel to *Resource Book for Rural Universities in the Developing Countries,* so much so in fact that it might be considered as Part II of that book. Like the *Resource Book,* it grew out of the senior author's experience under an AID contract in India and out of shorter experiences in Nigeria and Pakistan. It presents an analysis and discussion of university acts and statutes from many institutions in different parts of the world. (For a listing of these institutions, see Appendix III.) Its purpose is to disclose what things are included in acts and statutes and to express some views on what should be covered and on what seems best, together with alternative suggestions where appropriate. The authors hope to show how the legal framework of an institution relates to its educational purpose and the achievement of its goals. Often there is no sharp line of demarcation between a discussion of principles and a discussion of their application through legal provisions. If a reader finds himself questioning principles which the writers are attempting to incorporate into a university legal base, one recourse would be to the *Resource Book* for a discussion of why the principle is considered desirable.

With some exceptions, each section is an item about which there either is, or in the opinion of the writers ought to be, legislation or university statutes. Illustrative and statutory provisions are discussed and recommendations are made. It was not felt necessary to burden the text with citations, but in all cases there is identification of the act from which a quotation or example is drawn, and Appendix III is a list of institutions from which acts and statutes were procured. Most of the American court cases from which quotations or illustrative examples were taken are reviewed in the several books of M. M. Chambers, references to which are in Appendix II. The writers make no apology for discussing in some detail items which may seem relatively unimportant. An unfortunate mistake in framing a seemingly innocuous definition may be the basis for a celebrated cause in the later life of the university.

The last chapter pulls together the thinking of the authors in a pattern—not a model—for a university act and university statutes.

During the preparation of this book, Robert Caughey visited universities in Asia, Africa, and South America, discussing with both administrative and academic staff the functioning of their institutions under their laws and collecting university acts and statutes for study and analysis. Prior to the writing of this book H. W. Hannah spent almost three years in India helping with the organization and establishment of the Uttar Pradesh Agricultural University. Later he visited universities in fourteen countries in connection with the *Resource Book for Rural Universities in the Developing Countries*.

The writers believe this book, like the *Resource Book*, will be especially helpful to developing-country government officials, legislators, members of university governing bodies, administrative and academic staff, American contracting universities, and the members of contract teams. It should be particularly useful to those who have a responsibility for considering and drafting legislation and university statutes or amending existing legislation and university statutes. Established institutions as well as those in the process of establishment were in the minds of the writers.

CONTENTS

Chapter–3

The Corporate Nature of the University—Purpose, Powers, Functions 26

Chapter–4

The Governing Body—Selection and Structure 56

Chapter–5
The Governing Body—Powers and Duties   75

Chapter–6
The Chief Administrative Officer—Appointment, Tenure, and Conditions of Service   100

Chapter–7
The Chief Administrative Officer—Powers and Duties   109

Chapter–8

Budget and Finance   126

Chapter–9

Officers and Their Functions 144

Chapter–10

Educational Units—Creation, Structure, and Functions   168

Chapter–11

Academic Organization   181

Chapter–15

Staff—Appointment and Conditions of Service   239

Chapter–16

Nonacademic Staff—Employment and Conditions of Service   295

Chapter–17

Student Affairs   **306**

Chapter–18

A Pattern for a University Act and University Statutes   **344**

Appendixes 414

Index 451

CHAPTER – 1

The Scope and Purpose
of Legislation, Statutes,
and Regulations

1.1. INTRODUCTION

How can a university be assured essential freedom from unnecessary governmental interference and partisan political pressure? What procedures can be established to obtain and retain the best possible man as chief administrative officer? With what authority should he be clothed? What procedures can be established to assure selection of staff on a merit basis and to make it possible to procure the very best people for all posts in the university? What is the meaning of tenure and how can it be acquired? What are the grounds for dismissing a staff member? What are the procedures for discharging a staff member? What is his right to be notified? To appear and defend? To appeal? How can academic freedom be protected? How can staff participation in decision-making be assured? Who is qualified to enter the university as a student? What are the rights of students to organize? What procedures shall be established for dismissing students? What shall be the purpose of the university? In what programs shall it engage? Will public service be a responsibility and an objective? Will there be an integration of teaching, research, and extension? Will the university be unhampered in its management of finances and the establishment of an internal budget? Will the university have necessary freedom to acquire and dispose of property for the achievement of its objectives? If farm land is to be transferred to the university, will it have a free hand in the management of the farm, and what accountability will there be for income?

The answers to some of these questions depend wholly upon the act creating the university; the answers to others are influenced by legislative provisions. The importance of an act creating a university is generally underestimated. It may set a pattern which comes to be accepted—but which could have been a better pattern if the law had been better. Future development can be unwittingly stifled by laws which seemed right at their inception. Over time, institutions develop personalities, and come to be known for their major successes and failures. Universities gain reputations for many things; the composite picture or image is then viewed by those who would be served by the university. To an important degree the kind of students a university attracts depends on its personality and reputation. It can be a good university if it attracts good students, but it will not attract good students unless it is a good university!

University acts and statutes (the term used in this book for governing board "legislation") each serve a distinctive purpose. The legislative act should establish the university as a complete corporate entity with comparative freedom from government, should specify its powers and major functions and purpose, should provide for its principal officers and governing body, give it such legislative protection as seems required, and provide a basic administrative framework within which academic flexibility can be achieved. It is a mistake if the legislative act does not provide these essentials, but it is, perhaps, even a greater mistake if the act becomes too detailed and covers those things which should be left to the discretion of the board of control, the administration of the university, and the academic staff. Legislative detail can be stifling—particularly when it is wrong!

University statutes should be used to implement the application of the act by providing more of the detail necessary to give stability, establish understandable lines of communication and authority, protect academic freedom, define the roles of staff and students, and deal with a variety of internal matters on which there must be firm decisions. Like university acts, statutes may be either too detailed or too skimpy. Statutes tend to grow and change with the institution and should be viewed as working guides which are not irrevocable but which can be changed after reasonable deliberation and, depending on the subject matter, with the involvement of all appropriate individuals and bodies.

Three questions should always be asked in the consideration of university acts and statutes: Exactly what policy or principle do we wish to formulate? What is the best way to state it? At what level does it belong—legislative, board, academic council, or administrative?

Regulations, bylaws, or rules are completely internal and may be formulated and promulgated by any university body or authority. A code of student conduct, hostel rules, bylaws of the university senate, a business office manual, procedural rules of the board— these are examples. There must be general university regulations to augment certain provisions in the university statutes. These would be approved by the chief administrative officer and the board of control.

The value of any code of regulations, university act, or university statutes is seriously impaired if it is not published and made available to those concerned. University statutes and general university regulations should be published and made available to all staff members. There should be a plentiful supply of university acts for university administrative officers, board members, or anyone else upon request. Codes applying to students should be available to students.

1.2. GETTING LEGISLATION DRAFTED AND ADOPTED

Who should draft a university act? The answer depends on what we mean by "draft." If we refer only to the selection of the legal phraseology and the arrangement of parts and sections, then it is a lawyer's job. But drafting implies more than this. It includes agreement on ideas and their concise expression as well as good legal mechanics. The major provisions should be considered at length by those charged with establishing the university. Drafts of other university acts and of any "models" available should be studied for usable ideas and language. A record of such deliberations should be made and passed on to a small drafting committee of three or four persons. This committee should include a lawyer experienced in drafting legislation; the chairman or a designated member of the provisional body or other group fostering the university; an experienced officer from the Ministry of Agriculture, Finance, or Education; and, if available, an experienced member of a university contract team. Expert assistance may be requested also through the USAID mission office or from other sources. The draft produced by such a committee should be reviewed by the provisional body and by the solicitor (or the equivalent of this government officer) or someone in his office. If there is a legislative reference or drafting service, the draft should also be submitted to it for study. The chairman of the provisional body or fostering group should keep abreast of progress in drafting so that he can push for action when necessary; otherwise, the task may receive sporadic attention and consume too much time.

Drafting legislation is one thing; securing its adoption without serious compromise is another. In one country, inability to get legislation adopted led to the creation of a separate institute by administrative order. This may in some cases be a necessary and helpful step, but it does not provide for the stability contemplated when the institution is created by a legislature. But legislatures should also be interested in the view which government agencies take of a proposal. Certainly a desirable forerunner to presentation to the legislature of the draft for creation of the university would be agreement among the state agencies concerned that the legislation is sound and the institution is needed. Membership of state agency personnel on various committees essential to bring the university to life would, in part, provide for this. Likewise, involvement of state agencies in the drafting process would bring them into communication with those who will eventually need to urge the legislature to pass the law.

Legislators will raise many questions, some stemming from their own vested interest, but all requiring answers. They will inquire about location, cost, need, and duplication, and will ask why this institution needs more autonomy or freedom from government than existing government institutions. They will ask about qualifications for admission, numbers to be admitted, the cost of admission, tuition, fees, acceptance of students from other states or foreign countries, requirements for graduation, how standards are to be maintained, the qualifications of graduates for government service or for employment in private industry, how the university proposes to serve agriculture and farmers, and how much assistance it can expect from a central government or foreign sources. These are some of the questions; there will be many others. The legislators will want to know if the functions of government agricultural research and extension agencies are to be transferred to the university and if so, to what extent and when.

It is wise if as many of these questions as possible can be contemplated in advance and good answers formulated. Charts and visual aids are extremely helpful. It is particularly helpful if charts can be developed which show what the institution might mean financially to agriculture over a period of years. If, for example, it can be shown that a given number of extension agents will be trained over a period of, say, ten years, that these agents through their efforts will be able to increase production of a major crop by a given number of bushels per acre, that this will more than pay for the cost of establishing and supporting the institution—then a strong case can be made. Figures of this kind can be very forceful in convincing the legislative body that an idea is good. The legislative committee considering the "bill" may ask for particular people to appear before it. If they know a foreign expert is involved, they may want to ask him about certain features of the proposed law, particularly those which are different from university acts with which they are familiar. It is extremely helpful if individual members of such a committee and other influential members of the legislature can be brought into communication long before formal hearings are held so that explanations can be made in a more thorough and deliberate manner. Though a foreign expert may be involved in drafting the legislation and in making explanations, it would be unfortunate if this were to create the impression that the legislation is his idea and does not have the wholehearted understanding and support of the drafting committee and others who have been involved. It can generally be expected that legislators from the district in which it is proposed to establish the university will be strong supporters. In one Indian state, location was purposely omitted from the proposed act in the hope that all legislators would remain hopeful and hence favorably inclined.

1.3. GENERAL ENABLING ACTS

Some countries have constitutional provisions about universities. At the time of adoption in 1950, the constitution of India made three universities national universities and provided that parliament could include other universities in the same category. Provision is also made in the Indian constitution for the coordination and determination of standards in institutions for higher education or research. In some cases, as at the University of California, constitutions provide the charter for universities. Many constitutions express a national policy about education, sometimes in very general terms, sometimes with specific reference to higher education and the role of universities. Land or facilities may be granted, the institution may be given a name, immunity from taxation may be provided, the general purpose may be prescribed—these are some of the things which constitutions may contain. In the Latin-American countries, national constitutions contain most of the provisions which in other countries are left to the legislature. Most public universities, however, have been established by legislation and even where there are constitutional provisions, legislation is still essential to provide the specifics which cannot be contained in a constitution. It is probably safe to say that in no country are there constitutional provisions which would prevent an autonomous political unit within the country, state, or region from establishing universities of such character as their legislative bodies deem essential.

A more important question has to do with the establishment of universities under a general enabling act. Many people around the world and indeed in the United States assume that the land-grant universities were all established by the same law and that they are all uniform. It is true that a federal law, the Morrill Act, gave them their impetus, but they are still the creatures of their particular state legislatures. The Morrill Act stated that recipient institutions should achieve certain purposes in the field of higher education and that the federal government would provide generously for their establishment through the donation of land. The Morrill Act provided that these grants of land should go "to the endowment, support, and maintenance of at least one college where the leading object shall be, without excluding other scientific and classical studies and including military tactics, to teach such branches of learning as are related to agriculture and the mechanic arts, in such manner as the legislatures of the States may respectively prescribe, in order to promote the liberal and practical education of the industrial classes in the several pursuits and professions in life." [1] This was sufficient inducement to cause state legislatures to create colleges and to include among their objectives those expressed in the federal law.

Some governments have provided enabling legislation which goes much further in establishing the form and functioning of universities. There are areas in which provision for this kind of uniformity might be desirable—construction and finance, for example, or assurance of autonomy. Even the corporate framework for an institution might be spelled out by a common act, as in the National Universities Act of Peru. But the advantages of uniformity are outweighed by the need for a legislative expression of purpose and method pertinent to the particular university—this to be followed by participa-

---

[1] Act. of July 2, 1862; 12 Stat. 504 (7 USCA § 304).

tion of the faculty and staff in developing the institution under legislative provisions which preserve to them the freedom to implement educational policies and programs. It can be argued, too, that establishing a university is a distinctive endeavor which should be considered on its own merits and that a general enabling act might encourage the spawning of weak institutions. As a matter of fact, this is said to be happening in some South American countries. A general enabling act implies some surveillance, which may entail greater governmental control than is desirable on the one hand or which may, on the other, leave a gap in the essential legal framework for an institution.

A good university is an expensive endeavor. It should be given serious thought and should be established only when there is a clear need and when adequate consideration has been given. Legislation making funds or other resources available to universities providing they meet certain standards and are engaged in programs which the legislature encourages is another matter. The land-grant universities engage in a major extension activity and carry out a large number of research projects as a result of funds made available by both the federal and state governments, but particularly by the federal government and its agencies. But this support does not impose a pattern on an institution or cause it to sacrifice any policies it deems important.

A grants commission or a university education commission such as the Nigerian government has established can exert beneficial influence on universities by establishing standards for grants and support and by being a medium through which information about successful endeavors or organization in one institution can be carried to another. National planning for higher education and national support for research, extension, and other activities within universities are extremely important. But this is quite different from having a national uniform act under which universities can organize.

1.4. THE POLICY POTENTIAL OF A UNIVERSITY LEGISLATIVE ACT

One would hope that the most enduring feature of any university is its search for truth at all costs. But universities can exhibit this feature and still vary greatly in the services they render and the roles they play in the society of their times. It has been said that a

frequent recurrence to the principles of liberty is necessary to preserve democracy. Perhaps it can as truly be said that a frequent recurrence to the objectives for which a university was established is
essential to the preservation of its usefulness. In *Colleges for Our
Land and Time*,[2] Edward Danforth Eddy, Jr. quotes a passage from
the Northwest Ordinance which states that "religion, morality, and
knowledge being necessary to good government and the happiness
of mankind, schools and the means of education shall be forever
encouraged," and then quotes a remark of Daniel Webster about
this passage, in which he says, "I doubt whether one single law or
any law given, ancient or modern, has produced effects of more
distinct, marked, and lasting character than the Ordinance of 1787."
When a basic university law expresses a purpose and takes the
trouble to define agricultural education, it may have a meaning far
beyond that which is apparent in a cursory reading. The Morrill Act
set the stage for development of the whole American land-grant
university philosophy.

The Uttar Pradesh Agricultural University Act, for example, says
that the university exists "for the development of agriculture" and
"for the benefit of the rural people of Uttar Pradesh." It defines agriculture as meaning basic and applied science, soil and water,
crops and livestock, and the betterment of rural people. In the ab-
stract these statements may appear to be broad generalizations,
but when they are used to measure an activity of the university,
they are suddenly clothed with great meaning. It is important, therefore, that the basic act establishing a university contain a clear statement of objectives and a strong expression of policies to be pursued,
because these specifications may be the means through which a
future administrator of the university can hold the line against those
who would change the purpose of the institution. To cite an example
—much argument can develop over the role an agricultural university should play in research if the act creating the university fails to
make it clear that both fundamental and applied research without
restriction are to be prerogatives of the institution. Otherwise, it
may be argued by government agencies that the institution should
engage only in limited investigation to support its teaching program
and that the main outlay for research in all phases of agriculture
should go to the old, established government research agencies.

----
[2] Eddy, *Colleges for Our Land and Time* (New York: Harper and Brothers,
1957), p. 21.

1.5. THE GENERAL PROVISIONS OF A UNIVERSITY ACT

A division of the subject matter which seems to be common to many university acts, with variations, follows:

Part 1   Preliminary
Part 2   The University
Part 3   Officers of the University
Part 4   Authorities of the University
Part 5   University Funds
Part 6   Research and Extension
Part 7   Appointment of Teachers and Staff Members
Part 8   Statutes and Regulations
Part 9   Annual Reports and Accounts
Part 10 Miscellaneous or supplemental provisions

We believe a more complete division should include parts dealing with staff and students rather than "burying" the provisions concerning them in other parts of the act.

Without going into detail—which is the purpose of the remainder of this book—we can state that a typical university act:

Expresses a short title for the legislative act.

States the name and sometimes the location of the university.

Expresses the purpose and objects of the university and sometimes mentions subject matter to be included in its program—such as "agriculture, animal husbandry, and allied sciences."

Indicates the geographical area to be served.

Fixes the date on which the law becomes effective.

Defines terms (this is important—and helpful).

Establishes and incorporates the institution and states what officers and bodies constitute the corporation.

Expresses the scope of its borrowing power and its power to hold and deal with property.

Expresses guarantees about the right to admission, including any reservation which may be made regarding seats for women or special classes of people.

States how fees and tuition are to be determined and charged.

Expresses generally the powers of the university.

Gives state government the right to inspect facilities and the program of the institution and to require correction of shortcomings.

Contains special provisions which may apply only at the outset—such as how the first chief administrative officer shall be selected and how the first board shall be designated.

Expresses conditions for the transfer of other colleges or the functions of other government agencies to the university.

States who the officers of the university shall be, how they shall be selected, and what their functions are.

Defines and prescribes the composition and functions of university academic bodies.

Establishes an appointment procedure and the basic conditions of service for staff.

Specifies funds to be maintained by the university and general rules regarding financial management and accounting.

States how statutes and regulations are to be adopted and the subject matter which they shall cover.

Contains provisions about establishment of a retirement, pension, or provident fund.

Covers miscellaneous items such as filling vacancies, settling disputes, delegation of power, temporary appointments, and removal of difficulties.

The legislative act should be clearly divided into chapters, articles, or parts. These should be divided into sections with a complete table of contents included at the beginning of the act. Sections are easy to locate in the act if spacing is allowed between them and the title of the section is in the margin. A consistent and logical numbering system should be used.

Special attention should be given to those provisions necessary only at the outset so that anything of a temporary nature will appear in proper context and will cease to be operative after the initial conditions are fulfilled. Such provisions normally come at the end of the act. Insofar as possible, the legislation should allow for the kinds of activities in which the university might wish to participate over a long period of time and should insure its right to do so. For example, these kinds of questions may arise: Can other institutions be affiliated with this university? Can the university associate with other institutions and contribute funds for the maintenance of an association of colleges and universities? Can the university become a member of interregional or intercountry cooperative agreements which involve the expenditure of its funds and the use of its personnel? Are there any limitations within the university on cross-disciplinary research, teaching, and other endeavors? What is the university's position with respect to requesting and using foreign assistance, advisors, and expatriate personnel, not to mention the use of outside funds and grants?

If existing institutions are abolished or are absorbed by the new institution, provision must be made for the staff and even for the authorities of such institutions. There is a necessity also for preserving contractual rights and obligations other than those of faculty and staff. The act should be clear about these matters so that unnecessary fears and apprehensions will not arise and the transition can be as smooth as possible.

1.6. UNIVERSITY STATUTES

University statutes (which may be known as "ordinances" or by other names) deal with the internal functioning of the institution; hence, large numbers of people have an interest in them and should be permitted in appropriate ways to participate in their formulation or amendment. The process through which statutes are made and changed should be clearly outlined in the university act. Details regarding procedure are discussed in Chapter 5. They are so important yet are so frequently neglected that a special plea for their wise development and publication is made at this point.

The university act should contain a clear provision about the process for formulating and adopting statutes. Subject matter with which the statutes are to deal should be specified in the act with a general authority to develop other statutes as needed. The role which different university bodies are expected to play should be prescribed. When statutes emanate from the board of control, there should be provision for review by appropriate faculty bodies and staff members before they become final. When educational and academic matters are involved, statutes should originate within the principal academic body of the university. In the formulation of statutes, appropriate hearings should be held and time permitted for adequate consideration. The statutes should be printed and made available to staff members. Changes and amendments should be circulated to the staff and made available on request.

1.7. UNIVERSITY REGULATIONS

The purpose of regulations is to provide the ground rules, so to speak, for the activities of various bodies and groups within the university. The board will make its own procedural rules; the business office may develop a procedure manual; the physical plant department may develop a manual for its functioning and operation and the care and maintenance of its equipment; the dean of students may, through proper channels, formulate a code on student affairs and activities and even on student behavior within the university and hostels; the hostels themselves may develop rules regarding the use of rooms and facilities. The registrar's office, the bursar's office, the librarian, in fact all officers of the university in whom are focused responsibilities for rendering service of any kind will find it essential to develop some rules and regulations for a twofold purpose: (1) to make their services more available and usable by letting recipients know what, when, and how; (2) to protect their property by establishing guides for its use and their own time by ruling on the demands which are to be made. The standardization of procedures can save time in many ways.

By definition we have let "regulation" mean something that takes up where the university statutes stop. If regulations had to be approved by the board of control, they would simply amount to more detailed statutes and would not be as useful as they should be. However, certain regulations augment the university statutes and should be published with the statutes so that they are available to all who are interested. Many rules and regulations are of such general interest and importance that the chief administrative officer of the university will wish to approve them; for others of less consequence he may simply rely on his administrative officers to develop sound practices and the regulations which insure them. The board of control, acting as a university body, is privileged to develop its own regulations on any subject for which it has responsibility. This would include the making of rules and regulations for the furtherance of university statutes. This would not deprive the academic staff of privileges and prerogatives it should have, because the staff would still be involved in appropriate ways in the formulation of the statutes for consideration by the board. Presumably, rules and regulations could not change any rights or duties or privileges established by statute but would simply elaborate on them and further establish procedures to be followed. There would be no point in making all regulations of the university generally available because many of them would be of no interest to people outside certain channels of administration. A business office procedure manual, for example, would not be of general interest to the faculty. On the other hand, certain subjects such as a code on student affairs or activities would be of general interest and should be published for the benefit of staff and students.

Regulations will not be analyzed and discussed in this book. The basic university act and the statutes adopted under it provide the fundamental legal base for the university, and this is what the authors propose to discuss. But the impression should not be gained that regulations are not important. There may be times when enforcement of a shortsighted regulation can do more harm to the institution than any other one thing. A frequent complaint of students, for example, is that the university is too conservative and reactionary with respect to the according of certain student rights. This is an issue which is likely to continue into the foreseeable future. Regulations, more than the act and statutes, reflect the philosophy and temper of those currently in charge of the university and can be more readily changed. This is as it should be.

1.8. SOME SHORTCOMINGS OF UNIVERSITY ACTS AND STATUTES

Language, even well-drafted legal language, can never be an infallible purveyor of thought and intent. The poorer the draftsmanship and the more unfortunate the selection of words and language, the less reliability a document has. An examination of many university acts and statutes reveals the following shortcomings:

Illogical arrangement of chapters and sections.

The same subject divided and found in two or more places.

Policies or procedures insufficiently developed in the statutes.

Responsibility and authority not made correlative.

Important subject matter omitted.

Subject matter not indexed or subdivided into logical headings so it is easily found.

Omission of helpful cross-references.

Paragraphs that are too long.

The use of words of doubtful meaning.

Failure to define terms.

Language more legalistic than is necessary.

Too much detail.

Too little detail.

No list of contents.

Omission of dates and essential citations.

Faulty reference to other acts or legislation.

Failure to refer to essential acts or legislation which have a bearing on the university act.

Failure to change such things as words, dates, and numbers throughout an act when an amendment has made this necessary.

Amendments which do not logically mesh with current provisions of the act.

Too many special provisions to take care of all kinds of contingencies and particular situations with the result that the act or statutes are cluttered with provisions which tend to overshadow the real logic and purpose.

Failure to properly identify transitory provisions which are to become ineffective at particular times.

Failure of the legislation to establish essential forward-looking policies regarding such important activities as research, agricultural extension, and public service.

A statement about shortcomings should not be concluded without a reminder that the most carefully drafted act will have defects; something will be omitted, an unfortunate word will creep in, an unnecessary procedure will be required. As experience exposes weaknesses, the act will need amendment. Also, time will bring unforeseen needs, and changes or additions will become necessary. The board and the administration of the university should be prompt in submitting proposed amendments to an appropriate legislative committee so that the functioning of the institution will not be hampered by needless delay in removing legislative obstacles or in providing additional necessary authority.

CHAPTER – 2

Concepts and Functions
Which Depend on a Legal Base

2.1. INTRODUCTION

Universities have personalities. These develop over time and are a product of many forces, influences, and individuals. Though the personalities of institutions change with the men who constitute leadership, it is essential to the preservation of a university's character that certain elements of its personality be established and preserved by law. Without these assurances the institution may change character so frequently that its usefulness will be impaired and it will end up being a weak institutional personality. How centralized should control of the university be? How much control should government continue to exercise? What educational considerations should be left to the individual faculties of the university? Even physical arrangements provided by law can affect the answers to some of these questions. When an institution exists at more than one physical site, its character is immediately changed. This may be good or bad depending on how organizational problems posed by a physical separation are handled. These will be discussed in several places in this book. How strongly will a traditional and rigid university structure be supported by an institution's own graduates and those who have some hand in its destiny? Laws alone cannot change the character of an institution when its history and those who have been associated with it present a well-settled point of view about its purpose and function.

If it is a purpose of government to swing the institution from a position of relative insulation to one of public service, strong laws will be required, plus the right people on the job. In writing about African universities, Sir Eric Ashby points out that to be orthodox is to play for safety. He illustrates his point by saying that dozens of dons would recognize a first class in classics when they see one but that probably none would recognize a first class in Ibo land law. There was a time when pressure from students to participate in university government resulted in better instruction and facilities in South American universities. Now that universities in Latin America have become more responsible, the legal involvement of students in all phases of university government is regarded by many critics as a detriment. Likewise it has been pointed out that election of university officials for short terms might have been useful in getting rid of incompetent personnel at a time when there was a definite lack of dedicated and competent full-time staff members in Latin-American universities, but that this same policy has now become a road block to securing the dedicated and long-duration services needed.

Universities must function in a changing society, and the newer universities being financed by governments around the world are expected to deliver something which their predecessors could adamantly oppose—hence the need for a revamping of their laws and policies, so that values can be preserved, truth can be sought, and national aims can be achieved in the same environment and at the same time. What basic policies are essential to achieve these goals? In the *Resource Book,*[1] the author gave these answers:

In trying to decide what features of a university are essential to success, one must consider its mission. If the mission is that of good teaching, meaningful research, and service, the following seem indispensable:

A corporate board of management with delegated governing powers.
Independence from other institutions.
Adequate and liberal financial support from government.
Internal authority to determine educational policy and program.
Integration of research, teaching, and extension subject matter at the departmental level.
Power to appoint staff through regular administrative channels within the institution, upon approval by the board.
Syllabi and examinations developed within departments, with maximum freedom permitted to individual professors.
A scholarship and self-help program which will permit a maximum number of rural youth to attend the institution.
Extension education to be a major function, with departments involved in responsibility for subject matter.
Acceptance by all concerned of a philosophy of service to agriculture, aided by a system of advisory committees including educational, agricultural, and public leaders.

---

[1] H. W. Hannah, *Resource Book for Rural Universities in the Developing Countries* (Urbana: University of Illinois Press, 1966), p. 34.

The absence of any of these features can easily be so serious as to jeopardize the success of the whole venture. Good laws and university statutes can help in the establishment and preservation of these essential features.

The remaining sections of this chapter present and briefly discuss concepts and functions which can be influenced by a legal base. For the most part these sections are introductions to later chapters in the book where a more complete consideration is given to these subjects and illustrative sections from the laws and statutes of many institutions are discussed.

2.2. THE LEGAL NATURE OF THE UNIVERSITY

Like other corporations, the university is a legal person—a public legal person to be certain, but nevertheless, one clothed with the ability to do many things of both a legal and a nonlegal nature as though it were a sole actor. In "The Rights and Responsibilities of Universities and Their Faculties,"[2] it is said, "The modern university which evolved from the middle ages is a unique type of organization. For many reasons it must differ from a corporation created for the purpose of producing a salable article for profit. Its internal structure, procedures, and discipline are properly quite different from those of business organizations. It is not so closely integrated and there is no such hierarchy of authority as is appropriate to a business concern. The permanent members of a university are essentially equals."

The degree of independence or autonomy possessed by the university depends in part on the law creating it. If it is created by a state or regional legislature, then the central government will exercise no authority over it except to the extent that grants from the central government condition its activities or except for any overall constitutional or central legislative provisions which may govern universities generally. If a university is created by central government legislation, then it is the creature of that government and is responsible to it, and its freedom or autonomy will depend on the nature of that legislation.

Many of the universities in Europe and Latin America were established by papal decree. The earliest universities—those at Bologna and Paris, for example—grew out of the scholastic guilds

---

[2] *A Statement by the Association of American Universities* (March, 1953).

of teachers and scholars. Spanish universities were chartered by the king. Oxford's origins stem from the Bible lectures of Robert Pullen. Cambridge had its origins in the teaching of the Canons of the Church of St. Giles. Subsequent laws and their own internal structure have given all these universities a public character. Some universities are established by cities. Presumably they can be as independent and autonomous as those created by regional or central legislative authority. However, there may be general legislation, either federal or state, imposing certain guides or standards on all universities created by cities. Institutions created as private corporations would be subject to any general legislative act enabling them to organize. Enabling legislation might exist either at the provincial or central level or at both levels.

No matter how created, the relative independence or autonomy of an institution does not depend solely on the law. Public opinion, its own internal administration, and personalities in the government are important. A strong Minister of Education or Minister of Finance, for example, whether or not a member of the board of the institution, may exert a powerful extralegal influence on its functioning. Delays in appropriations, insistence upon certain budgetary and financial procedures, delays in sanctioning purchases or sales by the institution can all impair its independence as a corporation. Ministries and departments of agriculture, university grants commissions, national university commissions, and other bodies created to impose certain standards, make judgments about grants, or play a major role even in the organization of new universities must all be considered along with the university act itself. It should be clear from the legislation establishing the university that it is not intended to be an agency of any ministry of government. This will not coincide with the requirement in some countries that all governmental activities be assigned to a ministry.

2.3. GOVERNMENT OF THE UNIVERSITY—LEGISLATIVE

Given the university act creating the institution, how will major decisions and policies be established for its guidance? In other words, how will the internal legislative function of the university be discharged? Primarily this is a function of the board of control or management, but a function conditioned by the wishes and judgments of the staff of the university about what is appropriate in academic matters. It is important, therefore, that both the right to legislate and the right to participate in the formulation of internal legislative provisions be clearly authorized in the law and, to the extent necessary, further spelled out in university statutes.

2.4. GOVERNMENT OF THE UNIVERSITY— ADMINISTRATIVE

What is the basis for administrative decision-making and the exercise of administrative sanctions in the university? Legislation creating the institution and university statutes must be clear on this point. There must be no question about the authority of the chief administrative officer, though he may work with an elaborate system of committees established to counsel and advise him. Channels for decision-making and the implementation of decisions should be clear. This is a prime essential in establishing the legal base for the university.

The wording in some university acts implies that administrative functions shall somehow be divided between a board or other body and the chief administrative officer. This is not only confusing, but it may lead to encroachment on the administrative function of the chief administrative officer by a body which is supposed to decide policy and legislative matters. This problem is not unique to universities, it runs through the activities of government and, indeed, of private organizations. The philosophy which boards of control sometimes find it difficult to adopt is that of keeping "hands off" the administrative functioning of the institution and relying on the man they hired to do the job. If the board feels he is not "measuring up," the answer is not for the board to perform his functions but to find a man who can. Likewise, the chief administrative officer must master the art of delegation so that initiative and competence can be developed in his staff.

2.5. PURPOSE OF THE UNIVERSITY

The legislation creating a university must express its purpose. This should be broad enough to comprehend the depth and variety of activities in which the university will be engaged in the foreseeable future but not so broad as to be completely meaningless. A statement of purpose which is too detailed will invite debate about whether the university can do particular things and may very well serve to impede innovation. Preservation of a bias for agricultural development must be assured. A sound and adequate statement of purpose can help the university preserve the bias it needs if it is to be of real significance to agriculture and the rural people it is supposed to serve. The intent to integrate research, teaching, and extension should be clear. This integration can be accomplished, however, without impairing the right of the university to provide broad cultural education and to develop the full contingent of arts and sciences so essential to support agriculture. The statement of purpose should preclude the university from discharging regulatory programs or carrying on the kinds of administrative and "police" functions appropriate to a state agency. A good statement of purpose can serve as a guide for the life of the university. It should be worded with care.

2.6. EDUCATIONAL BOUNDARIES

In all the developing countries resources for education are limited. It is extremely important, therefore, that all educational institutions play an important role in fulfilling the total educational need without undue duplication and expensive overlapping. Mexico has a law governing agricultural education at all levels and dividing responsibility between federal, state, and municipal governments and private institutions. Such a law can be of great help in promoting agricultural education and conserving the resources with which to do it. The educational jurisdiction of an institution should be carefully delineated. This needs to be expressed in terms of the geographical areas served, the level of education to be provided, the educational programs or subject matter with which the university shall deal, and its freedom from undue restraint imposed by any government agency or other institution in carrying out its educational program. If it is to be in charge of agricultural research or agricultural extension, this function should be made clear and other institutions should not be permitted to duplicate its programs. Also, it should be designated as the recipient of government aid for research and extension to prevent "infighting" for such aid and to prevent it from being dissipated. The act creating the university should leave no doubt with respect to these matters.

2.7. ACADEMIC FREEDOM

In *The Rights and Responsibilities of Universities and Their Faculties,*[3] it is stated that

----

[3] *Ibid.*

The university is an association of individual scholars. Their effectiveness, both as scholars and as teachers, requires the capitalizing of their individual passion for knowledge and their individual competence to pursue it and to communicate it to others. They are united in loyalty to the idea of learning, to the moral code, to the country, and to its form of government. They represent diversified fields of knowledge, they express many points of view, even within the same department of instruction; they are not only specialists in various phases of the subject but men with widely differing interests and outlooks.

The necessity for academic freedom is recognized in universities throughout the world. However, its interpretation may vary considerably from one country to another or from one time to another depending upon political objectives and pressures of the times. The law creating the university can do no less than state that the university shall be free to pursue truth and those within it shall not be inhibited in any way from searching for the truth regardless of political and religious pressures which may exist at any time during the life of the university. The statement of such a legislative provision should capitalize on the past history of universities and on the fact that academic freedom has been recognized as a prime essential from the first appearance of any institution which could rightfully be called a university. Such a statement should be designed to protect the university from encroachments on this freedom both from without and from within. A more complete discussion of academic freedom and the responsibility which accompanies it appears in Chapter 15.

2.8. PROPERTY OWNERSHIP, ACQUISITION, USE, AND TRANSFER

Though the university is a public corporation, from which certain rights can be implied, it is not wise to leave all these rights to implication. To function properly and discharge a public service in the whole field of higher education, the university must have the right to acquire essential property, both real and personal, to hold title to such property, to lease it, to transfer it, and to deal with it in any way necessary to accomplish its purpose. Frequently, institutions are established without these rights being clearly defined in the original legislation, so that amendments are found necessary. Particularly is this true when the institution engages in projects such as housing where it may be necessary to charge rental fees and manage money accruing from rentals.

2.9. FINANCING

Certain rights and duties with respect to finance may be implied from the fact that the university is a corporation. The major activities in the field of finance should be plainly enumerated in a legislative act so that there will be no question about how the university will be expected to acquire funds, to account for funds, to borrow and pay interest, to invest, to manage major accounts, to audit, to prepare and receive approval of a university budget, and to engage in other activities which accord with sound financial management. The legislation should be flexible to allow for new procedures, new devices, machine systems, and other things which will change with time. The university should not be bound to an antiquated financial structure. It will, of course, take more than a basic law to insure sound, imaginative, and efficient financial management, but good law is essential to aid those who would innovate and keep the institution up to date. Insuring such management, along with procuring adequate funds, is a major institutional function. The right to finance through borrowing, including the right to issue bonds and pledge university property as security, must be based on specific legislative authority.

2.10. ADMISSION OF STUDENTS—NONDISCRIMINATION

There are many aspects of admission which should be left to university statutes and to internal regulations with which the faculty is concerned and in which it should have a hand. However, there are some basic assurances which should be made about admission to the university. These should not be subject to change by the board of control or the faculty. The guarantee of admission regardless of race, color, religion, national origin, sex, caste, or any of the other differences which do not determine one's capacity and will to become educated should be assured. Though the board and faculty should have a major hand in determining educational requirements for admission, the act creating the university should nevertheless contain a basic statement in this regard. Such a statement will perhaps have more value in the early life of the institution, when there is less internal ability to withstand pressures from the outside to get the university to admit or not to admit this or that kind of student. With age and achievement, the university will be able to hold its own on this score.

2.11. THE CONTRACTUAL RIGHTS OF STAFF MEMBERS

Certainty in the contractual relations between employer and employee begets confidence and is needed just as much in the academic as in the business world. Though the details on achieving academic tenure and on the contractual rights and obligations of staff members may be left to university statutes and internal regulations, the act creating the university should make certain basic guarantees to those who will become officers, staff members, and other employees. The right to have a written contract listing duties, rights, and conditions for participation in the university retirement or pension system; the guarantee that an employee will be discharged only for cause; and the right to notification and a hearing in cases of dismissal are all elements which should be included in the basic university act. The method of making appointments should be stated in the statutes so that the roles of the selection committee, administrative officer, the chief administrative officer, and the board are all known.

2.12. RECOGNITION OF THE MAJOR FUNCTIONS— TEACHING, RESEARCH, AND EXTENSION

The duty of the university to engage in an integrated program of teaching, research, and extension, with public service as a major objective, should not be left to the university statutes or internal regulations of the institution. The very reason why many of the new universities are being formed in developing countries is to achieve this kind of integration and commitment to service and to make a break with purely classical concepts. Therefore, the basic law must contain an adequate statement on this subject. In addition, there should be basic legislative provisions and guides on the taking over of government agricultural research or extension agencies, if this is involved, so that rights are guaranteed and so that the institution taking over such agencies will have a clear understanding of the conditions under which this is to be done.

2.13. THE BASIC INTERNAL STRUCTURE OF THE UNIVERSITY

Decisions regarding internal structure should insofar as possible be left to the board and to the faculty. However, there are elements in the internal organization of the university that help to commit it to an integrated program of teaching and research and to a public service philosophy. Other internal arrangements can be effective in preventing undue concentration of power in any one university body or official. These elements must be identified and clearly stated in the law creating the institution. One of the purposes of this book is to identify and discuss these elements as they emerge in the chapters which follow.

2.14. STUDENT GOVERNMENT AND STUDENT LIFE— STUDENT RIGHTS

Though the university statutes and internal regulations should be relied upon to establish the guides for student conduct and activity, the basic law creating the university should recognize the importance and the place of student government and student organization—and of individual student rights. Such legislation should be drafted so that it is both protective to the institution and reassuring to students. In many universities of the world there is a considerable amount of student activity labeled "political," "undesirable," and even "inimical to the functioning of the university." There are many causes for this, none of which can be cured by a legislative act. But this is no reason why there should not be a basic legislative provision designed to both assure and safeguard. If implementing statutes and internal university regulations supported by a sound university act are properly developed and adhered to, undesirable situations can be minimized and students can be urged to play a positive role in the life of the university.

2.15. ATHLETICS AND MILITARY TRAINING

Like many other matters, the athletic program of the university should be guided primarily by university regulations but the university act should contain at least two expressions of policy regarding athletics: one should impose a limitation on what might be called extremism in team sports; the other should give positive encouragement to athletics as a contribution to the cultural and physical development of students. These policies do not conflict.

The university act should state expressly the extent of the university's right to participate in any national officer-training or other military program designed for institutions of higher education. It is better if military training within the university is not imposed by law—but national policy may indicate otherwise. If such training is offered, the terms governing it should be so expressed that there is no doubt about what the institution can and cannot do. As a part of such a legislative provision there should be understandable criteria for those who are to be involved in such a program— whether or not the program is voluntary.

2.16. THE GRANTING OF DEGREES

The authority to grant degrees and by whom they are to be granted should be expressed in the legislative act. Academic requirements and other matters having to do with the granting of degrees should be left to statutes and internal regulations.

2.17. LONG-RANGE PLANNING

If an institution is to remain forward-looking and be of maximum service to its constituency, long-range planning is essential. The skill and thoroughness with which this is done will be determined by the competence of those who are responsible for it within the university. But all too often the necessity for long-range planning is overlooked. For this reason the legislative act, while it should not attempt to provide the structure for accomplishing such planning, should call attention to it and impose some requirement that this kind of planning be carried on.

CHAPTER – 3

The Corporate Nature
of the University—
Purpose, Powers, Functions

3.1. THE CORPORATE CHARACTER OF THE UNIVERSITY

The Uttar Pradesh Agricultural University Act provides that "The Chancellor and first Vice-Chancellor of the university and the first members of the board and the academic council and all persons who may hereafter become such officers or members so long as they continue to hold such office or membership are hereby constituted a body corporate." Legislative acts creating the new Indian agricultural universities generally have this provision. Some university acts do not state what officers or bodies constitute the corporation but simply state that the university is a body corporate. This is true, for example, of the University of Nigeria Law and of the law establishing the Rural University of the State of Minas Gerais in Brazil. The latter simply states: "The Rural University of the State of Minas Gerais is hereby established with independent juridical personality." Harvard University was launched under the direction of a board of overseers, but the president and fellows were designated as the corporation. Both the university and the separate colleges are corporate entities at Oxford and Cambridge.

Virtually all university acts state that the university shall be a body corporate, that it shall have perpetual succession and a common seal, and may sue and be sued by its official name. The charter for The Haile Selassie I University contains a somewhat eloquent statement of the same thing:

Now, therefore, We of Our special grace and certain knowledge and Our own motion do by this Our Imperial Charter for Us and Ourself and Our Imperial Successors grant and ordain that said university shall be one body politic and corporate in name and deed by the name of The Haile Selassie I University of Ethiopia and shall have perpetual existence with the common seal which may be adopted, changed, or varied at the pleasure of The Haile Selassie I University and with further powers and authorities but subject to the conditions and declarations in this Our Imperial Charter contained.

Some acts include the power to contract and to own and dispose of property in the statement constituting the university a corporate entity and giving it the power to sue and be sued. Others include rights with respect to property and contract in a general statement of powers and functions of the university.

An American work of law contains the following statements about the corporate character of a university:

While the terms are in a broad sense interchangeable, college and university are in a stricter sense distinct terms, the first meaning an institution of higher education devoted to the arts and sciences and the second a union of colleges and technical or professional schools. Colleges and universities are usually, although not necessarily, incorporated . . . .
The college or university or a branch or department thereof cannot sue or be sued as such unless it has in fact a corporate existence . . . . The public or private character and the control of a college or university are determined from its articles of incorporation and the statute authorizing its formation. A college or university is usually deemed to be a public institution or corporation and subject as such to the plenary control of the state where it was instituted by the state and maintained out of state funds or by means of the aid extended by the national or state governments . . . . Colleges and universities may be incorporated as either private or public corporations or they may be unincorporated. As organized under some statutes, they are mere instrumentalities of the state and not corporations. Educational corporations are designed to be perpetual and are not subject to the provisions of a general law limiting the life of corporations. The charter of a college or university is ordinarily subject to amendment.[1]

Some acts state that in addition to the powers included in its charter, a university shall have those granted to corporations in general. It probably does not matter just how or where the major rights and duties of the university are stated as long as the statement is adequate and unequivocal, but it is recommended that at the beginning of a university act there be a short and clear-cut provision making the university a corporate entity, giving it an official name, and empowering it to sue and be sued by this name.

It is probably not essential to name the particular officers or bodies which constitute the corporation. The essential fact is that the university, however constituted, is a separate corporate legal entity. The designation "body corporate" or "independent juridical personality" provides the proper legal connotation. The important

---
[1] 14 *Corpus Juris Secundum*, sections 1327, 1333, 1369. (This is an American encyclopedia of law which will hereafter be cited as *CJS*.)

thing is that the breath of corporate life be supplied whether by the constitution, a general universities act, the legislature, a royal decree, a charter, or by other competent legal authority, since a university cannot provide for its own corporate existence.

3.2. PURPOSE

Some universities have been created without any written statement of purpose. This may not be undesirable if one considers that all universities exist for a single major purpose—the advancement of the knowledge and understanding of man and his world—and that the very presence of the community of scholars which constitutes a university will cause this purpose to evolve. However, the newer universities are being organized with the hope that they will further the development of the country and meet a national educational need which has heretofore been neglected. These public service objectives seem to require a statement of purpose.

The University of Nigeria Law provides that the objects of the university are "to hold forth to all classes and communities without any distinction whatsoever an encouragement for pursuing a regular and liberal course of education, to promote research and the advancement of science and learning, to organize, improve, and extend education of university standard." The Uttar Pradesh Agricultural University Act states that the university has been established and incorporated for the purposes, among others, of "making provision for imparting education in different branches of learning, particularly agriculture, animal science, rural industry, agricultural engineering, veterinary science, home science, and other allied sciences, furthering the prosecution of research in all branches of learning, particularly in agriculture and other allied sciences, and undertaking extension programs relating to the aforesaid sciences." The Punjab Agricultural University Act contains a similar provision. The Revised Code of the University of the Philippines contains a broader statement: " . . . to provide advanced instruction in literature, philosophy, the sciences and arts, to give professional and technical training, and to encourage and undertake research and contribute to the growth and dissemination of knowledge."

Regardless of precisely how it is stated, there should be a provision on purpose if for no other reason than to help the new universities "hold the line" against those who urge that they revert to the traditional university pattern and thus de-emphasize the service, development, and rural improvement aspects of their endeavor. In some cases the purpose of the university appears under a listing of its general powers. In the West Pakistan Agricultural University Ordinance, under a listing of powers of the university, is included: " . . . to provide for instruction in agriculture, the basic sciences, humanities, social studies, and such other branches of learning as the university may think fit and to make provision for research and for the advancement and dissemination of knowledge in these subjects."

A statement of purpose should be neither too broad nor too restrictive. The Rural University Decree of the State of Minas Gerais in Brazil concludes its statement about teaching, research, and extension objectives by saying they shall be "adapted to the political development of the state." The act creating Iowa State University listed in detail many of the subjects to be offered, among them fruit growing, entomolgy, veterinary art, leveling, natural philosophy, and bookkeeping. A statement of purpose should not deny the university the right to enter any field of educational endeavor; the university must be able to add disciplines through its own internal processes of determination. It is essential that the statement of purpose contain a commitment to the whole rural economy and the development of agriculture. For this reason it is strongly urged that a statement of purpose contain language which commits the university to the development of an integrated program of teaching, research, extension, and service to its rural people and to its agriculture—without omitting language which will preserve the objective of providing a liberal education.

3.3. NAME

Though the title of the act itself may include the name of the institution, it is nevertheless desirable to include a section which specifically states what the name of the university shall be. Some examples follow: from the University of Nigeria Law, "The university is established under the name of the University of Nigeria"; from the Mysore act, "There shall be constituted in and for the state of Mysore a university by the name of the University of Agricultural Sciences"; from the University of the Philippines Ordinance, "The Governor-General is authorized to establish a university which shall be known by the designation of University of the Philippines, the same being organized under that name." Some of the Indian university acts state the official university name in the regional language. General university incorporation laws require an official name for the institution. When the name is specified in a university act it can be changed only by action of the legislature. While the naming of a university may seem a very obvious and natural thing to do, it is nevertheless an important consideration because contractual relations and agreements and official designations of many kinds will require a legal name.

Some American universities have been involved in litigation regarding their names. When clothing manufacturers, stationers, bubble gum fabricators, and jewelry salesmen wish to use the name of the university on their product to promote sales, a question of legal right arises. Some of the decisions in the American cases have been favorable to the institution; some have not. Columbia University won a suit to enjoin use of the name "Columbia Educational Institute" by a private agency. Perhaps this question is not likely to arise in most countries, however it would take only a few words to provide in the section of the act specifying the name of the university that this name shall not be used by any other institution or by any other individual or agency for any purpose whatsoever without the consent of the university. This would give the institution the right to intervene and enjoin the use of its name in those circumstances where its reputation or dignity is likely to be damaged.

3.4. LOCATION

University acts vary in the definiteness with which they locate the institution. Some are quite specific. The Mysore act, for example, states that the headquarters of the university shall be at Hebbal in the Bangalore urban district. The West Pakistan act states that the university shall be at Lyallpur. The Andhra Pradesh act fixes the headquarters and states that the university may extend to any place within a contiguous area of five miles. The University of the Philippines ordinance gives the Governor-General the authority to establish the university at any point he may deem most convenient in case he should decide not to establish it in the city of Manila. The Ahmadu Bello Act simply says that the university shall be established in northern Nigeria.

If the site is agreed upon before a university act is adopted, there is no reason why the act should not recite the location. When location is thus fixed, it cannot be changed except by legislative action. If it has not been agreed upon, then the act should indicate who has authority to select the site. The law will be adequate if it either designates the location or indicates in unequivocal terms that the board or some entity of government has the authority to select the location. If it is expected that the university might establish branches or experiment stations in other parts of the state or region, the right to do so could be expressed in a section on location of the university. The existence of this right in the absence of a legislative provision could be a debatable point and had just as well be put to rest in the act. In view of the mission of the new universities and the efforts they will be making in the development of agriculture, it would be wise to give them authority to establish branches or entities at such locations as the board deems desirable.

3.5. EFFECTIVE DATE OF ACT

It is helpful to know exactly when a university act becomes operative. In the absence of any statement in the act itself, it would be presumed to become operative on the date specified by law for other legislation to become effective. This might be covered by a general legislative provision, by the constitution, by custom, or by a rule of the legislature. Many acts, however, do contain a provision on effective date. Some state that the act shall come into force at once, others that it shall take effect on passage, and still others that it shall come into force on a date to be specified by the state government or by the governor or chancellor. Though the effective date of a university act may be indicated by a general law, it would seem desirable for the act itself to express the effective date. This, then, would be as far as anyone need look.

3.6. JURISDICTION OF THE UNIVERSITY

The land-grant universities in America think of the whole state as their campus. In a sense this would be true of any university in a developing country which has as its objective an integrated program in teaching, research, extension, and public service. The term "jurisdiction," in the sense of what the university does or whom it serves, will be defined in several places in a university act. While the assumption is that its service geographically is to the state or region creating it, many acts, nevertheless, contain a provision on territorial jurisdiction. The Andhra Pradesh act states that the agricultural university extends to the whole of the state of Andhra Pradesh. The Madhya Pradesh act gives the Jawaharlal Nehru Agricultural University "exclusive jurisdiction throughout the state to provide for instruction, teaching, and training in agriculture and allied sciences . . . ." The act creating the Ahmadu Bello University gives it the right to acquire property and construct buildings outside Nigeria. In some cases the new universities have been given exclusive jurisdiction to grant degrees in agriculture and engage in agricultural research and extension. This is probably a wise provision where applicable, and if another institution reaches the point where it can qualify, the law can be amended.

The term "jurisdiction" may be used in another sense—as meaning the campus area or that area which the university controls directly. In the absence of a provision covering this, there would be an assumption that the administration of the university and the board have the right to establish such rules and statutes as are necessary to provide security and to properly control activities in those areas which comprise university property. There is further discussion of security in Chapter 7.

3.7. DEFINITION OF TERMS

It is customary for both the acts and the statutes to contain a section on definitions. Such a section is helpful because it explains the meaning of a term as used in the act and hence may have an important bearing on future interpretations and, also, because it frequently permits the use of a single word in place of several in those places in the act or statutes where the term is used. The following terms are among those ordinarily defined in acts or statutes:

Academic council
Act
Agriculture
Authority
Board
College
Dean
Extension
Faculty
Government
Regulations

Statute
Student
Teacher
University

For the authors' definitions of these and other terms, see the Glossary (Appendix I). After acts or statutes are formulated, they should be studied to determine what words or phrases require definition.

3.8. RELATION OF THE UNIVERSITY TO GOVERNMENT

How independent is the university? This is an important question. Complete autonomy is not possible because a university is created by the people through its legislature and must be responsive to the people through that body. But no wise legislative body would wish to create an institution which could not operate truly as a university; neither would it choose to interfere unduly with such an institution once it is established and functioning. The decree creating the Rural University of Minas Gerais in Brazil states: "The university is guaranteed administrative, economic, disciplinary, and pedagogical autonomy as long as the directives and bases of national education are observed." There are many areas of government in which it is expected that politics will play a part, but this does not hold true for a university. Of course there will be internal politics—no institution exists without this—but reference here is to political influence by government or agencies of government on the university either in terms of financial support, who shall be employed or promoted, what projects are undertaken, or what kind of publications are issued. Even though there is no express reservation of power by government, it is understood that government nevertheless can change or even destroy the institution, and certainly it can hamstring its operation by not providing funds.

Typical provisions of an express nature are those designating certain members of government ex officio members of the board, naming the governor as chancellor or as honorary head of the institution, or providing for teams of visitation whose reports may influence the legislature. In some instances the chief administrative officer is appointed by government or by the head of state.

The Revised Code of the University of the Philippines provides that members of the board of regents except the president of the university are government officials or are appointed by the President of the Philippines; that the President of the Philippines, President of the Senate, and the Speaker of the House of Representatives shall constitute a Board of Visitors which may make visits to examine university property, courses of study, discipline, and the accounts of the institution, and report to the Congress of the Philippines on such recommendations as they favor; and that the Treasurer of the Philippine Islands shall be ex officio treasurer of the University.

The Uttar Pradesh Agricultural University Act provides that the state government shall have the right to cause an inspection of the university, its buildings, laboratories, and equipment, and to cause an inquiry to be made of any matter connected with the administration and finances of the university. The government shall request the board to take action on its recommendations and, if it does not, the government may direct it to do so. The act provides that the governor shall be the chancellor; that if any question arises as to membership on the board or on decisions made by authorities subordinate to it, the matter shall be referred to the chancellor whose decision will be final; and that the chancellor must approve all statute changes. The act also provides that the first statutes of the university be approved by the legislature.

The West Pakistan Agricultural University Ordinance provides that the governor shall be the chancellor. He may remove any person from the membership of any authority if such person is of unsound mind, has been incapacitated, or has been convicted of an offense involving moral turpitude. He may withdraw a degree conferred on any person by the university if such person has been convicted of an offense involving moral turpitude. He may cause an inspection to be made of the university physical plant, its teaching and other work, conduct of examinations, or any other matter connected with the university. After such an inspection, if the syndicate refuses to take action, the chancellor may cause such action to be taken as he sees fit. All proceedings of any authority are subject to annulment by the chancellor if he considers them not in conformity with the ordinance, the statutes, or regulations. The approval of the chancellor must be obtained for all university ordinances submitted by the syndicate. The chancellor appoints the vice-chancellor. The Agricultural Act of the State of Minas Gerais in Brazil provides that four things must be approved by the governor: the annual budget, the list of personnel (meaning the positions to be filled, not the personalities), the plan of salaries, and the statutes.

Other university acts from South America, Africa, and Asia contain similar provisions, though the individual acts vary considerably in the extent to which they vest powers in officers or authorities of government. It is said that the position of chancellor in the Indian universities is an honorary one, but a study of the university acts indicates that often it is considerably more than honorary. Under authority which has been granted, a chancellor (usually the governor of the state) could interfere substantially in the affairs of the institution. This is particularly true where the constitution vests the governor with interim authority to act for a legislature when it is not in session. Some acts give him the power to make official interpretation of the law and be the final arbiter. Apparently this authority has not been abused sufficiently to warrant any move to have such provisions excluded from acts creating new universities. After all, government is entitled to surveillance of an institution which it creates, and if it chooses to provide for such surveillance in the manner of the above provisions, it may be argued that this is its prerogative.

Of more importance is the relation of the university to government agencies, boards, or commissions created to pass judgment on grants and new programs and have a hand in the approval of budgets. Sometimes a fine line exists between a legitimate and necessary apportionment of public funds for the support and maintenance of institutions and the exercise of an arbitrary authority which discourages the establishment of new programs and curtails or modifies existing ones. Inasmuch as the legislature has the power to investigate the affairs of the university if it should ever feel such action necessary, it can be argued that it is better not to establish boards of inquiry in the law creating a university. No matter how benign such a board of inquiry might be, it stands as a constant threat and as a means whereby government can intimidate the university. The same is true of authority vested in the chancellor by the university act. Though he may not exercise the powers given him, the possibility exists. In one American state, Nevada, the creation of an advisory board to the board of regents of the University of Nevada was held void because the court regarded it as a duplicate body which was unnecessary and might threaten the authority of the board of regents. The court reached this decision even though the act creating the advisory body stated that nothing contained in it should be in derogation of the powers of the board. If the board is regarded as competent to deal with the affairs of the university, it should not seem necessary for a legislature to establish a series of checks and balances which, in the end, might serve only to impede.

In most developing countries it is certain that if more than one institution does not currently exist, more than one will exist in the future. This poses a problem of coordinating efforts, allocating funds, and determining what major phases of work should be undertaken in the different institutions. The necessity for a national university commission or overall university board seems implied. The legislation creating such a commission or body should give it the right to make determinations that have to do with the allocation of funds and the establishment of new lines of work—but not to participate otherwise in university affairs.

The relation of the university to agencies of state government, particularly to a Department of Agriculture or Department of Education, should be one of helpful cooperation without undertaking to carry on any of the administrative functions or control or regulatory work of such departments of government. The role of the university should remain that of imparting education in all its phases. Its manpower should not be used to accomplish routine duties or carry on any program which involves the applying of governmental sanctions. People cannot help but have some fear of an agent employed by government to enforce its laws, and their response to his educational endeavors will be conditioned and constricted. Perhaps the above concept need not be stated in the university act, but it could be expressed as a matter of policy in the university statutes. In some cases American land-grant universities have developed a memorandum of agreement with a state department of agriculture clearly delineating their respective fields of endeavor. There are many areas in which the department and the university should cooperate so that the agreement will have positive as well as protective aims.

If the university is located in a city, problems of university and city jurisdiction will arise—control of traffic and the exercise of the security function within the university, for example, are generally handled by university personnel. An understanding should be reached between the city government and the institution regarding their respective powers and duties. This understanding could very well be established as a matter of policy in either university statutes or administrative regulations.

A unique provision in the Punjab Agricultural University Act recognizes that it is possible to have forward-looking relations with government and that government itself might be able to benefit from the research effort of the university. This particular provision states that "The board shall submit to the government legislative proposals which it considers necessary for the betterment and promotion of agriculture based on the results of research conducted in the university." The research work of universities does frequently condition such legislation. However, it is not often that one finds recognition of this fact in a basic legislative or statutory provision.

Hopefully, the state or region in which the agricultural university is located will have an agricultural development council or its equivalent. The purpose of such a council would be to coordinate the activities of all public agencies toward a more efficient and imaginative development effort. The university should be an active participant in such a council, for by means of such participation, research, extension, and teaching could be coordinated with government regulatory programs and services to farmers. Also, advantage could be taken of government supply programs. If, for example, improved seed and fertilizer are high on the government's agenda, the university could prepare informational material and in other ways help extension personnel make the seed and fertilizer pay off in terms of farmer "know-how." As a member of such a council the university could, among other things, help "hold the line" against government's use of extension and educational personnel to carry out supply programs. Tempting as the supply programs are, participation in them is not a good idea, for maximum use of any agricultural supplies, whether seed, fertilizer, plant protection materials, better implements, or anything else, cannot be made unless the farmer understands something about their limitations and capabilities and how they can be used together to make more money for him. This is extension information and it is a prime function of the university—even if another agency administers the extension program. If such a development council is not in existence when the university is created, the university act itself could give the university leadership by providing that it shall foster such cooperative effort and provide the leadership in establishing and vitalizing such a council.

The federal or central government can play an extremely important role in university development through continuing grants for research and extension. This financial aid has been a dominant factor in making the American land-grant universities responsive to the needs of agriculture.

3.9. RELATION OF THE UNIVERSITY TO OTHER AGENCIES

As farmers' organizations and other special-interest groups grow in size and influence, they will ask a university to do many things for their constituents. Some of these requests the university can fulfill because they will simply imply an extension of the university's educational program or the tackling of research problems which have actually arisen and about which the university should be concerned. So the university should maintain close and friendly relations with all kinds of organizations in the hope that it can better understand its own function, make its research more realistic, and better serve the people of the state or region.

Sometimes special interest groups ask the institution to support them in views which are opposed to those held by other interest groups, or they may ask the university to engage in routine operations or functions simply as a matter of service to their members. These kinds of activities the university must avoid, because they involve political implications and the university must be impartial and ready to serve all in any legitimate way involving an exercise of its educational function. Furthermore, these activities mean use and dissipation of energy in a kind of work which by any definition could not be called educational. It is true, of course, that good research may sometimes involve a large amount of routine work such as testing, sampling, or just counting things, but in these cases the work is done for a purpose and there is an ultimate research objective in mind. When routine work is done only for the purpose of accomplishing the routine, the same cannot be said. This is an area in which it is probably not feasible to formulate legislative provisions; perhaps even university statutes are not needed. However, there should be a strong university policy regarding working with farm groups, developing local leadership, and doing everything in its power to increase the means whereby education can be spread. This philosophy should be exemplified in university regulations having to do with those segments of the university which deal with the public, particularly its extension service. When such a policy is expressed in a set of regulations, unnecessary detail should be avoided so that it will not be possible for a university staff member indisposed to render some service to say he cannot because the regulations prohibit it.

There is no way of predetermining certain judgments which the university will have to make throughout its life. As certain groups organize and gain power—labor, for example—the university will be asked to do things which could not have been envisioned in the beginning. Many American institutions have established schools or institutes of labor and industrial relations because pressure grew; it was pointed out that since the university is serving the agricultural community, it should also serve the labor and industrial communities. To some extent the university can be both protected and aided in these relations by a good statement of purpose or policy and by the inclusion of the proper language in a more comprehensive statement of powers and duties.

In time the university will need to establish proper relations with what might be called accessory or ancillary institutions and corporations—for example, a foundation to manage trust funds or an athletic association to handle the expenses, income, and other matters having to do with athletic programs for which charges are made and for which facilities are constructed. The university act should contain a clear statement regarding the right of the university to foster the creation of such entities and its relationship to them. Is the budget of the athletic association, for example, a part of the general university budget to be approved in the same manner, or is it that of a separate corporation with the university having only a more general surveillance? To what extent shall university procedures on employment, staff amenities, and other matters apply to these ancillary or accessory agencies? These are questions each institution will have to answer. But there is one principle which should govern in all cases—the university should retain sufficient control to insure the protection of educational objectives and the use of acceptable procedures.

3.10. CREATION FROM OTHER INSTITUTIONS

Sometimes a new university is created by changing the name

and functions of an existing institution. In addition, other institutions may be transferred to the newly created university either as university colleges, as constituent colleges, or under some other relationship. They may be merged with the new institution and lose their identity. The Andhra Pradesh Agricultural University Act provides that several named institutions shall be maintained by the university as university colleges. The Mysore University of Agriculture Sciences Act provides that two agricultural colleges and a veterinary college shall be disaffiliated from one university and maintained by the new university as constituent colleges. The date of transfer is that which shall be specified by state government in the official gazette. The Mysore law guarantees to students in an affiliated institution the right to complete any course of study which they were pursuing. Perhaps the right to complete "substantially the same course of study" would be better, thus allowing for some difference of opinion about what constitutes a "course of study."

Some acts provide for transfer to the new university of government agricultural research agencies and educational institutions maintained by the department of agriculture or animal husbandry. Such provisions may make transfers mandatory or may leave them to the discretion of state government. Some laws make the transfer mandatory but leave the question of timing to state government; this however, introduces an element of uncertainty. It would be better if some date were expressed by which the transfer is to be made—in two years, for example. Otherwise, the job may never get done and the uncertainty will be detrimental both to the research agencies and to the university. If such transfers are contemplated in advance, many interim steps can be taken to pave the way.

3.11. THE MULTICAMPUS UNIVERSITY—AFFILIATION

Should there be only one university with all other institutions being constituent (a part of the university and without separate autonomy) colleges? Should there be separate or affiliated (as separate autonomous units) institutions, but one major university for purposes of developing the syllabus, giving examinations, and granting degrees? Should institutions be developed completely independent of each other with such coordination and control as is deemed necessary achieved through a board of higher education or a national universities' commission? Arguments are not wanting for all these propositions and there is no inherent reason why any of them cannot work.

In some countries where there existed more than one institution, it seemed natural to make these all constituent units of a new university. This is probably the best solution, though it poses problems regarding good administration and the proper division of functions and authority. Shall there be one dean of agriculture, for example, with associate deans at the different geographical locations, or shall each institution have its own dean and shall the necessary administrative coordination be achieved higher up the line—at the vice-chancellor level, for example—with one vice-chancellor at the "home" institution and associate or pro-vice-chancellors at the other institutions?

The goal is an integrated and workable administration, proper coordination of effort, and conservation of resources without unduly restricting the freedom to carry on a program at any location and without making the staff at such location feel it is only "playing second fiddle" to those at the home base. In some cases the problem posed by geographical location has been solved by transferring institutions to the home campus, but generally this is not easily done. Pressures develop, for example, to keep a college of veterinary medicine where it is located.

Some university acts name the institutions which are to become a part of the university but do not state on what basis. The Punjab and Rajasthan university acts give the board authority to add constituent colleges. We believe this authority should be given with the proviso that recommendations first be received from the academic council and the chief administrative officer. In order that local initiative may be preserved, it is recommended that when a separate institution is a single college, the dean of the college be in charge of the campus and act as the chief administrative officer at that site. The direct channel then will be from the dean to the vice-chancellor or chief administrative officer of the university. An alternative is to make the chief officer at the separate college campus an associate dean responsible to the dean of the "home" campus college on educational matters and to the chief administrative officer through the dean on administrative matters.

Coordination of research, extension, and teaching efforts can be accomplished through the appointment of appropriate committees and through other devices which it is within the authority of the vice-chancellor to establish. It is assumed that there would be a uniform standard of admission, grading, credit evaluation and computation, and examination policies, so as not to complicate student transfers from one part of the university to another. If the separate institution is comprised of more than one college, then either a pro-vice-chancellor or perhaps one of the deans named as dean and pro-vice-chancellor to be in charge of the local campus would be feasible.

More difficult problems arise in the functioning of faculty bodies. There will be members of the university senate or council, for example, at the different geographical locations. Not only is it difficult for staff members to travel to the parent institution for meetings, but there will gradually develop the understandable feeling that some of their problems are separate, so that the staff at a particular location should be privileged to determine some of the answers for itself. At the same time there are overall policies to be considered and established by a university senate or council which require uniformity throughout and in the formulation of which all members should be involved. This is a matter which should receive continuous study, and university statutes should be framed to separate those functions which can be determined locally and those which must still be determined on a university-wide basis. This would relieve those at the outlying institutions of some frustration and would still preserve a feeling of unity within the university.

Problems will arise about courses and curricula. Shall all students complete a two-year general course at one location, then go to another for specialization? Shall there be duplication of courses—and, indeed, of departments—or shall animal husbandry be developed at one location, agronomy at another, agricultural engineering at another, and other branches at only one place? Arguments develop pro and con, and the solution which is most economical may not be best educationally. Having branches at different physical locations loses the multidisciplinary advantage of the university and the ability to give breadth to curriculum, but it encourages research and specialization in depth. Some compromises will be essential no matter how the question is resolved. Certainly students should not be "trapped" by a change in policy after they commence an academic program.

It has been argued that the new agricultural universities will find it difficult to achieve their purpose if they must accept the affiliation of any other college or university which desires to affiliate. It is argued that this tends to defeat at least one of the objectives in establishing the new universities—that of providing more freedom for the professor to teach and examine. The West Pakistan Agricultural University Act provides that "No educational institution situated within the territorial limits of the university shall, save with the consent of the university and the sanction of government, be associated in any way with or seek admission to any privilege of any other university established by law." This language would seem to force an educational institution within such jurisdiction to affiliate with the agricultural university and with no other institution in case it chooses to affiliate. However, the law does provide that with the consent of the university and the sanction of government, it may associate with or affiliate with some other institution. This same law provides that "Any educational institution situated anywhere in West Pakistan outside the territorial limits of the university may, with the sanction of government, apply to the university for being admitted to the privileges of the university and such institutions may, subject to conditions and restrictions as the university and government see fit to impose, be admitted to the privileges of the university." Here again, however, there are two provisos: that this be with the sanction of government, and with the implication that the university has the right to turn down the application for affiliation. With affiliation may come the necessity for the syllabus and the fixed examination. This is a policy question which must be answered in the light of circumstances existing in a particular country. The University of the Philippines is required to establish a system of affiliation under which private secondary schools or liberal arts colleges can be accredited by the university.

Unless there are compelling reasons why affiliation should be provided, it would seem best to excuse the new institution from this necessity at least until it has established itself. Any provision on affiliation should include a statement of the conditions under which an institution can be disaffiliated or disconnected from the university.

3.12. THE RIGHT TO CONTRACT—PROPERTY RIGHTS

How free should the university be to contract? Are there constitutional restrictions on incurring debt or raising funds? Does it matter with whom it contracts? How far in the future can the university commit its resources? The law should provide for a wide range of discretion with respect to all these questions. Reliance should be placed on the board to use the power to contract appropriately; attempts to limit the power by law are more likely to impede than protect. The University of Nigeria Law gives the university the same rights as an individual to make oral contracts. The power to contract necessarily implies the right to seek remedies for breach of contract and to be subject to suit for breach by contracting parties. However, it is customary for the law to provide that the university may enter into contracts and that it may sue and be sued by its corporate name. The Mysore University of Agricultural Sciences Act provides that in all suits and legal proceedings by or against the university, the pleadings shall be signed and verified by the registrar, and all processes in such suits and proceedings shall be issued to and served on the registrar. Many university acts have a similar provision, with the registrar generally being designated as the officer on whom process shall be served. Though there is no objection to having such a provision in a university act, it is not essential and, in its absence, service would be made on an appropriate officer.

The power to purchase, acquire, hold, sell, mortgage, and transfer property, both real and personal is obviously necessary. The following provision in the West Pakistan Agricultural University Ordinance is typical: "The university shall be competent to acquire and hold property both movable and immovable, to lease, sell, or otherwise transfer any movable or immovable property which may have become vested in or been acquired by it . . . ." The only limitation on the amount or kind of property a university may own should be one specifying that it shall be "for the purposes of the university." The board should be left free to determine purpose. The university must be able to accept property in trust and act as trustee. It must be able to accept gifts for a particular purpose, but must be free to judge whether or not the purpose is an appropriate one for the university. Also, with proper safeguards to protect a donor so funds or other property will not be capriciously diverted from their intended purpose, the university should reserve the power to sell trust property or make changes in use of the proceeds if the original purpose is no longer appropriate.

3.13. TAX LIABILITY

There is a theory that the state cannot be taxed; therefore, universities, being public corporations created by the state, should be exempt from taxation. But in some countries there may be qualifications based on the nature and purpose of particular property or activities and on the tax policies of the government. Also there may be constitutional provisions. The Peru National Universities Act, which is a general enabling act for public universities, provides that "The universities are exempt from the payment of any national or local tax, present or future. They shall have free postal and telegraphic service. The materials, machinery, and teaching and laboratory tools which they import for university purposes shall be free from any customs duty and its real estate is exonerated from the restrictions established by rental laws." Other university acts which were surveyed contained no provisions on tax exemption, though it is likely that as a matter of policy many of them would be in the same position as the Peruvian national universities. Some American universities continue to pay taxes on property as long as the property continues in use as an income-producing enterprise. One legal theory would require the payment of taxes on property used for proprietary purposes—as distinguished from educational purposes. But there is authority for the view that if the university has a legal right to hold and use the property, it should be immune from taxation on it.

There is no reason why the university act cannot clarify the tax responsibility. It can be argued that an institution which derives its resources from tax revenue should not have to pay taxes—since this would, in effect, make the burden of its support fall unevenly on the taxpaying public. We believe this is the better view and that the university act or a general legislative provision should give the university tax immunity. But interpretation will be necessary— and in many jurisdictions, even though the enterprise is related to the activities of the university or the property is held for essential university needs, the university may have difficulty making its case if the function is purely proprietary and a profit is derived from it. The sale and lease-back arrangements sometimes made between a university and a private industry may be legitimate and may imply immunity where an educational use of the property is made, but such arrangements are always suspect.

Theories about the tax immunity of a university may change as the university expands its functions and engages in more activities of a proprietary nature. Even many of its service activities, particularly when they involve the use of additional property and call for increased public services, may cause a change in thinking about immunity. The local tax problem is accentuated as a campus grows and the local community comes to feel the burden of supplying many of its services to the university. (Certainly there are offsetting factors, but these do not prevent local complaint.) This has been recognized by some American institutions, for example, and they have contributed voluntarily to the budget of such local enterprises as fire protection, police protection, streets and lighting, and sewage disposal. In some cases a distinction has been made between general taxes and assessments for local improvements, the university being required to pay the latter. While tax immunity may apply when the university commences functioning, it should be prepared for the day when such immunity may, at least in part, be eliminated.

3.14. TORT LIABILITY

The position of the university with respect to tort liability depends on whether or not it enjoys governmental immunity. Such immunity may be complete or partial according to whether a distinction is made in functions. If the function is "proprietary" as distinguished from educational, some jurisdictions would hold the institution liable for the negligent acts of its employees; if the function is educational there would be no liability. A further distinction may be made, depending on who is plaintiff—a "stranger" being permitted to recover while a student or other recipient of institutional benefits is denied recovery.

Any provision in the act creating a university should be framed in the light of the tort theory prevailing in the country, and this theory may be undergoing transition, as it assuredly is in the United States. If there is not governmental immunity, then insurance should be provided. The provision that the university may sue and be sued should not be taken to mean it has tort liability—for the liability to suit could be construed as that growing out of contract. Obviously it would not be within the power of the university to give itself immunity through university statutory provisions. None of the university acts studied contained any statement about tort liability; therefore, it can be assumed that the theory which applies to other public agencies applies to public universities in the country. In the United States some jurisdictions distinguish between private or proprietary "charitable" institutions and public educational institutions—but here we are concerned only with public institutions.

It is recommended that a section on tort liability, framed to accord with the theory existing in the country, be included in the act. If this means that the university can be sued by anyone, either for negligence arising out of its proprietary functions or for any negligent act, then adequate insurance coverage should be provided both for the institution and for the negligent employee. There are cases involving American universities in which liability for negligence depends on whether or not the institution is insured—the reasoning being that if insured, public funds will not be required to pay the claim; hence, one of the reasons for university immunity—protection of funds for educational purposes—will be satisfied even though the institution is held liable. But the gist of the action is negligence; there must be fault, and the plaintiff must be able to refute defenses which might be made—contributory negligence, status as a recipient, or assumption of risk, for example. In situations where the negligence of a contracting party is involved (supplying defective movable seating would be an example), the university may not be included as a party at all and the action may be against the contractors for negligence. On the other hand, the university may be joined as a defendant.

There is no limit to the kinds of actions in which a university might be involved, though obviously some are more likely than others. Laboratory accidents are frequent sources of litigation in American schools and universities. In such cases the extent and presence of supervision may be a controlling factor, assuming that the institution does not have immunity. Even if the institution has immunity, a negligent individual may be held liable to the injured party if his negligence is the proximate cause of the injury. If the university has a clinic and medical personnel, cases are, in time, likely to arise from this service. Negligence and malpractice of many kinds are claimed. The immunity principle still applies if it is present at all. There may of course be additional factors to consider in determining if there is liability—parental consent, for example, to a major operation on a student. This is an area in which a university legal counsel can be of great help in devising forms, waivers, and other documents which can protect the university without making it appear downright antisocial in the rendering of its services.

If there is a student newspaper, actions for libel may arise. In these cases there may be not only a question of immunity but a question as to who is the proper defendant. Many student publications in American universities are sufficiently separated from the university to cause courts to regard them as separate entities. In this case a university would not be a proper defendant in a libel suit. The kind of involvement which might make the university liable stems from such activities as advance censorship by the university, members of the university staff as advisers to the student publication, and other types of surveillance which, taken together, would permit a plaintiff to argue that the university was in position to control the contents of a paper but failed to do so. This is perhaps not the place to say it, but if the university exercises this kind of control, the student newspaper is probably not a very good one.

On-the-job accidents, particularly those which are likely to happen to nonacademic personnel, are another source of litigation. There may be public workmen's compensation laws in many countries which would cover university employees. As the agricultural universities acquire vehicles and are able to increase their extension activity, there will of course be claims arising from accidents caused by such vehicles.

Still another source of litigation arises from encroachments by the university on surrounding property. This may be either actual physical encroachment without having engaged in proper acquisition formalities or it may come in the form of a nuisance suit because the university's activities make the use of adjoining property untenable. In a 1926 Connecticut Supreme Court decision, Yale University was denied the right to erect a structure over a street to connect two buildings without the consent of city officials, on the theory that it would constitute a nuisance—even though the university owned the fee in the street. The more active the institution becomes, the more it extends itself to the public—and the more it invites members of the public to come to the campus, the greater is the need for a consideration of its position with respect to tort liability. Once again let it be urged that adequate insurance be maintained to fill any gaps which are not covered by a general or partial immunity theory or by any other constitutional or legislative provisions peculiar to the country.

There is a converse of university liability—namely, liability to the university. Certainly it has a right to sue for negligent damage to its property. However, when claims are made against its own staff members or students for damage caused in the discharge of their responsibilities, recovery is more difficult. It is argued that in such situations the university should be cognizant of the risk and should assume such as part of its normal functioning. This theory was applied in the case of an American university which attempted to recover for the alleged negligent operation of one of its aircraft by a student trainee resulting in the destruction of the aircraft. The university lost. There is further discussion of liability of the university to its employees in Chapter 16.

3.15. THE RIGHT TO ASSOCIATE

The very purpose of the university as an instrument of public service should mean that it can cooperate with all kinds of interest groups and can form judgments about the extent and nature of this cooperation. Labor, business, agriculture—many segments of the economy will wish to avail themselves of certain educational and research features of the university. At least it is hoped this will be true. There should be no question about the ability of the institution to involve itself with such agencies. The appropriateness of the involvement and the necessity to remain free from political considerations or from favoritism are always questions which must be considered. In the end, the good judgment of university personnel must be relied upon. The institution should be big enough to live with a few mistakes. It is better to cooperate and run the risk of criticism than it is to adopt a "hands-off" attitude resulting in a sterile program.

In the absence of specific authorization, what is the right of the university to associate in various degrees and varying commitments with other universities or institutions? Certainly there is some implied authority. It may be argued that so long as such association is in furtherance of the purpose of the university, it is legitimate— even though it requires a commitment of university resources. The consortium device has gained in usage among American universities without any additional specific legislative authority. It is probably safe to say, therefore, that a university in any part of the world has a certain implied authority to associate, cooperate, become a member of a consortium, or in other ways work with another institution or institutions in the achievement of legitimate objectives.

A more difficult question arises when the association involves some change in administrative structure. Such would be the case, for example, if a small institution asked simply to be made a part of a larger institution. This question will arise because as new institutions are formed and gain some distinction in rendering the kind of public service and in mounting the kind of educational program which the leaders in the country desire, there will be requests from smaller institutions to "team up" with it and to become part of it— the thought being that such smaller institutions can retain some essential identity but at the same time profit from the budget, prestige, and relationships of the larger institution.

There are sound arguments in favor of resisting such transfers until the new university has proved itself and is so well established that its objectives cannot very easily be shaken. But the time will come when serious consideration will need to be given to its relationship with other institutions, particularly smaller ones with limited resources. Rather than trust to the future for appropriate legislation, it would seem better to insert a provision in the act creating the university. This provision should require action by and the consent of both the main academic body, either council or senate, and the board of management. Certainly it should not be an administrative decision, and it would be unwise to permit the board to make such a decision without faculty action. Action by the above-mentioned bodies would insure thorough consideration of the advantages and disadvantages of the transfer and would afford greater protection to the new institution.

Though the right may be implied, it would be advisable for the act to authorize the institution to become a member of any association of universities or colleges established to permit institutions to pool their efforts in seeking appropriations and favorable legislation, and in dealing with other important public relations matters. The American Association of Land-Grant Colleges and State Universities, for example, has had a tremendous impact on the development of these institutions by protecting the integrity of their programs and by working to gain financial support and recognition for them. In addition to these functions, it has served as a medium for what might be called self-study and internal improvement. Though the right to participate in such an association is probably implied, it is so significant that a legislative provision which not only recognizes the right but encourages participation by the institution would be advisable. In Peru, the Inter-University Council has been created by law; in the Philippines there is the Association of Agricultural Colleges; Mexico has the National Association of Directors of Schools of Agriculture; and in India, the Association of Agricultural Universities is being organized. Colleges, departments, and other units of the university should likewise be authorized to cooperate with or associate with counterpart agencies in other institutions in the achievement of objectives or in expanding the impact of their programs. A university statute could authorize such activity and could require the execution and approval of appropriate memoranda of understanding.

Regional cooperation of universities in the developing countries through consortia or other devices is worthy of consideration. Such a pooling of effort will make possible programs which could not otherwise be initiated because of limited resources or inability to establish all lines of work which might be needed. Furthermore, such interregional organizations might attract outside funds and be of indirect benefit to the institution in broading the scope of its program. This could provide experience for staff members, be an outlet for graduate students, and in other ways benefit the institution. It is noteworthy that American universities with all the resources at their command, relatively speaking, are still interested in creating interinstitutional agencies.

3.16. THE GENERAL POWERS OF THE UNIVERSITY

Certain powers are essential if the university is to function effectively as a public corporation. The rights to sue and be sued, to enter into contracts, and to lease and manage property are indispensable. As a corporation, and hence an artificial legal person with stated educational objectives, the university will have many implied rights, but any necessary right or power which can be foreseen and about which there might be a legal question should not be left to implication. Fortunately for some American universities following World War II, state courts were liberal in implying that they should have the right to issue bonds, execute mortgages, and in other ways raise money to provide housing for returning veteran students and for necessary staff. In other situations and in some jurisdictions, however, this power or right was held not to exist without specific legislation.

Many of the new universities in developing countries are confronted with the necessity of acquiring property, building housing, charging rental, or at least including the rental value as part of the remuneration to staff members, and so need a range of power and authority which would not be necessary for a relatively static university in a large city. A university in a rural area will need to engage in a number of proprietary functions just to meet the reasonable needs of students and staff. Such proprietary activities might include the operation of a nonprofit store, services such as laundry and dry cleaning, the establishment of a school for the young children of staff members, even the operation of a cinema and recreational facilities regarded as essential in an isolated geographical location.

Two kinds of legal questions are posed by such activities: (1) the right of the institution to engage in them and (2) its tax and tort liability with respect to them. The legislation should be as explicit as possible with regard to both these important questions. Certainly the right to engage in proprietary functions which are deemed necessary to the operation of the institution should be left to the discretion of the board acting upon proper advice from the administration and staff of the university. A good argument can be made also that if the institution enjoys charitable or governmental immunity in the area of taxation and torts, it should enjoy this immunity all the way—that is, with respect to proprietary as well as so-called educational or governmental functions. After all, they are part and parcel of one overall endeavor, the object of which is education. Jurisdictions in America are divided on this point, as they very well might be in the developing countries; hence, clarifying legislation in the act creating the institution could go a long way toward preventing litigation and making the situation clear from the outset.

There is a further question having to do with the right of the university to assess students for services of various kinds. Theoretically, a tuition fee is supposed to take care of a student's contribution to the expense of operating the university, but many institutions, when hard pressed for funds and in need of some further service or enterprise, will look for internal means of financing. University constructed and managed housing with students and staff paying rentals is one example. Special student fees to help support athletics and, in at least one rare case, laundry services are other examples. Exactly what power the university has to engage in these activities should be decided in the light of the prevailing philosophy of the country and the likely needs of the institution. But here again it may be wise to be foresighted, so that if a right or power is needed, it will be available. At all times reliance should be placed on the good judgment of the administration and board of control to refrain from instituting activities which would not be feasible under current conditions.

Another power which a university may have, even though not specifically stated, is that of eminent domain. It is better, however, if the university act contains a provision on the right of eminent domain. It would be well to state that property may be acquired for future needs and managed in the meantime for income-producing purposes. Questions frequently arise with respect to the right of different public agencies in the same property. For instance, would the university have a right to acquire property from that held by a city, park district, or other public entity? Sometimes there is a general law stating which agencies are paramount. In drafting the university act, attention should be given to the general eminent domain law to see if it requires amending on behalf of the university. Then there should be a statement in the university act in accord with the provisions in the general eminent domain act. The converse situation should also be covered—that is, the right of other agencies to acquire easements in university property. May a city construct a drain through university property? May the highway authorities construct a road across the university farm? Certainly the university act should provide authority to contract with these agencies in situations where the administration and board are willing to yield the right requested, but in cases where the institution is unwilling, the law should state which agency is paramount. If the test is to be relative need, then the law should so state and should indicate guidelines by which the relative need is to be determined.

The general powers of the university as contained in the Uttar Pradesh Agricultural University Act and in the University of Nigeria Law are typical. Included are the following powers: to acquire, hold, and otherwise deal with movable and immovable property; to accept gifts, legacies, and donations; to enter into contracts, establish trusts, act as trustee, and employ and act through agents; to erect, provide, equip, and maintain libraries, lecture halls, halls of residence, sports grounds, and any building necessary or suitable or convenient for any of the objects of the university; to invest monies by way of endowment or in other ways and from time to time change or vary such investments; to borrow money and pledge the security of the university; to provide for instruction, research, and extension in all the areas of knowledge comprehended by the university; to hold examinations and grant degrees; to cooperate with other universities and authorities; to create academic, administrative, ministerial, and other necessary posts; to establish and collect fees and other charges; to institute and award fellowships, scholarships, and other forms of awards and assistance.

3.17. REMOVAL OF DIFFICULTIES—TEMPORARY PROVISIONS

In the early life of a university the staff and administrative personnel may not be present in sufficient numbers to meet legal requirements for some actions universities are required to take. As a matter of fact, the board of management may not be constituted for some time after the physical construction has commenced and the university is under way. In order that actions taken by a temporary administrator, a development board or body, and by faculty bodies not yet complete in membership be valid, the university act should contain a curative section. This is sometimes referred to as a "removal-of-difficulties" provision. For example, the Uttar Pradesh Agricultural University Act states that

The state government may, for the purpose of removing any difficulties in relation to the enforcement of the provisions of this act, by orders published in the gazette, (a) direct that this act and any statutes made thereunder, shall during such period as may be specified in the order, take effect subject to such adaptations whether by way of modification, addition, or omission as it may deem to be necessary or expedient, or (b) direct by whom and in what manner the powers, duties, and functions to be exercised or discharged under this act by an officer or authority of the university shall be exercised and discharged until such officer or authority is duly appointed or constituted, or (c) make such other temporary provisions as it may deem to be necessary or expedient.

It is generally provided that after publication such orders shall as soon as possible be laid before the legislature.

A statement similar to this should be included in a university act together with any more specific provisions which are required before the university is duly constitituted and has all its bodies and administrative officers functioning. The conditions under which a removal-of-difficulties clause or specific provisions pending final organization of the institution are to apply should be clearly stated so that there will be no question about when the special provision terminates and regular provisions in the university act prevail.

Though special sections in the act on removal of difficulties and temporary arrangements are important and should be included, there will nevertheless be many places in the act itself where the language should indicate that certain temporary arrangements are to prevail until a certain time and then permanent provisions are to apply. For example, in the Uttar Pradesh Agricultural University Act it is provided that the first vice-chancellor shall be appointed by the chancellor. This was put in the law so that a vice-chancellor could be appointed even though the board had not yet been constituted.[2]

The university act should state that the proceedings of university authorities or other university bodies shall not be invalidated by reason of vacancies or the presence of nonqualified participants at meetings. At the beginning it will not be possible to perfect the composition of all bodies.

3.18. INTERPRETATION—SEPARABILITY CLAUSE

When controversies develop over the fine points in a law, a statement in the law about interpretation may be very helpful. While some laws, lien laws for example, beg for strict construction, others need a liberal construction to be most effective. A section in the university act reminding those who must interpret it that it should be liberally construed to enable the university to achieve its overall objectives could be helpful. There should be a separability clause— a section stating that in case any part of the act is determined to be invalid or unenforceable, the remainder of the act shall not be affected.

----

[2] For a more complete discussion of temporary provisions, see Appendix V.

CHAPTER – 4

The Governing Body—
Selection and Structure

4.1. HOW GOVERNING BODIES ARE CONSTITUTED

The governing bodies of universities are known by many names. They range from syndicate, court, board of control, board of directors, university council, board of regents, board of government, board of trustees, and board of management to such designations as the overseers, or just plain "the corporation" or "trustees."

If anyone feels he knows exactly how to constitute the governing body of a university, then he has more knowledge and perhaps more confidence in himself than all the universities of the world combined. Though the authors did not make a special search of university acts and statutes to see if by chance any two institutions did constitute their boards in exactly the same manner, they are reasonably certain that no two ever did. On the other hand, they cannot help but feel that some methods of constituting the board are better than others. In this section we shall deal with just two questions—what kind of people are and ought to be selected for board membership, and in what manner should they be selected? A review of the laws of universities in Asia, Africa, and the Americas reveals that the following kinds of people have, in one institution or another, been included in board membership:

A variety of ex officio, co-opted, or organizational representative members, including secretaries, ministers and directors of education, agriculture, finance, community development, animal husbandry, horticulture, fisheries, and sometimes of other government agencies.

The chairman of lower or upper legislative house committees on education and agriculture.

Members of the lower legislative branch.

Members of the upper legislative branch.

Alumni of the university.

Representatives of various associations or organizations such as agricultural credit and assistance associations, registered engineers, state farmers' organizations, councils of agricultural education, state social welfare boards, and cooperative banks.

Members from local agricultural councils or political units.

Members of the faculty.

Student members, sometimes amounting to as much as one-third of the body (as provided in the Peru National Universities Act).

Apart from these kinds of members, the criteria for membership become quite general with, however, frequent statements about the kind of people who should be elected or appointed. For example, the law creating the University of Kentucky stated that the trustees should consist of a number of ex officio members and "twelve citizens of Kentucky, discreet, intelligent, and prudent." Among other statements which constitute guides are the following:

Eminent agricultural scientists.

Progressive farmers.

Progressive livestock breeders with experience and interest in scientific farming.

Distinguished industrialist businessman.

Distinguished manufacturer.

Distinguished trader.

Outstanding woman social worker.

A person interested in agricultural education and development.

Men of prominence and character in agricultural pursuits.

Citizens of character and distinction.

Reviewing all these criteria for membership, both ex officio and non–ex officio, one might conclude that two things seem important— securing competent people and attempting to secure representation from major areas of interest which would be concerned with the university.

It is probably not feasible to deal with the question of competency in a university act. One could express a hope for qualified members, as the Kentucky and certain other laws have, but in the end the question of competency must be judged by the appointing or electing authority—whoever that might be. The law, however, can contain helpful provisions regarding ex officio membership and the representation of areas of interest. One can argue that the board should not be loaded with ex officio members from government, though the presence of certain officers may be very helpful. Likewise, it does not seem a good policy to include members of the legislature. If this practice were followed throughout government, legislators would be making policy at two governmental levels.

Certainly the interests which ought to be represented may vary from one country to another; on the other hand, there are certain areas in both the public and private sectors of any country that ought to have a high interest in an agricultural university. If we assume some optimum number on the board, which the writers are willing at this point to set at thirteen, balance could be achieved with the following membership: secretary of agriculture ex officio; the secretary of either finance or education ex officio; the chief administrative officer of the university; two registered graduates of the institution (one woman and one man to be selected by the registered graduates or alumni organization); two members of the faculty to be elected by the faculty; two progressive farmers; two professional educators; and two members representing business and industry, labor, and the professions (these latter six would be appointed by the governor or chancellor; they should not be members of government). In some cases geography is included as a criterion and there must be district or local political unit representation. Inasmuch as some geographical spread can be achieved by wise selection, and since an expressed geographic requirement may very well prevent the best people from being appointed to the board, such a provision should not be included in the university act. In countries that have a history of student representation on the boards of management or control, it may be essential to continue such representation but, hopefully, to keep the proportion to a minimum. Students need to have a voice and be represented in many university bodies, but in view of the experience and qualifications which a good board member should possess, the board of control is not one on which such representation is useful.

Likewise, some of the objectives which an impartial and competent board can achieve are defeated if the governing body is composed entirely or predominantly of university faculty members. This is the case in some institutions where a university council is the governing body. Though some institutions having this method of control argue that it works very well, there is noticeable a higher degree of infighting and more frequent changes in the post of chief administrative officer. Continuity of good administrators and teachers is an objective, and yet a governing body which is so close to daily affairs that it can be unduly influenced by them does not seem to be the kind of body which will beget this continuity.

With respect to the second major question—how should board members be appointed or selected—the answer, drawn from study of the laws of a large number of institutions, would indicate that a diversity of methods, even in the same institution, would be desirable. Although in a few universities the board members or trustees are selected by a general election, this method does not seem to be widely used and, though it has worked very well with some institutions, could lead to political abuse. It is not recommended. Organizations which under the law are to have a representative on the board may, of course, engage in any method of selection they choose. The more common methods of securing board members are through:

Ex officio designation.

Appointment by the governor or chancellor with or without confirmation by a branch of the legislature.

Appointment by some other high government official—such as the Minister of Education.

Appointment by the court or judicial branch of government.

Designation of certain members by government agencies.

Selection of a stated number of members by legislative bodies from their own ranks.

Designation by other public and also private agencies of a stated number of members to be selected by such agencies.

Selection of representatives from the registered graduates or alumni by the graduates or alumni.

Election of faculty members by the faculty.

Self-perpetuation or selection of additional members by the board itself.

Nomination of deans or other faculty members by the chief administrative officer.

The writers hold no brief for or against any of these methods as long as the board achieves the kind of balance discussed earlier in this section. In the kind of board which was suggested, three members would be ex officio, six would be appointed by the governor (two each from three named categories with no requirement that such appointments be confirmed by the legislature), two would be elected from the faculty, and two, a man and a woman, would be selected by the registered graduates or alumni. With respect to alumni, some acts provide that until there are registered graduates, the registered graduates of institutions which have become a part of the university may qualify for membership on the board. In cases where no institutions have been brought in as constituent colleges and the university "starts from the ground," there should be a provision that these positions will simply be vacant until there are registered graduates or alumni and that in the meantime the functioning of the board shall not be legally impaired.

A practice worthy of consideration is that established in the Punjab Agricultural University law, which provides for a technical advisory committee to the board. Such a committee could contain representatives from those government or other agencies which have the most concern with the university—particularly in its early stages. The advice of such a group could be sought on all kinds of matters, from construction, finance, and physical development to the proper relation of the university with government research, extension, and other activities.

4.2. NUMBER OF MEMBERS

There is no more agreement among universities about numbers on a board than there is about the constitution of the board. In reviewing the acts of a large number of universities around the world, the number was found to vary from three to more than one hundred. How large should a board be? Large enough to represent the major interests with which the university is concerned and small enough to meet frequently and achieve some cohesion. Certainly there are factors more important to the functioning of the board than the number of members it contains. A small and uninterested board with members not coming to meetings would not be very helpful to the institution, whereas a much larger board with a high percentage of interested members could organize itself to be helpful. Probably the main argument against an extremely large board is that it is unwieldy, expensive in terms of travel, and bound to contain a certain number of uninterested members. Furthermore, if it is to be effective it will have to act through an executive committee which in a sense will become the real governing body—so that the larger board really amounts only to a panel from which the governing body is selected. Increasing the size of a board to get a quorum is self-defeating.

The board should be large enough to afford representation of important interest groups, though such representation should not be achieved at the expense of getting highly qualified, willing, and dedicated men on the board. In almost half the institutions studied the number ranged between nine and thirteen. Outside this range there were more institutions with larger numbers. We feel that the optimum size falls somewhere within this range. If it is felt in a particular situation that there should be a large number of ex officio government officials, then one would argue for a larger number of appointive, nongovernment officials so that the board would not be unbalanced in the direction of political influence. We do not feel that it is desirable to have a large number of government ex officio officers on the board—hence our suggestion that thirteen can be the optimum number.

How should the number be established and how can it be changed? Some self-perpetuating boards are able to vary their own membership. With respect to public institutions, we feel that the legislative act creating the university should specify the number and that the number be changed only by amending the legislation. After all, the board is the agency created by law to administer the affairs of the university, and it is presumed the legislature will have a sufficient interest in this body to wish to control its size and general composition. If the legislature wishes to provide for a board with a fluctuating membership, it could do so. This condition would prevail, for example, if the law specifies the university council as the governing body and the council has a fluctuating membership depending on the number of faculty members, students, deans or officers of administration who might at any particular time be qualified to serve on it. This is not likely to be the best method of establishing a board.

4.3. RESIDENCE REQUIREMENTS

Some laws require that all members of the governing body be residents of the state or political unit creating the university. Most university acts and statutes are silent on this subject. Rather than place any such limitation in the act, we feel that the converse should be stated, namely, that the law should specify that board members need not be residents of the state or political unit creating the university. First of all, under the provisions we have suggested for composing the board, it is not likely that many nonresidents would be appointed; on the other hand, their appointment should not be precluded, particularly in those cases where a small state or country with limited high-level manpower creates a university. In those cases it may be very wise to include one or more distinguished and interested educators from outside the country who have had experience in the country—providing it is possible for them to meet with the board often enough to make some impact. Also, a state or region may wish to include an appropriate officer of central government on the board or specify that an appropriate central agency (such as the Ministry of Education) designate a member to serve on the board.

The main argument in favor of a majority of the board and in most cases nearly all of the board being residents of the political unit is that the board is expected to be a working body meeting frequently to help the chief administrative officer resolve policy issues, and it is to be expected that citizens of the political unit will have a much higher interest in such questions and will be more willing to meet and thrash them out.

4.4. TERM OF OFFICE—REMOVAL

How long should the non–ex officio board members serve? In a few rare instances appointments are for life; in others, they are for as short a term as two years. A majority of laws provide for a term of from four to seven years, generally with the right of reappointment to succeeding terms. A consideration of the optimum length of term poses a dilemma. If the board member is a good man, everyone will wish to keep him for as long as he will serve. If he is an ineffective member, everyone will wish to get rid of him before his term is ended—no matter how short it might be. Since it is not feasible to draft a law which would specify one term for good men and another term for ineffective men, some compromise must be made. A majority of those concerned seem to agree that from four to seven years is a good compromise. The writers would like to suggest a six-year term with one-third of the appointive members going off each year. This staggering could be provided for in the beginning by law. Six years should be short enough to get some of the turnover which will produce new ideas and also to relieve enough of the burden of a nonpaying job to get good men. At the same time it is long enough for a member to become acquainted with the problems of the university and be a positive and productive member of the board.

Since ex officio members will, of course, serve as long as they hold their office, what is to be done about a member designated by an association or society who proves to be unfit? The organization could be asked to designate another member, but this raises legal questions. What is the right of the incumbent? Can or should the law give the appointing agency the right to recall a member once appointed for a designated term? Probably not, but suppose the member designated by an organization ceases to be a member of the organization while he is serving on the board. Does this automatically terminate his right to serve as a board member? Probably so.

Some university acts give the board the right to remove its own members, sometimes for stated causes such as conviction of an offense involving moral turpitude or participation in subversive activities. Other acts simply say "for cause," or say nothing at all. The writers recommend that the act provide for removal by the governor or chancellor of those appointed by him following a recommendation of the board to him and that the board be given the power under specified procedures to remove other members for cause, except ex officio members. The board should be empowered to develop its own rules with regard to removal of members. However, the law providing for the removal of members should specify the right to notice and hearing and representation by counsel if the member so chooses. Also, there should be a requirement that more than a majority of the board concur in the action—perhaps two-thirds or three-fourths. In addition, the member should have the right to appeal to the courts for a review of the board's decision. It is not recommended that moral turpitude or any other specific cause be listed in the law but rather that when a board member has for any reason become ineffective and unable to discharge the responsibilities of his position, the board itself be permitted to determine just cause for removal.

With respect to vacancies, the law should provide that the appointing authority or agency fill the unexpired term. The governing body should define "vacancy" in its procedural bylaws.

4.5. MEETINGS—MINUTES AND RECORDS—QUORUM

At least one university act requires the board to meet monthly; a few require meetings every other month; quite a large number require quarterly meetings; some require only an annual meeting and leave the matter of other meetings to the determination of the board; some simply say that the board shall meet at such times and as often as it may deem necessary. One can argue that if the board is doing its business properly, it should not be told how often to meet, and that if it is not doing its business properly, little good is accomplished by requiring a minimum number of meetings during the year. However, there would seem to be no harm in requiring quarterly meetings since it would be assumed that any active board would certainly need to meet at least this often. There should be a provision that special meetings of the board may be called by the chairman or by some minimum number of members such as three. The law should require sufficient notice of meetings, whether regular or special, and should also require that at special meetings only matters designated in the call be considered.

There is a general feeling that at least part of the meetings of the board should be at the university, if for no other reason than to make certain that board members see the university frequently, get more of the feel of it, and hence retain a higher interest in its affairs. Some acts or statutes require that one-half of the meetings of the board or that every other meeting be held at the university. There is probably no harm in having the act provide that at least one-half of the regular meetings of the board be held at the university.

Unless there are major policy issues to be settled, an active executive committee can transact much of the necessary business of the board and save all the members from coming to frequent meetings.

Opinions vary considerably about the public nature of board meetings. Some argue that all board meetings should be open to the public; others argue that none should be. The acts and statutes reviewed contained very little that is helpful on this subject. Certainly most acts and statutes do not prohibit board meetings from being public meetings—the question becomes one of general law regarding the meetings of public agencies and the right of such agencies to determine who shall attend. In the absence of some compelling law or custom in a country the best solution would be a provision in the act giving the board the right to determine when to hold closed meetings and providing that unless the board so determines, its meetings be open to members of the public.

The board should have the right to invite attendance by those who can be helpful in the resolution of problems before it. The law should so state.

There should be a provision in the law stating that proceedings of the board shall not be invalidated because of defective procedures in the appointment of any member. Also, to get the board off-center, its regulations should provide that any member may ask for a vote on any issue before the board. This does not necessarily mean a resolution of the issue, but simply that the member could cause something to be done. Other rules of order should be adopted so that motions to table, to delay consideration, to amend, or to refer to some other body for action would all be available as means of answering the demand for a vote. The board should have published rules governing its procedure at meetings and governing other activities in which it engages. These should not be a part of the university statutes.

Through its own rules the board should provide for adequate records and their publication. Here again an issue arises regarding the public nature of the minutes of the board. Provisions in acts and statutes are very meagre. The University of Nigeria Statutes require that the secretary open the minutes for the inspection of board members; the University of the Philippines act requires the secretary to distribute minutes to each board member within one week following a meeting. These laws would seem to imply that members of the public might not be entitled to inspect the minutes. However, since the governing body of a state university is a public agency, whether technically so designated or not, the records of its meetings should be available to all those who have responsibilities to discharge with respect to the university. This would include government officials and the legislature. However, we do not believe the law should require submission of all minutes to government or the legislature. How far beyond this one should go in making them available to the general public is a debatable question. Certainly there is no reason for their voluntary publication by the board. The better position would be that they be available to anyone asking to see them at the office of the secretary during regular business hours. It is always possible for the press and other agencies or individuals to publicize records of the governing body in such a manner as to cause problems for the university. The best protection against this is creation by the board of good public relations with the press and with other agencies and individuals most deeply concerned with the university.

The university act should state what constitutes a quorum for legal action by the board. Although a few laws specify that a majority of the board shall constitute a quorum, most laws specify a fixed number. Without designating institutions, here are some of the requirements: 6 out of 21, 3 out of 9, 6 out of 15, 9 out of 26, 6 out of 11, and 7 out of 12. In addition to specifying quorum requirements, some laws state that a smaller number may adjourn the meeting until there is a quorum. Requiring only a small number from a large board membership tends to defeat the main purpose of a board, that of interested and active participation in guiding the affairs of the university. Furthermore, this would permit an interested few to dominate university activities. If the board is of desirable size, the best provision would be one requiring a majority of the board as a quorum. If the board is larger, then it may be necessary to designate some number less than a majority. This number could very well fall within the range for an optimum board size of nine to thirteen. This would constitute a group large enough to prevent hasty or unwise action. Sometimes the law distinguishes between kinds of activity and requires a higher number for a quorum when matters such as the transfer of property or discharge of a chief administrative officer are being considered. There may be a provision that on some matters a favorable majority vote of the total board membership is required—not just a majority of a quorum.

The act should require adequate notice for all meetings of the board and provide that details regarding notice be contained in rules of the board.

4.6. THE CHAIRMAN OF THE BOARD

University governing boards are normally organized with a chairman or president, a secretary, a treasurer, and a few standing committees. Sometimes provision is made for the election of a vice-president or vice-chairman.

The chairman of the board holds an extremely important position with regard to the success of a university, particularly of a new university. The manner in which the board discharges its responsibilities will depend heavily on the interest and ability of the chairman. Not only must he provide leadership for the board, and in a sense for the institution itself, but he must also be able to take a strong stand against interference by government with the rightful autonomy of the board. Courage, then, should be one of his attributes.

Board presidents or chairmen are selected in a variety of ways. Three methods, however, seem to predominate: election by the board itself, appointment by the governor, and ex officio chairmanship as a responsibility of the chief administrative officer of the university. Some variations are ex officio chairmanship in an officer of government such as the Secretary of Education, chairmanship in the governor himself with the board electing a president or chairman pro tem, designation of the pro-chancellor as chairman, and complete silence on the subject. In this last case it is assumed the board will have the power to organize itself and name its own chairman. Many arguments pro and con can be made about these different methods of selecting a chairman. When any one of them produces a good chairman, it is a good method. When it does not, someone will argue that a different method ought to have been used. There is a theory that the board, being an independent body and in position to hire the staff of the university, should not have as its chairman a man hired by it to be chief administrative officer of the university. But there are arguments against this theory.[1] If one had to settle for just one method, which certainly is not necessary, he might argue for election or selection by the board itself. There seems no point in naming the governor as chairman unless it is clearly stated in the law that this is simply honorary and that a working chairman will be named. Also, it does not seem a good idea to name some other officer of government, the Secretary of Education for example, as ex officio chairman. Not only may this develop problems and tensions in the board, but it does not assure that the chairman will always be a man with a high interest in the university.

The term for which a chairman is selected varies considerably. If he serves ex officio, then the term lasts as long as he holds the position which makes him chairman. Terms for which the chairman is appointed vary from one to four years, with one and two years being most predominant. Some laws provide that the chairman cannot succeed himself or be appointed for a second term. It would seem desirable to specify a short term but with the right of reap-

----

[1] For a discussion of the pros and cons of having the chief administrative officer chairman of the board, see Chapter 7.

pointment. Good board members are likely to be busy people and a good chairman might not wish to be saddled with the job for too long a period. On the other hand, if he is willing, he can be reappointed. Where there are staggered terms for the board, bringing in new members every two years, one might argue that two years is a good term for the chairman. Otherwise, one would argue that a one-year term is better than a three- or four-year term.

It would seem that in all cases appointment or selection of a vice-chairman would be desirable whether or not the chairmanship is ex officio. The board may need to meet at times when the chairman cannot be present; the existence of a vice-chairman would make it clear who is to act and could lead to better prior planning before a meeting.

4.7. THE SECRETARY AND TREASURER

Who should be secretary of the board? A good man with clerical facilities readily available, preferably an administrative staff member of the university or an assistant to the president or chief administrative officer. In many universities in all parts of the world the registrar is named as board secretary. Occasionally the comptroller gets the job. Institutions having an office known as secretary of the university may name this official as secretary of the board. Though the position itself should not require full-time service, it is considerably more than a clerical job and should be discharged by someone with organizational ability and a grasp of the board's function. Furthermore, he should have free and ready communications between the board and the chief administrative officer of the university. Among his functions are those of maintaining adequate minutes and records; notifying members of the time and place of meeting; arranging for meetings; helping the chief administrative officer organize the agenda for each meeting and mailing out such agenda together with necessary supporting documents, reports, and materials so that board members can be informed in advance; and maintaining copies of contracts, renewals of contracts, records of staff members on leave, and other essential information which has to do with contractual relations between the board and members of the staff.

A strong argument can be made that the secretary should be a member of the chief administrative officer's staff, whether the registrar or not, and that he should be sufficiently freed of responsibilities through supplying him with additional help so that he can adequately discharge the responsibility as secretary of the board. He is not a member of the board, and therefore has no vote and takes no voice in the determination of policy matters. The secretary should not, either through design or default, be authorized to handle matters which belong to the board, the chief administrative officer, or to some other officer or authority of the university. The staff should not be made to feel that the secretary has any power of decision over them. In some instances the board may select a secretary from its own membership, and in at least one instance the secretary was made a full-time officer with the duty of maintaining an office at the state capitol, but this arrangement hardly seems wise or necessary. Also, asking a member of the board to serve as secretary tends to detract from his status and role as a member. The act should empower the board to appoint a secretary from among the officers of the university. His powers and duties should be specified in university statutes.

Some laws designate the chief financial and business officer of the institution as treasurer of the board. Though the title of treasurer may be applied to this officer, the term is more generally applied to one who simply has responsibility for safekeeping of the university's funds. This generally implies someone outside the university itself and not a member of the board. In some instances the state treasurer is named as treasurer of the board; in others, it may be an officer of the bank in which university funds are deposited. The law should require that the treasurer be bonded. The concept of the treasurer as a nonboard, nonuniversity staff member in a sense creates an additional check or safeguard on the management and use of funds by the university.

4.8. COMMITTEE STRUCTURE

Most university acts simply provide that the board may create such committees, either standing or special, as it may deem necessary or convenient for the proper performance of its functions. While this right may be implied, it is wise to have such a provision in the law. In those institutions where the chief administrative officer is a member of or chairman of the governing body, the law frequently provides that he shall be an ex officio member of all standing committees. This is realistic since either his assistance or that of some of his staff members will be needed by such committees.

The law should provide for the appointment of an executive committee, and should provide that it may act for the board between meetings, subject to confirmation by the board of any important policy decisions it may have been called upon to resolve in the interim. A usual provision designates the chairman of the board as chairman of the executive committee and specifies that two, three, or four additional members of the board shall constitute the committee. The additional members may either be appointed by the chairman or elected by the board, and the board should establish rules further specifying the functioning and authority of its executive committee.

Another standing committee frequently provided is one on finance. The chief financial officer of the university is included as a member and usually acts as secretary of the committee. The finance committee may have added to its membership the chief finance officer of the state or someone in his department. Its main purpose is to advise the board regarding the finances of the university, to study the budget and make recommendations, and to exercise some surveillance over the management of funds within the university. As described in the University of Nigeria Statutes, the Finance and General Purposes Committee functions also as an executive committee.

The Ahmadu Bello Act provides that the governing body may establish joint committees between itself and the academic senate. This could probably be done without statutory or legislative authorization, but it does seem wise to have a provision suggesting the possibility. Situations frequently arise in which such a joint committee could be of great service.

A good committee structure is essential for proper functioning of a governing body. Except for the designation of an executive committee and perhaps of a finance committee, it would seem best to leave the designation of others to the board through its own rules. A board attempting to emphasize agricultural development may wish to provide for a committee on agriculture. Others commonly established are committees on buildings and grounds, athletics, and future development. With or without specific organization, the board can certainly appoint such ad hoc committees as it needs and can call in such persons as it deems necessary to act in an advisory capacity on its committees.

4.9. CONFLICTS OF INTEREST

In none of the Asian, African, or Latin-American university acts and statutes surveyed were there any provisions on conflicts of interest of board members. This does not mean that such conflicts could not be recognized and that a board member could not be removed for such cause under some of the provisions contained in these laws and acts on removal. Many American university laws and statutes do contain such provisions. Typical is a provision in the laws of Illinois relating to the University of Illinois: "No member of such board shall hold or be employed in or appointed to any office or place under the authority of the board of which he is a member, nor shall any member of said board be directly or indirectly interested in any contract to be made by said board for any purpose whatever." The two main prohibitions seem to be against the employment of a board member by the board and against contractual or business relations between any board member and the university. The reason for such provisions is obvious though most board members, out of their own wisdom and good judgment, would not become employees of the board or engage in contracts with the university. Nevertheless, the writers feel that the act creating the university should contain a provision forbidding employment (except in the case of the chief administrative officer and the faculty members) of a board member by the board and forbidding contractual relations of a private nature between the board member and the university. American court decisions have held that such contractual relations are permissible unless prohibited by law.

There are other things which may reduce the effectiveness of a board member but which would not amount to conflicts of interest. Service on so many other boards and bodies that the member does not have sufficient time for the university; a government officer as ex officio member of so many university boards that he cannot possibly function effectively on all of them; active membership in organizations or associations which are strongly opposed to major policies of the university—these are examples of conditions which may detract from the ability of the board member to render impartial, diligent, imaginative, and faithful service to the university as a member of its board. But these things cannot and should not be legislated against; the only preventive is wise selection of board members.

Many American universities prohibit membership of a professor on the board on the theory that this would represent a conflict of interests. After all, the professor's contract is finally approved by the board. There are American court decisions holding that unless membership is prohibited, a professor may serve as a member of the board. It is the custom in British universities to have a faculty contingent on the governing body. Historically, the governing body in British universities was wholly internal. In many institutions, particularly those in Latin America, a preponderant number of the board or governing council may be professors. It would seem unnecessary to have any restriction in the law if the law specifies how the board is to be composed. There certainly should be no objection to the inclusion of faculty members on the board if the law does not permit their numbers to predominate.

There are American court decisions holding that for certain purposes board members are public officers and hence are prohibited from holding positions or engaging in activities which would conflict with this function.

4.10. PAY AND EXPENSES

In almost all universities board members serve without pay, and this is as it should be. A position on a university board is one of public service rather than employment. Since most universities could not compete financially with private business in attracting men with the leadership ability needed, they rely on attracting qualified men who feel that contributing to the development and growth of the nation's educational institutions is in itself adequate remuneration. However, these persons should be reimbursed for their reasonable expenses while engaged in the business of the board. Some universities have included a general provision in the enabling act authorizing the payment of travel expenses; others have authorized travel expenses and daily allowances. The writers found statutes of only one university which described in detail the rates at which board members were to be reimbursed. A general provision in the act requiring reimbursement for actual expenses is recommended. Further details should be left to the board for inclusion in its rules. Certainly the law should not specify rates or amounts, and it would be better if the university statutes did not.

5.8. APPROVAL OF COURSES OF STUDY AND QUALIFICATIONS FOR DEGREES

Courses, curricula, degrees—subjects near to the heart of all academic bodies. Should a governing board ever tamper with them? Not often and not very much if it is a wise board. But the board does have a mandate to see that the law creating the institution is carried out and that the subject matter prescribed by it is taught. If the law states that the institution shall teach agriculture and engineering, the board would not be discharging its legal duty if it sat by and watched the academics establish a liberal arts college. Even on this point, however, there may be a broad discretion with respect to subjects taught and colleges organized in a university. We have said many times in this book and in the *Resource Book* that the emphasis, the needed emphasis on agriculture in the new universities, should not preclude the addition of other areas of study which time will bring to the institution if it is to be in fact a university.

Despite such statements in university acts as "The board shall prescribe the studies to be pursued and the textbooks to be used," which cause academics to shudder, the educational direction of the university, its courses of study, its curricula, and requirements for degrees are well understood the world around to be in the domain of the academic council, which shall advise the governing body on academic matters and shall prescribe courses of study, the syllabus, texts for examination, and other essentials to see that students become educated. The law creating Stanford University contains an interesting passage on this point: "To establish and maintain at such university an educational system which will, if followed, fit the graduate for some useful pursuit; and to this end to cause the pupils, as early as may be, to declare the particular calling, which in life they may desire to pursue; but it is not binding if the president judges the student to be not fitted for the pursuit declared."

Since the principle is so well established that the academic council or senate is the proper body to deal with courses of study, curriculum, qualifications for degrees, and similar matters, there should be such a provision in the university act. This provision should grant the academic council the right to make determinations regarding (1) courses to be taught, (2) curricula and qualifications for degrees, (3) the degrees to be granted including post-

4.11. PROVISIONAL BOARDS OR COUNCILS

New universities require implementation. Someone must be on the job before the regular board is constituted. Some suggestions from the *Resource Book* [2] follow:

One device which has worked well is a small development group or development advisory body which can give guidance to a temporary administrator and can make those policy decisions which must be made at the outset . . . .[3] Interests which should be represented on such a body include the top government people in agriculture, education, and finance; the temporary administrator himself; representatives of agriculture; someone to represent the interest of women in the new university; representatives from foundations or aiding governments involved materially in the development of the university; and representatives selected simply because of their high interest in and appreciation of the educational process and of the need for it in their country. To be effective, this group should not be too large; perhaps fifteen should be the maximum number. The legislation itself should provide for such a group and for paying its travel and meeting expense until it can be replaced by the official board. If the advisory development body consists primarily of those people who served on the investigation commission, its members will be following the course of the legislation and will be eager to meet as soon as an act is adopted so that essential plans may be developed and the establishment of the institution expedited.

While the development body will have to make many decisions of a major nature, it should defer as many policy decisions as possible until such time as the board itself can act. In this connection it would be hoped that some members of the development advisory body would also become members of the first board of the university. Thus the continuity established at the outset would be preserved.

Legislation providing for the development body should also provide that actions taken by it shall have the same force and effect they would have if made by the board itself. Though the main function of the advisory body will be to consult with the temporary administrator and help him with policy matters, particular members of the board will be involved in other ways. The [state or regional] finance department will be concerned with resources for the university and with establishment of a budget. Public works will be concerned with how the university sets out to develop its physical plant; also, by law, it may have a supervisory role to play in this connection. Agriculture will be concerned for many reasons. This is why it is important that top administrative people in these branches of government be on a development advisory committee.

---

[2] Hannah, *Resource Book*, pp. 54-56.

[3] The legislature of Eastern Nigeria enacted a law authorizing the establishment of a provisional council appointed by the governor and having the power to do all things necessary for the establishment of the University of Nigeria in accordance with the provisions of the university act.

Except for any physical developments which take place prior to the establishment of the official board, it is not likely that decisions taken by the development advisory body will be irrevocable. With respect to physical development, it is essential that before decisions are made regarding construction of laboratories and facilities which will be used by scientists and research workers, some of these scientists and research workers and some department heads and deans be appointed. While it would be ideal if the board itself could have been established and could have made key appointments, this may not be possible, in which case, a development advisory body will need to establish appointment procedures and try to get at least a minimum number of key staff members on the job to give guidance to internal development.[4]

---

[4] For a more complete discussion of temporary provisions, see Appendix V.

CHAPTER – 5

The Governing Body—
Powers and Duties

Regardless of how authority may be diffused or what conventions and customs may become established, the ultimate authority with respect to a public university rests with the government which creates it. But there must be some entity legally responsible for the functioning of the university. This entity is the governing body created by law and known by different names. University acts vary greatly with regard to specifics—for example, the 1871 law creating the University of Arkansas required the board of trustees to submit an annual report which among other things should contain "a detailed and systematic account of the number of days worked, of 10 working hours each, of men and teams in the production of each separately treated crop." There are a number of similar requirements which indicate that the framers of the legislation wanted to be certain the public got its money's worth from the experimental efforts of the university. A more general and more typical statement is that in the Cornell University Statutes: "subject to the charter of the university and the laws of the state, the board of trustees shall have supreme control over the university, including every college, school and academic department, division. . . ."

Though the governing body is an independent legal entity with the power to protect the university from direct governmental interference and hence minimize political tampering, it may, under the law, go much further in intermeddling with the operation of the university than good judgment and academic practice would dictate. The board not only may, but must, delegate authority to its administration in recognition of its own inability to determine and resolve the complex and continuing problems of internal organization and educational policy. The community of scholars comprising the heart of a university is a jealous community in some ways and has come to feel that academic matters are its exclusive domain. Wise governing bodies recognize this and formulate statutes which protect the role of the academic community. The sections which follow discuss major responsibilities of the governing body as expressed in the laws creating universities. The discussion will indicate how authority is divided between the governing body and the main academic body and what statutory provisions have evolved.

5.1. SELECTION OF THE CHIEF ADMINISTRATIVE OFFICER

One of the first and most important jobs for any university governing body is the selection of the chief administrative officer. Details regarding the selection and the variation in legislative provisions on how it is to be done are discussed in the next chapter. Theories vary about whether the appointing authority should reside in the governor, the board itself, or the faculty. A search of the laws failed to disclose any making the position hereditary! Since the pros and cons of these various methods are discussed in the next chapter, they will not be discussed here. If the law lodges this responsibility with the board, such authority should be simply and clearly stated. Elaborate procedures and internal election processes should be avoided, both in the act and in the statutes. If the board makes the appointment, it should proceed informally, but thoroughly, involving appropriate committees of the faculty and from outside the university to screen the possibilities and eventually come up with the best man for the job.

An acceptable provision in the act is one which would simply state that the chief administrative officer shall be appointed by the board to serve at the pleasure of the board. Some assurance of faculty participation can be provided by a statement in the university statutes that "It will be the policy of the board to confer with a special committee named by the university faculty prior to selection of a new president." This provision appears in the statutes of Southern Illinois University. University of Ibadan Statutes provide that "The vice-chancellor shall be appointed by the council after consideration of any recommendation with respect to the appointment made within the period of four months beginning with the date when the office became vacant, by joint meeting of the council and the senate."

University acts frequently contain provisions in addition to the one which says that the chief administrative officer shall be selected to serve at the pleasure of the board. These may provide that his compensation shall be fixed periodically by the board, that he shall be responsible to the board, that he shall be a full-time officer, and that he may be removed from office by the board. Though these conditions may be implied, it is wise to pull them all together with power to appoint in one concise section of the law on the selection of the chief administrative officer.

5.2. FORMULATION AND ADOPTION OF UNIVERSITY STATUTES

Fortunately, much of the work of the university can go forward without written rules. But conventions and customs, important as they are in the life of the university, do not provide a satisfactory legal base for some of the rights and responsibilities of staff, administration, and students. University statutes should fill this gap while recognizing and perpetuating those widely accepted concepts which give universities their character. How should the statutes be made? What agencies and authorities are involved? What are the channels through which a proposition flows before it finally becomes a new statute, amendment, or an annulment of an existing statute? Two bodies are always involved—the governing body of the university and the academic council. Depending on the institution and the country, at least six other entities may be involved: government, the legislature, the chancellor, the Minister of Education, the chief administrative officer, and authorities within the university. Let us look briefly at the roles which different acts have prescribed for these last-named entities and then get back to a consideration of how the board and university authorities should interact in the formulation of university statutes.

In many universities, statutes must have the assent of the chancellor or governor before they become effective. Also, in some universities, particularly those in India, it is customary to involve government in the formulation of statutes, particularly the first statutes of the university, and to require that these statutes be laid before the legislative body or one house of the legislative body for a stated period of time before they become effective. In at least one instance, the University of Ibadan, the Minister of Education must confirm statutes which have been formulated by the university council and then place copies before each house of parliament for twenty days. Either house can annul the statutes during this period. Though sometimes not mentioned in the provision of a university act on formulation of statutes, the chief administrative officer and authorities within the university play an important role. After all, the chief administrative officer is the communicating link between the governing body and the academic council or senate. Also, since many of the statutes deal with administrative matters, some new statutes or suggested amendments will, in fact, originate with him. Likewise, college faculties or boards of studies are deeply concerned with those statutes which pertain to academic matters within their jurisdiction. Certainly no law should prevent the origination of proposals by such authorities—or by anyone in the university. All proposals should follow usual channels before reaching the governing body.

Let us return to a consideration of governing body and academic council responsibilities in the development of university statutes. One theory which runs through almost all of the laws, with a few exceptions where government has the sole right to develop statutes, is that the governing body is responsible for the formulation and adoption of those statutes which will make for effective functioning of the university. But just as pervasive as this theory is another—that the academic council or senate should have the right to formulate and pass judgment on all statutes which deal with educational policy or academic matters. The extent of the academic council's official involvement varies from the right simply to give advice or express an opinion on proposed statutes or statutory changes to the right of final approval on academic matters. A variation which seems to be common in many institutions still reserves to the governing body final approval of all statutes, with the requirement that those involving academic matters be first approved by the academic council. This certainly accords with the theory that legally the responsibility for all phases of university operation rests with the governing body; hence, if it wishes to exercise its authority, it may control any detail of academic life. In other words, it can act unwisely and still be within its legal rights.

In summary, we believe the following are principles which should be incorporated in the university act: (1) The power to make, amend, modify, or repeal statutes should be lodged with the governing body. (2) Any appropriate university authority or officer should have the right to propose or initiate statutes—this would include the chief administrative officer and his administrative staff, faculty boards, extension or research councils or committees, and anyone whose work is so affected by a statutory provision that he is in a position to judge it. (3) All proposals should go through regular administrative channels and finally be submitted to the governing body by the chief administrative officer with his recommendations. (4) All proposals which involve academic matters should follow regular academic channels, come to the academic council or senate for its action, and then go through the chief administrative officer to the board. This should be true of proposals originating within the university as well as those originating with the board itself. If the board has ideas about statutory changes involving academic matters, its proposals should likewise go to the academic council or senate for its action. (5) If the board finds it cannot approve statutes involving academic matters, it should, before taking action, refer the matter back to the academic council or senate through the chief administrative officer for reconsideration. (6) When any matters are sent back for reconsideration by the academic council or senate, when an unusually important statutory change is being considered, or when a major revision of the statutes is contemplated, there should be provision for establishment of a joint committee of the governing body and the academic council, the function of the committee being to study the problem and make recommendations. (7) There should be a requirement that university statutes be published and made available in sufficient numbers to supply members of the faculty and anyone else who requests a copy.

The statutes themselves should contain a provision distinguishing in some meaningful way academic or educational from other concerns and providing further rules or mechanics for getting statutes adopted. In many instances, for example, it is provided that there should be adequate time for all parties concerned to study proposals and that statutes cannot be adopted at the first meeting of the governing body or acted upon at the first meeting of the academic senate at which they are considered. The statutes should also provide that all authorities within the university can develop bylaws, rules, and regulations to govern their own activities. These should not go beyond the chief administrative officer for approval, though the board from its position of authority and control could annul them if it saw fit. Here again, we see a distinction between what the board is legally empowered to do and what it ought to do.

Finally, we see no reason to involve government in the formulation and adoption of university statutes. The law creating the university and delineating the powers and functions of its board and officers should express all the ground rules the legislature wishes to lay down. Beyond this, internal control and management should be left to the agencies created by the legislature. It should not wish to be concerned or to intermeddle, and, in our opinion, this holds as well for so-called first statutes as for statutes made later. If some statutory provisions are necessary before a board is properly constituted, the provisional council, temporary body, temporary administrator, or whoever is running the affairs of the institution prior to final establishment of the board should also be empowered to make such statutes as seem necessary. These, of course, can always be modified or changed by the board once it is appointed and functioning.

5.3. APPROVAL OF APPOINTMENTS AND SALARIES

Consonant with the theory that the board has final authority over matters having to do with the university is a provision appearing without exception in university acts—one giving the governing body the right to approve appointments and salaries of all personnel in the university.[1] In practice this authority is not as complete as it would appear, and other legislative and statutory provisions condition its exercise. Generally the principle is well established that the governing body only approves; it does not initiate appointments or even suggest the salaries for any appointees except for the chief administrative officer. There are some exceptions, particularly in Latin-American institutions where the governing body, generally a university council, does get into the details of appointments and passes judgment on all appointees even down to the most lowly.

While the board approves reappointments, promotions, leaves, resignations, and other changes in staff status, it does not initiate any of these. Thus, while its power to disapprove will tend to make the university administration exercise care in making appointments and fixing salaries, the initiation of appointments and

---

[1] See Chapter 15 for a discussion of appointment procedures and suggested statutory provisions.

the initial establishment of salaries remains with those who are most competent to judge. However, the governing body does have concerns that go beyond the right of approval. These concerns have to do with general policies regarding salaries and the establishment of salary scales, overall budgetary provisions for staffing and how this affects quality, distribution between ranks and numbers of staff who can be employed, tenure of staff and those conditions of service generally applicable throughout the university. For example, the board will no doubt wish to adopt statutes regarding definitions of full-time or part-time service, right of the staff to engage in outside activities, employment of relatives, and age of retirement. The board would not, for example, wish to become involved with the details of job descriptions, qualifications of appointees, or particular duties of staff members, although some university acts do place responsibility on the board to determine hours of service, compensation, and duties. This is something the board would wish to hand quickly to its chief administrative officer.

Though the selection and appointment process is discussed in detail in Chapter 15, it should be pointed out that the board considers only one man for a position, the one recommended by the chief administrative officer. The board should never be in a position to choose between two or more recommendations except when the university act provides for this with respect to key administrative positions. If the board disapproves a recommendation, then its action is referred back to the chief administrative officer who refers it to the department or college in which the recommendation originated, and in due course another recommendation will reach the board. In all cases, the initiation of an academic appointment should be through an appropriate committee. The selection and functioning of such committees are also discussed in Chapter 15.

It is desirable that the university act give the board authority to empower the chief administrative officer to make appointments which are: (1) below a certain grade (designation of instructor or below is quite common in American institutions), (2) below a stated salary level, or (3) of an urgent nature. In all instances where this right is given the chief administrative officer, there is a requirement that his action be reported to the board; hence, the board could still exercise its prerogative by objecting. However, if the law simply states that the chief administrative officer shall report such appointments, then the rights of the appointees are no doubt fixed and, even if the board were to object, they would be entitled to continue to the end of the term for which they were appointed. Urgent appointment implies someone above the minimum salary scale or rank, and it is generally provided that the board can disapprove such an appointment within a stated time period. Since the emergency appointee would accept the position presumably with knowledge of this right of the board, he probably could not complain if the board summarily dismissed him when his appointment was reported to it by the chief administrative officer.

5.4. APPROVAL OF UNIVERSITY BUDGET—FINANCE

One of the heaviest responsibilities of the governing board is securing adequate finances for the university. The necessity for action on this front is always present, though the most flourishing activity occurs before and during legislative sessions—usually annually or biennially, although government appropriations are sometimes made for longer periods. Between sessions the board must be concerned with the building of the budget for the next session and with acquiring funds from other sources such as the central government, aid-giving governments, philanthropic organizations, and institutional and private donors. In spite of this responsibility and its deep concern, a board does not formulate the university budget. As in the case of appointments to the staff, it either approves or rejects; however, in the case of the budget, which is a continuing process, it is possible to introduce what might be called operational or planning realism. There is no reason why a finance committee of the board, including certain co-opted members such as the financial officer of the university and a government finance officer, cannot formulate and agree on budgetary needs in cooperation with the chief administrative officer so that no drastic objections or changes will be likely when the budget is finally received by the board. More details on the formulation of the budget, the role of different individuals, and the functioning of a finance committee are contained in Chapter 8.

The university act should clarify the position of the board with regard to financial controls retained by the state or regional government. Maximum latitude should be given the university to develop its budget, expend the funds, and render an accounting. But in all these activities, it may be subject to certain state financial procedures and rules unless excused by the law. The extent to which it should be excused is a question of policy; certainly it should be relieved of anything which will hamper its operations. This is particularly true of procurement and meeting payrolls. If the payment of salaries or the securing of necessary supplies are held up because of state financial procedures, this is not good. On the other hand, certain uniform state practices and procedures may simply represent good business, and there is no reason why the university should not conform to them. Thought should be given to this in the formulation of the university act. The fiscal year of the university might be that of government; on the other hand, there may be a reason to have it cover a different period. The board should have authority to establish the fiscal year. The board, for example, may wish to make the fiscal year correspond in some meaningful way with the academic year. Also, the board will probably wish to fix dates for major budgetary processing so that it can have the required meetings and be prepared to present the budget to the legislative session at the proper time.

Among other authorizations having to do with finance, the university act should empower the board to: (1) appoint a treasurer and require that he be bonded, (2) select a depository for university funds, (3) exercise its judgment in the acceptance of specific grants for research or other purposes, (4) invest the funds of the university under such statutory provisions as may be adopted, (5) borrow for university construction without being subject to debt limits established for state agencies, issue bonds, or give other appropriate security for borrowing, (6) provide for auditing university accounts, (7) publish the budget and the accounts in such a manner and in such detail as it deems appropriate. It is possible to present the university's financial picture annually and accurately in an attractive publication which can be given wide circulation. This tends to create confidence and to enhance citizen interest in the university. A more complete discussion of the items mentioned above is contained in Chapter 8.

What role should the academic council play in financial management and development of the budget? It can be argued that most of the activity in this area is of an administrative nature and hence under the control of the university administration and the board. However, a most cursory glance at the purposes to be achieved by expenditures under the budget indicates a deep and continuing interest by the faculty in university finances. How can this interest best be expressed? Formally, it can be expressed through an academic council or senate budget committee and through college faculty budget committees. Such committees would not have any administrative power but by statute would be given the right to review budgetary requests and counsel with appropriate administrative officers regarding proposals. As a matter of fact, they would be asked by the administrative officers to review proposals and express their judgment. There have been instances in which such committees have instigated studies of salary scales and other matters which have proved to be of great value to the university administration. Sometimes this kind of activity has been carried on by a professors' organization. In the United States, the American Association of University Professors has been instrumental in instigating research having to do with the economic status of the university teaching profession. Informally, any staff member has the right to make his voice heard through appropriate channels on any appropriate subject, be it finance or something else. If he has a good idea or a valid criticism, it can be channeled through his department head and his dean to the chief administrative officer and eventually find its way to the spot where it can be effectuated—providing it is still considered to be a good idea!

Although the board works through the chief administrative officer, it will need to have close and continuous contact with the chief financial officer of the university. There should be a statutory provision requiring and empowering the chief financial officer to develop a business and financial procedure manual with rules and regulations covering procurement, expenditures, accountability, auditing, and other matters which are important in the day-to-day operation of the university.

To serve the university effectively, the board must maintain liaison and good relations with many officers of state government and with the managing personnel of grants commissions, national university boards, and other agencies concerned with universities.

5.5. CONSTRUCTION AND MANAGEMENT OF PROPERTY—CONTRACTS

Without exception, university acts prescribing the functions and powers of boards of management authorize the boards to hold, control, and administer property, to execute contracts, and to sue and be sued. The governing board as a corporate body holds title in trust on behalf of the state to achieve the purposes of the university act. There are American court decisions holding that failure to achieve these purposes constitutes breach of trust and redress may be had terminating the authority of the board and recovering the property. In the absence of specific prohibitions, the power of the board to control and manage for university purposes is quite broad. Questions are frequently raised regarding the authority of the board to hold property for future use and in the meantime make a proprietory use of it which may involve leasing or using for other income-producing purposes. When put to a test, this right has generally been upheld by the courts, and boards have been empowered to take care of future needs by wise and timely acquisition of property. University acts ordinarily provide for a wide range of authority over property through the use of such words as "purchase, sell, lease, devise, exchange, accept in trust." Although the board needs and generally has a broad authority, there are safeguards against the misuse or mismanagement of property. The board, for example, could not make a conveyance in trust or for a long period of time, thus delaying use of the land by the university beyond the time when it might be needed. Also, the courts would most certainly hold that particular kinds of uses would contravene public policy. And, too, if property is not used to achieve the educational purposes expressed in the law, even though it may be used for some different educational purpose, this is a violation of authority for which there is legal redress.

To what extent is the board bound by state government procedures with respect to certain aspects of land or property acquisition and management? Along with finance and budgeting, property custody and management is likely to involve some state laws unless the university act exempts the board from their application. Whether or not it should is a question which ought to be considered at the time the university act is drafted—even though it is possible to secure amendments later. Some uniform procedures prescribed by the state may not be objectionable; others may be.

An inventory system, property control and accountability, and final disposition or sale of depreciated items are among the things for which there may be uniform procedures. Acquisition has been mentioned earlier with the suggestion that the university be freed from any uniform procedures which would delay either the acquisition or sale of its property. Timely sale of products from a university farm, for example, cannot await extensive paper shuffling and a delayed approval.

How shall the power to contract be exercised? What contracts must be approved by regular board action? What contracts can be consummated by the chief administrative officer through delegated authority from the board? It is customary to provide that contracts involving an amount below a stated limit, which do not involve more than a stated expenditure in a year's time, which are for ordinary improvements or repairs to buildings, or which do not involve important policy considerations, and for which budgetary provisions have been made, may be executed by the chief administrative officer and reported to the board. Likewise, it is customary for the law to require bids on contracts involving more than a stipulated amount or that are for the procurement of particular kinds of property. All contracts must generally bear the signature of the chief financial or business officer of the university—those requiring board approval, the signature of the chairman or secretary or both. General rules of the University of Illinois contain a workable and sensible procedure under which contracts are drafted initially by the interested party—this may be a dean, a department head, a professor, an administrative officer, or even a committee—after approval of the idea by the proper academic or administrative authority. The contract is then submitted to the legal counsel—even here, however, there is a provision that the legal counsel need not scrutinize contracts which are long standing and which involve no major changes. After scrutiny by the legal counsel, the contract goes on to the chief administrative officer who can either disapprove it, approve it, send it back for further consideration, or, if it is a contract requiring board approval, submit it to the board.

The university may sue or be sued on its contracts; also, suits may be brought against it to enjoin the expenditure of funds under unauthorized contracts. Individual board members may be held liable for participating in actions which are clearly beyond the authority of the university or which amount to mismanagement of funds or property. They are not liable for honest, or perhaps even ignorant, mistakes growing out of the exercise of their discretion. The university may seek the same remedies as any other public corporation for breach of contract.

University construction involves a number of considerations, some of which may be covered in the university act, some by statutes, and other by rules or regulations of the comptroller and director of the physical plant or the estates officer. The university act is likely to contain a basic provision on bids, on the employing of architects to design university buildings, on borrowing and indebtedness, and on the acquisition of land. In some countries the public works department of the state or region may by law be empowered to construct university buildings. This may or may not be objectionable depending on how much latitude the university has in designing a building and getting the job done. One thing that cannot be required by law or statutes but which should stand very high among the objectives of the board is the achieving of a pleasing and distinctive campus. This can be done only through long-range plans which involve the efforts of good architects, landscape planners, and those who understand the functional aspects of the university physical plant. Some of the problems having to do with land acquisition are discussed in the next section. The power to borrow and incur debt is discussed in Chapter 8.

Protection of university property—security—is another responsibility of the board generally expressed in the university act. If it is not, it should be. University statutes and internal rules and regulations should provide the details for fire protection, police protection, traffic control, and control of personnel in the use of university facilities. There is a considerable overlap of these matters with student discipline and perhaps even more than a touching of the borders of academic freedom. For this reason, appropriate academic and administrative staff members should be involved in the formulation of statutes, rules, and regulations so that the university can achieve a desirable security without creating the feeling that it is a small police state.

What right does the university have to acquire land? Though the institution may be endowed with what seems to be an adequate land area, growth and the expansion of its activities will create the need for more land. Does the university have the right to condemn or acquire by eminent domain? Some university acts contain an express provision, either that the university may avail itself of the general eminent domain law and procedure or that it shall have the right under procedures and conditions expressed in the act itself. Many times, however, the university act is silent. The question then arises whether the university falls by definition within the group of public agencies which have the general right of eminent domain. American courts have so held with respect to a state university; they have held the opposite with respect to a private university. At any rate, the institution is in a precarious position with respect to this right unless something is said in the act.

There should be a provision in the act giving the university the right to avail itself of the general eminent domain law. It is in this connection that questions are likely to arise about the right of the university to acquire property for particular purposes. There are always some property owners who are quite adamant about yielding their rights in property to any public agency. One of the defenses they can make is that the land is not needed by the institution and that it would not be devoted to proper institutional purposes if acquired. Answering challenges by American property owners, the courts have held that land for student dormitories, faculty residences, the president's home, street railways, golf courses, and airports were all proper and upheld the right of the university to condemn. The writers did not pursue this subject into the laws or court decisions of other countries: the law and theory regarding condemnation or eminent domain and judicial interpretations should be studied in some detail by the drafters of a university act in any country, so that an adequate and sound provision can be included.

5.6. REMOVAL OF STAFF MEMBERS

The ultimate authority to remove any staff member of the university, from the chief administrative officer on down, rests with the governing body. Almost without exception, university acts so provide. This process, however, should never commence with the board except in the case of an action to remove the chief administrative officer. However, some acts do distinguish between administrative officers and other faculty members by stating that the process for removing deans, directors, or other administrative officers may issue from the board upon recommendation from the chief administrative officer. Presumably the board could exercise this right without a recommendation from the chief administrative officer if the act makes such a distinction between members of the staff. When this provision does occur, it is accompanied by a requirement that the staff member be furnished with a statement of the charges against him and the notice of a date for a hearing. This date should allow him sufficient time to prepare his defense and, if he chooses, to find and bring counsel. Some acts also state that with respect to any dismissal the board may use its judgment in fixing the date of dismissal in order that the staff member may have an opportunity to find other employment before his salary stops.

Statements regarding cause vary considerably from one university act to another. Some simply say "for cause," "for cause after investigation and hearing," or "for adequate cause," and make no further attempt at definition. Other specific causes sometimes listed are:

Conviction of an offense involving moral turpitude

Subversive activities

Unsound mind

Incapacity to function as a staff member

Gross misconduct

Inability to carry out duties for medical reasons

We recommend that the act go no further than stating "for adequate cause," and that the board determine in each case whether adequate cause exists. Attempts to state specific causes are likely to increase the staff member's vulnerability rather than his protection.

We do not believe the university act should contain details on procedures. We do feel that the university statutes should be complete in this respect. A discussion of cause and procedure in discharge cases appears in Chapter 15 together with a discussion of the right to suspend. A few university acts provide that when charges are brought against a staff member he shall have the right to ask for the appointment of a joint committee of the governing body and of the academic council or senate to hear his case. We think this is a good idea, but it should be so stated in the statutes.

In some countries and in some institutions the reaction one gets in discussing dismissal procedures indicates that staff members are already overly protected and that if anyone needs protection, it is the university. Certainly this situation may prevail, either because of legislative and statutory safeguards or because of unwritten policies and customs which have grown up in the institution. If this is true, then there should probably be a modification of laws or procedures back to the point where the staff member would be entitled to no more than "due process." Though this is a term which has come to have great meaning under the American constitutional system, we are certain it has its counterpart in all countries.

5.7. ESTABLISHMENT OF NEW UNITS AND BRANCHES

Though most university acts give the governing body the right to create new units, whether departments, faculties, colleges, divisions, institutes, or other formal organizations requiring separate budgetary provisions, a few university acts lodge this power with the academic council or senate. In between are those which provide either that the academic council shall first recommend the new unit before the board acts on its creation, or that the academic council shall have authority to make recommendations to the board regarding new units, the establishment of which involve questions of educational policy. Here again we are confronted with the divergence between law and practice. Theoretically, the governing body should have authority in determining the establishment of any new unit which requires separate or additional budgetary consideration. However, a wise board would never consider the creation of a new unit involving any question of educational policy unless there were recommendations from the academic council. The chief administrative officer should never bring to the board a recommendation for the creation of such a unit without having procured a recommendation from appropriate authorities or committees of the faculty. If the new unit is strictly administrative in character, then consideration by the academic council may not be implied, but recommendations from a special committee of administrators and perhaps of outside experts should be obtained.

College faculties and their boards of studies should have the right to initiate action on the creation of new departments or of new units affecting their college. These recommendations would then clear the usual channels within the university. It is important that the authority to create be clearly stated in the university act and that the procedure be delineated in university statutes. New institutions which are successful in their effort to serve the country are likely to experience rapid growth, and new units, particularly new departments and colleges, will have to be added. As the institution matures, questions will arise about the establishment of professional colleges and of intercollege agencies such as institutes, councils, or divisions which cut across college lines. Such units deserve careful consideration particularly from the standpoint of furthering research and expanding the service efforts of the university. The power to establish implies the authority to alter or to disestablish through the same channels and by the same procedures.

When the university needs to extend its efforts to another geographical location, creation of a branch is involved. In this case there is no question about affiliation or the status of the branch as a constituent college. It is an integral part of the university, though its separate physical location may require an administrative relationship like that of a constituent college. The procedures should not differ from those for the establishment of other units, except that more time may be consumed and more committees involved in making recommendations and working out some of the details which will lead to a better integration with the home campus.

In at least one instance the legislature of an American state became so concerned about the problems of the aged that it provided by law for the establishment of a university committee on gerontology in the state university. There have been other instances in which institutes and similar entities have been created in state universities by legislative action. However, this does not seem appropriate. The act creating the university may and frequently does specify the colleges or units with which the institution is to commence its academic life, but the creation of further units should be left to the internal processes of the university and appropriate action by its governing body. If members of the legislature feel that the university should be pursuing a field of study which it presently ignores, they can as citizens approach the administration or even the board with their suggestions. If the university feels that the new unit or line of work is not appropriate, it should not be forced to carry it out; if it feels that it is appropriate, then the legislation would not be necessary.

graduate degrees, (4) honorary degrees to be granted, (5) academic honors, (6) short courses, special courses, or other offerings of the university for nonenrolled students, (7) the establishment of new lines or combinations of work.

Technically, degrees are granted by the governing body. Laws generally provide that they shall be granted by the board on recommendation of the academic council or senate. Sometimes the law goes on to state that the graduate is then entitled to all the privileges which the degree implies. One act states that its degree is as good as that offered by any other institution. This reflects the self-confidence which many new universities need!

5.9. ESTABLISHMENT OF RETIREMENT, PENSION, AND INSURANCE PLANS

University acts generally empower the governing body to establish a retirement plan for university personnel. These are referred to as pension plans, retirement plans, superannuation schemes, or by other names. Probably the university act need go no further, leaving to the governing body such questions as which kind of plan is best, whether or not the plan shall be voluntary or mandatory, and whether or not the institution shall be a part of a state plan, providing such choice as possible. There is no question about the need for some plan from the standpoint of incentive, security, and just to meet the competition from other institutions in hiring good staff members. In many institutions a distinction is made between the academic staff and nonacademic staff or between those above and below a minimum wage level. Those below a minimum level do not contribute to a fund but are entitled after a minimum number of years of service to a gratuity based on years of service. Perhaps the gratuity system is necessary in many countries; however, it would seem desirable to have all university personnel under the same scheme regardless of the function they perform for the institution. In some instances nonacademic employees are civil servants and would participate in a state civil service retirement or annuity plan. If this is true, then a university plan would not apply to them. Temporary employees should be excluded, but if they become regular employees their rights in the plan should date from the beginning of their temporary employment.

In many universities group life insurance has been made available to staff members at attractive rates. Questions might be raised about the authority of a governing body to institute such plans for its employees. The provision in the act empowering it to establish a pension or retirement plan should also empower it to institute group insurance plans for its employees. Maintenance of health and accident insurance for employees and their families is quite common, and probably no question would ever be raised about the right of the governing body and the university to maintain such insurance.

In establishing a plan, and before any provisions are adopted regarding it, there should be a thorough study by a competent committee composed of board and university representatives, appropriate government officers, and outside persons with competence in the field. Following their recommendations, there should be a clear explanation of the plan which can be published and made available to staff members. Among the items which need to be resolved and then worded properly in university regulations are these:

Shall the plan be funded or not funded—that is, shall the institution's contribution be placed in a fund or shall there simply be an annual budget item sufficient to cover the institution's obligation to those who retire?

When will the rights of the participant vest—that is, after what period of time will he become entitled to the institution's contribution?

Is the participant's equity in the fund transferable to another institution? Does it draw interest?

To whom shall the plan apply—all employees, only the academic staff; and when—at the inception of employment or at some later date?

Shall the plan be mandatory or optional?

What are the rates of contribution for the participant and for the institution and in what manner can these rates be changed?

Are there any restrictions on who can be named as beneficiary, and what are the procedures for designating a beneficiary?

Will death benefits be payable?

Will it be possible to abate the retirement benefits which might otherwise be paid to create an annuity for a widow or other designated surviving beneficiary?

Under what conditions will it be permissible for a participant to withdraw a portion or all of his contribution?

What rules and provisions will there be on borrowing from the fund?

Will it be possible for the participant to convert a part of the fund to life insurance and reduce his annuity under the fund? (This is possible under the plans in Indian universities where the post office savings bank is used as a depository for the fund and for the contributions of individuals.)

Retirement plans cannot be established and forgotten. There will be a strong and continuous interest on the part of the staff in the plan and its benefits for them. There should be a standing committee with representatives of the governing body, the academic council, and the university administration to study the plan, make periodic evaluations, and recommend needed change. The staff needs to be kept informed through an appropriate publication. Someone in the business office with knowledge of retirement and insurance schemes should be designated as the officer to administer the plan. In large institutions this may come to be a full-time job with the need for trained clerical help.

One problem which has not been very well solved in any retirement system is how to meet the increased cost of living which besets retired staff members living on a retirement annuity established when living costs were lower. A formula could be evolved to increase the annuity payments of retired members, but unless money to meet these payments is accumulated by the fund itself, a direct appropriation would be required. If a cushion against increased cost of living is built up in the fund, then the contributions would either have to be greater or the basic annuity would have to be less. This does not seem like a very good solution. The best solution is inclusion of retired personnel when cost-of-living or "across-the-board" increases are provided in the budget. For further discussion of pension plans, see Chapter 15.

5.10. ESTABLISHING ADMISSION STANDARDS

Who shall be admitted to the university? Though by law and by practice this question is of primary concern to faculties and appropriate academic bodies, it does have its policy side. Many of the new universities wish to encourage attendance by young people with rural backgrounds. Many times the secondary institutions in which they received their education are not of the same quality as those from which city-born youth come. The right to admission, then, should be determined by factors other than the quality or course of study of the secondary schools. Nevertheless, the board is not an appropriate body to devise tests and criteria. Eventually it will have the right to approve or disapprove standards and procedures established by the academic council and appropriate officers of university administration.

The legislation itself should establish certain rights with respect to admission. It can provide that no one be barred because of color, race, place of origin, religion, sex, politics, or any other categorization which has nothing to do with ability. Some acts state that standards for admission shall be determined by the academic council subject to approval by the governing body. This is probably as far as the law should go. In many countries physical limitations are likely to impose a limit on numbers to be taken, either generally or in particular colleges or curricula of the university. Determinations about how to deal with such limits must be made within the university. The board, of course, will be concerned, because if physical facilities limit the numbers which the institution can accept, it may wish to make a strong case for more resources to permit expansion. Further details about admission requirements and procedures are discussed in Chapter 12.

The ultimate authority to discipline and expel students and regulate student conduct rests with the board. But though university acts so provide, it is well understood that these matters should be handled by the university administration, the academic council, and the various faculties—with appropriate representation of students on discipline and other bodies.

5.11. UNIVERSITY CALENDAR AND PERIODS OF INSTRUCTION

What should be the concerns of the governing body with periods of instruction and the university calendar? There are several. It will wish to be assured that a minimum number of days of instruction are accomplished, that vacation periods are not unduly numerous or long, that the public and particularly prospective students know what the terms are and on what dates they commence, and that there is to be a summer session or year-round operation. The board should have opportunity to consider operations well in advance so that budgetary commitments can be met. The burden of making all these determinations, however, should rest with the academic council and the faculty.

Generally there is a calendar committee of the council or university senate including members from university administration. The functions of such a committee are generally limited to determining the dates for opening and closing a period of instruction and for vacations during the period. Though no legislative provisions were found on this subject, there is an implication that the governing body would have the right to pass final judgment on periods of instruction and division of the academic year, particularly since these have budget implications. Most institutions do, however, have university statutes on the subject. For example, the statutes of the Mysore University of Agricultural Sciences provide that the academic year shall start approximately on July 1 or on such other date as may be recommended by the academic council and published in the university catalog. They also require that the university shall publish as frequently as may be deemed desirable or necessary a catalog containing, among other things, the academic calendar. The statutes of Harvard University go much further. They provide that, except in the case of the graduate school and the School of Business Administration, the academic year shall be divided in half. They specify the date on which the first and second half-year terms shall commence, when the annual commencement shall be held, when summer vacation begins, and which days are holidays. Each faculty, by a standing vote of its governing board, may fix the date for Christmas recess and spring recess. This much detail is not needed in a university statute. Authorization of the academic council to make these determinations and a requirement that they be approved and published is probably sufficient.

Institutions are frequently plagued about the division of the academic year. Several systems are in vogue. Among them are the semester system dividing the academic year into two long terms with sufficient time for a summer session if one is desired; the trimester system dividing the academic year into three shorter terms with a somewhat longer vacation period between the summer and fall terms; a quarter system of still shorter terms with three regular quarters and a summer quarter, the summer quarter frequently of shorter duration than the other three. Each system has its avid proponents, and many arguments can be developed for and against each one. Certainly there are questions more fundamental to the process through which a young man or woman is educated than how his academic year is divided—although admittedly this does have some importance. The board's concern in all this is considerable because finances, facilities, numbers of staff, and numbers of students who can be accommodated will all vary depending on length of periods of instruction and on the number of days out of the year the university operates. Though it can make its policies known, it must rely heavily on the good judgment of the faculty and administration of the university.

5.12. RELATION OF THE BOARD TO A BOARD OF HIGHER EDUCATION

Some countries and some of the American states have achieved coordination of higher educational institutions in one way or another. The state of California did it through a constitutional provision establishing one university for the whole state with as many physical locations as are needed. The state of New York solved it through legislation creating a state universities system. Peru solved it through the adoption of a national universities act. Perhaps the word "solve" should not be used, for though these different devices provide a coordinating framework, the solution of all problems of coordination does not necessarily follow. However, such coordination is a problem which now confronts or will confront all states, countries, regions, or political entities supporting more than one public university. Still another answer, particularly where institutions are already operative and the need for coordination arises, is creation of a board or commission of higher education. Such a board will naturally have several strikes against it because of the vested interests of institutional boards and university faculties. Nevertheless, such a board can play a solid coordinating role.

There is no question about the necessity for some device such as a board of higher education, and something more than friendly association is implied. Such a board or commission must be able to exercise certain sanctions. The most obvious have to do with budget, physical expansion, and the addition of major lines of work. Whether or not authority should go beyond these areas, even to the point where individual institutional boards could be dispensed with, is debatable. Where an institution has a history of operating with its board, strong arguments can be developed against change. These arguments deal mainly with communications, feelings, morale, the image of the institution, the responsiveness between its own board and its administration, and the void which would be felt if the point of control were further removed and were more closely allied to the politics of the state. This is not a subject which implies any provisions in a university act or in its statutes. We simply mention it in passing as something with which all universities may sooner or later be concerned. There are certain other overall bodies which can be of great help to universities. Some of these have been mentioned in other parts of the book. A grants commission can help immeasurably in advancing the research program, and a corporate building authority established by the legislature can be of great assistance in financing new construction.

CHAPTER – 6

The Chief Administrative Officer—
Appointment, Tenure,
and Conditions of Service

6.1. APPOINTMENT

How should the chief administrative officer be selected? (By "chief administrative officer" we mean the vice-chancellor, the president, the rector, the officer who by any title is the executive and educational head of the institution.) The answer: by any process which will get the best man for the job. A survey of university acts indicates that there is no fixed opinion on what process will best accomplish this end. In some cases the chief administrative officer is elected or appointed by a university council which may be composed solely of faculty members or may have a strong student representation. In other cases he is appointed either by the governor, the chancellor, a council of ministers, or the board of management.

Details regarding these methods of appointment vary by countries. There are at least four variations of the chancellor's power to select: he may do it directly; approve a nomination by the board; select one person from a panel; or after refusing selections, appoint his own choice. Some acts and university statutes specify in great detail how the appointment process is to be exercised. Others simply say that the officer shall be appointed by the board to serve at its pleasure. The Punjab Agricultural University Act provides that the first vice-chancellor shall be appointed by the state government and that subsequent vice-chancellors shall be appointed by the board in the manner prescribed. Several other Indian acts have a like provision.

Which of all these methods is best? Before attempting to answer, let us consider the conditions or circumstances which are likely to fill the position with the best man. First, there should be wide consideration of candidates. If only one person, such as the chancellor or governor, makes the appointment after consulting with only a few people, this objective will not receive adequate attention. Possible candidates may be found among members of the staff of the institution, alumni, successful presidents of other institutions, deans in other institutions, professors of administrative ability in other institutions, and able men outside the teaching profession. Advertising is not likely to be of much value in filling this position. Second, there should be a thorough discussion of the qualifications of the top few candidates, and they should be invited to meet members of the faculty and administration of the university. This is not likely to be done if the appointment is made by one person. Third, through appropriate committees there should be faculty involvement in the selection process, thus giving the faculty the assurance that it is represented and that its voice can be heard in the selection of the chief administrative officer. None of the methods of appointment or election would preclude this process if the university act and statutes provide for it. Some university acts do provide that the chief administrative officer shall be selected from a panel of names recommended—in some cases by the board or an administrative committee; in others, by the university council or other body which does have faculty representation. Fourth, when the choice has finally been narrowed to one man who is to be invited to become the chief administrative officer, the power to invite him, so to speak, should rest with that entity which has the widest concern for the university, the one which is least likely to put him under pressure when he assumes the job and to which he feels the least debt or obligation *because* he was selected. In other words, he should be able to feel that he was selected because he was a good man for the job and not because he had the right political affiliations or knew the right people.

Election or appointment by a university council or faculty body, particularly if it has student representation, puts the chief administrative officer under constant pressure. It sometimes gives rise to internal politics which history has shown results in short terms for chief administrative officers and an impairment of their ability to take bold action and make innovations which would be good for the institution. Selection by the governor, the chancellor, or an agency of government invites politics and favoritism and, though it may result in a good selection, it may also result in a political selection. The university deserves a greater guarantee than this provides against the encroachments of politics.

Perhaps the writers are showing a bias because of their association with American institutions, but they feel that the method most likely to produce a good man for the job is one in which the board appoints, not elects, and under which it discusses and finally invites a candidate whose name is one of a small panel presented to it by the faculty after the latter has engaged in a committee process which should be established by the university statutes. The formalism of an election by the board also begets politics and precludes a wide search for good candidates. In addition, it does not take into consideration the stake the faculty has in the selection. There should be nothing secretive about the selection of a chief administrative officer. The faculty itself, while engaging in the nomination process, and the board likewise, should welcome suggestions from any place about people who would qualify. If members of the board have ideas about whom they would like for chief administrative officer, these names should be transmitted to the chairman of an appropriate faculty committee so that the faculty can pass judgment on them before they come back to the board.

In summary then, the university act should provide that the chief administrative officer be appointed by the board to serve at the pleasure of the board. A provision that the chancellor has a right to approve—but not to appoint—a nominee of the board would not be objectionable, though it can be argued that by persistent disapproval he can force his will on the board. The act should contain a provision making it mandatory that the faculty be involved and should specify that the exact method of selection be spelled out in university statutes. The university statutes should provide a simple but effective mechanism for involving the faculty in the nomination process. Based on an unfortunate experience in the selection of a vice-chancellor for one Indian institution, it was recommended that the law be amended to eliminate the board from the selection process and give the power to the chancellor. The board was not even to have representation on the selection committee. But this is a cure that would be worse than the malady.

6.2. TERM OF OFFICE

How long should the chief administrative officer serve? As long as he is effective. How shall a judgment be made about his effectiveness? An obvious answer is that the agency appointing him should also be empowered to make this judgment. Some university acts do just this by providing that the chief administrative officer shall serve at the pleasure of the board or by specifying no term— which implies of course that the board may terminate his employment and appoint another man when it deems such action necessary. Many institutions specify a term of years, sometimes with a provision for reappointment, sometimes with no such provision. The agricultural universities in Pakistan and some of those in India provide for a term of four years with reappointment—in some cases providing for only one reappointment. Some institutions provide for a three-year term, others for five, some with the right of reappointment for one additional term, some with the right of reappointment without limitation.

In considering what is best to provide as a term for the chief administrative officer, two principles seem important: if he is doing a good job, it should be possible to keep him during the period of his effective leadership, be it three years or twenty years; if he is not doing a good job, it should be possible to relieve him and appoint someone else. The objection to a specific term with no possibility of reappointment or with reappointment for only one term is that a good man may not be able to hold the job long enough to be fully effective and give the university what he has to offer. Everything considered, it would seem best to provide in the university act that the chief administrative officer serve at the pleasure of the board. Next best would be appointment by the board for a specific term but with the power to reappoint more than once.

One vice-chancellor expressed the opinion that without having been appointed for a specific term he would have been discharged too soon. In view of the fact that he was performing effectively, this would have been a mistake. Thus, he would argue for a specific term during which he would feel free to innovate, solve problems, and advance the cause of the university. While his surmise about being discharged may have been correct, one cannot help but recur to the principle that the board is either to be trusted to perform its functions properly and guide the destiny of the institution or else is not to be trusted and hence is not the proper agency for control of a university. Certainly boards can abuse their authority, can be dominated by government, and for other reasons can fail to perform as a board should. The failure may become so pronounced as to call for government intervention, but this still does not argue for some different method of control which would place the university more directly in the channels of government.

6.3. QUALIFICATIONS

What can a university act or university statutes contain that will be helpful in assuring that the right man is selected as chief administrative officer? Judging the qualifications of any man is a highly subjective process, and the further removed from the technical the job for which the man is being selected, the more subjective the process. None of the university acts or statutes surveyed in the preparation of this book contained any statement about the qualifications of the chief administrative officer. This is probably as it should be since the qualities most important in a chief administrative officer are not likely to be measurable ones such as age or specific academic training. At least the writers are willing to let it rest there and recommend that no provisions be contained in the university act or statutes regarding the qualifications of the chief administrative officer. If the selection process is a good one and if he is appointed in the manner indicated, this is as much assurance as is possible about his qualifications. The *Resource Book*[1] contains a chapter about the chief administrative officer in which there is a discussion of the kind of man he should be and the qualifications he should have. Certainly experience, family, age, personal characteristics, and many other factors should be considered in detail during the selection process.

6.4. CONDITIONS OF SERVICE, SALARY, PERQUISITES

The Uttar Pradesh Agricultural University Act provides that "The emoluments and other conditions of service of the vice-chancellor shall be such as may be prescribed and shall not be varied to his disadvantage after his appointment." This is probably all a university act need contain, and there would seem to be no reason for university statutory provisions on the salary, conditions of service, or perquisites of the vice-chancellor or the chief administrative officer. Some acts simply specify that the conditions of service shall be such as are established by the board; others are completely silent on this subject. In some instances where the chancellor

---

[1] Hannah, *Resource Book*, ch. 13.

appoints the chief administrative officer, it is provided that the chancellor shall determine the terms and conditions of service. Perhaps there is some logic in this, but in our view it is not desirable to have the chief administrative officer appointed by the chancellor; hence, it would be undesirable to have his terms and conditions of service determined by the chancellor. A few acts mention salary or compensation and provide that it shall be fixed by the board.

There should be an understanding about such things as furnishing the chief administrative officer with a house (it has been held by American courts that free housing is not to be considered a part of his salary) and transportation; his liability, if any, for rent and other expenses; and other special arrangements. But these determinations should be made by the board and should not be formalized except as part of the board's regulations and hence as provisions in the contract of appointment. In view of the disadvantages which inhere when the chief administrative officer does not reside at the university, it is recommended that he reside there and that a university statutory provision so require. Harvard University, for example, has a statute which requires that the president live in the city of Cambridge.

6.5. VACANCY

Vacancy should be defined to mean more than temporary absence. It may arise through death, resignation, or discharge. Though some university acts contain no provisions on vacancy, and perhaps it is not of great importance that they do, there are, nevertheless, two questions which always need to be settled—and it might be helpful if the act contained a provision on them. One question has to do with filling the vacancy; the other has to do with carrying on the functions of the chief administrative officer until the vacancy can be filled. The Punjab Agricultural University Act provides that in case of a vacancy, the registrar shall report the fact to the board and the board shall fill the vacancy through the same procedure used to appoint a chief administrative officer, but "If the board's decision is not unanimous it shall be subject to confirmation by the chancellor." This act also provides that until the vacancy is filled, the registrar shall carry on the duties of the chief administrative officer. It is recommended that the university act contain two such provisions: one authorizing the board to name the official who shall act for the chief administrative officer when a vacancy occurs and the other providing that the board shall engage in the appointment process established by the act and statutes to find a new permanent chief administrative officer.

6.6 REMOVAL FROM OFFICE

The University of Nigeria Act provides that "The council may for adequate cause suspend the vice-chancellor from his duties or, subject to the approval of the governor in council, may terminate the appointment of the vice-chancellor." The Jawaharlal Nehru Agricultural University Act contains a rather elaborate process for getting first a no-confidence vote, then a resolution to the chancellor. The chancellor may then issue an order removing the vice-chancellor from office. Most university acts are silent on this subject, for when the board appoints the chief administrative officer to serve at its pleasure, there is an implication that it may terminate his appointment at any time it sees fit. When a specific term is designated, the board would be able to seek a new man at the end of the term. There would still be an implication, however, that for sufficient cause the chief administrative officer could be removed before the end of a specified term.

Attempting to state a cause for removal from office and establish a procedure for doing so presents the same problem as trying to put down qualifications for a chief administrative officer. Perhaps one could say categorically that if the chief administrative officer is unable to convince the board that he should continue on the job, then he should not be continued. Admittedly this may lead on occasion to harsh treatment of a good man, but a good man would not wish to administer the affairs of the university under a hostile board. Even so, it would seem that if the board wishes to discharge him, the chief administrative officer should by right have adequate notice in order that he may arrange his own affairs and seek other employment. The notice period should not be a long one because if the board feels that the chief administrative officer is damaging the institution, the damage should not be permitted to continue. An alternative would be suspension with salary until the discharge became final. This would be within the discretion of the board and a notice period would not be implied.

6.7. RESIGNATION

The Punjab Agricultural University Act provides that the vice-chancellor may relinquish his office by a written statement addressed to the board and ordinarily delivered to the secretary of the board two months prior to the date on which he wishes to be relieved. Inasmuch as the chief administrative officer of a university should not be expected to serve against his will, he should have the right of resignation. However, in fairness to the board, a notice period such as that provided in the Punjab Agricultural University Act is desirable. Even a shorter notice period would be acceptable if the act or statutes provide that the registrar or some other officer of the university shall act for the chief administrative officer in case of a vacancy.

6.8. LEAVE

It is logical to argue that if the chief administrative officer serves at the pleasure of the board, he should be granted leave at the pleasure of the board and no stated policy should be contained either in a university act or in university statutes. There must be some currency for this assumption since none of the university acts or statutes studied contained any provisions on leave for the chief administrative officer. However, since it is just as important that the chief administrative officer have leave as it is for other officers of the university, we believe the act should provide for annual leave to be determined by the board and included in his contract. During such period the chief administrative officer shall designate another university officer to act for him.

6.9. TEMPORARY DISABILITY

If the statutes provide that a designated university official shall fill the position of chief administrative officer in case of vacancy, they should also provide that the same official fill the position in case of temporary disability. Otherwise this matter should be left to the board's discretion. There would be no particular problem in this connection except when the chief administrative officer and the board disagree over whether he is under temporary disability. In most instances the board would rely on the opinion of the chief administrative officer. He might be hospitalized but still able to carry on his essential functions for a short while. On the other hand, he might develop a temporary mental illness which he himself would refuse to recognize but which would be apparent to the board. Decisions of this kind are certainly in the realm of the board and are not subjects on which either acts or statutes can contain any useful provisions.

6.10. ABSENCE

Suppose the faculty complains to the board that the chief administrative officer is seldom at the university, is never available to help them settle problems, and is continually absent from his office. Certainly this would concern the board, but it is not conceivable that any legislative or statutory provision could improve the situation. The chief administrative officer has to make many decisions about where his presence will be most helpful, and the board, in turn, will have to make a judgment on his decisions. If it feels he is neglecting his duties, then it should take the steps any good employer would take—first, try to rectify the situation and, if this proves impossible, replace the chief administrative officer. The chief administrative officer should be given authority in the statutes to designate an officer to act during his absences.

CHAPTER – 7

The Chief Administrative Officer—
Powers and Duties

7.1. GENERAL DIRECTION AND CONTROL OF UNIVERSITY AFFAIRS

Diffusion of the decision-making power does not work any better in an educational institution than it does in any other kind of organization. The authority of the chief administrative officer must be complete. The university act and statutes should eliminate any possibility that he can be bypassed and that individuals, authorities, or other bodies within the university can go directly to the board of management or to government. The Revised Code of the University of the Philippines provides that

Leadership in the university is vested in the president who shall be the chief officer of the university. He shall be ex officio head of the university faculty and of the faculty of every college or school or any other unit of the university. He shall have general supervision of all business and financial operations of the university. All officers and members of the teaching staff and employees shall be responsible to and under the direction of the president. He shall carry out the general policies laid down by the board of regents and shall have power to act within the lines of said general policies. He alone shall undertake to direct or to assign the details of executive action.

This is a clear and unequivocal statement of the authority and responsibility of the chief administrative officer. The decree of the Rural University of Minas Gerais in Brazil states succinctly that "The Rector is the central executive in charge of superintending all university activities."

Besides making it clear that the chief administrative officer is to be in sole charge of the affairs of the university, many acts point out also that he has a duty to discharge his functions and to discharge them well. Both the Andhra Pradesh and Mysore Agricultural University acts, for example, provide that it shall be the duty of the vice-chancellor to insure the faithful observance of the provisions of the act and statutes and that he may exercise all powers necessary for this purpose.

It would seem apparent that he should not have any interests which conflict with his ability to discharge his function as chief administrative officer, nor should he undertake to do time-consuming tasks within the university unless they are essential and contribute to the discharge of his duties. He might, for example, have an inclination to continue some teaching or research work if he were engaged in these before accepting the post. One would not argue against these activities if his time permited, but it is not likely that his time *will* permit.[1] If he has extra time, it would be better spent on a further study of his own job so that he can improve both internal and external communications and discharge in a better fashion the major responsibilities imposed upon him. He should have a well-organized office under the supervision of a skilled administrative assistant. It should be staffed with competent secretarial, clerical, and stenographic help. It is recommended that the university act contain a provision similar to that of the University of the Philippines', stating clearly that he is the chief executive and academic officer and that all functions channel through him. There is no need for the university statutes to reiterate such a provision, though there may be details of procedure which should be spelled out in them.

Many specific responsibilities could be listed: contracts, discipline, property management, annual reports, defining the duties of administrative personnel—the most important ones are discussed in the remaining sections of this chapter. Others appear in the chapters which follow.

Frequently overlooked, particularly in the early stages of a university's development, is the importance of good information so that the general public as well as those particularly interested in the affairs of the university can be informed. This parallels the chief administrative officer's duty to maintain appropriate and good relations with the legislature and officers of government. The decree establishing the rural university in the state of Minas Gerais in Brazil recognized this, a whole section of the act being devoted to provisions on a public relations service. Whether or not a separate officer would be justified in the beginning is doubtful, but someone should discharge the function. Such an information service could

----

[1] The law creating the University of Wisconsin provided that the president should "so long as the interests of the institution require it be charged with the duties of one of the professorships."

maintain directories, with names and addresses; organize visits to the university; prepare pamphlets, bulletins, and publications about the university; arrange for news releases and radio programs; receive official visitors and show them the campus; handle many of the complaints which would otherwise go directly to the chief administrative officer; collect data and interesting facts about the university; maintain a file which would build up a history of the university; and do many other things which would occur to an alert public information officer. One of the duties of such an officer, as it comes out in literal translation from the Minas Gerais decree is "to promote the integration of the university into public pastimes." If this means that the university should not be insulated from the pleasures of mankind generally, it is a good statement!

7.2. CHAIRMAN OF THE BOARD

Shall the chief administrative officer be the chairman of the board of management or control? Just as there are differing opinions about whether he should be a member of the board of control, there are differing opinions on this question. One argument is that membership on the board and serving as its chairman assures the chief administrative officer that problems needing consideration will be brought before the board and will be given consideration—and, furthermore, that he cannot be left out in deliberations of the board about major problems with which he is concerned. There is sometimes a fear, in the case of a strong-willed and politically minded board chairman, that conflicts will arise between chairman and chief administrative officer, and important issues will be detoured around the chief administration officer. Another argument is that since the board would rely upon the chief administrative officer to arrange the agenda and bring before it matters needing attention, he had just as well be a member of the board and serve as its chairman. Still another argument is that he should be chairman so that he will have the status necessary to deal with other agencies and with government officials. A major contrary argument is that the chief administrative officer is only an employee of the board and that the board should be organized to function with a chairman from its own membership. This argument is supported by at least three thoughts: (1) that it is not logical for an employee to be a member of the body which employs him and certainly not for him to direct its affairs from the position of chairman, (2) that holding both key positions gives him too much power, and (3) that the freedom of the chief administrative officer to present problems and viewpoints will be greater if he is not a member of the board and does not have to serve as its chairman.

However, there are some political facts of life to be considered, particularly when the university is young and needs strong leadership which can protect it from government agencies which would make encroachments, and also from ambitious and powerful members of the board itself. If the chief administrative officer is chairman of the board, his arm is strengthened in dealing with the board, in dealing with government, and in seeking funds. If the chairmanship is left to election from among the board members, the chairman might turn out to be a government official with selfish ambitions or someone from the private sector who would find it impossible to spare the time. There is a further argument too—that in the early life of the university the board will need to act on many matters and if the chief administrative officer is chairman he can make contacts and get jobs done without demanding from the board more time and travel than its members are able to spare. If, therefore, it is felt that the chief administrative officer should be chairman of the board, the writers recommend that the temporary provisions include a section stating that he shall be a member of the board and its chairman for some stated period of time, four years for example, after which he shall no longer be a member or chairman. This section might even state in brief the reason for the temporary provision. The writers feel that ultimately the chief administrative officer should not be either a member of or chairman of the board of control. However, there are American university acts making the president of the university president of the board; and if this arrangement is tried and works, then who are the writers to say "Nay!"

Where the governing body is a university council composed largely of faculty members and students with some outside membership and perhaps with some government membership, the answer may be different. But this is not a properly constituted governing body in the view of the writers and does not give the university the independence of action it needs. If a proper relationship is established between the chief administrative officer and his board, all the advantages of membership and chairmanship can be gained. If he needs to contact government or make a case before any other entity and there is any doubt at all about his authority to do so, the board can authorize him. It could even support him with a small delegation or subcommittee appointed for the purpose. To all intents and purposes he will still be in charge of meetings of the board because he will bring the agenda and present items from it. He can be assured this right by a provision similar to that in the University of Illinois Statutes which states that "The president shall attend meetings of the board and participate in its deliberations." Some other university acts make it his duty to present an agenda at all board meetings even though he is not a member. This will take care of the argument that unless the chief administrative officer is a member of the board a hostile board might meet without him. If there is hostility, the rest of the board could meet without him anyway—even if he is a member and chairman. He will have the advantage of some detachment if he himself does not have to act as chairman and push for action. The importance of his right to vote as a member of the board is more fancied than real. In most situations one would not expect a closely divided vote; hence, that of the chief administrative officer would be unimportant. If there is a heated policy argument in the board and a divided vote, the chief administrative officer would not want to be in the position of influencing the board's decision one way or the other—and should not have to do so by casting a vote.

7.3. BUDGET AND FINANCE, PROCUREMENT

A chief administrative officer is likely to please his board more by good money management and planning than by any other activity in which he engages. All of the university acts surveyed by the writers provide that this shall be one of his chief responsibilities. Typical statements from university acts are: "The vice-chancellor shall be responsible for the presentation of the budget and the statement of accounts to the board"; "He shall have general supervision of all business and financial operations of the university"; "The annual budget of the university shall be prepared in accordance with the rules approved by the president of the university"; "He shall be responsible for the presentation of the budget to the board." Proper discharge of this function requires a good finance officer, sound business organization, and the development of comprehensive fiscal regulations. Improper budgeting procedures can do as much as any one thing to destroy the will and ability to accomplish an integrated teaching and research program and the public service functions which the university should discharge. The university act, and particularly the university statutes, should contain essential directives to insure that a sound financial and budgeting process is carried out. These will be discussed in the next chapter which deals with budget and finance. At this point we simply recommend that the university act contain a provision similar to those quoted charging the chief administrative officer with the duty of handling the financial and budgetary responsibilities of the institution and presenting the budget and financial reports to his board.

Though the task of procuring necessary equipment and supplies will rest with the director of the physical plant and with other officers of the university, the ultimate responsibility, like all other responsibilities, rests with the chief administrative officer. Procurement of essential supplies, particularly chemicals and materials needed to carry on successful classroom and laboratory work, can become very important factors in the minds of teachers. Failure to take seriously this responsibility can do much to destroy faculty morale. The responsibility is stated quite well in the agricultural university decree of the state of Minas Gerais in Brazil: "To superintend the acquisition, the maintenance, and the distribution of materials as well as the control of their consumption and use."

7.4. APPOINTMENT OF ACADEMIC STAFF, OFFICERS, AND NONACADEMIC STAFF—SALARIES

As a matter of legal theory, the board can pass judgment on any decision made by the chief administrative officer. After all, he is the board's employee and has no power or authority separate from that of the board; he is its agent, so to speak, and hence, subject to its pleasure in any decision he makes, no matter how minute. But as a working principle, this is not tenable. If the board is to preserve its major functions of policy determination, financial and business management, and concern with other important areas having to do with the university, it must not become immersed in the details of administration. The appointment of staff and determination of salaries affords an example of how theory and practice coincide. Commencing with the basic assumption that the board has the right to approve all appointments and to approve the salaries of all staff members, we find that a considerable amount of discretion is given the chief administrative officer through custom, the university act itself, university statutes, and rules or procedures of the board. This does not mean, however, that some seemingly insignificant appointment might not become a controversial issue—even though it is an appointment for which the chief administrative officer is not required to seek board approval.

Most of the university acts studied provide that appointments shall be made and salaries determined by the chief administrative officer but that the board has the right to approve appointments and salaries. This means that the board cannot appoint staff members or determine salaries, and this is as it should be. The board can, however, refuse to confirm—in which case its chief administrative officer will have to come back with another recommended appointment. Details on academic appointments and on provisions which the writers feel should be in the university statutes are contained in Chapter 15. A discussion of nonacademic employment is in Chapter 16. The university act should provide that all appointments shall be made by the chief administrative officer and approved by the board. The statutes should then contain certain provisos, among which would be the right of the chief administrative officer to make temporary appointments, to make such appointments as are especially provided by the board without its approval (but to be reported), and to make appointments when emergencies occur.

The authority which must be given the chief administrative officer to make appointments and the board to approve them should not be taken as license for either the chief administrative officer or the board to intermeddle in appointments made by colleges and departments and other divisions of the university. Though the chief administrative officer may raise a question about any appointment, proper procedures will not involve him directly in staff selection thoroughout the university except for the major posts where the appointee reports directly to him.

7.5. DISCHARGE OF STAFF, PUNISHMENT, CENSURE

The right to appoint implies the right to discharge. Likewise, the right of the board to approve appointments implies the right to approve the termination of appointments for any cause. The university act should simply state that the chief administrative officer can institute proceedings for the discharge of any staff member for cause by following the procedure specified in the university statutes. The statutes should then state in detail what constitutes cause, the procedure to be followed, and the right of the staff member to be heard, both by an appropriate body of his peers and by the board. These procedures are discussed in Chapter 15.

The university act should also provide that under rules to be established by statute the chief administrative officer can take action short of recommending discharge. This would include suspension, censure, reprimand, or any other lesser punishment which might seem appropriate. The Revised Code of the University of the Philippines provides that "No member of the faculty, officer or employee shall be suspended or removed except for cause after an investigation and hearing shall have been had." But the president is given the right to suspend any member of the teaching staff, officer, or employee during the pendency of the administrative charges against him.

7.6. CUSTODY, USE, AND MAINTENANCE OF PROPERTY

Property management and accountability is another heavy responsibility of the chief administrative officer. One university act states that the chief administrative officer shall "Superintend the acquisition, the maintenance, and the distribution of materials as well as the control of their consumption and use." Some university acts go further than this in specifying just how this function is to be discharged. The Revised Code of the University of the Philippines charges the physical plant director with the immediate supervision of certain university grounds and buildings and implies that the responsibility for other areas rests with other officials of the university. It also provides that the custodianship of university buildings shall be lodged in the business executive and that the registrar shall have the power to allot classrooms. While these are not unreasonable provisions and certainly might be a fair statement of how the job actually gets done, it does not seem wise to insert this detail in the university act, especially without referring to the chief administrative officer as the final authority. It tends to becloud the fact that he is the final authority and might make another administrative officer of the university feel that he can act independently of the chief administrative officer.

The power to acquire and dispose of property and otherwise deal with its title rests with the board. The act should simply state that the chief administrative officer shall be responsible for the custody and use of all university property for the purposes of the university. Further rules for its custody and use should be developed in the university statutes. Some of these are set forth in Chapter 9 in the discussion of the director of the physical plant.

Some of the American states have added provisions to the law on universities prohibiting the use of any of their buildings by political organizations or by organizations described as anti-American or in other ways undesirable. The value of such a law is doubtful since it substitutes the judgment of a particular legislature for the judgment of the university community. Since a university community is supposed to be a place for the enlightenment of minds and the promotion of truth and thought, it would seem better to let this judgment rest with such a community even though its views might not at some particular time accord with those of the legislature.

The assigning of names to buildings sometimes gets to be an issue on a university campus. The Revised Code of the University of the Philippines provides that "University buildings, structures, streets, and other places shall have such names as may be given them by the president or a committee chosen by him." In the absence of such a provision, it is presumed that the board would approve the names suggested for university buildings—though the president would be expected to present recommendations after an adequate consideration has been given by appropriate bodies within the university. Opinions vary considerably about who should be honored by the naming of a building—whether male or female, the living or the dead, the political or the nonpolitical. It is probably better if the university act contains no recitation concerning this interesting enterprise. But the board may wish to express a policy in the university statutes.

7.7. CONSTRUCTION

The basic responsibility for acquiring university buildings and facilities, whether through purchase or construction, rests with the board. Provisions of university acts and statutes having to do with such contracts are discussed in Chapter 5. However, since the chief administrative officer is the employee and agent of the board, he does have responsibility. The university act should state that recommendations and plans for construction of needed new buildings shall be presented to the board by the chief administrative officer and that he shall be responsible through appropriate university agencies or bodies for construction. The act should also specify that in emergencies or for buildings costing below some stated amount, and if funds are available, the chief administrative officer can let contracts without prior approval of the board. Another provision should authorize him to negotiate with outside agencies, either government or otherwise, which might wish to make funds available for university construction.

7.8. AN ADMINISTRATIVE DESIGN FOR THE UNIVERSITY—RELATIONS WITH DEANS AND OFFICERS OF ADMINISTRATION

Adequate channels of communication, liberal and sensible delegation of authority, and the establishment of good relations with deans and other administrative officers of the university cannot be provided by law or statute, but they can be aided. The Revised Code of the University of the Philippines provides that "All officers, members of the teaching staff, and employees shall be responsible to and under the direction of the president." It also provides that "He shall be the official medium of communication between the teaching force, employees and students of the university on the one hand and the board of regents or board of visitors on the other." The statutes of Harvard University provide that the president shall "act as the ordinary medium of communication between the corporation and the overseers and between the corporation and the faculties." This is the theory under which the chief administrative officer functions. It is appropriate to remind him in the act or statutes that he is to be the official medium of communication.

The laws of Cornell University require the president to recommend to the board a plan for organization of the university. When adopted, the plan becomes the basis for official relationships throughout the university. After much consideration, five "Directorates" were established for the Rural University of Minas Gerais —teaching, research, extension, administration, and student assistance. There are many places in a university act and in the university statutes where a good administrative structure can be supported, but whether or not such a structure exists in fact depends upon the personalities, abilities, and desires of the chief administrative officer and his subordinates. It is essential that the chief administrative officer meet frequently with his deans and major committee chairmen and other officers to solve problems, discuss policies, and create the feeling that they are sharing in the decision-making process. This is how a sound structure and good communications are perfected. This implies having an administrative council to advise the chief administrative officer and discuss problems with him. All deans and other officers should be included—librarians, physical plant directors, deans of student welfare, and others are sometimes left out. University communications can be aided materially by such mundane equipment as interoffice telephones. Less mundane is the duty to make a continuous study of the internal structure of the university so that it can be kept functional.

7.9. HIS ROLE AS CHIEF EDUCATIONAL OFFICER

The Indian agricultural university acts generally state that the vice-chancellor is the principal academic officer of the university and chairman of the academic council. Some of them provide that he shall be responsible for the close coordination and integration of teaching, research, and extension. Though the obligation to act as chief educational officer of the university is apparent, it is well to have this duty stated in the university act. Financial affairs, the building program, and outside problems of many kinds can very easily use up the time the chief administrative officer should have to think about the educational program of the institution and keep abreast of educational progress. He may even be accused of forgetting students and their needs: does he know how the counseling program is functioning, how efficient the registration process is, how the admissions plan is working? A reminder that promoting the cause of education within the university is one of his main objectives is not amiss. Frequent meetings with faculties of colleges, interest in the committee activity which has to do with the educational process, and high interest in the functioning of university bodies are all essential. Though institutional growth may bring the appointment of an academic vice-administrator, the chief administrative officer must not relinquish his position of leadership.

7.10. HIS RELATION TO UNIVERSITY BODIES AND AUTHORITIES

Most laws make the chief administrative officer a member of and presiding officer of various university bodies and faculties. Many laws make him presiding officer of the academic council. Certainly his position entitles him to be considered a member of the various faculties and of their boards of studies, but this does not mean he should come to meetings and dominate them. The fact of his membership has some meaning, certainly, but his membership should not be used to intimidate. His relationship to and feelings about any faculty body should be such that he can receive criticism without bristling and going on the defensive. This implies his keeping a close and understanding ear to campus issues.

He may wish to be a member of certain university committees—an extension advisory or research advisory committee, for example—but such membership should be limited because the function of administrative committees is to serve the administration and thrash out problems for the chief administrative officer without his having to be involved and concerned during their deliberations. Membership on very many committees would take all of his time. Making him chairman of administrative committees would, in a sense, tend to defeat their purpose. He should, however, be interested in the committee structure, have some judgment about membership on different committees, and know which staff members are already heavily loaded with committee activity. He may oftentimes be helpful by appearing at a meeting to explain some policy matter or issue which he knows that the faculty or administrative body will be considering, but here again, the purpose for his appearing should not be to sway the faculty or body to a point of view or to otherwise dominate its proceedings. The writers cannot, for example, wholly subscribe to the Columbia University Statutes, which provide that "The president shall be the chairman of the university council and of every faculty and administrative board established by the trustees. His concurrence shall be necessary to every act of the council or of a faculty or of an administrative board unless after his nonconcurrence the act or resolution shall be again passed by a vote of two-thirds of the entire body at the same or at the next succeeding meeting thereof. . . ."

7.11. USING COMMITTEES—AN ADMINISTRATIVE COMMITTEE

Though the chief administrative officer by virtue of his position is a member of the various faculties and university bodies, he could not possibly attend all their meetings or preside over them even if he wished to do so. His time would not permit. He should have a committee or administrative council composed of his deans and other administrative officers. Many problems need to be worked out at this level, and discussion is required on many matters which are not policy items for consideration by the general faculty—budget matters, for example, and new fiscal or accounting procedures which may have been provided by state government. These things require explanation and are simply examples of the many items which a chief administrative officer can handle best by meeting with those who are directly responsible to him.

In some instances a council of deans has been established, and one of its functions is that of advising the chief administrative officer on academic matters. Certainly this is proper, providing the chief administrative officer does not rely on the council of deans to make decisions which should be referred, initially at least, to the faculty and staff. Since such a council would be purely advisory, it can be used in such a way as to augment the chief administrative officer's knowledge and understanding without invading the sphere of proper faculty activity and decision. Some chief administrative officers have used such councils to good advantage. The vice-chancellor at the University of Nigeria has made a practice of meeting weekly with the council of deans and discussing the various problems which have arisen. Such a council could be established by university statutes, with the outline of its functions left to the chief administrative officer and the council itself. The chief administrative officer should have the right to appoint such ad hoc or standing administrative committees as he deems necessary.

A permanent record of committee appointments should be maintained in the office of the chief administrative officer so that particular staff members do not get overburdened with committee activity—and also in order that the chief administrative officer can make or suggest better selections for committees. There is sometimes a tendency to use the older, experienced staff members almost exclusively, without giving the younger staff members an opportunity to engage in committee activity and gain the experience and insight which will make them more valuable in the decision-making process.

A standing committee on the future development and direction of the university should be provided by university statute or act and appointed by the chief administrative officer. While some institutions appoint such committees at irregular intervals and publish their reports, this is such an important activity that it should not be left to chance. Also, it has a continuing aspect which is overlooked when there is no mandate that such a committee be established.

Another kind of committee which many institutions, particularly universities trying to serve agriculture and the public, have found useful is the advisory committee. These committees may exist both at the university and college—or even at the departmental—level. While the details should be left to regulation, the university statutes should require the establishment of such committees and designate that they be comprised of interested and able members of the public. The statutes of the University of Illinois, for example, provide that "The president of the university may recommend to the board of trustees the appointment of consultative committees to advise the colleges and schools and other divisions of the university."

7.12. POWER TO DELEGATE

Delegation of authority does not mean escaping responsibility. It means that an administrative officer is willing to turn over some functions to others and then stand by their decisions, or if this is not possible, at least to protect them as though he himself had made the decision. This does not come easily for many administrators. However, the authority to delegate must be provided because the chief administrative officer of a university cannot do all the chores himself. His ability to delegate freely—and wisely—and still to be recognized for his leadership is the mark of a good administrator. Certain acts which need to be delegated are of a recurring nature and need to be delegated on a continuing basis. The statutes of the Orissa University of Agriculture and Technology provide, for example, that "The president shall, as soon as possible, prepare a scheme for delegation of administrative powers to other officers of the university and obtain approval of the board to such a scheme of delegation." Such a provision is desirable. It supplements the statements of duties of officers of the university expressed in the act and statutes. Along with delegation should go express authority to develop rules and regulations for the efficient discharge of duties.

7.13. ANNUAL AND OTHER REPORTS

The Revised Code of the University of the Philippines provides that "The president shall prepare an annual report to the Board of

Regents on the work of the past year and the needs for the current year. He shall also present to the board the annual budget of the university with estimates of income and expenditures." Similar provisions are contained in other university acts, sometimes with the requirement that the report be submitted to the board some specified period before an annual meeting. Such a requirement would not be necessary for a board which meets regularly, but there should be a requirement that the report be submitted to members of the board in time for their study and consideration before the meeting at which it is to be acted upon. In view of the fact that the board will present certain information and facts about the university when it makes a case for the budget before government, there would seem to be no necessity for requiring an annual report to government. In addition to reporting to the board, the chief administrative officer should be interested in having prepared simplified factual statements which would be of interest to the general public and create more knowledge about the university in people throughout the state —a publication showing, for example, how many students are enrolled and in what courses of study, the number of professors, the internal organization of the university by colleges and departments, major research in progress, numbers reached in extension work, and a simplified statement of the university's resources including its sources of income and its expenditures. Many of these facts and figures are newsworthy in their own right and could be used to good advantage by an alert public relations officer.

7.14. MAINTENANCE OF DISCIPLINE

Virtually all university acts charge the chief administrative officer with the maintenance of discipline. Though one would assume that this refers to student discipline, there is no such limitation in the expression in the acts, so that, presumably, it applies to discipline in general, though necessarily there must be a different set of procedures for exercising discipline over the staff and over students. The acts express this duty in different ways—some with modifiers such as "due maintenance of discipline," and others by including certain elements of the procedures to be used. It is recommended that the university act charge the chief administrative officer with the duty of maintaining discipline but that the procedure be contained in university statutes. Suggested statutory provisions are discussed in Chapter 17.

7.15. THE SECURITY OF THE UNIVERSITY

None of the university acts or statutes surveyed contained any provision on police or fire protection or the general preservation of order in the university—except for an occasional reference to fire protection under the duties of an estates officer or physical plant director. Certainly there is an implication that the chief administrative officer acting through appropriate university officials has this responsibility. There have been instances where failure to realize the extent of the responsibility has been detrimental to the institution. We recommend, therefore, that the section in the act stating the general responsibilities and functions of the chief administrative officer contain a statement that he be responsible for maintaining order, for the security of university property, and for the security of staff, students, and other persons rightfully within its confines. Inability of the University of California to effectively control non-student agitators under existing laws led the legislature to enact a law making it a misdemeanor to interfere with the peaceful conduct of campus activities. Free speech and political advocacy are still permitted however—as they should be.

7.16. ROLE IN THE FORMULATION OF STATUTES

In at least one instance a university act provides that the chief administrative officer shall formulate the first statutes subject to approval by the chancellor or governor. However, the customary role of the chief administrative officer in the development of statutes is to act as intermediary between the academic council and the board of control. This does not deny him the right to initiate statutes, providing he refers them to proper academic bodies before they come to the board for discussion and approval. His role is explained in more detail in the discussion of the formulation and adoption of university statutes contained in Chapter 5. He is in a different position with respect to internal rules and regulations: over these he must have the power of approval.

7.17. EMERGENCY POWERS

Typical of provisions in the Indian agricultural university acts giving the chief administrative officer emergency powers is that contained in the Jawaharlal Nehru Agricultural University Act which states: "In any emergency which in the opinion of the vice-chancellor requires that immediate action be taken, the vice-chancellor shall take such action as he deems necessary and shall at the earliest opportunity thereafter report his action to such officer, authority, or body as would have in the ordinary course dealt with the matter." This act does contain a proviso, however, that any such emergency action taken by the vice-chancellor shall not commit the university to any recurring expenditure for a period of more than three months. Also, if such emergency action affects any person in the service of the university, that person is entitled to appeal to the board through the appropriate officer, authority, or body of the university. We believe that a section similar to this should be contained in the university act, but that the provisos included in the Jawaharlal Nehru Agricultural University Act are not necessary inasmuch as the emergency action taken will in due course be subject to review by the board. Furthermore, any staff officer or employee of the university who claims injury because of the emergency action can make use of the usual channel of appeal. If the chief administrative officer is to be given emergency powers, then a minimum of limitations should be imposed upon him. The board or any interested party will always have a right through proper procedures to determine if an emergency really did exist. If it didn't, then the chief administrative officer acted without authority and his acts are void. At least one act uses the language "In an emergency arising out of the business of the university," thus intimating that a definition of emergency is always in order and that it must concern the business of the university. If the emergency power is wrongfully used, the university would not be legally bound, and if damaged, could seek redress against the chief administrative officer and any third parties who may have benefited from its exercise.

CHAPTER – 8

Budget and Finance

8.1. THE CHIEF FINANCIAL OFFICER [1]

The act creating the Orissa University of Agriculture and Technology states that the comptroller shall be a full-time officer of the university appointed by the board. He shall manage the property and investments of the university and advise in regard to its financial policy. He shall be responsible to the vice-chancellor for preparation of the budget and statements of accounts for presentation by the vice-chancellor to the board. The statutes of Orissa and most other universities generally develop in detail the specific functions, powers, and duties of the comptroller. The Udaipur statutes list seventeen distinct functions; the Orissa statutes, sixteen. Comparable listings of functions and duties occur in many other university statutes in other parts of the world. The title of the chief financial officer is not always comptroller; others are bursar, business officer, business manager, controller, and finance officer. In any case, the position implies responsibility for developing the budget and handling financial and business affairs.

Some university acts provide that the comptroller be appointed by the board. This is likely to give him the feeling that in some respects his authority is equal to that of the chief administrative officer. This is particularly true if the law, besides allowing for his appointment by the board, bypasses the chief administrative officer and makes the comptroller directly responsible for specific functions. Better administrative theory and practice would indicate that the comptroller be appointed by the chief administrative officer, as are other officers of administration. All such appointments, of course, are subject to approval by the board.

Though the act and university statutes can say very little that is helpful about qualifications for this position, the chief financial officer ought to be a man of high business and administrative ability. In the beginning, when the institution is smaller and he will

---

[1] For a comprehensive and detailed discussion of the functions of a university business office, see Hannah, *Resource Book*, ch. 10.

have to look after more of the details regarding accounts, payrolls, disbursing, student fees, and other items, one would argue for a man with considerable technical training. Certainly one with accounting and business office experience would be implied. He should have the ability to meet with legislative committees and state finance officers and explain the budget to them. As the institution and the job grow, administration and personnel handling become more important, leaving more of the purely business and technical responsibilities to be taken care of by subordinates.

The comptroller or chief financial officer should make a constant study of the business organization and the kind of service it renders to the university, of the relations between his office and other offices on the campus. He should try to institute up-to-date methods, employ competent personnel, and do a good job of reporting and informing. Clear instructions to deans and department heads are of great help during the budget-making period. He should see that a business office procedure manual is prepared, kept up to date, and made available to all personnel in the university who need to know about the policies and procedures of his office.

The remaining sections in this chapter discuss major responsibilities or divisions of work in the areas of business and finance. Others not dealt with under section headings but discussed elsewhere in the book have to do with maintenance of the physical plant (sometimes a function of the comptroller) and the role of the comptroller with respect to university contracts and property acquisition, in maintaining service records of university staff members, and in managing student loan and scholarship funds in cooperation with other university officers. Under some acts or statutes he is also secretary of the governing body or administrative council. Though all acts and statutes impose a reporting duty on the chief financial officer, few of them give any intimation that his duty includes informing the public. Much understanding of the institution can be brought to members of the public through a brief but informative annual report of the financial operations of the university. Many universities do this. The University of Illinois, for example, publishes annually an attractive brochure entitled *Your Money, Your University.* In just a few pages with good photographs and concise language, the highlights of university functioning are portrayed. One page entitled "The Year in Statistical Summary" would in about two minutes' reading time give any interested citizen the answers to many questions about the cost of his university, where its resources originate, and how they are being used.

8.2. FUNDS

Many university acts require the establishment of a university general fund into which will be placed appropriations from state or regional government and funds from other established sources. Disbursements for the ordinary expenses of the university are made from this fund. University acts may specify other funds to be created or leave this determination to the board. Other funds sometimes specified are a pension fund, a student loan fund, capital or plant fund, and an endowment or gift fund. Since the purpose of a special fund is to help keep particular income and its use segregated and accounted for, it would seem that beyond specifying the establishment of a university general fund, the act should leave these determinations to the board acting on advice of the chief financial officer and university administration.

Particular funds may be needed depending on the kinds of income received by the University and on the kinds of activity in which it engages. Whether or not petty cash funds should be maintained, for example, is a question of policy and need and should be settled within the institution. Even statutory provisions specifying funds seem unnecessary. These can be established by regulation or as a part of the business office procedure guide and can be approved by the governing body. In the absence of state funding or control, the university will wish to establish a fund to protect contributions to a retirement or pension system. Also, where the university produces income, as it will when there is a university farm or when publications are sold, separate funds may be needed to make a proper accounting and to protect the future use of such income. Whether or not particular income can be segregated and reused within the institution or whether it must be covered into a general fund is a question which may depend on provisions in the university act or on the law of the state or region and its applicability to the university.

8.3. A FINANCE COMMITTEE

A finance committee is of sufficient importance that we feel the university act should provide for it. Without specifying exact composition, the act should require membership from the board and from the state or regional department of finance, with the university business officer included as a member and designated as secretary. The chief administrative officer should be an ex officio member. The chairman should be a nongovernmental member of the board. Six is a desirable number of members and allows for two each from the board, the university, and government.

8.4. BUDGET PREPARATION AND APPROVAL

The university act should require the chief administrative officer to submit an annual budget to the governing body for its consideration and approval. University statutes should state that responsibility for the preparation of the budget rests with the chief financial officer. Statutes should further require that the budget shall include allocations to the various administrative units of the university down to and including departments and that, when appropriate, all budgets submitted contain separate allocations for research, teaching, and extension. The business office procedure manual should contain standard instructions and forms for budget preparation. These must be studied and kept up to date. The heart of the budget process is firm, adequate, and understandable information provided in sufficient time to allow each unit to consider proposals from lower units and eventually to consolidate a budget for the university which represents the best judgment possible with no one feeling that he did an inadequate job for lack of time or information. Many conferences and consultations will need to take place. Good administrators will involve several of their key people in the budgeting process. These things, of course, cannot be written into the law or statutes, but they can, to a degree, be reflected in the kinds of provisions contained in the business office procedure manual and in the correspondence issued by the business office and sometimes by the chief administrative officer.

8.5. APPLICABILITY OF STATE GOVERNMENT REGULATIONS AND PROCEDURES

The degree of control exercised by state or regional governments over university finances and business affairs varies greatly. Except for those universities established under a national or state constitution which exempts them from certain controls, the legislature may provide that some university fiscal functions be subjected to the same regulations as state agencies. This may mean, for example, that a state auditor, treasurer, director of finance, property control officer, or budgetary commission may exercise a substantial—and sometimes embarrassing—amount of jurisdiction over the university's financial affairs. Universities must be accountable to the state, and the legislature certainly has some discretion in determining how this accountability shall be met. Designating the state treasurer as a treasurer of university funds is not objectionable in itself; neither is providing for a general audit by the state auditor. The theory is, however, that the university is a separate autonomous body with a particular broad objective to achieve and that its board should have a wide discretion in managing its affairs. Once the university budget is approved, then the better theory is to hold the university accountable to the state for expenditures in accordance with its budget and not to give any state official such as an auditor the right to make constant objections to proposed university expenditures. Many university acts require that statements of accounts be maintained and submitted at specified times to the state auditor. Where state auditors have held up payment and a controversy has arisen, American courts have almost uniformly held for the university. In one case the auditor refused to approve payment for ceremonies incident to the inauguration of a new president. The court held that the auditor could not interpose a discretionary authority over disbursement of the university's funds.

If there is any question about the right of the university to be free of objectionable state controls in procurement and sale, this right should be included in the university act. This does not mean that it need be excused from uniform procedures—bidding, use of forms, and other elements—which would still be under the control of the university. In a few instances a state board of higher education or its equivalent has been given authority to develop standardized forms, accounts, and records applicable to all universities in the state or region.

With respect to approval of the university budget, it has been held by American courts that the governor cannot delete certain items and approve the remainder, that he must either veto or approve the budget in toto. Though many legislatures provide for continuing fixed amounts for the university, sometimes as a general appropriation, sometimes broken down for specific purposes, these continuing appropriations cannot be binding on succeeding legislatures. However, they may come to be morally binding and a reliable source of income. There is some doubt about the wisdom of separate appropriations from the legislature for particular activities in the university. A much stronger argument is for approval of one consolidated university budget presented by the administration of the university. Administrators are opposed to pressure from within the university to get special recognition, unless the pressure is exerted on the administration and stops there. The presentation of a single university budget is a sound procedure, and in the long run will enable the university to make a better case for more resources. The policy should be against earmarked funds from the legislature. Sometimes, however, legislation provides that a portion of the state property tax or of the state school tax or that even a separate university tax on all property in the state shall be used to create a capital or building fund.

If a general state law, one on purchasing, for example, is not to apply to the university, the university act should so state. American courts have held that funds coming to a university from nontax sources should be under no surveillance by the state. Also, it has been held that payment to the university for loss under an insurance policy maintained by the university from nontax funds is the sole property of the university and not subject to the usual state audit controls.

The university act should require that those who handle funds be adequately bonded and that proper safeguards in the disbursement through signature requirements, the channeling of vouchers, and other procedures be established and published in the regulations of the comptroller. As universities grow in size and develop more complex and efficient internal structures, there tends to be a lessening of state control and surveillance and a recognition that universities really are different from other branches of government—that they have been established to accomplish distinctive objectives and should be given maximum freedom to accomplish these objectives.

8.6. COLLECTION AND USE OF TUITION AND STUDENT FEES

Authorization for making a tuition charge and assessing student fees should be contained in the university act. This is probably as far as the act should go. University statutes, however, should either fix the tuition fee or state that the tuition shall be such as is established by regulation. If there is to be a higher tuition for non-residents of the state or region, this should be authorized by statute. Authority should also be contained in the statutes for assessing and collecting necessary student fees. Inasmuch as policy issues may arise with regard both to the amount of tuition and the amount and use of student fees, the academic council should be asked to advise on these matters, though it should not have final authority over the fixing of either tuition or fees. These should be established by the university finance officer after consultation with appropriate university officers and an administrative committee appointed by the chief administrative officer to study and make recommendations regarding tuition and fees. There should then be approval by the board.

The statutes should contain a general provision on the purpose for which fees are collected. It should not be too restrictive because new needs will arise. However, there should be an expression of policy indicating that students are supposed to get value received for fees collected from them. For example, is it legitimate to use student fees for building construction, operating a laundry service, carrying on an athletic program, or augmenting the library? Such issues have been before American courts many times and the general theory is that if the charge is reasonable and is used for something which benefits students, it is valid. Usual fees are those for health and medical service and insurance, use of library, use of laboratory equipment and supplies, use of textbooks where the institution supplies them, travel in connection with courses or field work, and sometimes, for a program of cultural events. These should not be listed in the university statutes but should be established by regulation based on a statutory authorization.

Apparently it is valid to provide for no refund of student fees regardless of circumstances. At least many university acts and statutes make no provisions for refunds. It is recommended, however, that the university statutes contain a provision that refunds can be made as established by university regulation. There should then be regulations drafted which permit a student to recover a portion of his tuition and fees in case he leaves the university for other than disciplinary reasons. Many institutions make such provisions and establish a date during the term, sometimes more than one date during the term, for making partial refunds.

Some university acts provide for free tuition or only partial tuition charges to indigent students or others in specified categories. Some of the laws establishing American land-grant and other state universities provided for free tuition to residents of the state. This policy has been generally abandoned. Sometimes the legislature provides that there shall be one or more free tuition scholarships from legislative districts to be based on competitive examinations. Still other acts and statutes establish a work program under which it is possible for a student to earn a portion or all of his tuition. Such free tuition scholarships or partial exemptions will be upheld, according to American court decisions at least, if the classification of recipients is not arbitrary. Frequently statutes or regulations use the number of credit hours or courses per term as a basis for charging tuition and provide that staff members of the university, members of their families, or certain other categories may take courses without paying the charges.

8.7. GOVERNMENT GRANTS

A legislature is not bound to make appropriations promised by its predecessor. The university act, therefore, cannot assure the university of a fixed income beyond the term of the legislature establishing it. As a matter of practice, however, many legislatures, particularly central government legislative bodies, do establish formulas under which stated amounts—sometimes with an annual increment—are to be distributed to specified universities or educational institutions. Once the grants are commenced and institutions rely on them, it may be difficult for a legislative body to fail to provide them though legally it is not bound to do so. Such grants may be absolute and unconditional or they may be conditional. If a condition is attached, it must be performed to entitle the institution to the appropriation. Following the establishment of the American land-grant institutions, several acts of congress provided for continuing funds for specific purposes, particularly for agricultural extension and agricultural research. Though these laws are fairly broad in scope, they nevertheless impose conditions on the use of the funds. Government then has the right to verify through audit that such funds are used for the purposes specified.

Though money paid to a university from a state or regional treasury is derived from taxes and in theory belongs to the public until it has been appropriated by the legislature, money donated by a central government to a university for specific purposes never becomes a part of the public funds of the state or region and a state or regional legislative appropriation of such money to the university is neither proper nor necessary. Hence, questions regarding its use and procedures for disbursing and accounting are solely between the university and central government. Recurring grants from central governments are many times handled by a grants commission or other body in position to make judgments about allocation of the funds.

If land is granted to the university, stipulations regarding minimum price and method and time of disposition may be included as conditions in the grant. If so, they must be met to qualify the university for the benefit. Such conditions did accompany land granted by the Congress of the United States for the establishment of the so-called land-grant institutions. If any money or property is offered to the university from government under conditions which are contrary to the general educational policy or purpose of the university, then there is but one alternative—to refuse the grant.

Though local taxing bodies are not likely to offer much assistance to universities in the developing countries, it may be useful to know that in American court decisions the right of such bodies to use their tax money in this manner has been upheld—even though benefits would not flow back to the local unit in direct proportion to its grant. As an example, many county governments in the United States have supported the land-grant university's extension program through appropriations from county boards or commissions.

8.8. GRANTS FROM FOREIGN GOVERNMENTS AND FOUNDATIONS

The university act should permit acceptance of aid from any source under any conditions which are in keeping with the functions of the university. However, questions of national policy are likely to be involved in gifts from foreign governments or foundations. Must the aid be channeled through central government and be allocated under conditions imposed by it, or can aid come directly to the institution? Presumably, the central government will not impose conditions which are at variance with the purpose of the aid-giving government; otherwise, the funds would not be made available. It seems, however, that at times the controls imposed by central governments closely approach this line. Grants from foreign foundations, particularly those carrying on major operations in the country, can be made with more freedom, though even here a central government can impose conditions. But a foundation is even less likely than a foreign government to make aid available if it cannot accomplish the objectives it has in mind. Regulations developed by the chief financial officer should contain details on accepting, using, and accounting for grants from foreign governments and foundations.

8.9. ACCEPTANCE OF GIFTS AND DONATIONS

Laws creating the University of Alabama required that the law school be supplied by the Supreme Court of the state with its secondhand and superseded volumes and that the school be supplied by the Secretary of State with ten copies each of the Alabama Code and the State Supreme Court reports. The university is probably under a duty to accept these lavish gifts—even if it does not have shelf space for them! University acts creating public institutions provide that gifts or grants for any legitimate purpose may be accepted by the university, provided they are not accompanied by conditions contrary to the policies of the institution. Such a gift or grant, for example, should not give the donor any right to participate in university affairs.

University statutes may provide for appropriate means of recognizing donors or grantors, such as designating specific funds by their names. The Purdue University Act states that "The trustees of Purdue University are hereby granted authority to receive, accept, hold, administer, and use any property transferred by gift, bequest, or devise with such terms and conditions and with such obligations, liabilities, and burdens as are imposed, when in the judgment of the trustees it is in the best interests of the university." The statutes of some universities authorize staff members to conduct preliminary negotiations with prospective grantors with the prior knowledge and approval of an appropriate administrative officer. This simply recognizes that many gifts to universities are made because of the outstanding activities of its staff members. Though such a statutory provision is not essential, it might encourage staff members to follow up on possibilities. A common provision is one requiring the chief administrative officer to submit the question of acceptance to the board if the amount involved exceeds a stated figure or if acceptance would involve additional expenditures or onerous conditions on the part of the university. Statutes should also require that when art objects are offered to the university, an appropriate committee advise the president on their value and whether or not they should be accepted. Generally, the business office maintains a separate fund for gifts and donations. Whether or not such a fund is maintained, there must, of course, be accountability for use of income from the gift and for disposition of the corpus should this become necessary.

American courts have held that a promise or offer to donate or contribute to a university is binding and enforceable if liabilities have been incurred by the university in contemplation of the gift. A written agreement from the donor in which it is stated that the gift is for valuable consideration may be of probative value if an issue arises. In other American cases the courts have upheld gifts by American citizens to foreign universities over the objections of disappointed relatives—even when the name of the foreign university was misspelled!

8.10. TRUSTS

Many gifts to universities are encased in trusts. These raise some special problems. As with other gifts, universities are empowered by law to accept trusts providing their conditions can be legally and economically met. This is a determination to be made by the university administration and approved by the board and is an area in which the services of legal counsel are required. Apart from challenges raised by disgruntled heirs about proper execution of the trust instrument, questions most frequently arise about achievement by the university of the purpose of the trust and the right of the university to dispose of the corpus of the trust and use the resulting funds. The writers are not familiar with theories which have resulted from trust litigation in other parts of the world, but the American courts have been quite liberal in their definitions of purpose. Under the *cy pres* doctrine, though the specific purpose of the trust cannot be carried out, any related purpose which the court determines would have satisfied the desires of the creator of the trust is acceptable.

Princeton University, for example, was able to accept and use a large sum of money which according to the trust document was to be used for the publication of a more or less unintelligible mass of material left by the donor. But he did have a general purpose in mind which the university claimed it could accomplish without publishing his notes. The court agreed. In another case the trust was accompanied by a complicated mechanism for administering an essay contest. The university did not employ the mechanism but in the opinion of the court had accomplished the benefactor's purpose in other ways and the trust was sustained. The court said, "Equity will presume that the donor would attach so much more importance to the object of the gift than to the mechanism by which he intended to accomplish it that he would prefer to alter the mechanism to the extent necessary to save the object."

Trusts with odd and eccentric provisions will be upheld if the purpose is appropriate and the trust can still be administered. In one case the awarding of scholarships under a trust was made to depend on golf scores; it was upheld by the court. Further on the subject of scholarships—the courts have said that neither indigence nor excellence need be expressed in the granting instrument as conditions for receiving benefits.

Universities should be wary about accepting trusts which tie their hands. If property is to be held in perpetuity or cannot be mortgaged, leased, or sold under any conditions, then it probably should not be accepted. University statutes should contain provisions on conditions which make a trust acceptable. This makes it easier for those who need to explain to a donor the reasons why there must be some flexibility. In some cases such a provision is contained in a university act. The laws creating Purdue University, for example, provide that the board may, if not inconsistent with the terms and conditions of the gift, sell or otherwise dispose of real property and invest or reinvest it to accomplish the uses which may have been designated in the gift. In such cases a separate fund is required. Some laws require that no university or other public agency can dispose of land or real estate held in trust without an opinion of the Attorney General on the validity of the sale and approval of the Governor following an evaluation by appraisers appointed by him.

Sometimes donors are not certain of the exact designation of the institution to which they wish to leave property. There should be a provision in the university statutes that gifts shall not fail because of misnomer or informalities when the intent of the donor is clear. Decisions indicate that courts are likely to support such a provision.

8.11. INVESTMENTS

The university act should provide that the board can invest funds of the university in proper securities. There may be a general law conditioning the right of a public university to make investments and defining the kinds of investments which are acceptable, in which case, of course, the institution is bound. Nevertheless, the university act should contain a reiteration of the general law giving the board the right to invest under the conditions expressed in it. Different conditions may attach to grants from the central government. There is a general rule that a trustee may not invest funds in his own obligations. This may not apply to central government grants. Some American institutions have established a separate corporate body to accept gifts and make investments. In some cases there may be a corporate authority empowered to do this for all educational institutions. If the governing body has money to invest, a foundation fund or its equivalent should be created. If the employees of the university have established a credit union, the university may wish to invest funds in this—providing it is legally possible. In any event, the chief financial officer of the university must assume investment as one of his responsibilities and be prepared to give the chief administrative officer and the board sound information and advice.

8.12. DEPOSITS

Unless the university act conditions the right, the board may select the depository for university funds. Sometimes the law states that deposits shall be in a "scheduled" bank or in some other approved depository as defined in the law. Though the act may give the board discretion in selecting a depository, it should state that funds must be deposited. This ought to be obvious, but in view of the archaic business procedures which still prevail in some universities, it is worth the words necessary to put it into the act. American courts have held that in the absence of direction from the board, the treasurer may deposit university funds in such banks as he chooses or may withdraw the same at his pleasure subject to liability on his bond. We do not feel that such discretion should be placed with the treasurer.

8.13. PAYROLL DEDUCTIONS

Many universities in the developing countries have improved their business procedures to the point where they are able to render certain financial and bookkeeping service to the staff. Making deductions for income tax is an example. Though the right may be implied, there should be a university statute giving the chief financial officer authority to make income tax and retirement system deductions and any other deductions authorized by the payee. These would include insurance and other charges made by the university. At the rural university in La Molina, for example, staff members are able to make purchases of meat and other products from the animal husbandry store and have the amount deducted from their monthly check.

8.14. PURCHASING AND LETTING CONTRACTS

These subjects are discussed in some detail in Chapter 5. The letting of contracts should be accomplished under rules developed by the board, supplemented by regulations of the chief financial officer. Certain basic principles must be established by the university through regulations—particularly the conditions under which bidding is invited. If there are general provisions applicable to the university, these should be reiterated. Purchasing is one of the major responsibilities of the chief financial officer. Provisions in the university statutes should place this responsibility with the chief financial officer acting in accordance with such general state laws or regulations as may apply. There should be a purchasing agent in his office whose functions and duties are described in a business procedure manual. The purchasing agent should cooperate with the manager of a central supply or stores office in keeping up the stock of expendable items. Clearly delineated procedures and a supply of necessary forms in all offices where requests originate help greatly in expediting purchases. Precise instructions on how to prepare vouchers and what channels to follow for approval should likewise be available in all such offices. A discussion of the business procedures involved in purchasing and letting contracts appears in Chapter 10 of the *Resource Book*.[2]

8.15. BORROWING

The right of the board to borrow money for purposes of the university on the security of property of the university is contained in

---

[2] Hannah, *Resource Book*, ch. 10.

most university acts. Some state that borrowing must be from government-approved sources. Some limit the purposes for which money may be borrowed. Along with the power to borrow should go the power to issue bonds, charge for services (housing, for example), and retire indebtedness in any approved manner.

Depending on the law in the particular country, issuance of bonds is sometimes conditioned by detailed legislative provisions. Many questions arise about the legality as well as the worth of bonds issued by a public agency: lenders will feel that their protection lies in a strict adherence to the law, in the opinion of competent legal authority that the university has the right to issue bonds, and in the assurance that proper procedures were followed. If the law creating the university does not empower it to issue bonds and it wishes to use this security and fund-raising device, the legislature should be asked to amend the law.

With respect to short-term loans to meet obligations pending receipt of funds, there should be rules of the board and of the chief financial officer under which these can be accomplished in the regular course of business. If the university is subject to a maximum debt limit imposed by general law, legislation will be necessary to excuse it from this limit. Interest rates, method of issuing bonds, and other conditions may also be expressed in the general law; if they are not, the university act should authorize the board to make such determinations, and further details should be contained in university statutes or regulations.

In connection with borrowing, the chief financial officer of the university should know what remedies are permitted the lender. American courts have held, for example, that a mechanic's lien law does not apply to property of the university. Whether or not such immunity exists in other countries depends on the law regarding claims against public agencies and the theory under which the university holds property. The purpose of the property might also have a bearing. Here is another place where a distinction might be made between so-called governmental or educational functions and proprietary functions. Some laws require approval of government to any transaction under which the board borrows and pledges the security of the university.

8.16. DISBURSING AND ACCOUNTING

Many of the earlier laws creating universities contained lengthy and specific provisions on how the university should account for funds. We do not believe the act need express any of the details, but it should empower the board to collect, disburse, and account. Details of all these operations should be contained in a business office procedure manual. The manual should contain forms to be used and procedures to be followed together with the rules on such things as establishing petty cash funds, cosigning checks, and verifying the receipt of funds. Generally there is in the business office a bursar's division to discharge these responsibilities. The legitimacy of expenditures is always open to challenge from the state auditor, the board, or any interested taxpayer. The bursar, or his equivalent, should be an experienced and efficient officer. Also, he must have tact and understanding. Sometimes, for example, impatient staff members advance money of their own for a research project. The question of their repayment then arises. The courts have held that repayment may be allowed if there is no collusion and the money was spent for a legitimate purpose. The bursar will need to deal wisely with many "irregular" situations.

8.17. AUDITING

The role of the state with respect to surveillance over university funds and accounts is discussed earlier in this chapter. Regardless of any rights which the state auditor may have, the university act should empower the board to establish a system of audits. University statutes should then impose on the chief financial officer the duty of establishing an auditing division and determining the rules and regulations under which it shall function. *The University of Illinois Rules of Organization and Procedure* state that the auditor shall "(1) Verify by audit the transactions and records of all officers and employees responsible for the receipt or expenditure of money, for the keeping of accounts, or for the custody of property, (2) Review accounting systems and business procedures, test the effectiveness of the system of internal controls, and assist in the installation of new procedures, (3) Audit or cause to be audited the accounts of all organizations required to submit financial reports to the university." This would appear to be an adequate statement of the auditor's responsibilities. It is recommended that a similar statement be included in the section of the statutes or of the business procedure manual providing for the appointment of an auditor and defining his duties.

8.18. UNIVERSITY TRAVEL

Some university acts contain detailed provisions on travel, including rates and items which can be claimed. This is a mistake. If there are general laws and regulations on travel applicable to university employees, they are not to be reiterated in the university act. If there are no laws or detailed regulations applicable to the university, then the act should simply empower the board to develop them. The board in turn should leave such determinations to the university administration for inclusion in a business office procedure manual and for approval by the board. Even the university statutes should go no further than to provide that the university shall reimburse for actual and necessary expense of travel on university business for which proper approval has been obtained. Certainly the right to recover for necessary travel should not be confined to administrative officers of the university. Some staff members—agricultural extension supervisors and specialists, for example—cannot accomplish their work without traveling.

8.19. STUDENT ORGANIZATION FUNDS

Though it may run counter to the measure of independence which student organizations feel they must have, many university statutes or regulations provide that the university controller or business officer shall act as treasurer of student and other organization funds. This is regarded as a service to the organizations, and sometimes the statute or regulation makes it discretionary with the controller. In any case, such accounts are kept separate from university accounts and the organization funds are kept separate from university funds. Handling of student organization funds by the university business office is likely to be an aid rather than a detriment to the organization, but it certainly is not a policy matter of high priority.

8.20. INSURANCE

Insurance in connection with a retirement or pension fund has already been discussed, but there are other kinds with which the university must be concerned. If there is a state workmen's compensation act or its equivalent applicable to nonacademic employees, the university may by law be required to participate in it. Use of university vehicles requires the maintenance of liability insurance. There must be fidelity insurance or bonding to protect the security of funds in the hands of various university personnel.

Insurance against fire and other property damage may be necessary. It is possible even to obtain "interruption" insurance to protect the institution against the loss of tuition, fees, and rentals. This latter kind of insurance is not likely to apply to a public institution. The board should be empowered by law to make determinations about insurance needs and procure the insurance which it feels necessary. It should, in turn, by university statute, pass this responsibility on to the chief financial officer. If the institution is large enough, a separate insurance officer may be needed. Insurance against property damage is generally not carried by institutions when investment in their physical plant reaches the point where annual premiums exceed any probable loss. This same principle does not apply to fidelity or liability insurance, though under the immunity theory the need for liability insurance may be problematic. This matter is discussed in Chapter 3 under the tort liability of a university. Health and accident insurance for both staff and students has been mentioned previously, but is discussed further in Chapters 15, 16, and 17.

CHAPTER – 9

Officers and Their Functions

A full complement of university officers is no assurance of good administration. In Chapter 7 we alluded to an administrative design for the university and discussed the necessity for good communications between the chief administrative officer and his deans and officers of administration. No university officer works in a vacuum. Weakness in the organization of any office and delay in accomplishing the functions assigned to it tend to weaken the whole administrative structure, making it more difficult for other officers to discharge their functions in an efficient manner. Though the university act and statutes can designate the officers to be appointed and delineate their functions, the achievement of team effort and a feeling of cohesion between officers of administration depend on the personality and administrative ability of the chief administrative officer and other key officers.

To achieve effective functioning in his own office and throughout university administration, some freedom to choose and to change personnel must be granted the chief administrative officer. Though appointments to administrative positions are subject to approval by the governing body, such appointments do not carry tenure; they are quite generally for one, two, or three years with the right and, in fact, the expectation of reappointment. For many administrative positions selection committees are not used, though they may be, and in at least one institution the law requires them. It is generally expected that the chief administrative officer in consultation with others will select the man he wants and ask the board for approval. When other officers of the university employ administrative assistants or administrative staff not in the category of nonacademic personnel, they will select the persons they want and ask for approval by the chief administrative officer who will, in turn, secure board approval. In a few instances major officers such as the comptroller may be hired directly by the board. But when this means bypassing the chief administrative officer, it is not a desirable method.

Since the position of chancellor is ordinarily an honorary one and is designated by law, it would hardly be considered an office. The same holds for pro-chancellor where this is an honorary position. The Minister of Education or Minister of Agriculture is sometimes accorded this post. Those acts creating the position provide that the incumbent shall act for the chancellor when the latter requests. If there is any fear that a minister may be hostile to a new university, making him pro-chancellor might be a good move! It is customary for the university act to list certain offices and then state that others may be created by university statutes. There are differences of opinion about the echelon in which particular officers belong. Some authorities will argue, for example, that the director of physical plant should be a subordinate of the comptroller, that a personnel officer or director of nonacademic personnel should fall under some other officer of administration, and that a university farm manager should come in about a third or fourth echelon of administration under some department head. Size, maturity, and scope of activity of the institution have a bearing. In the early years, when the institution is small and its resources are limited, many officers may be obliged to carry on dual roles and the question of administrative echelon will not arise until these roles can be separated. Since status and salary are involved, the question is an important one to individuals concerned. The size and nature of a job will vary too, depending on the kind of institution. The hiring and retention of qualified nonacademic personnel, for example, becomes extremely important as the institution increases the scope of its research program and has a need for more technicians and skilled workers.

Certain administrative procedures are common to all university offices—budget preparation, hiring of nonacademic personnel, and processing of travel vouchers, for example. These details will be omitted from the discussion of functions and responsibilities contained in the remaining sections of this chapter. The roles which most of these officers play are discussed in more or less detail in other parts of the book under chapters dealing with major segments of university activity in which they play an important part. The duplication of description, however, is not wholly unintentional, for one of the purposes of this chapter is to present a quick view of all the major areas of university functioning.

Lest a discussion of legal and operational considerations becloud the central purpose of university administration, this quotation from the statutes of the University of the Philippines is appropriate: "The administrative agencies and offices of the university function primarily for the purpose of serving the educational program of the institution. Their relationship with the faculty should, therefore, be on the basis of sympathetic and intelligent interest in the work of all departments with due consideration to the policies and needs of the institution as a center of learning."

9.1. VICE-POSITIONS TO THE CHIEF ADMINISTRATIVE OFFICER

How much assistance and what kind of assistance does the chief administrative officer need beyond that provided by university administrative officers and his own personal staff? In the beginning he may need only a good assistant to serve more or less in the capacity of an aide. This kind of assistance can be of great help. Names used to describe the post are administrative officer, establishments officer, administrative assistant, executive assistant, and aide. Executive assistant implies a somewhat higher status than administrative assistant; likewise, administrative officer and establishments officer suggest more responsibility. The latter officer may have a great deal to do with university structure and personnel.

As the tempo of university activity increases and more pressure is felt in the office of the chief administrative officer, there will develop a need for additional officers to be in charge of separate activities—personnel and the university press, for example. This may take care of some moderate increase in activity but as the institution continues to grow, problems will increase. Eventually sheer volume of work and diversity of responsibilities in the chief administrative office will create a demand for high-level help. At this stage, consideration will need to be given to a vice-position. Generally, when a single position is created, it is one in which academic affairs center. However, all are not of this nature. A single vice-position may be one of general responsibility or it may be for some function other than academic—business affairs, for example. Among the names used for such a position are the following:

Principal
Dean of Faculties
Dean
Executive Dean

Vice-Rector
Deputy Vice-Chancellor
Pro-Vice-Chancellor
Executive Vice-President
Provost
Vice-President and Provost
Vice-President for Business Affairs
Vice-President of the University

Southern Methodist University has a "vice-president for university life." Another position found in some institutions is secretary of the university. Such a position may include both internal and external responsibilities. Generally the emphasis is on external relationships and communications with state, national, and other agencies. Sometimes these kinds of responsibilities are lumped together under a vice-president or vice-position for external affairs.

Separate physical locations may call for one or more vice-positions. In this case the vice–chief administrative officer may be in administrative charge of a branch or constituent college of the university. When more than one vice-position is created, a second one is likely to be for business affairs. Those institutions which have a full complement of vice-positions are likely to have four: one each for business affairs, academic affairs, external affairs, and student affairs. Some institutions have a vice-position for external studies under which falls responsibility for all extramural work and administration of the summer school. The order creating the Rural University at Viscosa in Brazil divides the administrative responsibility into five directorates with an executive dean for each.

Since the chief administrative officer must delegate to any vice-position a considerable portion of his responsibility, he should have the right to nominate the people for these positions. The university act should so provide. When a vice-position is created to be in administrative charge of a branch or constituent college, the faculty at such location should participate in the nomination process through appropriate committees just as the faculty of the university should participate in the nomination of a chief administrative officer. All vice-positions, however, must be approved by the governing body. Terms and conditions of service should be prescribed in the university statutes. As with other administrative positions, they should not be for indefinite tenure but for a definite period of from one to three years with the right of reappointment.

9.2. DEANS OF COLLEGES OR FACULTIES

The Andhra Pradesh Agricultural University Act states that "There shall be a Dean for each faculty, to be chosen in such manner and for such period as may be prescribed. The Dean shall be the Chairman of the Board of the faculty and shall be responsible for the faithful observance of the statutes and the regulations related to the faculty and for the organization and conduct of the teaching, research, and extension work of the departments comprised therein." This is probably as much as the act need contain. While it is not recommended that the statutes set forth a complete job description, they should delineate major duties.

Typically, university statutes list the following as duties and responsibilities of a dean: (1) the organization and conduct of teaching, research, and extension in his college, (2) observance of university statutes and rules, (3) formulation of college policies, (4) submission of reports to the chief administrative officer, (5) conducting meetings of boards of studies and of his faculty as presiding officer, (6) supervision of the registration and progress of students in the college, (7) allocation of office space and the educational use of buildings and rooms assigned to his college, (8) being the medium of communication for official business of the college with other authorities of the university, with students, and with the public, (9) representing the college in conferences (or designating a representative), (10) preparing and submitting the budget of the college, (11) granting casual leave and authorizing travel, (12) procuring necessary equipment and supplies for the college, (13) exercising necessary jurisdiction over land assigned to the college for research and experimental work, (14) being responsible for the administration and operation of the university farm if this function is assigned to him.

His major objectives, which cannot be delineated in the university act or statutes, are to achieve an effective integration of the teaching, research, and extension responsibility of his college and to see that manpower in the college is wisely used, that students are challenged, that research is aimed at solving problems, and that the extension program actually reaches and affects people. Internally, of course, he is the chief officer of his college directly responsible to the chief administrative officer and a member of the latter's administrative council. As its representative within the university, he will be expected by his faculty to get the college's fair share of university resources and otherwise protect its interests among other colleges and entities of the university.

Deans are chosen in various ways and for various terms. Sometimes they are elected by the faculty, sometimes by a college council; in rare instances they may even be appointed by the governor. The most usual method and the one recommended is appointment by the chief administrative officer and approval by the governing body. A selection committee composed partly of faculty in the college and partly of outside members should participate in the selection process. Some institutions provide for a term as long as five years with the right of reappointment, some for as short as two or three years with no right of reelection or reappointment. The deanship should not carry indefinite tenure but it should be possible for a good man to hold the job long enough to be effective. The dean may have indefinite tenure as a professor, which rank he would retain while dean. His tenure as dean should be longer than two or three years. Perhaps the best method is for the university statutes to provide a term of two years with the right of reappointment. A dean who is subject to the whims of a faculty body and who can be ousted by their vote is in a precarious position. The job is so important that its occupant should not be changed by whims. A college, particularly a college of agriculture which establishes an image in the eyes of the public, requires good and continuing leadership. Others besides just students and members of the faculty have a stake in it.

9.3. DEPARTMENT HEADS [1]

Though the structure of a department is discussed in the next chapter, the function of a department head cannot very well be outlined without emphasizing the necessity that a department be a permanent administrative unit from which can flow a coordinated program of research, extension, and teaching. The responsibility of an agricultural university or of any university attempting to solve pressing problems standing in the way of development in the country cannot be met by having a large number of small one-

---

[1] Technically, a department head is not an "officer." He is not responsible to the chief administrative officer but to the dean of his college. This is also true of a college director of instruction. But these positions are so important that they are included in this chapter for discussion.

professor departments where theoretical research is jealously guarded. The department should be a primary educational unit dealing with all phases of activity in the subject matter involved in the department. It is important that university statutes clearly define the nature of a department and prescribe the method of selecting the head.

In some institutions department heads are elected by the faculty or by the faculty council; in others they are nominated by the dean following a selection process, and the name of the nominee is then forwarded to the chief administrative officer and the governing body for approval. We believe this latter method is best. In some institutions the department head is referred to as a chairman and the position is considered as one which should be rotated by election among professors in the department. This may be satisfactory for departments that engage in no extension activity and that have a limited research program and a small staff. It can be argued that they do not particularly need the continuity and strength which a continuing head and an efficient administrative organization could provide.

University statutes contain a variety of statements about the duties of a department head. We feel that the following should be incorporated in the statutes: a general statement that each department shall have a head whose appointment, powers, and duties shall be as prescribed in the statutes and who shall be responsible to the dean for the proper organization and working of the department. Without elaboration and detail, additional provisions should be included giving the department head responsibility for:

The administrative organization and conduct of work of the department.

Formulation and execution of departmental policies.

Reporting on teaching, research, and extension activity in the department.

General supervision of work of students in the department.

Preparation of the budget.

Responsibility for departmental funds and property.

Responsibility for use of departmental space and land areas.

Responsibility for necessary liaison with the director of extension and the director of research.

Cooperation with the dean of the graduate school with respect to the work of graduate students in the department.

Nomination of staff members for the department following a selection process.

Though the department head will normally be a professor and will have indefinite tenure as a professor, he should be selected as a department head for a specific term with the right and expectation of reappointment. Terms vary from one to five years as with deans, some with and some without the right of reappointment. The position should not pass automatically to the senior member of the department, though personnel in the department should be considered first in the selection of a new head. Likewise, it should not be a short-term assignment without the right of reappointment. Departments are expected to grow; to develop policies; to develop strength in their teaching, research, and extension efforts; and to have their own meaning to the agriculture of the state or region. These goals can be realized only through competent leaders who can hold their positions long enough to accomplish important departmental objectives.

9.4. DIRECTOR OF INSTRUCTION [2]

This is a position which may exist either at the university or college level. At the university level it is likely to be a vice-position— one of those discussed in the first section of this chapter. As colleges grow, the responsibilities of the dean may reach the point at which some division is indicated. This is particularly true in colleges of agriculture which have an unusually heavy program in research and agricultural extension. It is quite common, therefore, to have an officer under the dean in charge of each of the three major branches of work. These officers may be known by various names, such as assistant or associate directors, assistant or associate deans; or, as the institution grows, they may be directors and deans, and the person who would normally be dean of the college may become a vice-president for agriculture and related affairs. Functions, however, remain essentially the same. University statutes should provide for (but not outline in detail) this kind of organization when it is needed, following a recommendation from the faculty of the col-

---

[2] See footnote 1.

lege and approval through the usual academic and administrative channels.

The extent to which a director of instruction is a "line" officer or a "staff" officer is one which should be determined within the college. His authority should be understood by all who deal with him. Department heads, for example, need to know who has the authority to make initial determinations about appointments, salaries, travel, and other matters with which they are concerned. A director of instruction for a college should be nominated by the dean following recommendations from an appropriate search committee composed partly of members of the college faculty and partly of members outside the faculty. Being an administrative position, the post should be for a definite term, such as two years, with the right and expectation of reappointment. The director, of course, may be a professor in one of the departments and have indefinite tenure as a professor.

Probably the university statutes should go no further than saying that the director of instruction shall have such duties as are delegated to him by the dean or, if he is a university officer, by the chief administrative officer. As is the case with all positions, however, it is desirable to have a job description indicating the broad objectives of the position as well as the major functions to be performed. These descriptions should be developed and become a part of either university regulations or those of the particular college. The University of the Philippines developed a comprehensive statement of the functions of the different directors under the dean of the college of agriculture. Such a statement can serve a useful purpose for many people. Furthermore, it provides a basis for reevaluation of the job and improvement of the relationship between various officers in carrying out the total work of the college.

9.5. DIRECTOR OF RESEARCH

The new agricultural universities in India and many other universities provide for a director of research. There may be such a position also at the college level. Since Chapter 13 is devoted to research organization and functioning, details of these relationships will not be discussed here. Some comments about the nature of the position are, however, appropriate. A director of research, whether at the university or college level, is not a czar. He is a coordinator, a suggester, a finder of resources, a repository of information about the total research program, an assistant in publication matters, a disseminator in conjunction with the extension program, an advisor to the chief administrative officer on all major policies having to do with research; he is many things but he is not a director of those who are carrying on research work. The fear of direction many times arises when the position is even discussed.

The university act should provide for the position of director of research at the university level; the statutes should provide for (but not require) the appointment of such an officer at the college level. As with other officers, the job description should be left to regulations. University statutes should indicate only the major functions of the university director of research. Among these would be the following: coordination; advice to the chief administrative officer and other personnel about research policies and procedures; study and recommendations on the research budget; assistance in the search for personnel; assistance in publication; encouragement of cross-disciplinary research; discharging for the chief administrative officer his responsibility for field stations and separate research facilities, maintenance of computer, statistical, and other services established for the whole university; representing the chief administrative officer in discussions and consultations having to do with grants and contracts for research; responsibility for the wise use and allocation of land for research and other research resources of the university; making appraisals and evaluations which will help establish goals for the university and its colleges; consulting with the deans—or with department heads if he is a college officer— on appointments, promotions, and salaries of the research staff. Though in an agricultural university it can be argued that the university director of research should be an agricultural scientist, he should not be appointed by or be subject to approval by the dean of the college of agriculture. A part or all of the deans may serve on a selection committee, but the director should be appointed by the chief administrative officer and be responsible solely to the chief administrative officer.

9.6. DIRECTOR OF EXTENSION

Many of the American land-grant universities have two extension programs—one in agricultural extension and one in general university extension. Federal emphasis on and funds for agricultural extension account for this situation. Ideally one would argue for an overall university extension program under a director of extension with, however, a decided emphasis on agriculture since a major responsibility of the new universities is agricultural development and bringing the results of research to rural people. Emphasis on agriculture can be achieved by starting with a director of agricultural extension in the college of agriculture and letting the institution grow in its program and efforts to the point where a director of extension for the institution could be appointed —with agriculture constituting a major segment of the total program. Still another possibility is to start with a director of university extension but provide that he shall be a person trained in agriculture and responsible to the dean of agriculture for an agricultural extension program.

We believe that the university act should provide for the appointment of a director of extension responsible to the chief administrative officer. Qualifications and functions can be spelled out in the university statutes so that the needed emphasis on agriculture will be assured. The overall philosophy of the university and the kind of personnel it is able to hire mean more than the formal organization. If an institution feels it should be able to depart from what seems like the ideal paper structure to function instead by means of some compromise, and if this decision is based on an earnest desire to serve agriculture, then one should not quarrel with the compromise.

Sometimes the position is designated director of extension education or director of extramural studies. The name shouldn't matter as long as agriculture comprises a major part of the extension effort and the university engages in the right kind of activities. The Uttar Pradesh Agricultural University Statutes provide that "The Director of Extension shall plan and execute all extension programs and activities in cooperation with the deans of the colleges and the directors of schools." The act should provide that he be nominated by the chief administrative officer following an appropriate selection process and that he be approved by the governing body. Some acts state that he shall be a full-time officer technically trained in agriculture. He should be a member of the university council or main academic body. The statutes should provide, among other things, that he shall be in charge of all extension education activities and that he shall cooperate in developing the extension education program for students and graduate students in the university.

Among other activities which may be stated briefly in the statutes are the following: coordination of the university's extension effort with that of the central government, state, or region; supervision of field activities of the university extension staff; development of visual aids and other extension teaching materials; planning and executing an information and publication program; cooperation with the director of research and with the various colleges and departments so that research information can be made available for extension purposes at appropriate times; conducting special training schools for officers of cooperatives and other government employees carrying on specialized jobs in agriculture; planning and holding field days and events at the university to attract farmers and special interest groups; cooperating with the deans of colleges in developing courses which have needed extension education content; maintenance of good relationships with farmer groups and outside agencies having an interest in the research and extension program of the university. Further consideration of the extension function is contained in Chapter 14, which is devoted wholly to this subject.

9.7. CHIEF FINANCIAL OFFICER

In the preceding chapter the functions of the business officer or chief financial officer were discussed in some detail. The university act should provide for the appointment of a business or chief financial officer to be responsible to the chief administrative officer for business and financial matters. Suggestions regarding the content of a provision in the act and of the university statutes are also discussed in Chapter 8. Several of the officers listed and discussed, such as the physical plant director and the personnel officer, are sometimes subordinates of the chief financial officer. Nevertheless, they are included in this chapter because we feel their functions are important enough that, eventually at least, they should not be under the jurisdiction of the comptroller or the chief financial officer. The method of appointment of the comptroller and of other officers is discussed in Chapter 15. As a matter of terminology, "bursar" is sometimes used to mean chief financial officer. Ordinarily, however, the bursar is a subordinate of the chief financial officer in charge of collections and disbursements. Other names by which the business officer or chief financial officer is known are comptroller, business executive, general director for administration, and vice-president for business affairs.

9.8. PHYSICAL PLANT DIRECTOR

Maintenance of the physical plant and the installation and maintenance of needed utilities are frequently neglected. Many times this is because the responsibility is not centered in anyone; in other cases it is because the responsibility is centered in an officer who already has a full-sized job and has not been given the resources to develop the staff necessary for a proper discharge of the university housekeeping function. We recommend that the university act provide for a full-time officer under the chief administrative officer to be appointed by the latter with the approval of the governing body to be in charge of all physical plant activities as prescribed by university statutes. In the Indian universities this officer is frequently known as the estates officer. Sometimes he is referred to as superintendent of buildings and grounds. The name does not matter; centralization of functions in a competent man, an adequate staff, and funds for him to accomplish his job do matter.

Many of his activities involve cooperation with deans, department heads, and other officers of the university. In some cases an appropriate administrative committee appointed by the chief administrative officer can help in achieving needed coordination. Like the library, the physical plant of the university exists to promote education and though the physical plant director needs authority to carry out many of his functions, his authority should not be so extensive as to deny any legitimate educational use of university property. In the management of hostels and other facilities for students, there must be close cooperation with the dean of student welfare. University statutes reveal an extensive assortment of responsibilities varying greatly in detail, and though many of these should be listed in a university statute, others should be left to university regulation. There may be a change of opinion about which officer should discharge certain detailed functions—it is easier to reallocate if these duties are not expressed in a statute. Following is a list of responsibilities included in university statutes:

Construction and maintenance of roads, fences, and lands of the university.

Maintenance of utility services.

Maintenance of fire protection.

Provision for architectural and planning services for the university.

Preparation of the capital budget of the university.

Maintenance of proper accounts.

Allotment of space.

Repair, construction, and maintenance of university buildings.

Maintenance of university security.

Supervision of the use and the maintenance of university vehicles.

Provision for a waste disposal and sanitary system.

Management of the telephone, mail, and messenger service.

Issuance of keys.

Responsibility for food service.

Operation of a central store for university office supplies.

Maintenance of an inventory of university property.

Provision for physical arrangements and security for university functions.

As we stated earlier, there is necessity for cooperation between the physical plant director and many other officers of the university. Otherwise, sore points can arise about jurisdictional rights. The university farm is an example. To what extent shall the physical plant director have the right to exert control over vehicles, equipment, and supplies having to do with the farm as opposed to the right of the farm manager? From what budget will funds come for repairs and replacements of certain items—the budget of the physical plant or that of the university unit involved? Regulations should be developed to answer such questions.

9.9. LIBRARIAN

Statutes of the University of the Philippines provide that "There shall be a university librarian appointed by the Board of Regents on the recommendation of the President. He shall administer the university library and the branch libraries in colleges and schools, divisions and departments, and perform such other duties as may be assigned to him by the President." We think this is a good statement, but it should be included in the university act. In addition, the act should state that courses and professional training in library science should be under the jurisdiction of the librarian. In some institutions the librarian is called director of university libraries and dean of library science.

The university statutes should contain provisions on the appointment of a university library board or committee, the chairman of which would be the university librarian. This committee would assist in preparation of the budget, in studying library needs, and in making recommendations. The statutes should also provide the method of appointing branch librarians and for establishing branch libraries. Though these should be under the jurisdiction of the university librarian, the faculties involved should have some voice in determining the location and type of service and in selection of the branch librarian. The statutes should require an annual report on the condition of the library including information on acquisitions, volume of use, future needs, and other matters. The librarian should be a member of the academic council.

Many statutes in specifying the duty of the librarian to maintain the university library state in addition that library services should be organized in the manner most beneficial to the needs of teaching, research, and extension personnel. It is obvious that good library service cannot be established by a university act and university statutes. Sound organization and procedure can be provided, however. Good library service results in large measure from adequate training and education of the personnel involved. Frequently librarians are underpaid and are offered no encouragement to improve their professional ability. This is a mistake. The least the university can do is establish a salary scale and personnel policies which will attract good librarians. Although there should be an overall university library board or committee, there is no reason why the academic council or senate should not have its own committee on the library or why individual college faculties or the board of management should not have library committees. The library is more likely to be hurt by lack of attention than it is by overattention.

9.10. DEAN OF STUDENT WELFARE

There are other names for the dean of student welfare, among them being dean or director of student affairs, dean of students, or just simply dean. In some cases this position is created by the university act, in others by university statutes. The Punjab Agricultural University Act provides that

The Director of Student Welfare shall be a whole-time officer of the university and shall be appointed by the Vice-Chancellor with the approval of the board. The Director shall have the following duties: (1) To make arrangements for the housing of students, (2) to direct a program of student counseling, (3) to arrange for the employment of students in accordance with plans approved by the vice-chancellor, (4) to supervise the extracurricular activities of students, (5) to assist in the placement of graduates of the university, (6) to organize and maintain contact with the alumni organization of the university.

Statutes of the University of the Philippines provide that "There shall be a Dean of Student Affairs appointed by the board on recommendation of the president who shall coordinate the operation of the units in charge of student personnel services, student help, student organizations and publications, student residences, athletics, physical education, and other extracurricular activities subject to the general supervision of and under such regulations as may be promulgated by the president of the university." University of Nigeria statutes provide that the dean of student affairs shall consult with and be advised by a board of student welfare. Among additional responsibilities which may be placed with the dean are communications with parents and guardians concerning students, obtaining travel facilities for holidays, administering health services, food services, and student loan and scholarship programs. A few institutions place responsibility for a student work program with the dean of student welfare.

As the number and variety of educational programs increase—athletics, physical education, alumni affairs, and an officer training or national cadet corps, for example—some responsibilities will be placed with separate officers, either under the jurisdiction of the dean of student welfare or under the chief administrative officer. Also, as numbers of women increase, a dean of women will be needed to function under the jurisdiction of the dean of student welfare. University statutes should be worded so that these changes are possible.

Frequently there is misunderstanding and friction between the office of the dean of student welfare and the various college officers regarding authority over different aspects of student life and activity. By and large the college offices deal with academic affairs concerning students, while the dean of student welfare's office handles nonacademic affairs. However, these two activities are not completely distinct; they overlap in many ways. The university statutes are not the place for a delineation of functions, but certain basic university regulations should be developed which clarify the relationship between the college and the office of the dean of student welfare. The dean of student welfare should be a member of the academic council.

Psychiatric treatment, if available, should be a part of the university health program administered by the dean of student welfare. Counseling, guidance, and testing relate closely to the responsibilities of colleges and of college deans and should be coordinated with their functions whether established in the office of the dean of student welfare or as a separate unit under a vice-director of academic affairs. It is helpful if the university statutes require the dean of student welfare, in conjunction with other university officers, committees, and appropriate representatives from the students and student organizations, to develop and keep current a code on student affairs and activities. The dean of student welfare should not be given authority to censor student publications nor should he have the power to approve or disapprove the specific activities of student organizations. He may and should bring such matters to the attention of the university administration, but the university should avoid a reputation for undue interference with student affairs. Rather, it should try to foster worthy ones.

9.11. REGISTRAR

Without exception, either university acts or statutes provide for the appointment of a registrar, sometimes under different titles such as dean of admissions, dean of admissions and records, registrar and recorder, or director of admissions. The university act should provide for the position and should state that the registrar shall be responsible for administering the university's admission program, registering students, maintaining student records, and performing such other related functions as may be designated in the university statutes or by regulations. There is sometimes a tendency to load the registrar with responsibilities unrelated to his function. This should be avoided.

The status of the position varies considerably between universities. In several instances the registrar is the officer designated by act or statute to act as chief administrative officer until an appointment can be made when there is a vacancy. In many universities he is given a large number of chores to perform, all below what might be called the policy level—for example, he may be required to organize the office of the chief administrative officer and manage its personnel. Along with this may go the duty of assisting the chief administrative officer in the general administration of the university, except for academic and financial affairs. Quite often he is designated either by the university act or by statute as secretary of the academic council, and frequently as secretary of the governing body. Some statutes state that he shall attend meetings of the chief administrative officer's administrative council.

We do not feel that it is logical to name the registrar as second-in-command, so to speak, to take over the post of chief administrative officer in case of vacancy. Rather, we feel this service should be performed by a senior dean of a college if there is no vice-position to the chief administrative officer. We do feel, however, that the registrar should be a voting member of the academic council and of any other university authority in which the university statutes give him membership. Designation as secretary of the governing body does not entitle him to membership. We believe that such designation should be left to statute rather than stated in the university act. Among specific duties contained in university statutes are the following: administration of entrance examinations; registration of students; preparation of necessary forms and maintenance of student records including their safekeeping and protection from unauthorized use or examination; assessing tuition and student fees; publication of a university catalog, university register, timetables, course descriptions, admissions information, and similar materials; maintenance of a record of registered graduates and a current record of student drop-outs and transfers; preparation of examination schedules; publication of a university calendar; and service and acceptance of service of legal process.

The registrar performs a variety of essential functions, many of which must be accomplished under the pressure of meeting deadlines. This calls for good organization and adequate information to all concerned. Development of a registrar's office manual is extremely important. Many institutions have recognized this and have asked for expert help in the organization of the office and in the development of a manual.

9.12. MANAGER OF THE UNIVERSITY PRESS

The university act should empower the chief administrative officer to establish a university press and appoint a manager to be approved by the board. This may be a modest operation in the beginning, serving mainly either to produce or contract for the printing of necessary university publications such as timetables, official registers, and catalogs. Eventually the press should accept worthy manuscripts for publication from members of the faculty and others, and render assistance to colleges, departments, and units of the university in the preparation of printed materials. The university statutes should provide for the appointment of a university press board to advise the director or manager of the press and to pass judgment on manuscripts or books and other publications the quality of which must be judged by the press. The manager should be authorized to arrange for contracts with authors and for royalties. Such contracts should be subject to review by the board and approval by the university legal counsel.

Besides printing and design, a press may render a number of valuable services to the institution. Some university presses have started paperback book series. Under a competent and imaginative manager the press can come to have great meaning for the institution and can help establish its reputation. It should be especially concerned with gaining a hearing for authors whose works have importance and quality but lack the wide appeal required for commercial publication. The press should not have authority to interfere with the right of colleges, departments, and other units in the university to produce extension materials or to duplicate and mimeograph. By the same token the press should not be charged with responsibility for a central mimeographing and photographic service or for similar responsibilities which may involve a large volume of work where the emphasis is on factual information and timeliness rather than quality. The university press will produce income. This should be handled in accordance with procedures established by the chief financial officer of the university.

9.13. TREASURER

In some institutions the treasurer discharges all or a portion of the responsibilities which fall to the university business or financial officer. But most institutions keep the position of treasurer distinct. We believe this is right because it separates the day-to-day business and financial management of the university from the safekeeping of its funds and other paper assets and, in a sense, provides a double check on the security of funds and investments and on their proper use. Some of the early laws creating the land-grant institutions provided for the appointment of a treasurer from the staff. This did not become a general practice. As a matter of fact, some institutions provide that the treasurer shall not be a member of the governing body. In many institutions he is an officer in the banking establishment which has been selected as the depository for university funds, and he is not an officer of the university but of the board. Some laws provide that the treasurer of the country, state, or region shall be the treasurer of the university. This is true, for example, in the Philippines and many American states.

We believe that some of the provisions in the Cornell University Statutes would make a desirable provision in a university act. They provide that the treasurer shall be appointed by the board on recommendation of the president and that he shall have four major functions: (1) administration and management of investments under guidance from the investment committee, (2) custody, control, and safekeeping of funds, securities, deeds, and documents of title, (3) the collection and receipt of money payable to the university, (4) deposit of university funds in a banking institution designated by the investment committee. To avoid conflict, function (1) should be correlated with the functions of the chief financial officer, and function (3) should be omitted and left as the sole responsibility of the chief financial officer. Either the university act or statutes should authorize the appointment of a deputy treasurer when necessary. There should be a requirement that the treasurer and any deputies who might be appointed be bonded in a sufficient amount to protect the university.

9.14. NONACADEMIC PERSONNEL OFFICER

Most university acts and statutes omit any reference to the nonacademic employees of the university or to any officer who might have something to do with their employment and welfare. One exception is the order creating the Rural University for the State of Minas Gerais in Brazil. It provides for a personnel service and for the appointment of a personnel officer, then lists twenty distinct functions to be performed by this officer. We believe that the university act should provide for the appointment of a director of nonacademic personnel to perform such functions as may be prescribed in the university statutes and required by the chief administrative officer. Even the statutes need not contain as much detail as the Minas Gerais order—they should simply provide that this officer is responsible for the administration of policy and rules relating to the employment, compensation, and working conditions of nonacademic employees. There should however, be regulations developed (perhaps as a manual) which further specify the functions of this office. Provisions in the Minas Gerais order would be quite appropriate for such a manual. Some of the duties of the director of nonacademic personnel as stated are:

Promotion of recruitment.

Selection through competition and examinations.

Establishment of training courses.

Orientation and help in adjusting to work.

Reviewing and administration of plans for job classifications.

Study of salaries and promotions.

Preparation of appointment forms and papers.

Maintenance of registers of skilled and other applicants.

Consideration of questions having to do with the rights, benefits, duties, and responsibilities of nonacademic employees.

The drawing up of personnel contracts.

Provision for physical and mental examinations of employees.

Management of cases of discharge, transference, and other personnel problems.

When the institution is small the function of director may be discharged by the chief administrative officer's assistant or by another university officer such as the registrar or physical plant director. But as the institution grows and the need for more nonacademic help increases, particularly the need for skilled help, there should be a full-time position. A more complete discussion of the employment and conditions of service of nonacademic personnel is contained in Chapter 16.

9.15. OTHER OFFICERS

For a number of reasons—size, extent, and nature of functions, university administrative patterns in the country—there may be a need for several officers not listed and discussed above. Among these are the following:

University Legal Counsel

Sometimes this function is performed by the Attorney General or his counterpart in state or regional government. Eventually the university will need its own legal counsel. In the meantime it may need to hire legal service.

Director of Public Information

This position may be filled by someone in the office of the chief administrative officer. It is a function which deserves attention from someone with training and ability in the field.

Farm Manager

Many agricultural universities have farm land to manage. Efficient use of this land, not only for income-producing purposes but as a demonstration to the public, is extremely important. This means that a competent manager should be employed. There should be a section in the university statutes stating that the management will be placed under the dean of agriculture and that a competent manager shall be appointed by the dean, subject to approval by the chief administrative officer and the board. We suggest placing responsibility for management in the college of agriculture because the skills and knowledge needed for successful management should be present in the college and there is more likelihood that they will be exploited if the manager is closely identified with the college. The statutes should also provide that land being used for income-producing purposes and that devoted to research and experimentation shall be kept distinct, and that the farm manager shall have no jurisdiction over the latter. Additional land for experimental and research purposes may be taken following recommendation by appropriate committees. Methods of accounting and reporting on farm operations should be agreed upon between the farm manager and the chief financial officer of the university.

Director of Institute and Director of School

These officers would function like the deans of colleges and would be directly responsible to the chief administrative officer.

Purchasing Agent

This officer is sometimes not under the chief financial officer of the university.

Auditor

This may be someone appointed by the board to function apart from the internal auditing which should be carried on by the chief financial officer. He would not be an officer of the university.

Controller of Examinations

This office still exists in some institutions which give external examinations.

Establishment Officer

We found this officer provided for only in Pakistani universities, though he may be in others. His function in a university is similar to that performed by an establishment division in government. It has to do with organization and personnel.

Secretary of the University

In some instances the functions of the secretary are almost entirely centered on board activities; in others the position is more general and resembles an assistant to the chief administrative officer.

9.16. UNIVERSITY RECORDS

Many of the officers discussed in this chapter maintain records having to do with staff and students of the university. Grades, loans, disciplinary action, certification for degrees, applications for admission, aptitude test scores, honors, payment of tuition and fees, book loans, and health records are examples of recorded material. To what extent are these records confidential? What information must be divulged to appropriate agencies? How are the rights of individuals affected? The laws in some countries define public records and require that they be available for inspection by any citizen during regular office hours. There is great variation, however, in the definition of public records and in the circumstances which permit a citizen to see such records. Also, a distinction exists between kinds of records. Hospital records, for example, are regarded as highly privileged; student grade records would not be so considered though they are of a confidential nature and would be subject to a qualified privilege.

A review of American court decisions indicates that, with the exception of hospital and health records, the university can divulge information from its records when the following circumstances exist: (1) the information is requested and not voluntarily offered, (2) it is given to a person having a real interest in the matter and a need to know, (3) the information given does not exceed the scope of the request, (4) the information is given in good faith and not with intent to damage the individual.[3]

---

[3] From "The Confidential Nature of Student Records," a paper given by Robert B. Meigs, Legal Counsel, Cornell University, at the Second Annual Conference of the National Association of College and University Attorneys (1962).

With respect to hospital records, the general theory is that the hospital owns the records and has a right to their possession, but that the patient has a property right in the information contained in the records. This would entitle him to inspect them and to exercise his discretion in authorizing others to inspect them. Many times insurance companies wish to inspect such records. There is a trend toward giving the right to insurance companies to inspect such records without authorization of the patient when their liability may depend on the information. At any rate, records maintained by the university hospital, health service, or clinic should be carefully prepared and kept beyond periods of time established by statutes of limitations for personal actions.

We believe the university act should provide that all records which are required to be kept or which are necessary to the discharge of the function of any office of the university be available for inspection under such regulations as may be established by the university, and that such records need not be regarded as highly confidential except insofar as the university determines by statute. The university legal counsel should provide other university officers with a statement of basic policy about university records and should be required to give them his opinion when asked.

CHAPTER – 10

Educational Units;
Creation, Structure,
and Functions

_____

10.1. UNITS DESIGNATED BY LAW

Should the act creating the university specify colleges and departments which shall comprise it? Some acts simply say the university shall have such faculties as may be established by statute. The University of Nigeria Act, on the other hand, provides for the establishment of thirty-six colleges, including nursing, midwifery, and diplomacy. It also provides that there shall be one or more of seven listed faculties. Many of the acts creating the American land-grant institutions specified in great detail the subjects to be taught. At the time this seemed proper. It can be argued that if the new institutions are to emphasize agriculture it is well for the act to provide for those colleges which will insure this emphasis— agriculture, veterinary science, agricultural engineering, home science, and basic arts and sciences, for example. The act should then provide, as almost all of them do, that additional faculties, departments, or units may be established as prescribed by university statutes. The main reason for listing any colleges in the act creating a university is to provide some assurance that its major educational objectives will be carried out. We feel this is as far as the legislature should go. An attempt to provide a complete list of colleges and any designation of departments will impose a rigidity on the institution which could deny growth in proper directions and remove much of the discretion from the place where it belongs—in the faculties and academic bodies of the university. If existing institutions are to become constituent colleges, these should be designated in the university act together with a provision that the rights of staff members and students of such institutions shall be protected when the transfer is made. The act should also indicate the date for transfer in case it is not effective upon adoption of the university act.

As decisions are reached to establish new colleges and their establishment is approved by the governing body, there should be a university statute recognizing their creation. Though departments should be approved by the governing body following recommendations from the faculty concerned and from the academic council, there need be no statutory provisions for individual departments. Unless the act so stipulates, a college or unit established by the act cannot be abolished by university statute. An amendment to the law would be required. On the other hand, when the law provides for a particular unit and the board does not establish it, legal action may be brought to compel its establishment. In Kansas the board of regents was compelled to establish a school of mines provided for by legislation as a result of a mandamus action brought by a citizen. Nebraska court decisions held that the board was compelled to establish an agricultural experiment station at a place designated by the legislature and to comply with a new law requiring the establishment and operation of a hog cholera serum plant. On the other hand, courts have held that legislation attempting to impose upon the board of a university the responsibility for establishing or carrying on functions having no relation to the purpose of the university is void. Also, when a university charter is based on a constitutional provision, the legislature has no authority to compel it to establish or remove units. In a Michigan case it was held that the university could not be compelled to remove a medical college to the city of Detroit.

We recommend that the act giving the university authority to determine what colleges and departments shall comprise it also give it the right to establish these units at geographical locations where it determines the services to be necessary. This assumes that the main university will be located at the site designated by the legislation or determined in the manner provided by legislation.

Long after the university is established there is frequently a tendency for legislators to require the establishment of a particular unit in which the legislature, or at least some of its members, have a high interest. This may be a college, a department, an institute, even a committee. The Illinois legislature, for example, passed a law requiring the establishment of a committee on gerontology in the University of Illinois. Such legislative activity should be resisted because it invades the proper sphere of the university. If the university agrees that the function is a good one, legislation is not required; if the university does not agree, it should not be compelled to yield to legislative pressure.

10.2. AUTHORITY FOR CREATING NEW UNITS

The law creating the University of the Philippines provides that "The Board of Regents may establish such colleges and schools as it deems necessary." The East Pakistan Agricultural University Act provides that "Statutes may provide for the establishment of teaching departments and constituent colleges." The proposed Ataturk University Act provides that "The academic council shall formulate, modify, or revise plans for the constitution or reconstitution of departments of teaching, research, and extension." The acts creating the Indian agricultural universities generally provide that the establishment, abolition, or amalgamation of educational units shall be determined by the academic council. Some require government approval. This is not a usual provision, nor is creation of new units by legislative action a usual procedure. We believe that the authority for creating new units—whether teaching, research, extension, public service, or some combination of these; whether traditional colleges or departments or newer cross-disciplinary institutes or study centers—should rest initially with the faculty or university body most concerned. Ultimately the proposal to create a new unit should reach the academic council where it may be approved, disapproved, or returned for revision. Though the governing body must have final authority, it should not contravene the actions of the academic council unless there are compelling budgetary reasons. This policy should be established in the university statutes.

Where there is a national universities commission, as in Nigeria, or a board of higher education, as in some of the American states, final approval of new units may rest with this body. The purpose is to prevent duplication of facilities and hence extra expense to the taxpayer, and also to insure that before new units are created they are given adequate consideration and are located in those institutions which can best foster their activities. The existence of this higher authority with the right of approval or disapproval does not alter the procedure which should be used within the university in determining whether a new unit should be proposed. An exception would be the creation of an administrative unit with no academic functions. In this case the chief administrative officer should have the right to propose its establishment and get approval from the governing body. Proposals to the governing body regarding academic units should always be based on a study and recommendation by the faculty or faculties concerned and the academic council or senate. Definition of "new unit of instruction," "unit of research," or similar phraseology is necessary when a higher authority has the right to pass judgment on their establishment. New programs for master's or doctor's degrees, and even for undergraduate majors, generally fall within the definition.

10.3. THE COLLEGE

The largest educational and administrative unit within the university is the college. It should comprise those departments or divisions which are best served by their inclusion within it. Its academic affairs should be governed by its faculty. It is both an educational and administrative unit responsible for teaching, research, extension, and public service. A dean is its chief educational and administrative officer and is responsible for all phases of its program. The concept of the college as a firm administrative unit with responsibility for an integrated program in teaching, research, and extension is fundamental if the university is to be an important factor in agricultural development. The term "faculty" is sometimes synonomous with college. It is more meaningful as a designation of the academic staff of the college. The role of a college faculty is discussed in Chapter 11. In many institutions boards of studies play an important role. These, likewise, are discussed in Chapter 11.

University statutes should define the educational jurisdiction of the college and define its faculty. The faculty generally consists of the dean and his associates and all staff members above a designated rank together with representation from other university units participating in the program of the college. The chief administrative officer is regarded as a member of all college faculties. If there is a vice-position in charge of academic affairs, this officer, likewise, would be a member of all college faculties. In delineating its educational role, statutes generally provide that the college has jurisdiction over the following: determination of its curricula; establishment of new courses; establishment of its research program; planning its extension activities; handling of academic matters concerning students—including a determination of their status, certifying them for degrees, determining majors and giving general advice and counsel; and jurisdiction over all other educational matters falling within the scope of its programs. Subject only to such university regulation as is necessary to achieve full use of facilities, the college should be given jurisdiction over buildings and land necessary for its program.

University statutes should provide for a college executive committee of from three to five members to be elected annually by the faculty. It should be advisory to the dean and subject to call either by the dean or a majority of its members. It should serve as an important liaison between the dean and the faculty. University statutes should empower the college faculty to determine its rules of procedure, appoint such committees as it deems necessary, and select its own secretary. Meetings of the college faculty should be presided over by the dean. The dean may, either informally or through more formal arrangements, establish an administrative committee composed of his associates or assistants and department heads. The university director of research and director of extension might with their consent serve as ex officio members.

10.4. THE DEPARTMENT

University statutes should provide that the college shall function with such departments as are recommended by its faculty and approved by the academic council and the governing body. The statutes should further provide that each department shall carry on a program of teaching and research under the supervision of a department head and, where appropriate, a program of extension and public service. The department is the primary unit of education and administration. It is established to carry on programs of instruction and research in a particular field of knowledge. It should have the fullest measure of autonomy consistent with the maintenance of college and university educational policies and correct academic and administrative relations with other divisions of the university. The department is the basic unit for originating courses and giving initial consideration to curricula leading to degrees. It does not have authority to determine requirements for a degree, but it should have the right to indicate what subject matter and how much should be included in the programs of students majoring in its area of work.

Some institutions still operate under the theory that a professor is in essence a department. In many South American institutions a chair professor is the primary academic unit. There may be arguments in favor of this kind of organization but, as has been previously explained in several places in this book and in the *Resource Book*, it is not possible with this kind of departmental fragmentation to achieve the integration of teaching, research, extension, and public service so essential if the college is to discharge its responsibilities to the public. It is better to start with a few comprehensive departments and let time, experience, and growth indicate what new ones are needed. University statutes should provide for a departmental executive committee of from three to five members to be elected by the faculty of the department. As stated earlier, we believe a department head named by the dean after due consultation is more conducive to long-time program development than a chairman elected at frequent intervals by the faculty.

No matter how departmental lines are drawn, they are always artificial. Man divides knowledge into what he believes are workable compartments, but discovery and experience continually press for recombinations. The urge for interdisciplinary research is a response to realism. Another response is represented by the increasing tendency to group related departments into large divisions—the life sciences, the physical sciences, the social sciences, the humanities—and thus create greater cohesion. Such divisions become academic and administrative units and are created through the same processes as a new department. The division partakes of some of the authority of both the department and the college. The delineation of authority should be clearly indicated in the proposal for creation of a division; otherwise there will arise jurisdictional problems requiring the expenditure of valuable time on issues which could have been put to rest.

10.5. THE GRADUATE COLLEGE

Graduate education, or postgraduate education as it is sometimes called, must be provided early in the life of the university. Such education, however, implies strength and depth in the departments offering it. No department, therefore, should receive approval for offering graduate work until it has the requisite staff and facilities. Statutes of the Mysore University of Agricultural Sciences provide that "The university shall have authority to offer postgraduate instruction and research training leading to the degree of Doctor of Philosophy at such future time when adequate staff and facilities become available as determined by the academic council and approved by the board." The right to establish a graduate program and a graduate college is no doubt implied, but we feel the university act should contain a provision authorizing such establishment when it is recommended by the academic council and approved by the governing body. Further details should be left to university statutes. Since the graduate school or college is the training ground for needed research workers in agriculture, there will be a desire to establish it as soon as possible. It may be many years before a substantial number of departments are strong enough to offer a graduate program, but some of them will probably qualify in a few years. As a matter of fact, if resources are available for hiring competent staff and obtaining needed scientific equipment, some departments may be able to offer graduate work almost from the beginning. The decision, however, should be left to the judgment of the academic council and should not be predetermined by law or independent action of the governing body. As the university matures and departments become stronger, more of them can be brought into the graduate fold.

There is a close relationship between the graduate college and its functions and the university director of research and his functions. Many American institutions do not have a separate director of research except at the college level. The dean of the graduate college is regarded as automatically fulfilling this role. But where the institution has both officers, there should be a clear delineation of functions. This should be possible through properly framed statutes. The primary concerns of the graduate college are training for advanced degrees and the production of research workers. The primary concern of the director of research is coordinating and fostering experimentation and investigations which will contribute to the economic and social development of the country, particularly to agricultural development. The Universidad Agraria in Peru combines both efforts in a general institute of research and advanced studies. We believe that when there is a university office and director of research, the graduate school, graduate college, division of advanced study—or by whatever name it is called—should focus on advanced training and should be involved only with such research as pertains to advanced degrees, and that the university statutes should so provide.

The statutes should define the faculty of the graduate school. It is generally composed of the chief administrative officer, the vice-president for academic affairs (if there is one), the dean of the graduate college, the director of research (if there is one), the deans of colleges or directors of schools and institutes, the full professors in the university, and such other members of college faculties as the graduate council may approve for giving graduate instruction and supervision. Graduate college staff members are members of college departments in the university. Statutes generally provide that an advisory council shall be elected by the graduate faculty. Sometimes it is provided that a part of its members shall be elected by the graduate faculty and the remainder appointed by the chief administrative officer in consultation with the dean of the graduate college. In a few institutions the council is wholly ex officio, consisting of the dean or director of postgraduate studies, deans and associate deans of colleges, director of research, and director of extension. This may suffice early in the life of the university but it will not satisfy for very long the desire of the graduate faculty to participate through their own representation in the affairs of the college. Some statutes require that, however constituted, the council have at least one member from each college. We believe that such a provision should be in the statutes. Though decisions of the council carry great weight, final authority must rest with the dean.

The statutes should recognize that the two entities concerned with graduate education are the graduate college and the undergraduate college departments. While the graduate faculty should be empowered to establish standards of admission and the requirements for receiving advanced degrees, the department should have the right to establish additional admission requirements, both in terms of academic achievement and subject matter, for those graduate students who ask to do their work in the department. The department obviously would not have authority to waive language requirements or such other requirements as have been established by the graduate faculty for all graduate students. Many important policies need to be settled and rules and regulations developed to implement them. As soon as possible the dean of the graduate college should publish rules and regulations of the college based on a study made by appropriate committees of the faculty and recommendations received from the departments and colleges. The university catalog or register should contain a clear statement of the requirements for admission to the graduate college. The supervision of certain graduate student affairs—discipline, for example—is a function of the graduate college. Generally there is a final appeals committee or body in the university to which all student disciplinary cases may go. This would apply to graduate students as well as to undergraduate students, but the committee or disciplinary body of original jurisdiction would be established in the graduate college. Only those activities and regulations of the dean of student welfare which are appropriate would apply to graduate students. In many instances, specific exceptions should be made.

Some statutes provide that the recommendation of the dean of the graduate school be secured before appointing to the staff of any department any person who may be expected to become a member of the graduate school faculty and offer graduate courses. This has the effect of giving advance notice to the department that it is not the sole judge of the qualifications of a new appointee for membership on the graduate faculty. On the other hand, statutes generally provide that the graduate college council or executive committee shall have the right to recommend members to the graduate faculty; hence, a recommendation in advance by the dean is in a sense a prejudgment. Such a recommendation should be made informally, but as a statutory provision it conflicts with the prerogative of the council. Since graduate courses are taught in college departments, colleges and departments are presumed to know what the requirements are for membership on the graduate faculty and to be so guided in making new appointments.

Responsibility of the graduate school in the general area of research is discussed in Chapter 13.

10.6. INSTITUTES

The statutes of Columbia University provide that "There shall be institutes established as approved by the university council and authorized by the president for the purpose of coordinating and developing research and teaching in special fields, particularly those of interest to more than one department. The direction of each institute shall be assigned to a coordinating committee or to an administrative committee consisting of a director and members nominated by the president and appointed by the trustees to serve for a term of three years." Research involving more than one department and calling for teamwork between several individuals is becoming more and more common. The quotation above shows how one major university has tackled the problem. There are other ways, but the establishment of institutes which cut across college and departmental boundaries is a recognized and successful method. Statutes of the University of Illinois provide that "For the development and operation of teaching, of research, of extension, and of service programs which are horizontal or intercollege in their scope and which can not be developed under existing administrative agencies, there may be created such institutes, councils, divisions, or other agencies as are warranted. The creation of such horizontal agencies shall be by the same procedure as for colleges." We believe that a provision similar to the ones quoted should be included in the statutes of the university so that such units can be established when needed.

Many times when a new university is established or an older one is reorganized, an existing institute may be made a part of it. This should be provided in the act, and there should be a statute containing essential details about the structure and functions of the institute. This is particularly important if changes are desired. The law creating the Ahmadu Bello University in Northern Nigeria contains two separate schedules—one for the Institute of Administration and another for the Institute of Agricultural Research and Special Services—detailing the objects and internal structure of these institutes. Such provisions preserving the purpose and organization of an existing institute help assure its continued successful functioning and give a feeling of security to its staff.

10.7. OTHER UNITS

Among units not previously discussed and for which there may be a general legislative or university statutory authority are the following:

A Division of General Studies

This unit may be organized like a college and enroll students, or it may be established as a service division to offer courses in general education to all students in the university. It may even be established under the jurisdiction of a college of arts and sciences. The academic council should determine if there is to be a division of general studies, and if so, its purpose, organization, functions, and relationship to students in the university should be clearly stated in the university statutes.

Military Unit

If the institution offers military training, either for qualifying reserve officers or simply as a training program, it will have a unit of military science and tactics. In some ways such a unit resembles a department. It is likely, however, that it will not be placed under the jurisdiction of any particular college and hence will be directly under the chief administrative officer, one of his vice-officers, or, possibly, the dean of student welfare. Also, since the program is carried on in conjunction with the armed forces, the staffing of the unit and many of the rules and regulations for carrying out its program will be provided by the Ministry of Defense or armed forces branch of the central government. There should be a university statutory provision describing the purpose and organization of the unit and providing for cooperation with government. If the program is voluntary, university statutes should state the prerequisites for student enrollment in the program. Such determinations and others bearing on the educational content of the program should be made cooperatively by the faculty of the military unit and the academic council within the framework of requirements imposed by the central government.

Citizens' Advisory or Consultative Committee

Some American university statutes provide for consultative or advisory committees to the colleges, schools, or other divisions of the university. Many universities have a general committee or citizens' committee advisory to the institution. In some instances departmental advisory committees have been established. This is a method of bringing outside or citizen judgment to bear on the functioning of the institution. It seems particularly important to have such advisory bodies when the university and its colleges and departments are trying to be responsive to the need for development and the solution of social and economic problems. Such citizens' committees composed of individuals who have demonstrated leadership in their fields and who are interested in the success of the university can have a beneficial effect on research and educational programs and attitudes within the university.

Alumni Association

Such an association may or may not have a legal tie with the university. Sometimes the university act authorizes the institution to establish such an organization and designates an officer of the university as secretary. We believe the act should so provide.

Accessory Associations or Corporations

Universities frequently become concerned with activities which are ancillary to their main function. Also, they frequently find that the accomplishment of some of their regular functions can be expedited by creation of a separate corporation or entity to hold and administer funds or to accomplish particular lines of work. The university act and statutes should contain a general provision permitting the organization of such entities. Without discussing details, the following are some of the kinds of accessory organizations which have come to play an important role in the functioning of universities:

Research foundations
Housing corporations
University clubs
Athletic associations
Publishing companies
Cooperative book and supply stores
Elementary schools for staff members' children
Special organizations to administer trusts
Building corporations

The legal relation of the university to these various organizations is not always clear. In each case it depends on the facts. Sometimes the courts have found that a separate corporation is after all a "mere instrumentality of the university" and have looked through the separate corporate existence to the university. This has been true of athletic associations and housing corporations, for example. Other ancillary organizations may seem further removed and a court might very well find that they are not legal instrumentalities of the university but do have a separate existence and are responsible in their own right, both in contract and tort.

Patronships

An interesting feature of the Peru National Universities Act is a provision for patronships:

The linking between each university and the community shall be in charge of a patronship whose function shall be to encourage the increase in the patrimony of the respective institution, to increase enrollment, and to facilitate university information about problems whose study and solution are required by the country or by the particular region. The patronship shall organize a creation of funds for the maintenance of students of modest economic conditions. The patronship shall be composed of representatives of the various activities interested in national development. It shall include professional women in its number. Its members shall not receive remuneration. Each patronship shall issue and approve its own bylaws and it shall set forth the manner in which it shall be composed.

CHAPTER – 11

Academic Organization

There are generally three levels or tiers of government in a university: the board or governing body, the academic council or academic senate, and the college faculties with their boards of study. In many institutions the department has achieved a status which would make one conclude that there are four tiers. In some institutions, particularly those in Latin America, many of the functions of a governing body and of an academic body are combined in a university council.

11.1. MAIN ACADEMIC BODY OF THE UNIVERSITY

With few exceptions the main academic body of a university is either the academic council or the academic senate. There are other names for university-wide faculty organizations: the "assembly" in the Universidad Agraria at La Molina is composed of faculty and students and is concerned primarily with university statutes and the election of a rector and a vice-rector; the "congregation" in the University of Nigeria and Ahmadu Bello University is composed of all members of all faculties, meets infrequently, and is more an advisory than a legislative body; Ataturk University has a "council of professors" which serves as the main academic body. Without exception, the acts creating universities provide for an academic council or academic senate or a main academic body by some other name. Some acts go no further than this. Most of them, however, specify in some detail the composition of the main academic body, with a provision that other members can be added as provided in university statutes. Also, most acts specify in some detail the functions of the main academic body with the statement that it shall have such additional powers and functions as are specified by university statute. Generally the act leaves sufficient discretion with respect to both composition and functions that a desirable academic organization can be achieved. There are a few instances where the law specifies that the academic council shall consist almost entirely of deans and officers of administration with little or no faculty representation. This is a mistake. The law should permit flexibility with respect to size, membership, and internal organization.

In the beginning many academic bodies were so small that they could meet at frequent intervals and discuss many intimate details having to do with the life of the university. But as a university grows, the academic body must grow in size, and eventually some system of representation will be needed. Many American universities, for example, include all professors as members of the academic senate. In the larger universities this results in a body of about 1,000 members. This is hardly the kind of deliberative body which can meet frequently and perform all the functions which the university act and statutes accord it. Yet, paradoxically, the need for wise consideration of issues by an academic council or senate increases as the university administrative structure grows in size and complexity, for the latter can very well come to dominate the activities of the university. This does not mean that university administrators are designing and wicked; it only means that if the faculty of the university is not organized so that it can express its views and be a potent force in the educational process, the administration will feel that it has to assume the responsibility. In a few instances it was observed that an administrative council (as opposed to an academic council) or an executive committee of a university senate composed almost entirely of administrators had, in effect, supplanted the main academic body. This is opposed to both wisdom and custom in the internal ordering of university affairs and is the kind of situation which the faculty of the university should guard against.

How should the main academic body be constituted? Let us look at the provisions for three widely separated institutions. The statutes of Harvard University provide that "The University Council consists of the President, Professors, Associate Professors, and Assistant Professors of the university and such other university officials as the Corporation, with the consent of the Overseers, may appoint members of the council." The University of the Philippines Act states that "There shall be a university council consisting of the President of the university and of all instructors in the university holding the rank of Professor, Associate Professor, or Assistant Professor." Statutes of the Uttar Pradesh Agricultural University provide that "The academic council shall consist of the deans of the colleges, the director of the school, director of the agricultural experiment station, director of extension, the heads of departments or persons acting in the foregoing positions, all professors in the university, and five staff members to be selected as determined by the academic council." These statutes also provide that membership on any standing committee of the academic council shall be open to any member of the faculty and when a faculty member is serving on such a committee, he is considered to be a member of the academic council. Some American university statutes have a similar provision. We believe this is desirable and should be included in the statutes.

Regardless of how the academic council or senate is composed, we believe that all important administrative officers of the university should be ex officio members. Their numbers would never permit them to dominate a meeting of the main academic body, while their presence could be extremely helpful in answering questions and expediting the consideration of many matters. Some statutes give emeritus professors the right to attend meetings and discuss issues but not to vote. We feel this is a desirable provision. In at least one institution certain government officials such as the director of agriculture, the director of animal husbandry, and the director of the education department are included as members of the academic council. We do not feel that this is a wise provision. Certainly good relationships should be maintained with these officers through appropriate personnel and activities of the university, but they should not be involved in its government. Universities which are primarily affiliating institutions will have staff members of other institutions on the academic council.

There are different ways of meeting the problems imposed by size, though none are wholly satisfactory. Those institutions which include all academic ranks in membership on the main academic body may reduce the size by cutting out one or more of the lower ranks. This would be unpopular with the lower ranks. Another way would be to decide on the optimum number and then provide for elections on a proportionate basis from the different faculties of the university. This would be democratic but, again, would probably be resisted since it would mean nonmembership for many who had previously been members. Still another method is to let the main academic body grow in size according to the formula originally established but have most of its activities carried out by a smaller executive group elected by the membership. This could be a relatively large body of, say 100 out of 1,000, or it might be a much smaller group which can operate like an executive committee. Still another partial solution lies in the increased use of committees so that problems presented to the main body at its meetings will have received thorough consideration and can be presented with recommendations plus arguments pro and con. The danger here lies in the tendency toward apathy on the part of the main body and too great an enjoyment of the feeling of power on the part of the few important committees. For many reasons, including some solution of the problems of size and representation, the academic council or senate should formulate a sound constitution and bylaws and then give consideration to both at frequent intervals so that they can be kept operational for the achievement of the main objectives of the academic body.

Without exception university acts or statutes provide that the chief administrative officer shall be the presiding officer or chairman of the academic council or senate. He has the right to vote if he is so disposed and in some instances is given a casting or second vote in case of a tie. When the statutes provide for a vice-position, it is usual for them to contain a statement that in the absence of the chief administrative officer the second-in-command shall preside. Some statutes contain even a further provision that if the second-in-command is also absent, a senior dean or a dean selected by the academic council or senate or some other member of the academic council or senate shall be designated by that body to act as chairman. Though such a provision need not be in the university statutes, the rules of procedure for the council or senate should state that when it meets as a committee of the whole, it shall also elect its own chairman for such meeting.

Almost as universal as the designation of the chief administrative officer to act as chairman of the main academic body is a provision that the registrar shall act as its secretary. We believe the main academic body should be given the privilege of electing its own secretary. It may elect the registrar, but even if it does not, he can cooperate with the secretary in supplying mailing lists of staff members, office help to duplicate materials, and clerical assistance to make distributions, and perform other chores which are necessary. Perhaps the statutes should not contain such detail but at least the regulations or procedural rules of the main faculty body should provide that the secretary keep adequate minutes and distribute them, that he prepare and mail out an agenda and supportive materials in advance so that members can pass judgment on their content, and that he perform certain other functions which will expedite and make meetings of the main academic body more effective.

Statutory provisions on meetings vary considerably. Some require monthly meetings, some regular meetings, some quarterly, some every two months, some only one at the beginning of the year, and others leave the matter entirely up to the main academic body. The statutes should and generally do contain provisions on special meetings stipulating that these can be called by the chief administrative officer or by a stated number or percentage of the main academic body. University of Nigeria Statutes provide that ten members can call a regular meeting of the main academic body. It is quite common for university acts to state that the procedures of the main academic body and the frequency of meetings shall be as determined by university statute. An important statutory provision is one requiring adequate notice of meetings and providing that when any important policy matter is to be considered it shall not be finally determined by a vote until the meeting following the one in which it is introduced and initially discussed.

The statutes should stipulate the quorum necessary for carrying on business. Some are silent, which would mean, presumably, that the main academic body can establish its own rules regarding a quorum. Many statutes do contain a provision designating a majority, one-half, one-third, a fixed percentage, or a stipulated number of members as a quorum. As membership increases it is difficult to get a majority or any stated percentage present for all meetings. Perhaps in the beginning a majority for quorum requirement will be satisfactory, but as the size of the body grows, it may be necessary to amend the statutes and provide for some fixed number.

Another statutory provision which is useful is one stating that nonmembers may be co-opted for committee membership or for meetings of the main academic body in which their knowledge and experience may be helpful.

University statutes should empower the main academic body to appoint such standing and ad hoc committees as it deems necessary and to co-opt nonmembers for such committees. In some institutions, senate or academic council committees are appointed by the chief administrative officer. We believe this is a usurpation of a prerogative which the main academic body should have. The chief administrative officer will be interested in the activity of many of these committees. There should be friendly liaison between his office and committee chairmen so that needed information can be obtained and so that the committees will feel free to invite members of administration to sit with them when this is helpful. In some institutions the academic council or senate appoints an advisory committee to the president. Such a committee can serve a useful function. Probably the most important standing committee of an academic body is one on educational policy. There should be others on the library, student discipline, and academic freedom. In their attempt to emphasize agriculture, the newer universities in India have provided for university council or senate standing committees on research and extension. The academic body should be the judge of its committee needs and should wish to have standing committees to deal with problems which have a continuing important policy aspect.

What are the powers and functions of the academic council or senate? As a matter of legal theory, the governing body must have final authority over all matters, including academic or educational matters. As a matter of history, good procedure, and wisdom, it should not choose to exercise its authority in those areas where the faculty is more competent. Some university acts or statutes provide for a delegation of such authority to the main academic body, thus indicating that unless an unusual situation arises, the governing body shall keep "hands off." There are American court decisions holding that actions of an academic senate to which authority had been delegated by the board were binding if not arbitrary or in violation of law. Certainly the main academic body is privileged to advise the administration or the governing body on any matter whether or not such a provision is contained in the university statutes. A provision that its approval must be obtained on all matters having to do with educational policy before the administration or board can act is a vital safeguard.

A study of many university acts and statutes discloses the following list of subjects over which the academic council or senate has been given authority (obviously its authority is not complete with respect to all these subjects because other university authorities, bodies, committees, and administrative officers are involved):

Courses of study.

University calendar.

Designating examination periods.

Designating holidays.

Determining the date of commencement.

Matters of educational policy concerning more than one college or unit or that are of a general nature.

Establishing the requirements for degrees.

Determining what degrees shall be offered.

Establishing rules of discipline.

Determining admission requirements.

Recommending candidates for degrees.

Academic affairs and educational policy.

Determining standards of academic performance.

Determining the educational relation of the various colleges.

Approving new units.

Awarding honorary degrees.

Developing policies for awarding fellowships, scholarships, medals, and prizes.

Establishing postgraduate teaching.

Policies regarding research and extension.

Recommendations on distribution of grant money.

Establishing policies for libraries and library service.

Proposing statutory changes or amendments and approval or disapproval of those statutes or statutory changes having to do with educational matters.

More details could be added, but this list should illustrate the scope of activity of a main academic body in a university. Perhaps it is well for the university statutes to list in some detail the functions of the main academic body to help indicate the division of authority between it and the faculties of the colleges. On the other hand, jurisdiction over many educational areas is divided between the colleges and the main academic body and there should be some possibility of clarifying and realigning without changing the university statutes. In many institutions there is a statutory provision protecting the rights of faculties by providing that the academic council or senate shall not act on a matter concerning any particular faculty until it has a recommendation from that faculty. This, together with a provision that the main academic body cannot change a proposal sent to it by a faculty but can only send it back and recommend changes, eventually either approving or disapproving it as it comes from the faculty, offers substantial safeguards to the faculties.

11.2. FACULTIES

University acts sometimes specify the colleges and thus the faculties of the university. More often they provide that the university shall have such colleges and faculties as are provided in the university statutes and that the composition and function of faculties shall be as determined. We believe that this is the better kind of provision. Though "faculty" may designate the academic staff in a particular discipline, regardless of college, we believe the term should be used to designate the academic staff of a college as defined in statutes and regulations. In many institutions a college faculty functions primarily through a board of studies, a smaller group of the faculty—either designated by statute or determined by the faculty itself. Determination of function and composition of such boards of study should be left to the faculty and the academic council with their recommendations finally expressed in the university statutes. There may also be a university-wide board of studies but this seems unnecessary if the academic council is properly constituted.

Statutes of the University of the Philippines provide that the body of instructors of each college or school shall constitute its faculty. It provides that members of another faculty giving instruction in the college may attend the faculty meetings of that college. Graduate assistants are not members of the faculty but are accorded the right to attend faculty meetings and take part in its deliberations. The dean is ordinarily designated as presiding officer of the college faculty and chairman of the faculty board of studies where the latter is provided. The number of meetings to be held, the procedure for calling meetings, and the rules for conducting meetings should be left to the faculty to determine and express in its own constitution and procedural rules. These should not be contained in a university statute.

In defining a faculty, statutes frequently provide that it shall comprise the academic staff of such departments as may have been assigned to the college. In addition they generally state what academic ranks and what additional staff members or university officers shall comprise the college faculty. Statutes generally provide that the faculty of the graduate college shall consist of those professors and staff members from all departments who have been approved to teach and supervise graduate work in addition to the deans of colleges and certain administrative officers such as the director of research, the chief administrative officer himself, and others. In some Latin-American institutions a college council composed partly of professors and other designated staff members from the college and partly of students supplants the faculty and board of studies as the academic agency for the college. The over-all authority of a college faculty, board of studies, or college council depends not only on the particular statutory and regulatory provisions, but on history and the theory prevailing about the autonomy of a college. In most American universities the college is clothed with less authority than its counterpart in Europe and in many other parts of the world. An increased emphasis on the university as an instrument of social and economic betterment seems to result in a tightening of administrative organization which tends to move more major decisions to the university level. This is unavoidable and it is not bad, providing the role of the college and its faculty is preserved and the college faculty is given an effective voice in the government of the university.

Among the functions of college faculties (whether or not there is a board of studies) specified in university acts are the following:

Determination of entrance requirements for courses of study in the college.

Determination of courses of study to be pursued for degrees.

Recommendation of candidates for degrees and other titles.

Administration of the educational and internal life of the college within the limits prescribed by university statutes and rules.

Assistance in the registration of students.

Academic counseling and advisement.

Development of courses, the place and time for offering them, and the instructors who will teach them.

Preparation of course outlines or syllabuses.

Management of the examination and grading of students.

Recommendation to the academic council on the abolition, amalgamation, or establishment of departments.

Coordination of its work with other college faculties and the academic council.

Recommendations to the academic council on matters affecting educational policy in the university.

Recommendations which will lead to a better integration of the teaching, research, extension, and public service responsibilities of the college.

Frequently, reference is made to the "faculty of the university." Sometimes this is not defined. It is a useful term, however, because there will certainly be occasions when the whole faculty and staff of the university will be addressed or called into a meeting. The terms "congregation" and "assembly" serve this purpose. "Faculty of the University" defined as to membership can also serve such a purpose. We recommend its inclusion in the university statutes.

Regulations of the college should provide for departmental faculties and identify them as such. In many institutions certain departments are larger than some of the smaller colleges. Though their status is lower, problems of organization, representation, functioning, and morale are just as great. In such instances good departmental organization may be just as important as good college organization. As we mentioned earlier, the faculty of the graduate college, acting through its graduate council or executive committee and the dean should develop rules and regulations for the graduate college. Frequently the faculty of a school or college of basic sciences and humanities is not accorded a degree-granting privilege. This stems from the view that its offerings are really service courses for those who are qualifying in other fields. This is understandable, but we feel it is a mistake. If an institution has a faculty of arts and sciences it should be a full-fledged faculty in every sense with the right to enroll students and grant degrees; hence we see no reason why its faculty organization should differ from that in the other colleges. In a university committed to development and to aiding agriculture, college faculties have real problems to tackle. The organization and philosophy of the college should be such that its faculty can deal with such problems and help in their solution.

11.3. BOARDS OF STUDIES—COLLEGE COMMITTEES

The Ahmadu Bello Act provides that "In each faculty a faculty board shall be established which shall, subject to the provisions of this law and statutes and subject also to the direction of the senate, regulate the teaching and study of and the conduct of examinations connected with the subjects assigned to such faculty, deal with any other matters assigned to it by the statutes or by the senate, advise the senate on any matter referred to it, deliberate on any matter affecting the work of the faculty and report to the senate thereon." This act further provides that the vice-chancellor and deputy vice-chancellor shall be members of every faculty board and that composition of each faculty board shall be determined by the statutes of the university.

University acts do not always provide for faculty boards; this is frequently left to statutes. When there is a provision in the university act, it generally states that there shall be a board of each faculty, the constitution and powers of which shall be prescribed. We do not feel it is essential to provide for a board of studies since, in the absence of such a provision, the faculty can organize, appoint committees, and perform the functions which a board would perform. Creating a board of studies seems to place an unusually large amount of authority with those members of the faculty who constitute it. While it is true that a large faculty may need to delegate much of its decision-making to smaller bodies, it should have the privilege of deciding how this shall be done. A properly constituted college courses and curricula committee can achieve all the objectives of a board of studies in preparing integrated and well-balanced courses of study.

A faculty which has an extensive responsibility for teaching, research, extension, and public service will need more than one strong committee to discharge its functions. A faculty board may be satisfactory from a purely academic standpoint but, as historically constituted, hardly serves the purpose of a faculty. We believe that a properly constituted college executive committee augmented by essential standing and ad hoc committees represents sound organization. Certainly one such committee should be a courses and curricula or educational policy committee. There is oftentimes much discussion about the nature of a college executive committee. Frequently such a committee is composed of the dean, his associates, and department heads. Admittedly the dean is entitled to such a forum but it is in essence an administrative group and does not have a representative voice for the faculty. Occasionally efforts are made to cure this deficiency by providing for a few elected faculty members. This may change its nature somewhat, but it remains an administrative committee.

We believe that the faculty of a college deserves an important committee or body on which it is represented in strength and from which will emanate ideas and suggestions to the dean of the college about any matters affecting the functioning of the college. Boards of studies constitute a partial answer. If, however, the executive committee is not constituted so that it can reflect the voice of the faculty, there should be a general policy and development committee or its equivalent. We feel there should be two major committees—one to advise on general policy matters and another to deal solely with courses, curricula, and the educational content of the college's offerings. Depending on size and scope of program, many other committees are implied: library, student relations, extension, research, graduate program, social, faculty program, extramural studies. These are some that may be useful, even necessary.

11.4. OTHER ACADEMIC BODIES

The Udaipur University Act provides for a staff council composed of the dean, department heads, college librarian, and designated instructors. It is authorized to elect new members to the boards of studies and to the academic council, to advise the dean on administrative and academic matters, and to approve the college budget. Such a council would need to have a mixture of executive, policy, and advisory functions resembling, perhaps, an executive committee more than a policy or advisory committee. As we suggested earlier, the dean should certainly seek the advice of his administrative officers and should have an administrative council or its equivalent. This body, however, does not supplant the need for a faculty committee advisory to the dean on college policies and another to deal with courses, curricula, and educational policy matters of the college.

As we indicated earlier, departments also need academic organization and committees advisory to the department head and also for the consideration of courses and educational policy matters. The department, particularly a large department, should have an organization somewhat like that of the college—except on a less formal basis and without some of the committees which would be required only at the college level.

When the university has important elements at more than one geographic location, the problem of coordinating academic activities is complicated. The problem of a divided council or senate has been discussed earlier in the book. There will no doubt need to be some delineation of functions for each segment of the council or for each separate council if that is the way they are organized. One device for getting them together on university-wide issues is a coordinating committee or council whose function is to get the different councils or segments of the council together on recommendations to the governing body.

Though good academic organization at the university, college, and department levels would provide advisory avenues for the faculty, there may be some merit in establishing advisory bodies or committees by university statute. Where this has been done the statutes generally provide for a university advisory council, a university research advisory committee, a university extension advisory committee, college advisory committees, and departmental advisory committees. Such committees may be set up so that they are largely of an administrative nature, or the staff may be given an important role in electing membership. If they are to provide an effective link between the faculty and the administrator who is being advised, they should contain a substantial faculty component.

Though not official organs of the university and hence not academic bodies in the legal sense, voluntary faculty organizations can play an important role in the life of the university. As voluntary organizations they are freed of any restraints or definitions of function which may be included in a university act or statutes and will be inhibited only by their lack of energy and judgment in accomplishing great good for the institution and for their own membership.

CHAPTER - 12

The Teaching Function

12.1. INTRODUCTION

It may be said that a university is no better than its teachers. In one way or another everything discovered through experimentation must, or at least should be, taught to somebody else.[1] This is one of the arguments in favor of integration of the teaching and research functions. Good teaching cannot be legislated or provided by university statute, but many things affecting teaching can be settled in a university act and its statutes. These are discussed in the sections which follow. The method of appointment and conditions of service of teachers are discussed in Chapter 15. If the institution intends to supplant the use of external examinations and a fixed syllabus, a number of terms will need to be defined either in the university statutes or in university regulations approved by the academic council. Some requiring definition are: credit hours, clock hours, grade, grade point average, academic probation, and other terms which have to do with the student's academic progress and right to receive a degree. Worth noting is the fact that more and more institutions are becoming concerned about the teaching and learning processes in a university and are engaging in research to learn something about them.

12.2. ADMISSION REQUIREMENTS AND QUALIFICATIONS

Who shall be admitted to the university? Every student who has completed his secondary education? Only the intellectual elite—as determined early in their school career? Only those who pass tests prepared and given by the university? In many of the developing countries with limited resources, and following the pattern of British higher education, universities have catered to an intellectual elite. The urgent need for manpower for development is swinging them away from this concept. On the other hand, there must be standards; there must be quality control. What shall they be?

----

[1] Some of the elements which make for good teaching are discussed in Hannah, *Resource Book*, ch. 19.

Typical of provisions either in land-grant university acts or in their statutes or admissions regulations is a provision in the law creating Kansas State University requiring that every student who has completed his high school education and has a certificate to that effect from his principal shall be admitted to the university. Statutes of the Universidad Agraria in Peru state that "Any student who passes the entrance examination and fulfills the requirements set by the pertinent bylaws shall have the right to enroll and matriculate in the university. The entrance requirements for the university shall be established in such a way that there be no other admission criteria than those based on the ability and preparation of the candidate." Regardless of such provisions, the increase in numbers of students completing secondary education has imposed upon universities the necessity of limiting in some way the numbers to be enrolled. If the policy of government is still to admit all who have completed secondary education, then the only answer is more public universities, junior colleges, and other postsecondary institutions. Though this may still be the policy, increased facilities for higher education of all kinds have not materialized even in the affluent United States in time to keep large public universities from being overcrowded. Hence, some additional criteria for admission are implied.

Before discussing criteria and qualifications, it should be stated that there has been general acceptance by institutions around the world of the policy that anything which is not related to the particular individual's capacity to perform at the university level shall not become a qualification for his admission. Sometimes the constitution of the country, but more frequently the legislation creating the university, provides that no one shall be denied admission because of race, color, religion, or national origin. Some universities include sex in this list. The Indian universities include caste. Some also state that political opinion or affiliation shall not be a bar to admission. We recommend the inclusion of such a provision in the university act unless there is a constitutional or general legislative provision applicable to all universities. Even so, we believe it might be wise to reiterate such provisions in the university act. Also, if there are any gaps in the constitutional or general legislative statement, these can be filled in the university act. There may, for example, have been a change in feeling about sex being a bar. If so, the university act could assure the right of both sexes to attend.

Divergent positions have been taken on the question of age. The University of the Philippines Statutes and the Kansas State University Act, for example, provide that no student shall be denied admission to the university by reason of age. The law creating Michigan State University, on the other hand, provides that "No student shall be admitted to the institution who is not fifteen years of age." And the University of Nigeria Statutes provide that "A person shall not be admitted as a student of the university unless he shall have attained the age of seventeen years on the first day of the academic year in which he is admitted." We do not believe there should be any legislative stipulation about age although the legislature undoubtedly has the authority to stipulate so long as the age designated is not unreasonable. Seventeen years seems close to the border. Certainly the specification of an age beyond that of most students who have completed their secondary education would be arbitrary and unreasonable. Though the youthfulness of an applicant for admission may at times indicate that a university is not the ideal environment for him, we feel that it should not be stated as a legal bar. On the contrary, we recommend that the university act provide that no student be denied admission by reason of age.

What shall be the criteria for admission and who shall establish them? If there is to be a residence requirement, it should be established by the university act, and university regulations should define residence. We do not believe a university act should deny admission because of nonresidence but that it should authorize the establishment of differential tuition rates and educational qualifications for admission if the pressure for admission by residents makes this necessary. Though the governing body exercises final judgment, the right to fix requirements for admission to the university generally rests with the academic council. Rules of admission developed by the council or senate are not normally placed in university statutes but after adoption are published as university regulations and are included in the university register or catalog. We believe that the university act should authorize the governing body to determine standards of admission and that the governing body in turn should adopt a statute empowering the academic council to develop rules. Among the qualifications and requirements which may be expressed in the rules are:

Completion of secondary or precollegiate education
Accreditation of the secondary school attended
Academic achievement or rank of the applicant
Subject matter completed at the secondary level
Ability on achievement tests in lieu of secondary education
Score on entrance examinations given by the university
Physical ability to attend classes
Freedom from communicable disease
Freedom from serious mental disorder

The courts have held that it is proper for a university to require health examinations and deny admission to an applicant who fails to present a certificate showing he has been examined and that he is free of any communicable disease. It has also been held that the university may require inoculation for specified diseases as a prerequisite to admission.

An institution may have to deny admission generally or to specified colleges, departments, or programs of study when capacity is reached and physical facilities will not permit additional students. In this case, numbers will have to be limited in some nonarbitrary fashion such as priority of application among all those qualified or secondary school achievement or rank. Students may be denied admission for other reasons. If, for example, there is a required military training program and a student refuses to participate, his admission could be denied. Also, there are some necessary formalities—forms to be filled out, for example, deadlines to be met, and fees to be paid. An applicant who fails to submit the proper forms, to pay required advance fees, or to request admission at the beginning of a regular term may fail to gain admission.

If the lack of social and educational development among tribal and other groups in the country seems to justify, it would be proper for the act creating the university to insure a given number or percentage of places for applicants from such groups. Many Indian agricultural university acts contain such a provision.

Questions will arise about residence unless there is an adequate definition and a will to make reasonable interpretations of the definition. Many married students in American universities have had difficulty convincing the authorities that the university is their place of residence and that they are therefore entitled to the privileges accorded residents of the state.

The individual colleges or faculties of the university have a right to make additional requirements for admission to their program. The College of Engineering, for example, should not be compelled to admit a secondary school graduate deficient in mathematics. The Udaipur Agricultural University Statutes recognize this right through a provision that "Admission requirements for entrance in the university, including admission to advanced training and a continuance of students as such, shall be laid down by the academic council on the recommendation of the board of studies."

Statutes of the University of the Philippines require that every student shall sign a pledge promising to comply with all the rules and regulations laid down by competent university authority. Refusal to sign the pledge is sufficient cause for denial of admission. While it may be proper and useful to require applicants to sign such a pledge, we do not believe it should be provided by the university act or its statutes.

Among the prerogatives of the academic council should be that of determining if the secondary institution of the applicant meets acceptable standards. If there is an accrediting body, either public or voluntary, the university could accept its judgment. With very few exceptions university acts or statutes place the right to determine admission requirements with the academic council. We believe this is the way it should be.

Though the governing body—or through delegation, the academic council—may develop rules for admission, the regulations must be reasonable. One university statute states that the applicant must possess such additional moral and educational qualifications as shall be determined by the dean of student welfare. This is not an acceptable provision since it places with the dean of student welfare a discretion he should not have. Requirements that a student must reside at the university and that he cannot belong to a fraternity or private club have been struck down by American courts. The establishment by a public university of unreasonably high tuition fees, thus excluding many students who might be qualified academically for admission, would constitute an arbitrary and an unauthorized act.

In summary, the legislature has the right to guarantee admission to all who can meet educational requirements. In addition the act may contain stipulations about residence and age. The governing body has the right to determine admission requirements and qualifications but as a matter of history and good procedure will delegate this authority to the academic council. The administration of the university, particularly the registrar or dean of admissions, should confer with appropriate committees of the academic council in the formulation or change of such requirements. Many matters which have to do with admissions concern the individual faculties and colleges. A useful device is a committee or council of the associate deans in charge of resident instruction. Such a body can develop many useful procedures and give wise counsel to the registrar.

University statutes should authorize the registrar, acting on recommendations from college faculties and the academic council, to allow transfer credits for work done by students in other institutions. Statutes should also authorize the use of proficiency examinations to establish credit for transfer students. There should be special provisions permitting the completion of courses of study by students enrolled in colleges which become constituent units of the university.

Admission standards for graduate students should be established by the graduate council following recommendations from the graduate faculty and approved by the academic council. Individual departments must be given the right to determine such additional requirements as they feel necessary for their graduate students.

12.3. ADMISSION PROCEDURES

Teachers in the university are concerned with admission and registration procedures. Many of them will serve on committees and perform other functions relative to admission or registration. Also, as advisers to particular students they will be concerned with the registration of these students. Statutes authorizing the registrar to administer an admissions program and provide for the registration of students should authorize him to request such academic help as may be needed to get these jobs done. Registration procedures should be thoroughly described and communicated to all concerned. They should be reevaluated and revised after each registration period. The procedure for admissions, the forms involved, and communications required should be thoroughly outlined in the university register or catalog so that a prospective student will know what steps to take to gain admission. Regulations of the University of Ibadan require candidates to complete appropriate forms by a specified date and to attend the university for interviews or such tests as may be set to assess their suitability for admission. Statutes should provide that the registrar be responsible for administering entrance examinations, evaluating secondary school records, and conducting such admission tests as may be approved by the academic council. Information about fees, tuition, loans, and scholarships should be included in the university catalog or official register. Separates or "tear sheets" of pertinent information should be available for mailing to applicants.

12.4. PRESCRIBING METHODS OF INSTRUCTION— SYLLABUS—TEXTBOOKS

The teacher should have freedom to teach a course in the manner he deems most effective. Interference with this right may constitute a breach of academic freedom. The scope of academic freedom is discussed in Chapter 15. There are, however, some financial implications. If laboratories, laboratory equipment, field plots, animals, implements, and tools are required, there must be budgetary allocations. University statutes should give the faculty of the college the right to make these determinations.

The decision about the way a course should be presented is primarily a departmental matter with heavy reliance being placed on the individual instructor. Though deans, directors of resident instruction, and other administrative officers may urge the use of modern techniques such as films, taped discussions, television, programmed instruction, language laboratories, and others, the decision to use these techniques must be made within the departments. Statutes of the University of the Philippines provide that

The lecture method shall be used only when it is clearly a good method considering the subject matter, the skill of the lecturer, the objective of the course, the maturity of the student body, and the physical facilities that are available. The lecture-discussion or small lecture method shall be used when a certain amount of student participation under the affirmative leadership of the lecturer is desired. The seminar method shall be used when what it desired is open discussion under relatively loose instructional leadership. The tutorial method shall be used only when its justification is abundantly clear.

This is a good statement about the suitability of different modes of instruction, but it hardly seems appropriate to convert it into a statutory mandate.

Where the external examination system prevails and the university is an affiliating agency, firm provisions must be made for the development of a syllabus covering each subject. Students demand it as a matter of right so that they can determine limits beyond which they are not required to go in preparing for the examination. The syllabus does not have this meaning or importance when each instructor grades his own students in courses taught by him. The course outline becomes important, but it does not occupy the same sensitive position as the syllabus. University statutes should provide that new courses or major course revisions or the joint offering of courses by more than one department be initiated by the instructor or instructors involved, approved by the department or departments and the college or colleges involved, and approved finally by the academic council. Department heads, deans, and the chief academic officer of the university should have the right to review, and where appropriate, recommend the involvement of other departments or units. Also, if there are budgetary implications and the means are not available, they must have the right to veto a proposal for this reason. Good administration and good liaison between administrative officers and faculty bodies will lead to the kind of understanding which results in a high correlation between budgetary allocations and faculty desires.

Many of the earlier laws establishing universities gave the governing body the right to determine what textbooks should be used. No modern governing body is likely to desire this burden. University of the Philippines Statutes provide that the president shall establish rules under which a committee shall approve textbooks to be used and prices to be charged for them. Selection of the materials (including textbooks) to be used in teaching a course should be primarily the responsibility and right of the teacher. If it is a course taken by many students and a whole segment of a department is devoted to teaching the course, the textbooks and teaching materials will probably be common to all sections of the course. Certainly the university act and statutes should leave such decisions to the faculty.

In many countries the lack of suitable indigenous textbooks poses a problem almost as important as that of who shall determine which ones to use. Though one would not ordinarily recommend a statutory provision on the subject, the production of such books might be stimulated by a statute providing an incentive in terms of royalties or additional compensation for those who are willing to expend the effort required in their preparation. The Indian agricultural universities are greatly concerned over this matter and have asked for and received expert help in the preparation of textbooks by Indian professors.

12.5. COURSES OF STUDY—CURRICULUM

The responsibility for developing course content should rest with those who are experts in the field, and the individual instructor should have a considerable degree of freedom in making changes and revisions. But who decides what combinations of subject matter taught in the university will produce graduates with the desired education? This in turn poses at least two major questions, both of which go to the heart of the institution's educational effort: (1) in what competencies, professions, or specific areas of knowledge shall the students be educated, and (2) what combinations of subjects will produce the desired educational result? The legislature may set guide posts for the first, but obviously it cannot predetermine the second; therefore, the answer is not to be found in the university act. Nevertheless, detailed and constrictive provisions are sometimes included in university acts. Likewise, it is not to be expected that the governing body can reach any working conclusions about these questions, though it is quite common for the law creating a university to give the governing body the right to determine courses of study and curricula. A wise board will as quickly as possible provide by university statutes that these determinations be made by the respective faculties and the academic council of the university. This is as far as a statutory provision ought to go, though some statutes contain details about such things as the form for submitting course proposals and the date by which course outlines must be published. Internally, a fine balance is needed between the rights and judgments of departments, colleges, and the main academic body of the university.

The statutes should provide that the academic council shall approve, disapprove, or return for further consideration college faculty proposals on courses of study and curriculum. It should not have authority to alter such proposals. Each body plays an important role. No determinations about courses and curricula are ever made with finality because the fund of man's knowledge and his opinion about the parts of this fund which will produce an educated man in any area change constantly. Producing graduates competent to aid agriculture on all fronts requires cooperation and understanding among all elements of the university. If, for example, one objective is to educate teachers of vocational agriculture, university units teaching agriculture, professional education, psychology, and the arts, sciences, and humanities will all be involved. It is necessary that there be working rules and that these be widely understood by staff members. College committees or boards on courses of study or curriculum are beset by enough uncertainties—reducing some of these to propositions which can be considered, changed, rejected, or supplanted can save time and improve the functioning of such boards or committees. The determination of courses of study and curricula will continue to be an intriguing business because the opinions held about the proper education of man are at least equal in number to professors participating in the process.

12.6. EXAMINATIONS AND GRADING

When the external examination system is used, extensive provisions are frequently made both in the university act and in the statutes regarding the framing of examinations, preparation of syllabuses, and conducting of examinations. Faculty boards of study and the academic council are given important roles. If there is to be an external examination system, such provisions are essential. Sometimes the registrar is placed in charge of conducting examinations. Some statutes provide that the chief administrative officer has the power to appoint from panels of names submitted by boards of study the paper setters and examiners for all examinations in the university. Provision is sometimes made for an officer known as the controller of examinations. We do not believe that the use of the syllabus and an external examination is conducive to the kind of teaching and learning it is hoped will take place in universities oriented toward the solution of social and economic problems and the development of agriculture.

The Punjab Agricultural University Act provides that

The university shall gradually establish an internal system of examinations for all levels of academic pursuit. The examinations shall be held on a continual basis providing for formal, short-term, mid-term, and final tests. Detailed procedure of examinations and conditions of eligibility for the award of degrees and diplomas shall be laid down by the academic council on the recommendations of the boards of studies. Until the new system of examination is prescribed, the existing system laid down by the Punjab University with such modifications as may be considered necessary by the academic council on the recommendations of the boards of studies shall be deemed to have been adopted by the Punjab Agricultural University and shall continue to be enforced.

The Mysore University of Agricultural Sciences Statutes contain this revealing section: "In view of the interruption of the teaching and research program of the teachers and officers of the university as a result of conducting external examinations in other institutions or universities, the University as a general policy shall discourage the acceptance of external examinerships."

We believe there should be a statutory provision recognizing the right of the instructor to grade students in his course and empowering the colleges and departments to study grading patterns until there is some common understanding of the system and equitable assignment of grades. The Mysore statutes contain this provision: "The course grade earned by an enrolled student shall be determined by the teacher who is in charge of and conducts the course in accordance with regulations proposed by the board of studies and approved by the council. Consideration shall be given by the teacher to daily class performance, interim examinations, terminal examinations, and other factors specified in the regulations."

Though statutory provisions are not essential, regulations should be developed by the registrar with advisement from the colleges defining grade values and methods of determining a student's academic standing. There should be provisions also for recording grades, computing averages, and issuing transcripts and grade records. College offices will have to keep more records, make more computations, and advise students more closely under an internal examination system. The registrar with advice from appropriate committees of the colleges should be empowered by statute to evaluate grades and courses from other institutions and determine the standing of transfer students. College regulations should require instructors to furnish grades at the completion of a course and perhaps at other times when the standing of a student must be determined. They should also cover such subjects as make-up examinations, absence from final examinations, retaking examinations, computation of academic standing, academic probation, and dismissal for academic reasons. Statutes of the University of the Philippines provide that no instructor may be required to furnish grades in any course more often than twice a semester or term. This does not need to appear in the statutes, but it would be desirable as a college regulation. The finality of the grade assigned by an instructor should be protected, and no committee or higher authority should be given the right to question except when it can be shown that the instructor was motivated by malice or acted capriciously.

12.7. TEACHER-STUDENT RATIO–CONTACT HOURS

University of Illinois Statutes provide that "The responsibilities to the university of full-time members of the academic staff are held to be fulfilled when a teaching load appropriate to the rank and program is carried, an appropriate amount of productive scholarly research, aid in a program of public service, and a reasonable share of committee assignments is performed." Though seldom expressed in university statutes, most institutions have a rule or an understanding that a given number of contact hours with students by various categories of teachers constitutes a full teaching load. The formula for determining the number of contact hours varies depending on whether the teaching involves laboratory instruction, field work, lecture, or discussion. The contract of employment may specify the amount of teaching which constitutes a full load. We feel that teaching loads in terms of contact hours (depending on type of instruction) should be expressed in university regulations and included in contracts of employment.

Related to clock hours of teaching per instructor is the ratio of instructors to students. Though university averages in this regard are deceiving due to the research involvement and other activities of most teaching members of the faculty, they may nevertheless be used for or against the university at budget-approval time. A university regulation defining teacher-student ratio and expressing the factors for determining it could go a long way in explaining erroneous impressions which sometimes arise. We do not believe there should be a statute or a university regulation attempting to establish either a minimum or maximum number of students who should sit in lectures, discussion periods, or other types of instruction. The general feeling is that laboratory and discussion classes should be kept small, and that the size of lecture sections or periods where films, tape recordings, or certain kinds of programmed instruction are used may be limited only by physical facilities. If it is felt desirable to express a hope and a policy, there would be no harm in framing a university statute which would state that the university shall strive to insure competent and inspired instruction throughout—that standards with respect to clock hours of teaching, numbers of students in classes, distribution of ranks of academic staff within departments, and space and equipment necessary for classrooms and laboratories shall be established. It might also state that a continuing study shall be made of the use of classroom and laboratory space in order that all university facilities be used to maximum advantage.

12.8. CERTIFYING FOR DEGREES

One American work of law states that

While the granting of degrees is a matter resting largely in the discretion of the college or university authorities, a student ordinarily has the right to pursue his course of study to its completion and to receive his degree on successful completion of the course with due observance of reasonable regulations as to attendance, deportment, and other matters and the college or university may not arbitrarily deny him a degree. Ordinarily, one matriculating at a college or university establishes a contractual relationship entitling him, on compliance with reasonable regulations as to scholastic standing, attendance, deportment, and payment of tuition, to pursue his selected course of study to completion and to receive a degree or certificate awarded for successful completion of such course. But the ordinary rule is subject to modification by university regulations assented to by the student. A college or a university may refuse a degree to a contumacious student or to one who has not complied with all the conditions required, but a college cannot arbitrarily and without cause refuse examination and degree to a student who has complied with all the conditions entitling him thereto.[2]

Statutes of the Universidad Agraria in Peru provide that each college of the university shall set forth in its bylaws the degrees or professional titles it awards and that such bylaws shall establish the requirements for obtaining the degree or title. The statutes further provide that students who have complied satisfactorily with the program of study and other requirements established by the college shall be certified for the corresponding degree or title. Statutes of the Ahmadu Bello University provide that the faculty board for each faculty shall make recommendations to the senate for the award of degrees, diplomas, certificates, and other distinctions in the faculty. Statutes of the Mysore University of Agricultural Sciences provide that each board of studies shall be responsible for recommending

---

[2] 14 *CJS.* § 1338

that degrees be conferred on students who have met satisfactorily the requirements of the faculty and of the university. It further states that in order to earn a bachelor's degree, a student shall complete the sepcified number of course credits and, in addition, shall in the judgment of the faculty possess good moral habits and a high standard of honesty. The Punjab Agricultural University Statutes provide that the conditions under which students shall be admitted to the degree or diploma shall be such as are laid down by the academic council on the recommendations of the boards of studies of the individual faculties. University statutes should provide that the faculty of the college in which the student is registered for a degree certify him for his degree.

12.9. GRADUATION REQUIREMENTS

The university act should empower the board to approve graduation or degree requirements, and the board should by statute provide that the faculties of the university and the academic council establish such requirements. This accords with the provisions in most university acts and statutes. The University of the Philippines Act provides that the university academic council shall have the power to fix requirements for graduation and to recommend students or others to be recipients of degrees. They further provide that no student shall be recommended for graduation unless he has satisfied all academic and other requirements prescribed for graduation. These statutes also contain much detail about the payment of graduation fees, completion of records, completion of work in physical education, military science and euthenics, and other matters which should not be in the university statutes but which should be left to internal regulations and rules.

The Mysore University of Agricultural Sciences Statutes go further than most in specifying a curriculum applicable throughout the university. They state that "The curricula shall include courses in basic sciences and humanities, concerned basic agricultural sciences, courses in closely related fields, courses in a major field of specialization, and elective courses, all of which provide opportunities for a student to gain basic and usable knowledge to make him capable of dealing reasonably well with all facets of agriculture and rural life and especially with the particular activities for which he has taken special courses." This is certainly a good statement of educational objectives and if having such a statement in the statutes will help make the graduates the kind of people this statement says they should be, then by all means it should be a part of the university statutes.

Graduation requirements should be established by regulation and published in the official register or catalog. Such a regulation should express the credit or clock hours of work in common subjects required of all students in the university plus any other general university requirement such as field or extension work in an agricultural village, completion of a minimum number of clock hours in a student work program, and completion of a military training requirement for those required to participate. Also, there may be a general grade point average established by the university as the minimum for graduation. In addition to expressing general university requirements, the register or catalog should also state the additional requirements of each college including a listing of the curricula of the various colleges and the subject matter required for their completion. Columbia University Statutes state that the university council has the power to prescribe by concurrent action with the appropriate faculty or administrative board the conditions upon which degrees shall be conferred and to recommend candidates for such degrees.

Many times there is a requirement that a minimum amount of the academic work required for a degree be obtained at the university. Such requirements are expressed in different ways: some state that the final year of a student's work shall be done at the university; others require that some minimum proportion of his total work be done at the degree-granting institution. Sometimes both formulas are used. Generally a lesser amount of total work in the university is required if the student completes his last academic year or last term at the university. Such a requirement should be stated in the university statutes and published in the university register or catalog.

12.10. HONORS

Many university acts state that the governing body shall have authority to award honors, prizes, and other academic distinctions. Since this activity falls in its sphere, there should be a university statute authorizing the university council or senate to establish the conditions under which such awards shall be made. The conditions for such awards should be recommended to the council or senate by an appropriate committee of that body working in cooperation with committees of the various faculties. In some countries "honors" may refer to an academic program rather than to quality of performance.

12.11. CONFERRING DEGREES

The statutes of Purdue University provide that "Upon the recommendation of the president of the university and the faculty, the board may confer upon students completing the prescribed courses such degrees as may be deemed appropriate." The board is also authorized to confer postgraduate degrees and honorary degrees, the latter to be conferred only on recommendation of the president. Some statutes state that the degrees shall be conferred by the president or chief administrative officer under the authority of the governing body. Perhaps this latter provision is more realistic and would in most cases have more meaning to the graduate.

The recommendation of candidates for degrees following their certification from the college in which they did their academic work is a function of the academic council. Almost without exception such a provision is contained in university acts or statutes. A sample is that from the Punjab Agricultural University Statutes which provides that "The academic council has the power to recommend candidates for diplomas, degrees, and certificates to be conferred by the university."

The recommendation of candidates for honorary degrees is a prerogative of the academic council and should be recognized in an appropriate university statute. The law establishing the University of Kansas provided that "No strictly honorary degree without corresponding literary or scientific attainments shall ever be granted by the university." And the University of Nebraska Act provided that "No degree shall be conferred in consideration of the payment of money." These admonitions to the faculty should not be necessary. It should not be mandatory that the academic council confine its recommendations to men with academic backgrounds. Many of the Indian university acts provide that recommendations for honorary degrees shall be confirmed by the chancellor.

Though any public university established by law undoubtedly has the right to confer degrees, even though there is no specific provision authorizing it to do so, we feel the university act could empower the institution to award appropriate degrees. An American work of law states that

A degree is any academic rank recognized by colleges and universities having a reputable character as institutions of learning or any form of expression indicative of academic rank so as to convey to the ordinary mind the idea of some collegiate, university, or scholastic attainment. The conferring of degrees or the issuing of diplomas or certificates except by duly authorized institutions is sometimes prohibited by statute. A college incorporated under a general law authorizing the incorporation of colleges has implied power to grant diplomas as this right is one of the characteristic features of a college. A university may not properly issue diplomas to students without requiring necessary attendance and is guilty of fraud in so issuing diplomas to be used as a basis for securing state license to practice a profession.[3]

In many developing countries fraudulent institutions—"diploma mills"—will thrive unless there is legislative control. Only in recent years have the American states achieved some measure of necessary control. The enactment of appropriate legislation is recommended to protect public and legitimate private institutions and unwary citizens.

12.12. CONVOCATION

Degrees are ordinarily conferred at a gathering known as convocation, commencement, or by other appropriate names. University acts which make the governor the chancellor of the university ordinarily provide that he shall have the right to preside at convocations when present. Candidates for degrees are expected to be present but may be excused for good cause. A statutory provision would not seem essential, but there should be a regulation so stating. Some university acts provide for an annual commencement. The statutes of Harvard University fix the date. Many institutions now find it necessary to hold more than one commencement during the year to accommodate those who qualify for degrees at the end of different terms. Probably a statutory provision is not necessary, but if there is one it should permit the holding of more than one graduation ceremony during the year. If there is no statute, there should be a university regulation. Instances have been cited where a convocation or commencement was not held because the chief administrative officer was away or was too busy. This is not a good enough reason for cancelling a ceremony which has great meaning to many of the graduates and to their families. The statute or regulation should require that the event be held.

---

[3] 14 *CJS*, § 1337

12.13. EXTRAMURAL CLASSES, ADULT CLASSES, NIGHT CLASSES, AND CORRESPONDENCE COURSES

University teachers are often hesitant about participating in teaching programs outside the classroom. Correspondence courses, for example, are very expensive because they consume so much teacher time per student. Frequently teachers are asked to participate in such programs with no additional compensation. Some of these areas will be taken care of by an extension program—adult classes, for example. All the others—extramural work, night classes, and correspondence courses—imply offerings for university credit and must be handled by competent members of the academic staff. Certainly the university has authority to engage in such programs without any specific provision in the university act. We feel, therefore, that if the act provides adequately for the extension function, these other areas can be left to university statute and internal rules and regulations. To make the situation clear and to protect staff members who might be asked to devote extra time to grading correspondence course examinations or conducting extramural or night classes, we recommend that there be a statutory provision authorizing these educational undertakings by any faculty on approval of the academic council and that teachers who participate be paid for the extra time they devote or be given released time from their regular duties.

12.14. INSTITUTIONAL STANDARDS

Many university statutes state that the chief administrative officer has a general responsibility for maintaining satisfactory academic standards in all university units and that the academic council shall be responsible for the maintenance of standards of instruction, education, and examination. Such provisions are good statements of policy, but they are wholly internal. When an institution goes off the syllabus–external examination "gold standard," the critics will ask, "What assurance is there that standards are being maintained and that degrees granted will be equal in quality to those granted by other institutions?"

The final answer is performance by the graduates of the new institutions. A recognized external body with the ability to examine institutions and give them a rating is a partial answer. Such an activity has been undertaken, for example, by the Indian Council of Agricultural Research for the agricultural universities in India. A university education commission or similar higher body which has some surveillance and authority over universities would be in position to insist on certain standards for all institutions. There is no reason why a university cannot engage in useful self-study or self-examination through appropriate committees including in their membership some persons from outside the university. Many professional associations provide a partial answer by passing judgment on the facilities and staff of institutions in which members of their professions are being trained—professional engineering, medical and veterinary medical associations are examples. We think there should be a university statute authorizing and encouraging the chief administrative officer to establish, with the approval of the various faculties and the academic council, a system for self-study and evaluation.

CHAPTER – 13

Research Organization and Functioning

13.1. THE SCOPE OF RESEARCH

The Uttar Pradesh Agricultural University Act provides that "An agricultural experiment station shall be established in the university. It shall have responsibility for research, both fundamental and applied, in all faculties." Other Indian agricultural university acts contain similar provisions. The proposed Ataturk University Act adds a clause stating that research will be "directed to the solution of problems handicapping the development of Turkey." The law establishing the University of Wisconsin stated that "The Board of Regents shall have the power and authority to encourage scientific investigation and productive scholarship and to create conditions tending to that end."

Following adoption of the Hatch Act of 1887 providing funds for the establishment of agricultural experiment stations, the American states passed laws establishing such stations in the land-grant institutions. The laws of Massachusetts provided, for example, that "The trustees shall maintain at the college an agricultural Experiment Station and shall use therefore the land, buildings, and equipment heretofore acquired therefore and owned by the Commonwealth. Such station shall be a part of the college." This same law goes on to express in detail the nature and scope of experimental work to be undertaken. It was quite obvious that the framers of the legislation were interested in practical and useful experimentation. Among the investigations which as a matter of law they declared should be made were the causes, prevention, and remedies of diseases of domestic animals, plants, and trees; the history and habits of insects destructive to vegetation and the means of abating them; the composition of both foreign and domestic fertilizers, their values and adaptability to different crops and soils; and the comparative value of green and dry forage.

The name "experiment station" came to be used in America because the federal law fostering research in the land-grant universities used this term. The experiment station has come to encompass all the research which some institutions carry out. Those unacquainted with the special meaning it has acquired in the American land-grant institutions rightly consider it a narrow term and one which does not adequately express the whole research responsibility of a university. We recommend that the basic law giving the university authority to engage in research, both fundamental and applied in all its faculties, omit the use of the term "experiment station" except in reference to the right of the university to establish such stations, both at the university and at other locations as a part of the total research effort.

A properly framed law authorizing the university to engage in research on a broad front, and particularly to engage in that research which will aid agricultural development and the betterment of the agricultural population, is extremely important. In one country the established research agencies challenged the right of the new university to engage in any research except that which might be considered a part of the teaching program. The university was able to protect its right by pointing to the law defining the scope of its research activity and also by relying on official reports in which was expressed the philosophy that the university should not be limited in its research efforts. If, as is hoped, the new agricultural universities become the center and focus of all major agricultural research activity in the state or region, they should not be bound by any narrow definition of the research function.

13.2. DIRECTOR OF RESEARCH

The Andhra Pradesh Agricultural University Act provides that "The board shall appoint a Director of Agricultural Experiment Stations. The Director shall initiate, guide, and coordinate all agricultural research and be responsible for the efficient working of such stations." The Udaipur University Act provides that the director shall:

a. Initiate, guide, control, and coordinate all research activities of the university in the different branches of learning.

b. Formulate research programs, proposals, and projects in consultation with the several deans and associate deans.

c. Keep records

d. Receive reports of progress

e. Consolidate such reports

This listing of functions fails to mention at least two important elements—the relation of the director of research to the dean of the graduate college, and the role of the faculty in making determinations about the research program. These will be discussed in the next section.

Primarily, a director of research for the university should discharge the responsibilities which would otherwise fall to the chief administrative officer. In a sense, therefore, it is a vice-position for the research function. However, in many institutions the dean of the graduate school has assumed this role. If the act provides for a director of research and there already exists a graduate school which has become the focus for the research effort, jurisdictional problems are bound to arise. We believe there is a place for both a director of research and a dean of the graduate school. University statutes should clearly delineate their functions. In Chapter 9 we discuss in some detail the functions of a director of research, and in Chapter 10 we discuss provisions of the university act and statutes relating to the graduate school. These things we can say about the office of director of research: [1]

The basic and important role played by departments of the university must be recognized.

The role of the graduate college in bringing graduate students into the research activity must be protected.

The freedom of research workers to propose and determine the content of research projects subject to reasonable controls from the financial standpoint must be protected.

The director's office should become the repository of all essential information about research projects, grants, financing, and other research matters.

The director's office can encourage and help research workers in many ways—maintenance of a data processing center, providing statistical services, and offering expert assistance in the experimental design of projects are examples.

He should not have authority to veto projects but he should be able to raise questions resulting in reconsideration and improvement or perhaps sometimes in a decision by the department to abandon

----

[1] For a comprehensive and rather exciting statement about the objectives, activities, and possibilities of an office of director of research, see Appendix VI.

the project. Close cooperation with department heads and deans is implied.

Some university statutes place responsibility for management of a university farm in the director of research. We see no reason for this. Insofar as lands are taken for research or experimental purposes, they will become a part of the research program. Lands which are not so used should be clearly separated from those which are and should be managed on a commercial basis. Responsibility for management should be placed with the dean of agriculture. If, however, the farm is large, and hence an important source of university income, there may be a feeling that the manager should be directly responsible to the chief administrative officer, in which case a small committee advisory to the farm manager should be appointed by the chief administrative officer.

13.3. THE ORGANIZATION AND COORDINATION OF RESEARCH

Research is basically a departmental function. It is at this level that it must be coordinated with teaching and extension so that each can benefit from the other. Statutes of the Orissa University of Agriculture and Technology provide that the heads of departments shall maintain close liaison with the director of research and arrange for the allotment of lands and facilities necessary for carrying out projects. They also provide that research programs shall be conducted by appropriate departments through the members of the staff and the students of the department. They further state that the department shall be the primary unit of education and administration.

In coordinating research, therefore, and in establishing lines of authority for funds accountability, approval of projects, reporting, publishing, and other activities, the department must be assured of its preeminent role.

Statutes of the Jawaharlal Nehru Agricultural University in Madhya Pradesh provide for a research council consisting of the director of research, all deans and associate deans, the director of extension, the director of postgraduate studies, the librarian, and two department heads to be nominated by the director of research. This body is advisory to the director. A council of postgraduate studies is also established with the director of postgraduate studies as chairman, with deans and associate deans, the director of research, and the director of extension as additional members. This kind of liaison between the graduate college and the director of research should be helpful. Something of this nature is necessary in those institutions where both positions exist. Many of the Indian agricultural university acts provide for a research advisory committee which performs about the same functions as a research council. Another type of organization is a university research board, generally existing under the aegis of the graduate school. Its purpose is to assign research funds, review applications for outside grants, and advise the chief administrative officer and dean of the graduate college on matters relating to research. When there is a director of university research, the research board, if established, should be under his chairmanship with the dean of the graduate college as a member or perhaps vice-chairman.

Purdue University provides for an advisory committee, all the members of which are representatives of agricultural organizations and associations in the state. Advisory committees established by the Indian agricultural university acts are usually internal, though the state director of agriculture may sometimes be included as a member. Some university acts provide that the academic council shall be responsible for the planning and development of research activities. Though this is probably not a necessary provision in a university act, the statutes should provide that all educational policy matters touching research should be referred to the academic council for its study and recommendations. Since the graduate college sets admission standards for graduate students and the standards which must be met by departmental graduate programs, it plays an important role even though there is a university director of research. The director of research can enhance the whole graduate program through the services, technical advice, and coordinating effort he can provide as a part of his responsibility.

At several points in this book mention has been made of the need for interdisciplinary research. Many institutions have established centers or "task force groups" for this purpose. This kind of research is indispensable. We suggest in Chapter 10 that there be statutory provisions making it possible and encouraging it. Internal memoranda or agreements between cooperating units should be reduced to working documents which can be improved as more of this activity takes place.

13.4. EXPERIMENT STATIONS

Some of the Indian agricultural universities have established an experiment station as the agency for the total university research effort. As we explained earlier in the chapter, this term was no doubt borrowed from the American land-grant universities in which the term was used because it appeared in the federal act making funds available for research in agriculture. We have suggested a more restricted use of the term. The proposed Ataturk University Act states that the university "Shall establish such laboratories and field stations for research as the university shall deem necessary." Similar provisions are contained in many university statutes—sometimes in university acts. Though specific authorization to establish experiment stations at different locations in the state or region appears in many acts or statutes, the university probably has this right without specific authorization. Its inclusion, however, makes the point perfectly clear and also indicates that it is something which ought to be done.

All states or regions maintaining an agricultural university have a diversity of agricultural conditions. Research in many subject areas such as soils and crop production cannot be done satisfactorily unless research workers can function at appropriate geographical locations. Some of these outlying areas may be simply field plots or demonstrations; some may be research stations at which particular crops are studied intensively; others may comprehend a broader program designed primarily for the area. These latter are sometimes referred to as substations.

There should be no question about the status of university personnel employed in research away from the university. The Udaipur University Statutes put the matter to rest by providing that staff located at various substations shall be on the rolls of the different colleges, schools, and departments or divisions pertaining to their discipline. The director of university research should have administrative supervision of such outlying research stations or should have authority to delegate the responsibility.

13.5. RELATION TO GOVERNMENT RESEARCH

One of the features of the American land-grant university system which has appealed to those responsible for establishing the new agricultural universities in developing countries is the centering of agricultural research in the university. There is nothing to prevent the legislatures in the American states from establishing agricultural research apart from the university, but with minor exceptions state legislatures have not chosen to do so. It has come to be generally understood that state departments of agriculture will carry on regulatory and control programs and that the state universities will be responsible for research. In the American states this applies to virtually all kinds of research, not just agricultural research.

In the developing countries a considerable amount of research has been established by state or regional departments of agriculture, animal husbandry, fisheries, forestry, and related agencies, and hence there is a history of involvement by these agencies. Thus, when newer agricultural universities were established, there was already a large investment in agricultural research. Opinions vary about the advisability of transferring all of this research to the new universities. The Andhra Pradesh Agricultural University Act states that the government shall order the control and management of all government institutions conducting research to be transferred to the university within three years. Other acts require such transfer at some future date to be determined mutually by the university and the government agencies involved. Still other acts make it permissive in stating that the state government may on such terms and conditions as are agreed upon with the vice-chancellor or chief administrative officer transfer to the university with the consent of the board such research institutions as state government may deem necessary and proper. Still other university acts are completely silent on the subject.

We believe that the university act should provide for such a transfer either within some specified time period such as three or five years, or on a date to be established later by the legislature. If discretion is left with the state, the transfer may never be made. If it is left with the university or is mandatory, it may mean transfer before the university is equipped administratively or otherwise to handle such agencies. Probably the most impartial judge is the legislature—hence our suggestion. Until such a transfer is made, or in case it is not made, we recommend that the university act contain a provision like that in the Udaipur act providing that "Between the university and several departments of state government there shall be kept and carried on in the manner agreed upon between the board and the state government a regular exchange of all information concerning research programs, proposals, and projects and concerning knowledge gained through research." In Chapter 3 we discuss the desirability of a coordinating council with the university playing a major role in its development and functioning.

Another feature of the American land-grant university is its relation to the federal or central government in carrying on agricultural research. It has come to be more or less understood that the system can function effectively if it is assumed there are three major kinds of research needs in agriculture: those which are nationwide in scope, those which involve several states in a region, and those which are primarily the concern of a particular state. Under the system which has evolved, the federal government through the United States Department of Agriculture carries on a major program of research on subjects in the first category. For the second category, a regional organization has been established involving universities which are interested and concerned through representatives from their experiment stations working in cooperation with the federal agricultural research service. The latter provides funds and some supervision. Projects are carried on, the results of which will be of value to all the participating states. Many subcommittees and research teams are formed. For research in the last category— that of primary concern to the state—there is some federal assistance but the states rely heavily on their own resources. These are not "neat" categories but they do have suggestive value in a developing country which is trying to accomplish a "breakthrough" in agricultural research with limited resources and facilities.

Though the right may be implied, we believe it is important that the university act contain a provision authorizing the university to accept central government assistance for research and to cooperate with the central government in regional or other research endeavors.

13.6. FINANCING RESEARCH

In many universities the most important step which can be taken to bolster agricultural research is internal budgeting for it. Many university budgets do not contain specific items for research at the departmental, college, or university level. We discuss budgeting procedures in Chapter 8 and will only reiterate here that a budget is supposed to help the university achieve its major objectives. Research is a major objective. It will not be pursued satisfactorily until there are funds earmarked for it. Otherwise, the whole institutional budget can be absorbed in the teaching program and for other needs. We recommend that the university statutes contain a provision requiring the university, college, and departmental budgets to contain specific allocations for research and providing also that contracts of employment of the academic staff indicate the proportion of time they are to spend on research.

The internal budgeting and management of funds for research is one problem; procuring funds is another. A provision in the statutes of the University of Illinois states: "It is the policy of the university to encourage research on the part of all persons and groups within the several faculties. Such encouragement includes the endorsement and support of acceptable proposals of outside contracts or grants." This statutory provision further points out that outside support for research must be integrated with the regular research functions of the university and that acceptance of contracts or grants involves substantial internal cost to the university—hence consideration must be given before such contracts or grants are accepted. The statutes should further require that rules and regulations governing the acceptance of such grants and contracts be developed as part of the business office procedure manual.

Many universities have fostered the establishment of a research foundation as a separate corporation to receive and administer funds, handle patents, make allocations to units of the university, and accomplish other objectives. In some institutions, the research advisory committee makes recommendations for allocation of grant money or of a university research contingency fund. The council of the graduate college and a university research board are other agencies sometimes used. University statutes should provide that such entities may be created and state generally their composition and functions. Regardless of any administrative devices which may be established to receive and allocate funds or to perform other functions, the academic council still has the right to pass judgment on major policies involving research, and the governing board must still be the final authority. Research workers and research units in a university can sometimes be asked to do strange things which amount to no more than routine testing or performing some function for a commercial concern simply because the concern does not wish to buy the equipment and hire someone to do it. Faculty judgment is important in "holding the line" on such activities.

13.7. THE RESEARCH STAFF

The University of the Philippines Act provides that a university professor may be assigned to do research work on the subject or subjects of his specialization in any college or unit of the university. The Orissa statutes provide that "The teacher shall teach, do research and extension education work and such other work relating to the university as may be required." When a staff member is employed, there should be an understanding about the division of his time between teaching, research, and extension or other university activity, and this should be stated in his contract. The method of appointment and conditions of service of the academic staff for research are discussed in Chapter 15. The employment and conditions of service of nonacademic staff are discussed in Chapter 16.

We would like to emphasize again that well-trained and dedicated nonacademic staff are extremely important in agricultural research. Animals, facilities, and equipment of great value are under their immediate care, not to mention sensitive experiments which can fail completely if those in charge do not properly carry out routine functions demanded by the experiment. We were told of one cattle-feeding experiment which went awry because the attendant who fed the cattle felt sorry for the lots that did not get silage and "on the sly" remedied this omission. Reliable non-academic employees do not materialize because of any provision in a university act or statute, but they can materialize through a sound program for nonacademic personnel established pursuant to a statutory provision requiring that there be an office of non-academic personnel under the supervision of a competent director.

13.8. PATENTS AND COPYRIGHTS

The patent policy of a university may derive from legislation, the university statutes, regulations of the governing body, or regulations of a research board or other university authority. The attention which universities have paid to patents and copyrights varies from an unwillingness to be concerned at all to detailed and formalized policies and procedures. What justifies a patent and copyright policy? Several things: the fact that public funds, facilities, and equipment are used; that the staff member making the discovery is paid by the university; that, due to the nature of university research, the discovery is likely to be something in which the public would have an interest. These are some of the reasons— but they do not rule out in all cases some right of the professor-inventor or professor-writer to a portion of the royalties which may accrue. Judgments about the nature and extent of this right should be made by some competent group or university authority acting in accordance with a clear statement of policy.

The statutes of Columbia University provide for a corporation known as "University Patents Incorporated." This corporation has authority to apply for and take out patents and to accept by assignment patents, patent applications, royalties, licenses, or rights covering discoveries, inventions, or processes whether produced by members of the university staff through use of university laboratories or otherwise. The corporation may also accept assignment of trademarks, proprietary names, or copyrights of literary works owned or produced by members of the university staff or others. Statutes of the University of Illinois provide that

The principle is recognized that the results of experimental work carried on by or under the direction of the members of the staff of the university and having the expense thereof paid from university funds or from funds under the control of the university belong to the university and should be used and controlled in ways to produce the greatest benefit to the university and to the public. Any member of the staff of the university who has made an invention as a direct result of his regular duties on university time and at university expense may be required to patent his invention and to assign the patent to the university, the expenses connected therewith to be borne by the university.

With respect to contracts for research with outside agencies, statutes and regulations of the University of Illinois provide that patentable discoveries resulting from such research are the property of the university to be used for the benefit of the university and the public, but if such discoveries have commercial value the sponsoring agency may receive preferential consideration in the administration of the patent. Exceptions are made when the contracting party is an agency of government. It is further provided that a discovery or invention shall be submitted to the university patent committee for study. The university patent committee is a subcommittee of the university research board. When it makes a recommendation to the board of trustees or governing body, the board may do one of three things: release the patent to the dis-coverer or inventor, retain the patent in the university, or release it to a contracting agency in case the patent was developed under a contract research arrangement. If the patent produces income, university regulations provide that the university patent committee shall make a recommendation to the president about the propor-tion of the income which may be assigned to the inventor. As a guide, the regulations indicate that this should usually fall between 10 and 15 per cent of net income but that in unusual cases it might be as much as 25 per cent.

There is some feeling against compulsory assignment of patent rights to a university. It can be argued that a staff member who makes a patentable discovery has gone beyond the performance of duty which entitled him to his university salary and that he should have some discretion about what to do with the discovery. Arguments on the other side point out that most staff members are not in position to get their discovery patented due to the expense and management involved; also, that the discovery is likely to touch the public welfare in some way, and the university has at least a moral obligation to see that it is turned to the public good. This is particularly true of patentable discoveries in the field of public health; many institutions have special provisions about such discoveries. We feel that the stake of any university in a discovery made by one of its staff members on university time and through the use of university facilities justifies a provision in the statutes or in the law compelling assignment to the institution. The statutes should then provide an adequate mechanism for determining the equity of the inventor in the discovery and for providing some remuneration to him in all cases where the patent produces in-come. This policy should apply likewise to both graduate and undergraduate students if they make discoveries while engaged in their studies in university laboratories. The act or statutes should state specifically that discoveries made outside the university and on the individual's own time are not subject to the university's patent policy.

Though many institutions seem to get along without any patent policy and new institutions may feel there is no necessity for any provision on the subject, they should hope and expect as their research programs expand and gain more depth and meaning that patentable discoveries will be made. It is wise to have a policy established in advance. If there is a state board of education or a higher governing body for universities, the policy might be established at this level and be applicable uniformly in all public higher educational institutions. Even in the absence of any such higher body the legislature could establish a uniform policy, leaving with the institution some flexibility to work out details and further contractual arrangements with staff members. University contracts of appointment should incorporate by reference its patent and copyright policy and should include a citation to the law or university statutes.

Most institutions have no policy regarding copyright because it is generally considered that the author has the sole right either to perfect the copyright himself or assign it to a publisher. But along with the increase in sponsored research has come an increase in the number of contracts with outside agencies, governmental and otherwise, to produce reports or written materials for a monetary consideration expressed in the contract. Under these circumstances the staff member or members who work on the project are paid for producing the written material. When such material lends itself to copyright, questions arise about relative rights of the university, the sponsoring agency, and the professor-author. Many American universities have adopted a policy similar to that in effect at the University of Illinois. It provides that "The right to copyright a work or to assign this right to a publisher normally belongs to the author of the work. However, when the author is specifically commissioned by the university or one of its departments to prepare a manuscript or report, the manuscript and all rights to it shall belong to the university." This policy encompasses work commissioned or subsidized within the university as well as work resulting from outside contracts with the university. For example—what are the author's rights in an extension education circular or in an agricultural research bulletin? Policy established at the University of Illinois states that such may or may not be copyrighted at the discretion of the department issuing the work. A university committee on copyrights and recordings administers the policy. As with patents, provisions are also made for sharing royalties with the author. This policy also applies to films, video tapes, and other materials which have been produced with university facilities, resources, and financial support. All books published by the university press are copyrighted by the press, and the author's royalty, if any, is expressed in a contract with the press.

While it is important to have a policy recognizing the university's contribution to written materials produced by members of its staff, a more important consideration for institutions in the developing countries is how to encourage staff members to prepare written materials, particularly textbooks, laboratory manuals, and other aids essential to good teaching. It is not inconsistent to establish both policies—one insuring the institution's right in materials expressly commissioned by it or produced with its resources and another encouraging staff members to write textbooks, manuals, and classroom aids through a bonus plan or some scheme providing for extra compensation. When a faculty member is willing to produce such materials, it could be expressly stated that the copyright, if any, shall belong to the author.

13.9. PUBLICATIONS

One of the early laws relating to Michigan State University contained this provision:

The several professors of chemistry, zoology, botany, agriculture, horticulture, and veterinary science shall each at least twice in each year, not excluding the president and other professors, prepare for publication an article embracing such facts as they may deem of public importance, a copy of which shall be simultaneously sent to each and every newspaper published in the state and to such persons as the state board of agriculture may think proper, said professors to so arrange that at least one of said articles shall be sent out as above provided the first week of each and every month in each and every year.

Though this may remind one of the adage "you can lead a horse to water but you cannot make him drink," it expresses in no uncertain terms the thought that if the professors are hired and equipped to make discoveries important to the farmers of the state, they shall not keep their findings secret.

Though the conflict may not be tempestuous, there is in every institution a difference in the philosophy about publication between those doing research and those engaged in agricultural information activities. The former wish to withhold all information until the project is completed and then publish a learned monograph; the latter wish to popularize and disseminate any findings that might create interest whether or not they are conclusive. Who shall decide how much and when? Statutes of the Mysore University of Agricultural Sciences provide that "The director of re-

search shall require and supervise the publication of research results." The government decree concerning the organization of the
Rural University of Minas Gerais in Brazil states that the general
director of experimentation and research shall have the right to
select the experimental and research projects to be published.
Neither of these statements is very helpful. They imply an authority in the administration which the academic community would
not accept without considerable interpretation.

We believe a statutory provision encouraging the publication
of research results through bulletins, scholarly articles in journals,
and other means is important but that, beyond this, control of
publication should be left to rules and procedures developed
within the university. Generally this is considered a departmental
matter. Most departments have a publications committee. There
should be such a committee at the college level if not at the departmental level. The purpose of such committees is to improve
and to encourage, not censor and suppress. Only good judgment
and a right philosophy in the department or college will produce
this kind of committee activity. Through working together toward
common objectives the research worker and the extension worker,
particularly the extension worker in the field of information, should
reach some understanding about the proper use of information
derived from experimentation and research.

13.10. POLICY ON CONSULTING

Successful research workers who get to be known in their field
may be asked by government agencies or private industry to serve
as consultants either on a regular basis or with respect to some
particular project or problem. Since they are employees of the
university and are expected to render their services to it, this
raises a policy question on which there should be a university
statutory provision, such provision to be incorporated by reference
in contracts of appointment. Further discussion of policies on consulting and suggested statutory provisions appear in Chapter 15.

13.11. LAND AND IMPROVEMENTS FOR RESEARCH

Governing bodies should have authority to acquire such land
as is needed for research and other educational purposes—by
eminent domain, if necessary. This authority of the governing body
is discussed in Chapter 5. Also, the governing body has the right

to accept land and improvements which may come to the university if and when transfers of other governmental research agencies are made. For that matter, it has the right to accept a gift or donation of land from anyone for research purposes so long as the gift or grant is not accompanied by unacceptable conditions.

Problems sometimes arise concerning the allotment of land among departments and research agencies of the university and the taking of land from other uses for research purposes. The converse of this latter problem may arise—that is, the taking of land in use for research and experimental purposes for other university needs. Any change in the use of university land and improvements should eventually be approved by the chief administrative officer. The process through which recommendations for such changes are made should involve all of the people concerned. The director of research should make an initial decision on allotments or transfers involving the research function. His decision should be made after he has received recommendations from the departments, colleges, or other units concerned. There may be conflicts between colleges or departments, in which case he may feel the need of a special committee to make a recommendation. We believe the university statutes should contain a provision empowering the director of research to make recommendations to the chief administrative officer on the allotment and use of lands for research purposes after he has conferred with appropriate departments and units of the university. It will still fall to the lot of the chief administrative officer to determine between a recommendation from the director of research and a counter recommendation, for example, from the director of the physical plant department.

CHAPTER – 14

Extension Organization
and Functioning

14.1. THE SCOPE AND PURPOSE OF
UNIVERSITY EXTENSION [1]

Most of the developing countries are making an effort to reach farm people with information which will help them increase production and improve the communities in which they live. For the most part, these programs have been undertaken by departments of government with the leadership frequently resting in the central government and the states or regions playing a cooperating role.

Creation of new agricultural universities in many parts of the world has raised questions about the part the university should play in a community development or extension program. Many educators and government officials in these countries have viewed with favor the responsibility which American land-grant universities discharge under the cooperative federal-state agricultural extension program. In the United States there was no problem in making the land-grant colleges or universities the focus for extension activity because no other extension activity existed for farm people at the time the Smith-Lever Act[2] creating the cooperative program was passed. The situation in the developing countries is different; the problem becomes one of fitting the new institutions into the ongoing extension program. This raises policy questions regarding the scope of the university's program. Shall it take over the total extension effort for the state or region and, if so, what central or federal government financial aid can it expect? Shall it administer a block of villages or a geographical area as a participant in the government program? Shall it restrict its activities to the education of extension workers and to the dissemination of extension information?

----

[1] For a discussion of the responsibility of an agricultural university in developing an extension education program, see Hannah, *Resource Book*, ch. 22.

[2] Act of May 8, 1914; 38 Stat. 372 (7 USCA §§ 431-438).

One of the most concrete answers is found in the Punjab Agricultural University Act which provides that "The university shall be responsible for the agricultural extension functions in the state which are primarily educational in nature and for imparting training to the future extension officers for the national extension block and instructors for the extension training centers. All subject matter extension specialists shall be members of the staff of their respective subject matter sections in the university and shall work in close coordination with the state departments of agriculture, development, and cooperatives." The Andhra Pradesh Agricultural University Act states that the university shall establish an agriculture and home science extension service under a phased program covering the entire state, the objective being eventually to transfer the extension function for the state to the university.

Although most other acts creating the newer agricultural universities charge them with the responsibility for carrying on an extension program, most of them do not go as far as the Andhra Pradesh act in providing for a transfer of responsibility to the university. The decree for the estate of Minas Gerais in Brazil gives the university a coordinating function and lists as one of its purposes the integrating of the extension projects already existing in the state. The Uttar Pradesh Agricultural University Act simply says that an agricultural and home science extension service shall be established in the university to make useful information available to farmers and housewives and to help them solve their problems. It gives no indication of jurisdiction or scope. The Peru National Universities Act provides that in each university there shall be a university extension department, but the listing of functions for such a department seems to be confined to the organization of courses for professional training, programs of technical advice, and practical courses for adults including lectures, speeches, plays, auditions, and other cultural activities. The Udaipur University Act distinguishes between extension functions primarily educational in nature and those which have to do with supplies, services, and regulation.

Many American universities have two extension programs—one in general university extension and another in agricultural and home economics extension. This dichotomy exists because of the federal Smith-Lever Act and the appropriation of federal funds for an agricultural extension program. A policy question confronting the new universities is how to combine the needed emphasis on agricultural extension with a university general extension program involving all colleges and departments. As we have stated earlier, theory favors one extension program with each discipline in the university assuming the importance which conditions in the country indicate. Under such a theory it would be expected that agriculture would constitute the dominant subject matter of the extension program for many years. We believe that a university act should provide for the following:

1. A university extension service responsible for making educational resources of the university available to qualified persons who are not students in residence.

2. The education of personnel for the government community development or extension program.

3. The establishment of a strong agricultural and home economics extension program as a major part of the university extension effort at the outset.

4. The coordination of all extension agencies operating in the state under the leadership of the university.

5. A recognition of the philosophy that the whole university is in a sense devoted to public service and that all staff members should in varying degree consider themselves purveyors of facts and information which will be helpful in the developing economy of the country.

One of the early acts concerning Purdue University seems to charge the whole faculty with some such responsibility in this language: "In order to promote home study and reading on subjects relating to rural life and the principles of agriculture, the trustees and faculty of Purdue University shall encourage and direct farmers' reading courses and publish and distribute circulars and pamphlets of information on the above subjects as may seem profitable in promoting the agricultural interests of the state." Even the trustees were expected to help the cause! The definition of extension included in the university act should not inhibit educational programs in which the university wishes to engage. The language accompanying federal grants for agricultural extension work in the United States has from time to time required interpretation. Even so, new laws and amendments have been necessary to enable the land-grant institutions to enlarge their extension clientele and engage in new programs. Certainly, work with urban people in activities involving the social sciences should not be denied. With respect to leadership and overall control of the extension program, we believe the university should earn this right. If a state or regional program already exists, legislation would be required when and if the transfer is to be made to the university. If no such program is in existence, then by its own efforts the university could establish a position of leadership and mount an extension program which would eventually encompass the whole state or region.

14.2. DIRECTOR OF EXTENSION

The qualifications, appointment, and duties of the director of extension are discussed in some detail in Chapter 9. We would like only to reiterate here that he should be a highly competent man, skilled in dealing with people and educated professionally in agriculture. With growth of the university and development of the country's agriculture, other phases of university extension may assume greater importance, in which case a director with a different educational background might be selected. We believe, therefore, that qualifications for the director should be expressed in a university statute so that they can be more readily changed if at some future time there seems to be a need for changing them.

14.3. COORDINATION AND ORGANIZATION—STAFF

Though we believe that the critical need for agricultural extension makes it important that the first extension directors in the university have an agricultural background and that particular attention be paid to developing a strong extension program in colleges of agriculture, veterinary medicine, animal husbandry, and home science, the director should nevertheless be appointed by the chief administrative officer and should be responsible directly to him. This we believe will make for better administration. Internal coordination of the extension program is achieved primarily in two ways: (1) by the provision that departments and colleges shall engage in teaching, research, and extension—hence, department heads and deans of colleges are responsible for extension work in their units—and (2) through an arrangement under which all extension subject matter specialists are members of their respective departments insofar as their subject matter competency is concerned but are also members of the extension staff with regard to general administration of the program, scheduling meetings, travel, and engaging in activities through which their subject matter knowledge is brought to the people. Under this arrangement, which in our opinion should be established by university statute, subject matter specialists sit in departmental meetings, participate with other members of the staff in affairs of the department, and keep abreast of the departmental program. By rubbing shoulders frequently with their research and teaching colleagues they are able to apprise them of problems in the field and contribute to realism in the research and teaching program. Some extension specialists may even have joint appointments under which they accomplish some research or do some resident teaching.

The Uttar Pradesh Agricultural University Statutes provide that there shall be extension specialists in such departments as may be recommended by the academic council and approved by the board. Extension specialists shall hold academic rank and be members of the staff of the department, but in carrying on field activities they shall be under the supervision of the director of extension. The Punjab Agricultural University Act provides that all subject matter extension specialists shall be members of the staff of their respective departments. The Udaipur University Statutes make it permissible to employ extension specialists jointly for research or teaching.

University statutes should authorize the director of extension to employ through the regular appointment process such administrative and supervisory staff as he deems necessary. Through appropriate rules and regulations, extension specialists and supervisory staff should be given a high priority in the use of university vehicles. These are costly in the developing countries and are not likely to be in plentiful supply. Nevertheless, extension workers cannot achieve their objectives unless they can travel to their clientele.

In many agricultural universities the statutes provide for an extension advisory committee. Sometimes this is wholly an internal committee such as the one for the Uttar Pradesh Agricultural University. It is composed of the vice-chancellor as chairman, the director of extension, director of research, and deans of the colleges. It advises on coordination of the university extension program with state and national programs, allocation of funds for extension, and ways and means of increasing the effectiveness of the university's extension program. In some cases these committees are advisory to the chief administrative officer; in others the statutes state that they are advisory to the director of extension. The Udaipur University Statutes provide that there shall be an extension education advisory committee consisting of the vice-chancellor, the Development Commissioner for Rajasthan or his representative, a representative of the State Farmers' Forum, the director of agriculture, the director of animal husbandry, the director of primary and secondary education, and, from the university, the director of the agricultural experiment station, the director of extension, and the deans and associate deans of colleges and schools. This illustrates quite a different type of advisory committee, one which can very well serve as a coordinating body for state agencies since it includes the heads (or their representatives) of the departments of state government most concerned.

We believe there is a distinctive role for each type of advisory group and that the university statutes should provide for each— one to be completely internal and thus helpful with more of the operational details of the program, the other to be largely an external committee which can express views on policies and on the effectiveness of the university's program.

One of the primary responsibilities of the university in the extension area is to educate extension workers. This involves formulation of a proper curriculum, administration of the curriculum, advisement of the students enrolled in it, and provisions for advanced work. In the beginning a committee on extension education could prepare and administer a curriculum, but as the program grows, a full-fledged extension academic department will be needed.

Much of the success of the university extension program will depend on the relations it is able to build with local groups and with local government. This was one of the keys to the success of the extension program as carried out in the American land-grant universities. These relations are even more important in developing countries because extension is generally conceived as much broader than agriculture and involves the whole concept of community development. We believe that university statutes should recognize this by encouraging cooperation with local groups and providing that insofar as possible the activities of the extension program of the university be carried out through such groups. There may be particular local agencies in a country which can be named in the university statutes. The University of the Philippines has given special attention to this kind of liaison through establishment of a Farm and Home Development office as a part of its program. Within recent years rural area development has become one of the prime functions of the extension program in the American land-grant universities. It is important also that local extension workers cooperate with the teachers of vocational agriculture. These men can greatly augment the program if proper relationships are established with them. This also should be recognized by a provision in the university statutes.

14.4. RELATION OF EXTENSION TO NATIONAL AND STATE PROGRAMS

The Andhra Pradesh Agricultural University Act provides that "The government shall endeavor to secure proper coordination between the departments of the government and the university in the conduct of research and extension work and may render necessary advice to the board in that regard." This is unusual as a provision in a university act, since it imposes a duty on government rather than on the board or the university. The objective is laudable, but we believe the university act should state that it shall be a responsibility of the university to work toward coordination of the total extension effort in the state or region and to take the lead in achieving such coordination. It would be helpful if legislation relating to a government (nonuniversity) extension service imposed a duty on it to cooperate with other agencies including the university. The Mysore Agricultural University Statutes place the responsibility for coordination with the director of extension in the university. The law creating the Rural University of Minas Gerais in Brazil also places this responsibility with the extension directorate of the university. Some of the Indian agricultural university statutes make the agricultural universities responsible for both basic and refresher training of government extension officers and instructors. In addition to provisions which we have suggested for the university act and statutes, we believe the statutes should provide that as soon as possible the university initiate a field extension program cooperating where possible with state and regional or national programs, and also that the university give basic and in-service training to qualified government extension employees.

Though it may not be an appropriate subject for a university act or its statutes, we feel it is extremely important that there be an extension coordinating council with representation from the university and from all agencies of government that have anything to do with the extension program. This should include representatives from the national as well as from state or regional governments.

14.5. EXTRAMURAL AND CORRESPONDENCE COURSES

Provisions regarding these courses are discussed in Chapter 12. We believe that through regulations and internal administrative arrangements the responsibility for fostering and managing such courses should rest with the director of extension and that teachers for such courses should be recruited from the various colleges and departments through arrangements to be made with deans, department heads, and the personnel involved. There is a need for coordination of effort and for firm rules which make it clear where the right and responsibility rest. If, for example, the extension service is charged with making arrangements for extramural and correspondence courses, individual colleges or departments should not be permitted to establish such except by working through the extension service. There must be division of effort and division of cost between the extension service and the academic units involved. The rules and policies under which this is to be done should be clear. The University of the Philippines law places all extension and extramural work as well as the summer school under a vice-president for external studies. When extramural and correspondence courses are offered for credit, graduate work should be included after it is established in the university. The university business office will be involved because fees and tuition will be charged for some courses. Also, there frequently are misunderstandings about how to handle income from short course registration fees and other extramural sources. There should be cooperation with the registrar's office because credits earned by those who take correspondence or extramural courses must be made a matter of record.

14.6. FIELD DAYS AND DEMONSTRATIONS

In an attempt to emphasize the extension responsibility of an agricultural university, the act itself many times expresses in detail the activities which should comprise the extension function. Field days and demonstrations are frequently mentioned. Though one might argue that a legislative provision should be more general and that perhaps even the university statutes need not express the particular ways in which an extension program is to be carried out, there is a purpose to be served in this instance by including some detail in the university act. Those in the developing countries who have given thought to the role of the university in national or community development realize that universities have traditionally not been responsive to social needs but have sought for themselves an insulated position. Anything which will cause a university to break out of its shell in order that it may be more useful is worth trying. Certainly the demonstration method has been an important feature of the successful agricultural extension program carried on in America. This was particularly true in the early days when there were more skeptics than believers. In the developing countries, demonstration is likely to be for a long time the most effective tool of the extension worker. It is not bad to mention it—even in a university act.

14.7. SHORT COURSES AND OTHER ACTIVITIES

Arguments frequently arise about the proper level for the educational effort of a university. There is an inclination to be critical of educational offerings for people who would not be qualified for admission to the university. Fingers may be pointed and the remark made, "That institution is just a trade school." Experience has shown that a university can be many things to many people. It can have high academic standards and turn out people with fine professional training and at the same time teach typing, practical vegetable gardening, badminton, and weight lifting. It can give short courses to secretaries of cooperatives, rural youth, farmers, homemakers, rural bankers, and village headmen without losing its dignity or ability to educate at other levels. Many university acts and statutes make it perfectly clear that short courses for farmers and others shall be a responsibility of the university through cooperative effort of the extension director and the academic departments. The university should have authority to issue certificates to those completing non-college level work and diplomas to those completing college level work less in quantity than that required for a degree.

The law for the Rural University of Minas Gerais in Brazil states that the university shall coordinate, orient, and control intensive extension courses for farmers. The Mysore statutes require that the extension education council shall make recommendations for short courses for nonstudent rural people and that the director of extension shall supervise off-campus programs dealing with short courses for cultivators and training for nonstudents. The Orissa statutes state that the university shall, subject to conditions laid down by the academic council and approved by the board, offer diplomas in various courses including diploma courses for farmers. With proper planning, university facilities can be made available for much short course activity. Vacation periods and the interim between terms offer possibilities. If resources and staff are available, the institution may establish a center for short courses and many other activities which can operate throughout the year and accommodate several groups at the same time. The University of Nigeria, young as it is, has established such a center. Panchayat schools in India and short courses in the Institute of Administration at Zaria for all levels of local officialdom in Northern Nigeria are other examples. There is no limit to the good a university can do if it is willing to supply its extension and public service arm with resources, qualified personnel, and imagination.

CHAPTER – 15

Staff—Appointment
and Conditions of Service

In his book *The Colleges and the Courts Since 1950*,[1] M. M. Chambers states: "Members of the teaching, research, and administrative staffs of colleges and universities are employed under contracts for personal services. This is true in both private and public institutions. As to the inception, duration, termination or breech of the contract, the old and comparatively simple principles of the law of contracts are applicable. The simplicity and harshness of these rules are modified considerably in institutions having legally enforceable tenure regulations which specify in detail under what conditions a contract of indefinite duration may be entered into and terminated."

With few exceptions, university acts, statutes, or internal regulations require that the contract be written. The Jawaharlal Nehru Agricultural University Act, for example, provides that "Every salaried officer and teacher of the university shall be appointed under a written contract which shall be lodged with the vice-chancellor and a copy thereof furnished to the officer or teacher concerned." We believe that this is a necessary provision in a university act. University statutes should contain additional detail about the content of contracts, and the contracts themselves should be improved with time until they contain definite statements about most of the policies and conditions which apply to a staff member so that the extent and nature of the service required can be determined from his contract.

It should be clearly understood, and the contract should state, that appointment is not binding until it has been approved by the governing body. Many times prospective appointees assume there is a binding agreement when negotiations have been completed for their appointment. Certainly there is a strong moral obligation on

---

[1] M. M. Chambers, *The Colleges and the Courts Since 1950* (Danville, Ill.; The Interstate Printers and Publishers, Inc., 1964), p. 77.

the university at this point, and only infrequently would the board reject a recommendation from the chief administrative officer—but the possibility exists and legally it may lead to unhappy results. The written contract should refer to other policy documents such as the university statutes or general rules and regulations and state that applicable provisions are included in the terms of employment. Specifically, the contract should cover such items as (1) duration of the academic year for which services are required, (2) duration of the service period and vacation allowances when the period is other than for the academic year, (3) right of the appointee to engage in other occupations during the period between academic years, (4) salary and the method of its payment, (5) duration of the appointment, whether on indefinite tenure or for a specific period of time such as one year or two years, (6) the appointee's status with respect to university retirement system and insurance program, and (7) division of the appointee's time between teaching, research, extension, administrative, or other functions.

There should be maintained at the university, either by the secretary of the governing body or by the chief financial officer, a complete file of contracts with staff members. In addition to a contract file there should be maintained a personnel file for each staff member containing essential information about his experience, educational qualifications, and scholarly achievements.

Though faculty members are employed under contracts with the governing body, questions have been raised in the American courts about their status as public officers. Opinions have varied depending apparently on the legislative language creating the faculty positions and on the nature of the positions themselves. If the legislation states that a particular position can be abolished by the legislature, then, to a degree at any rate, the incumbent is like a public officer. Also, if the appointee occupies an administrative post in a university agency created by specific legislation, he may be regarded as an officer. The Arkansas Supreme Court so held regarding the vice-director of the agricultural experiment station. In holding that a faculty member was not an officer, the Supreme Court of West Virginia made the interesting remark that "A professor, learned and distinguished as he may be, is an employee of the board of regents."

As a matter of terminology, the writers generally employ the term "staff" to mean "academic staff." In proper context, however, it may mean "nonacademic staff" or "administrative staff." Some prefer not to use the term "staff" in connection with nonacademic personnel. Officers are simply those members of the administrative staff whose positions are established by the act or statutes. Some will also have an academic rank.

15.1. METHOD OF APPOINTMENT

If universities in the developing countries are to fulfill their obligations as instruments of progress, they must be able to hire qualified personnel and in so doing compete successfully with other institutions and government agencies. Their ability to do this hinges primarily on three things: salary, conditions of service, and appointment procedures which in every case permit them to search for the best man for the job. Certainly they should not be limited to prospects disclosed by advertising the post—though advertising may very well be one of the devices used to disclose prospective candidates. This section will deal with appointment of the academic staff. Chapter 4 deals with the selection of the governing body, Chapter 6 with appointment of the chief administrative officer, Chapter 9 with appointment of other officers of the university, and Chapter 16 with the hiring of nonacademic employees.

Though clear lines of distinction cannot be drawn between the various methods used by universities to procure staff members, five general methods are discernible: (1) a system under which recommendations originate in the department following the activity of a selection committee and are then transmitted through department head, dean, and chief administrative officer to the board for its approval—in this pattern there are several variations having to do with the composition of selection committees, the number of nominees for the position to be carried forward to different administrative levels, the position being filled (whether administrative or purely academic), and the final authority of the board; (2) the system commonly used in many developing countries under which the position is advertised and filled by the decision of a selection board or a committee which has final authority; (3) election by university and college councils through a secret ballot or through competitive examinations conducted by these bodies; (4) through civil service and operation of the seniority rule; (5) appointment by a government official or a government board.

Of these methods, the last two are least acceptable since the governing body and the faculties of the university are not involved in making recommendations. The third method does involve the faculty and frequently students, particularly in the Latin-American universities, but it incites more political activity than we feel is desirable in filling an academic post. The second method is not satisfactory because a selection board should not be the final authority in making academic appointments, even though the recommendations of the selection board are subject to approval by the governing body. Selection committees should be used and advertising should not be ruled out as one method of discovering candidates, but we believe the use of selection committees and of advertising should be part of a process which emphasizes "combing the field" to find the best man, which places more responsibility with administrative officers in the university, and which puts the whole selection process in motion again if there is disapproval of the recommended nominees at any administrative or at the board level. Hence, we favor the first general method. The proposed Ataturk University Act states it rather well: "Subject to the provisions of this act, the members of the staff of the university shall be selected by the head of the department, recommended by the dean, and appointed by the rector with the approval of the board." We would add to this the requirement that nominations be first made by an appropriate selection committee.

With few exceptions, legislation creating the newer universities in developing countries provides that academic positions shall be filled strictly on the basis of merit and that no appointment shall be made unless there are recommendations from an appropriate selection committee. We visualize the following steps in making an academic appointment and recommend that a university act permit this process and that the statutes establish it in sufficient detail to insure its use:

1. The appointment of an appropriate selection committee to recommend a panel of names to the administrative officer under whom the appointee will serve. Selection committees, boards or commissions are constituted in a variety of ways. Some are standing committees with both ex officio and appointive members. Some selection boards have membership outside the university; some consist entirely of nonuniversity members. Sometimes they contain members of the governing body. The Ahmadu Bello University Act lists seven categories of persons to serve on selection committees or boards and then makes different combinations of these categories

depending on the position being filled. In a few institutions the chief administrative officer is chairman of all selection committees for professors. This might work during the early years of the institution when the faculty is small, but we do not believe it is a good policy.

We propose that the selection committee should be advisory to the administrative officer in whose department or unit the appointee is to serve; hence, it should not be a standing committee but should be constituted each time a position is to be filled. We do not believe there should be governmental members on such committees. After all, appointment is university business. Likewise, the head of the unit in which the appointee is to serve and the unit head's administrative superior should not be members of such a committee. They will have their opportunity to consider the work of the committee, counsel with it, and, if need be, ask it to give further consideration to candidates. When another university officer such as the director of research or director of extension is concerned with a position, the statutes should require that the selection committee confer with him and that the head of the unit in which the appointment is being made also confer with him before carrying a name forward to his administrative superior.

We believe a selection committee of five members represents an optimum size. This will allow for some membership from the unit in which the appointee is to serve, some from the college, and some from other appropriate units of the university. We believe the administrative officer in whose unit the appointee will serve should have the privilege of constituting the selection committee. This means a department head should constitute the committee for appointment of a professor or position of lower academic rank, that a dean should appoint the selection committee for a department head, and that the chief administrative officer should appoint the selection committee for deans and other university officers who serve under him.

2. After the committee is appointed and has had a conference with the appointing authority, it should go to work. In a few instances university statutes or regulations require that consideration first be given to candidates who are members of the staff of the university. This is good practice whether or not it is stated in a statute or regulation, but at the same time the committee should be gathering information about possible candidates outside the uni-

versity and deciding whether or not it should use the advertising procedure to augment its search. Many things can be done to disclose possible candidates. An imaginative committee will think of them. After it has completed its consideration of all the possibilities which have come to its attention, it will present the top candidates —probably not more than three—to the appointing administrative officer.

3. The administrative officer and the committee should meet and discuss candidates to help the former decide which name he shall recommend. At an appropriate time, in the judgment of the appointing officer and the selection committee, candidates may be invited for informal interviews and to meet members of the staff. This procedure can be embarrassing if it is not properly handled. The situation is somewhat different from the one in which interviewing is part of the appointing process and for which formal arrangements are made. For example, regulations of the appointments and promotions committee of the University of Ibadan provide for a university assessment and interviewing panel which interviews and assesses all candidates for appointment.

4. The name of the candidate finally decided upon by the administrative officer shall be recommended through administrative echelons for board approval.

5. The board will either approve or disapprove. This holds also for administrative officers between the appointing officer and the board. If, for example, the chief administrative officer does not approve of the nomination by a dean for a department head, he should simply disapprove it, not appoint somebody else.

6. If a candidate is disapproved at the board level or at any other level, the original recommending authority should be notified so that the selection and recommendation process can take place again. This may involve either the same or a new selection committee depending on the discretion of the initial appointing authority.

We see no reason for involving the board in the selection process, whether it be an academic or administrative appointment. In some cases the board has the exclusive right to appoint the registrar and controller. We do not believe this represents good policy.

Some concessions may need to be made in view of the history and custom in a country. It may be necessary, for example, to secure a release for a professor whom the university wishes to appoint who is on the staff of another institution or has a government appointment. In some cases more reliance may have to be made on the advertising method because motives might be mistaken if letters are written and contacts made with large numbers of people and organizations in an attempt to disclose candidates. Proper constitution of the selection committee can help on this score. Evidence of a reluctance to break with all past practice is contained in the Udaipur University Act which states on the one hand that all appointments of teachers shall be strictly on the basis of merit and on the other that the head of a department shall be the senior professor, or if there is no senior professor, the senior associate professor. The Orissa University of Agriculture and Technology has a similar requirement with the proviso, however, that the department head may be chosen on a basis other than seniority if the president, for reasons to be stated in writing, so decides.

No matter what system is evolved and made firm in the university statutes, it will not succeed very well unless there is confidence in it. We believe confidence can be created by a system in which appointments are made without unnecessary delay and on a basis of merit, in which there is participation by the faculty in the selection process, and in which the governing body—though it is the final authority for all appointments—does not itself make any appointments except that of the chief administrative officer. A provision like that appearing in the statutes of one university that "If no one is acceptable the board shall take such action as is necessary," does not contribute to confidence in the appointment process.

15.2. QUALIFICATIONS

Should there be any provisions in a university act regarding the qualifications of staff members? How much detail should be contained in the university statutes? Without exception, the acts creating universities empower the governing body to employ the necessary number and kind of staff. Frequently the statement goes no further than this. Sometimes, however, it expresses the method of employment by stating that recommendations shall come from the chief administrative officer and that the board will approve or confirm. Sometimes the act names specific positions to be filled—director of research, director of extension, and comptroller, for example —but generally without any provisions in the act regarding qualifications. The right to employ staff would probably be implied even if not expressed in a university act.

Perhaps the most important objective to be accomplished through a provision in the university act is the elimination as qualifications of those things which have no bearing on the individual's ability. The West Pakistan Agricultural University Act provides that "No person shall be excluded from membership of any of the authorities on the sole ground of sex, race, creed, or class and it shall not be lawful for the university to impose upon any person any test relating to religious belief or professions so that he may be admitted as a teacher." The law creating the University of Wyoming stated that there shall be no sectarian or partisan test for employees and teachers. Both the university act and statutes of the University of the Philippines provide that no religious tests shall be applied and that religious opinions or affiliations of instructors shall not be subjects of inquiry. Though the language in university acts varies considerably in defining the factors which shall not disqualify, the intent seems clear, and such expressions in university acts are quite general in all parts of the world.

We believe the act should contain such a provision and that it should include an expression of factors which are not to disqualify —color, religion, political affiliation, caste, and sex, for example. In addition, we believe that citizenship and residence should not matter and that the university act should so state. There would be no question then about the right of the university to hire a professor from another state or region or from another country.

Sometimes university acts contain a provision about health examinations and physical fitness. Physical capacity to perform is always essential. We do not believe it requires expression in a university act. It should probably be in university statutes, not because it might otherwise be neglected, but because it then serves notice on all prospective staff members that they can be required to submit to physical examination. Some statutes contain lengthy and detailed requirements on this subject stating how the costs of different elements of the examination shall be handled, the dates by which particular examinations are to be completed, and the method of reporting the results. This kind of detail should be left to regulations of the university health department. If the university knowingly contracts with a professor who has a disability, it is likely to be bound. In one American institution a crippled professor was knowingly hired. Later, when the university decided that his employment was not a good idea, it failed in an attempt to discharge him during the contract term.

With respect to qualifications which staff members should possess, most university acts provide that recommendations on qualifications shall be made by the academic council. Some provide for approval of such recommendations by the chief administrative officer and by the governing body. Frequently there is a provision permitting a departure from stated qualifications when such is felt necessary and is approved by the chief administrative officer. We feel that both these provisions should be in a university act—that is, one empowering the academic council to make recommendations regarding qualifications and another empowering the chief administrative officer to depart from these on the advice of an appropriate university authority. In many countries good staff members are scarce, particularly for certain posts requiring training in areas which have not been popular with students studying abroad. In the beginning it may be necessary to depart from fixed standards in order to find persons to fill certain positions. It is possible, after all, to express qualifications in such a way that no one can meet them.

Statutes of the University of the Philippines require that every recommendation to the board of regents for the appointment or promotion of staff members shall contain a complete statement of their qualifications, training, service, publications, research, and other matters which may be required by rules of the university. Statutes of the West Pakistan Agricultural University are quite detailed. Contained in them are such phrases as the following:

Good basic degree in the basic arts and sciences
High rank from a recognized university
High specialist qualifications
Ten years of successful teaching or similar experience
Demonstrated ability to conduct original research and to interpret research through publications
Acceptable personal characteristics and good moral character
Three years of successful teaching or similar experiences as lecturer
Potential research and teaching ability
Evidence of ability to identify and solve problems in agricultural education and to stimulate and guide postgraduate students
A thorough knowledge of agriculture and rural conditions

However, there is a saving statement at the end of all this detail:

"The prescribed qualifications shall be treated as guide lines and while advertising posts it shall be indicated that the university authorities may select a candidate who does not possess the stated qualifications but is regarded as otherwise eminently suited for the position."

Many statutes express an educational requirement in terms of degrees held. Some require a minimum number of years of experience of a defined type—for example, the statutes of the Universidad Agraria at La Molina require an appropriate degree and five years' experience for a professor, a professional title or appropriate academic degree and three years' experience for an associate professor, and an appropriate degree plus one year of experience for an assistant professor. The proposed Ataturk University Act contains similar provisions except that the experience requirements for professor, associate professor, and assistant professor are ten, seven, and three years respectively. We do not believe the act or statutes should contain this kind of detail. Statutes of the University of Illinois provide that "In determining appointments to and salaries and promotion of the academic staff, special consideration shall be given to those of the following factors which are applicable: (1) teaching ability and performance, (2) research ability and achievement, and (3) general usefulness or promise thereof to the university." We believe this is an appropriate kind of statement for the university statutes.

15.3. DURATION AND AMOUNT OF SERVICE— RESIGNATIONS

Should all initial appointments be for only one year and on a trial basis regardless of the rank of the appointee? Some institutions have such a policy, but competition for good staff members may bring compromise. After a trial period—if there is one—for how long should contracts of appointment be written? In some institutions professors are appointed for five-year periods, associate professors for three, and assistant professors for two. The acquisition of "indefinite tenure" depends on rules which vary from one institution to another. These are discussed in the next section. It is not customary to give those serving in administrative positions "indefinite tenure," though some such persons may have a professorial rank in the university and have "indefinite tenure" for this reason. However, the statutes of Harvard University provide that deans and certain other major administrative officers are appointed without express limitation of time. The term of office of the chief administrative officer is discussed in Chapter 4. In some institutions department heads and deans are appointed for one- or two-year terms with the expectation that they will be reappointed. Initial terms are likely to be longer when these officials are elected by a university or college council; otherwise, the politics behind the election process would be likely to produce a rapid turnover. The Peru National Universities Act, for example, provides a three-year term for such officers following their election by college councils.

In many American institutions, administrative officers are appointed for two years. Statutes of the University of Illinois provide, for example, that "The dean shall be elected biennially by the board of trustees on nomination of the president. On the occasion of each election, the president shall have the advice of the executive committee of the faculty concerned." The intent of this statute is to give the faculty a voice in determining whether or not a dean should be continued in office. We recommend such a provision in the university statutes. More important than the exact period of service specified in a contract are the provisions on appointment, reappointment, and termination. Statutory rules which preclude politics, both internal and external, from these processes will help insure the continuity of good staff members.

Contracts of employment should state what is meant by a year's service. A professor was employed at the University of Illinois for a year—without further specification. The university made no claim to his services during the summer months between academic years but reduced his pay because he was employed by another institution during those months. The issue was litigated and in an 1898 decision the Supreme Court of Illinois held for the professor. University of Illinois statutes now provide: "The terms of employment of the academic and administrative staff as defined in the University of Illinois statutes shall be explicitly stated by the nominating officer indicating that the services are required for the academic year, twelve months, the summer session, or other stated periods."

Hours of service required from the academic staff are left to rules and regulations, custom, general understanding, or the staff member himself—though statutes of the University of the Philippines do contain some specific provisions. They provide that full-time members of the faculty shall be on duty a minimum of forty hours each week—the only exceptions being faculty members in the conservatory of music and in the school of fine arts and architecture, for whom twenty-four hours per week suffice. There is further provision for either punching a time clock or signing in and out. We do not believe this kind of detail should be included in university statutes or even rules or regulations applying to the academic staff. Perhaps we are not being wholly realistic, but our reason is that the nature of the academic endeavor, whether teaching or research, is such that it should be engaged in only by those who require no schedule of minimum hours to induce full performance.

Many university acts and statutes contain no provisions on resignation, though the right to resign may be implied from portions of the act and statutes dealing with appointments and conditions of service of the staff. Where general conditions of service apply, as in many of the Indian universities, rules and regulations do exist, and unless a staff member secures a release before he leaves one institution or agency to go to another, he may sacrifice all the security and benefits he has accumulated from previous service. Where it prevails, this is a fact which should be recognized in university statutes or rules. In many institutions, resignation seems to be accepted as a matter of right with the implication that some reasonable notice should be given. However, statutes of the University of the Philippines contain these rather detailed provisions:

No resignation presented by any member of the faculty shall be considered unless notice thereof has been given to the president through the dean or director concerned, at least sixty days before it takes effect. No resignation shall take effect until the services of a successor or a temporary substitute have been secured. Failure to report to duty six months after appointment without the president's written permission automatically cancels the appointment. The above rules shall not apply to resignations on account of serious illness or when in the judgment of the president it is in the interest of the university that the resignation be accepted to take effect immediately. Acceptance of a resignation does not carry with it any waiver of the financial or property obligations of the person concerned to the university.

The Jawaharlal Nehru Agricultural University Act provides that officers, except deans, may resign by letter addressed to the registrar. The resignation becomes effective in three months unless accepted sooner by the authority competent to fill the position.

Problems are not likely to arise when the resignation takes effect at the end of a regular contract period of employment. Regulations for the internal administration of Purdue University provide that "An appointment may be terminated by the appointee by resignation, but it is expressly agreed that an appointment will not be re-signed after July 1 for the succeeding academic year without permission of and upon conditions approved by the president of the university." When a staff member submits an immediate resignation, questions arise about his right to salary and the right of the university to seek a remedy for breach of contract. Judging from the lack of litigation, universities apparently seldom seek such a remedy. There are, however, American court cases holding that when a staff member submits an immediate resignation the university is not liable for further salary payments. Resignation at the end of a regular term can sometimes be accomplished by not signing a contract for the next year. It has become standard procedure in many institutions to mail contracts to staff members and ask to have a signed copy returned before some deadline date prior to the beginning of the next academic year. This is a good practice.

We do not feel that there is need for a statute containing details on resignations. Internal business procedural rules incorporated in the contract should suffice. If something more is desired, both the Purdue and Philippine statutes are sound. Whether a resignation occurs at the end of a regular term or during the term, it is presumed there will have been conversations between the staff member and his department head or other administrative superior and the institution will not be wholly unprepared for the shock of losing him.

Competition for good staff members has led some large universities to inquire into the reasons why staff members resign. Committees called "Exit-Interview Committees" or other indicative names have been established, either by the university administration or by the academic council, to interview staff members who leave the service of the university. Though in a new institution with a small faculty this may seem like an unnecessary procedure, we recommend it as a matter which should receive timely consideration by the academic council and the chief administrative officer.

15.4. TENURE

Simply defined, "tenure" means the right to hold. The term is commonly used with reference to rights in land and rights in an office or position of employment. In academic parlance it means the right to hold a position of appointment or employment in the university, and academic usage has clothed it with the additional meaning of "permanent." So when a professor is asked if he has tenure, he is really being asked if he has permanent tenure. This raises two questions: how "permanent" is permanent tenure, and how is it acquired?

In a sense, the purpose of academic tenure is to give academic employees of the university the insulation from political and other whims which government employees enjoy through civil service. Though the reasons may differ, the object is the same. Academic tenure is inseparably linked with due process and academic freedom, both of which are discussed in the sections which follow. In this section we shall discuss some of the statutes and regulations which have been adopted by universities and those policies which we believe should be embodied in the law.

Why should a university have tenure rules or regulations? Because in the absence of rules, tenure would be uncertain—at least it would be in American universities. In *Tenure in American Higher Education*,[2] the authors state: "Legal protection of tenure is insubstantial. Judicial reluctance to decree specific performance of 'personal service' contracts, charter provisions authorizing discharge at will, disclaimer and finality clauses, confusing uncertainty in the written plans of some institutions, the complete absence of formal plans in others, the vagueness and inconclusiveness of termination criteria, and retention of ultimate decisional authority by most governing boards—all underscore the hazards of reliance on judicial protection of tenure." American courts have held that the well-publicized policy of the American Association of University Professors on tenure and the customs of institutions in the accrediting organization to which a university belonged were of no avail to a professor in the absence of a statement in his contract or in university statutes, rules, or regulations. Statutes of the University of the Philippines state that repeated appointments do not create a presumption of tenure. As a principle of contract law, this is no doubt sound in the absence of provisions under which repeated appointments do lead to tenure.

There may be general laws or provisions in the university act

---

[2] Clark Byse and Louis Joughin, *Tenure in American Higher Education* (Ithaca, N. Y.: Cornell University Press, 1959), p. 136.

itself limiting the ability of the university to establish tenure—a law stating, for example, that the board cannot enter contracts of employment which extend for more than one year and that such contracts can be terminated without notice or cause. Certainly such harsh provisions should not appear in the university act or in a general law which might apply to university personnel (in case they are regarded as government servants—a position against which we will argue later).

What can universities provide in their statutes or rules to create a desirable tenure situation for the academic staff? Schemes which have been devised and placed in the statutes vary from the simple to the complex. The statutes of Harvard University provide that "All officers of instruction are subject to removal by the corporation only for grave misconduct or neglect of duty. Subject to the foregoing, professors and associate professors and deans and certain other major administrative officers are appointed without express limitation of time unless otherwise specified." This varies from the usual provision in that deans and administrative officers are generally not accorded indefinite tenure. The Peru National Universities Act provides that "Teaching in the state universities is a public career and the teachers shall enjoy the benefits which attach to the national magistrate and to other civil servants." The law further provides that professors shall be confirmed in their posts after the first year of teaching if their performance has been satisfactory, but such confirmation is good only for five years, after which they are subject to reelection by the college council. The bylaws of Cornell University provide that professors and associate professors shall be elected by the board by ballot for an indefinite term, or if without ballot, for a definite term of years. Assistant professors, research associates, and extension associates are appointed for terms of three years, senior research associates and senior extension associates for terms of five years. Other academic ranks are appointed for one year. Maximum periods of service within the assistant professor and instructor grades are also established.

The University of the Philippines Statutes establish a pattern under which instructors are appointed for one year, after which they may be reappointed for another one- or two-year term. At the end of three years, their contract automatically terminates unless a temporary appointment is renewed or they are reappointed with tenure. Assistant professors are appointed initially for three years, after which the same kinds of decisions and possibilities exist as for instructors. Professors and associate professors are appointed initially for a five-year period. After that they may be reappointed for a stated period or on permanent tenure. The University Code of Purdue University provides that "Except where appointment is for a limited term, it shall continue from year to year without further notice. Such appointment may be terminated by the university for causes relating to the conduct or the efficiency of the appointee or because of the discontinuance of the department or work to which the appointment is related." This applies to all academic ranks but leaves with the dean, department head, or other unit head the discretion to recommend appointment for a limited term or let it continue from year to year. This does not seem a satisfactory arrangement from the standpoint of the staff. The statutes of Columbia University state that "Professors and associate professors are officers appointed for full-time service without a stated term." The president may recommend appointments for a stated number of years.

University of Illinois Statutes provide that appointments as professor or associate professor shall be for indefinite terms and that assistant professors, instructors, and research associates shall be appointed for definite terms under a seven-year probationary period, following which, providing adequate notice is given as described in the statutes, they may be discharged. If such notice is not given, they acquire indefinite tenure in their positions. They may, of course, be promoted to the next rank. These provisions represent the substance of the policy advocated by the American Association of University Professors which has been adopted with variations by many universities. Some institutions have an "up-or-out" policy— which means that if the individual is not promoted at the end of a probationary period, he must be dismissed. We feel it is wise to allow the additional alternative of retaining such a person in his current rank but on indefinite tenure. In the end, the quality of the staff will depend on the good judgment and decisiveness of department heads and deans. Requiring that a man be discharged if he is not promoted is, in a sense, excusing his administrative superior from making a timely judgment about him. Administrative superiors should not be excused from making such judgments; it is one of their important functions.

In summary, we recommend the following: (1) that the university act require the establishment of a sound tenure policy, (2) that the university statutes establish such a policy involving (a) permanent tenure for some or all of the professorial ranks and (b) permanent tenure for other ranks after a stated probationary period and following failure to give notice of termination, (3) determination of tenure for the staff of institutions brought into the university as constituent colleges as though the college had always been a part of the university—thus giving its staff members the same time advantages as those appointed directly by the university, (4) a definite statement about the administrative staff (the policy is generally against indefinite tenure; we believe this is best, though if an administrator has an academic title he should retain tenure in the academic position), (5) if there is any likelihood that academic posts in the university will be considered as "government offices" with the result that an incumbent would no longer have a job or any contractual rights in case the position is abolished, there should be a provision in the university act declaring that posts in the university are not government offices. If this last is in conflict with the application of civil service or of a policy such as that expressed in the Peru National Universities Act that "Teaching in the state universities is a public career," then it may be necessary to thresh out some compromise at the legislative level. We believe that teaching and doing research in the university are vitally important callings in the developing countries and that they deserve the protection, encouragement, and continuity of effort which indefinite tenure can give.

15.5. ACADEMIC FREEDOM

Academic freedom is the right to pursue truth. It applies both to institutions and to members of the academic staff within institutions. A university should not be an island of conformity but rather a mainland of stability in which eruptions can take place without destroying the institution. In a 1956 United States Supreme Court decision,[3] Mr. Justice Frankfurter said, "It is the business of the university to provide that atmosphere which is most conducive to speculation, experiment, and creation. It is an atmosphere in which there prevail the four essential freedoms of a university—to determine for itself on academic grounds who may teach, what may be taught, how it shall be taught, and who may be admitted to study."

---

[3] Sweezey v. New Hampshire, 354, U. S. 234, 250 (1957).

In the same case, Chief Justice Warren said, "To impose any strait-jacket upon the intellectual leaders in our colleges and universities would imperil the future of our nation. No field of education is so thoroughly comprehended by man that new discoveries cannot yet be made. Particularly is that true in the social sciences where few if any principles are accepted as absolutes. Scholarship cannot flourish in an atmosphere of suspicion and distrust. Teachers and students must always remain free to inquire, to study, and to evaluate, to gain new maturity and understanding. Otherwise, our civilization will stagnate and die." Sir Eric Ashby states that "Academic freedom is not a personal privilege. It is an essential freedom to enable university teachers to do their jobs with integrity. It guarantees no teacher will be victimized in any way by reason of what he teaches or writes unless it is contrary to the laws of the country. The strongest argument for it is not the appeal to tradition; it is the appeal to empiricism. Where academic freedom is disallowed, universities always fail." [4]

The Encyclopedia of Social Sciences states: "Academic freedom is the freedom of the teacher or the research worker in higher institutions of learning to investigate and discuss the problems of his science without interference from political or ecclesiastical authority or from the administrative officials of the institution in which he is employed unless his methods are found by qualified bodies of his own profession to be clearly incompetent or contrary to professional ethics." [5] The *Statement of Principles of the American Association of University Professors* asserts that

(a) The teacher is entitled to full freedom in research and in the publication of the results subject to the adequate performance of his other academic duties. (b) The teacher is entitled to freedom in the classroom in discussing his subject, but he should be careful not to introduce into his teaching controversial matter which has no relation to his subject. (c) The college or university teacher is a citizen, a member of a learned profession, and an officer in an educational institution. When he speaks or writes as a citizen he should be free from institutional censorship or discipline, but his special position in the community imposes special obligations.

Perhaps this is enough definition. What has been provided in university acts and statutes?

----

[4] Sir Eric Ashby, "A Contribution to the Dialogue on African Universities," *Univ. Quart.* (Dec. 1965), p. 82.

[5] I *Encyclopedia of Social Sciences* (1030), 385.

While academic freedom, subject to some variations in definition and meaning, is a principle which has received universal recognition in the university world, legislative and statutory expressions on the subject are scanty. For a number of reasons, one no doubt being the "closeness" of American public universities to the governmental structure of the state and to the groups and agencies which they serve, one finds more statements in American university statutes than in those of foreign universities. In our search through the acts and statutes of universities in the developing countries we found only two references. The Peru National Universities Act states that the colleges and professional schools shall assure free teaching and they shall set forth conditions for exercising it. Statutes of the University of the Philippines are quite comprehensive on the subject. They guarantee the teacher freedom in the exposition of his own subject in the classroom or in addresses or publications—but there are prohibitions against inculcating sectarian tenets in teaching, discussing in the classroom controversial topics not pertinent to the course of study that is being pursued, and conduct which would give doubt concerning fitness for his position.

Many American universities incorporate in their statutes the definition of academic freedom contained in the official statement of the American Association of University Professors. Statutes of the University of Illinois state that

It is the policy of the university to maintain and encourage full freedom within the law of inquiry, discourse, teaching, research and publication and to protect any member of the academic staff against influences from within or without the university which would restrict him in the exercise of these freedoms in his area of scholarly interest. In his role as a citizen the faculty member may exercise the same freedom as other citizens without institutional censorship or discipline. He should be mindful, however, that accuracy, forthrightness, and dignity befit his association with the university and his position as a man of learning and that the public may judge his profession and the university by his conduct and utterances.

These statutes also give the faculty member a right to a hearing before the university senate committee on academic freedom and tenure if he feels that he is being denied the full enjoyment of the academic freedom which it is the policy of the university to maintain and encourage.

In the absence of legal provision, what preserves academic freedom? It exists because of tradition and because it resides inherently in the functions of teaching, learning, and research. The spirit of academic freedom can be created within an institution without law; it cannot, conversely, be created by it—but it can be preserved by law. In England, in Latin America, in many parts of the world, academic freedom exists without express stipulation. In America, where statements on the subject have apparently meant more, the courts have had little to say about it and many times have scarcely recognized its existence. However, when an institution has a definite policy stated in its act, statutes, regulations, or perhaps partly in all three, courts would be bound to take it into account. We believe the university act should contain a statement that principles of academic freedom shall be recognized throughout the university. University statutes should contain provisions embodying ideas like those expressed in the statement by the American Association of University Professors, the University of Illinois Statutes, and the statutes of the University of the Philippines. No doubt there are other sources just as good, perhaps even better, but we believe these contain the essentials. The exact wording of the statute must be accomplished in the light of conditions prevailing in the country without compromising basic principles.

Though the university may guarantee academic freedom to the individual through either written or unwritten policies, it may have its institutional freedom curtailed by unwise legislation. The right to foster and encourage organizations, espouse student movements, and invite speakers and groups to use university facilities should rest with the judgment of the university. The pressures of the times frequently lead legislatures to respond to what they regard as a public demand for control of the university's freedom in matters like these. Students and their organizations should also enjoy academic freedom. This is discussed in Chapter 17. It should be pointed out that university autonomy is not academic freedom. A university can have the desired autonomy but, through its own internal policy, deny academic freedom. Furthermore, the enjoyment of academic freedom may vary between faculties in the university or even between departments. This is another reason why a firm statement on the subject in the university statutes can stand as a protection to any staff member regardless of his department or college. It should be pointed out, too, that the university is expected to operate within the general charter or framework provided by legislation. It is not denial of institutional academic freedom to hold the university to the major objectives expressed in the act.

15.6. DISCHARGE AND SUSPENSION—CAUSE AND PROCEDURE—ACADEMIC DUE PROCESS

Who has the power to discharge a faculty member? And in what manner and for what reasons? One-half of the fifty-one American colleges and universities whose charters and basic laws were analyzed by Edward C. Elliott and M. M. Chambers[6] in 1934 provide that the governing body shall have the power to discharge. Interesting variations were disclosed in the language giving the boards this right. A breakdown discloses the following:

Six boards were given the right to remove at pleasure with no statement about cause, notice, or hearing.

Eight boards were given the right to discharge "when the interests of the university require."

One legislative provision stated that the board has "full power to suspend and remove."

Another stated that the board has the right to "displace and remove" as it deems the interests of the college require.

The board of the University of Arkansas was given the right to conduct a hearing and compel testimony with judicial power to issue process and compel witnesses to appear.

In three cases the board was required to vote—in one case a majority being sufficient; in another, two-thirds being required; and in another, a majority but with the safeguards to the faculty member that the board could vote only when (a) two-thirds of the board members are present, (b) due and timely notice has been served, and (c) the vote is taken at a succeeding or adjourned meeting following the one in which the matter was introduced.

Except for those boards which were empowered to discharge "when the interests of the university required," further specification of cause was made in only four instances. These were:

"For misconduct or breach of the laws of the institution."

"For misconduct, neglect of duty, breach of the law of the institution, or for any reason the majority may deem sufficient."

----
[6] Edward C. Elliott and M. M. Chambers, *Charters and Basic Laws of Selected American Universities and Colleges* (New York: The Carnegie Foundation, 1934).

"For good and sufficient reasons."

"For cause."

What is the position of a staff member when the board is given an unqualified right to discharge? It seems that unless there are implied constitutional safeguards of due process, the right is absolute and no cause need be stated. Many boards which have been given an absolute power have nevertheless developed statutes or internal rules which do provide for notice, hearing, and other safeguards. American courts have varied in their opinion about the validity of such statutes, some arguing that they are in derogation of the board's absolute right. The better, though not necessarily the predominant, view is that if the board establishes safeguards, they then become a part of the contract of every staff member and the staff member can insist that they be observed as a contractual right. Certainly the move in American universities is toward establishment of rather thorough safeguards under the general heading of due process. If there is doubt about the validity of such provisions, an amendment of legislation vesting the absolute right in the board should be sought.

We believe the board as the ultimate authority regarding university affairs must have the right to discharge, but that the act giving the right should state that it may be exercised only for cause and under procedures to be established by university statute. The act should further state that cause shall be defined by statute. This would make it the duty of the university to develop procedures and define cause and would make it possible to revise both in keeping with improved practices and procedures.

How should cause be defined and what procedures should be established? The University of the Philippines Act provides that no member of the faculty, officer, or employee shall be suspended or removed except for cause after an investigation and hearing. It states that if the conduct of a teacher in his classroom or elsewhere gives rise to doubts concerning his fitness for his position, the question shall in all cases be submitted to a committee of the faculty and that in addition he shall be entitled to a full and open hearing before the board of regents if he desires. It also provides that the president may suspend or remove administrative officers after a hearing but without prejudice to their right to appeal to the board of regents. The Punjab Agricultural University Statutes state that no penalty, dismissal, removal, or reduction in pay shall be imposed unless the employee has been given a reasonable opportunity to refute the action taken against him. It further requires that the cause or causes shall be reduced to a definite charge which shall be communicated in writing to the employee. Hearing, the right of cross-examination, and other procedural safeguards are provided. However, these statutes deny the right of the employee who has been charged to engage legal counsel.

The West Pakistan Agricultural University Statutes list several causes—some reasonable, some in our opinion not reasonable—which may give rise to any one of a number of penalties. Among them are (a) inefficiency, (b) infirmity of mind or body, (c) indifference to duty, (d) exercising unwholesome influence on the academic, moral or corporate life of the university, (e) an assumption that the staff member is corrupt because he or his immediate family possesses resources or property disproportionate to his known sources of income or because he has assumed a style of living beyond his ostensible means. Another cause is listed—engaging in a trade, business, or occupation which in the opinion of the appointing authority interferes with the performance of his duties and without securing prior permission of the appointing authority in writing as required. Actually this amounts to breach of contract. Any violation of laws, statutes, or regulations which are incorporated as part of the contract might amount to breach and hence constitute cause for dismissal unless lesser remedies such as reprimand or suspension are provided.

The Ahmadu Bello University Statutes provide that "good cause" shall mean conviction of a criminal offense involving moral turpitude, gross misconduct, and inability to carry out duties. Statutes of the Universidad Agraria in Peru state that causes for separation are neglect of university duties, fulfillment of duties with notorious deficiency, conviction of crimes for which one loses his civil rights, moral incapacity, or use of the teaching position to endorse a candidate in a political campaign. Statutes of the University of Illinois provide that tenure may be terminated by honorable retirement, acceptance of resignation, or dismissal for due cause. They further state that due causes shall be deemed to exist only if

(1) a faculty member has been grossly neglectful of or grossly inefficient in the performance of his university duties and functions or (2) with all due regard for the freedoms and protections provided in the

statutes, the faculty member's performance of his university duties and functions or his extramural conduct is found to demonstrate clearly and convincingly that he can no longer be relied upon to perform his university duties and functions in a manner consonant with professional standards of competence and responsibility.

What should constitute cause? Opinions vary considerably. If the definition is wordy and general, it becomes meaningless. If it is too particularized, it may and probably will deny academic freedom. If moral turpitude is a cause, it immediately induces a conflict of opinion about the state of current morality and the right of one, particularly a staff member of a university, to advocate change. We believe that if the statutes go further than to say "for good cause"—which then makes the matter subject to review by a court—they should simply say, "for failure to perform his functions for the university" or "for incapacity to perform." This latter would permit evidence of conduct to be admitted as a factor but only as a factor in determining if the staff member is incapable of performing.

What procedures should be established by university statutes? What constitutes academic due process? Though "due process" has come to be a technical phrase in the United States, the principle, whatever name it is given, is recognized in all legal systems. It means simply the procedures designed to protect the individual and produce the best judgment when his security and freedom are threatened. In some countries it might be called natural or fundamental justice. It should involve less formality than court proceedings but enough formality to bring out the facts and permit them to be challenged in an orderly way. The purpose is to protect the staff member and the institution at the same time. The American courts have held that even in the absence of any prescribed procedure, certain reasonable procedures will be implied. It has been held, for example, that there was not due process when proceedings of the governing body were irregular according to its own rules, when a quorum was not present, when improper notices were sent, when proceedings were hasty and insufficient, when there was unequal treatment of adversary parties, when the board failed to take a vote, and when it did not delay the vote until an adjourned meeting as prescribed in its own rules.

What steps can be provided by the university statutes that will promote due process? We believe there should be provisions on the following:

1. A requirement that conciliation be attempted before any charges are filed. This should be the first step. Many problems can be solved if the parties confront each other frankly in the beginning.

2. A requirement that if charges are to be made they must be made by the chief administrative officer and that he will not make them until he has consulted with an advisory committee of the faculty. Preferably this should be an elected committee—it may be either standing or ad hoc. This permits discussion and a certain amount of "cooling off," following which a settlement of the matter may be made without commencing discharge procedures.

3. Proceedings should be instituted by delivery to the staff member of an adequate statement of charges which also gives him relevant information about applicable laws and statutes, procedures to be followed, his rights, and the time for a reply to the charges.

4. A staff member should have the right to both legal and academic counsel.

5. His cause should be heard by a faculty committee, preferably an elected committee. It should be stated that the burden of proof is on the chief administrative officer to make a case for dismissal.

6. There should be requirements regarding the hearing procedure, the calling of witnesses, the making of a record.

7. An appeal should be provided to the governing body.

What are the rights of a faculty member who does not have tenure? Though there is no duty to renew his contract, can he make a case if he can show that the failure to renew stemmed from improper considerations? Admittedly it is more difficult for the nontenure appointee to make a case, but even in his situation due process is implied. If the institution chooses to give reasons, they should be the right ones. If the appointee can show that prejudice, malice, or gross misinformation motivated the decision not to reemploy him, he should be permitted to throw his case into the channels of due process as discussed above, after which the same rights would apply.

We have mentioned earlier the possibility that an appointee may be regarded as holding an office, in which case he can lose his job through abolition of the office. If this happens, there is no recourse. But a converse situation may arise: if the attempt is to remove the officer rather than abolish the position, he will have the same rights as other government officers. These may be controlled by a civil service act. Conceivably he could have protection regardless of provisions in the university act and university statutes. In another section we argue against the application of civil service to the academic staff of a university; hence, we do not feel that this avenue should be relied upon either as a means of protecting or getting rid of a staff member. In some countries, states, or regions, there may be a constitutional right to due process or its equivalent applicable to universities. If so, this would apply to the administrative staff and to the academic staff without permanent tenure as well as to the academic staff with permanent tenure.

It should be mentioned that many statutes provide for penalties other than discharge; suspension is a common one and generally means that the staff member will continue to be paid until the outcome of dismissal proceedings is known. Other penalties which have been provided are reprimand, censure, reduction in rank, compulsory retirement, reassignment of duties, withholding of salary increases, and withholding of promotion. A few institutions even impose fines or monetary penalties. We believe dismissal, suspension, and official reprimand are the only appropriate penalties. If the staff member is not discharged, his promotion and salary increases should depend on performance; they should not be withheld as a penalty. There is something about a reprimand, too, that smacks of bad human relations. But as a means through which the administration can dissociate itself from statements or actions of a staff member without discharging or suspending him, it should be provided in the statutes. Even so, we would point out that a university gains stature not by reacting immediately to public complaints about its staff members but by protecting unpopular staff members and assuring them that conformity is not a prerequisite of security.

There is some earlier discussion of removal of staff members in Chapter 5. Removal of the chief administrative officer is discussed in Chapter 6.

15.7. GRIEVANCES AND DISPUTES OVER TERMS OF EMPLOYMENT

In the preceding section we discussed the legislative and statutory procedures and safeguards having to do with the discharge or imposition of other penalities on a staff member. What recourse should there be for the staff member who has complaints against the university? The Uttar Pradesh Agricultural University Act provides that "Any dispute arising out of contract between the university and any officer or teacher of the university shall on the request of the officer or teacher concerned be referred to a tribunal of arbitration consisting of one member nominated by the board, one member nominated by the officer or teacher concerned, and an umpire appointed by the chancellor." This statutory provision declares that the decision of the tribunal shall be final and that no suit shall lie in a civil court. Such requests are deemed to be submissions to arbitration and the general arbitration act of the state of Uttar Pradesh applies.

The statutes of Southern Illinois University provide that

In case of difficulty or complaint, each member of the university faculty and staff shall have the right to use the channels provided for the settlement of grievances. In general, personnel problems should be solved within the organization at the level at which they arise, and in no case should individuals outside the university internal organization be asked to pass on such difficulty until established university channels have been exhausted. Academic staff members may appeal through the regular academic channels . . . if any member of the university faculty staff feels he is unjustly or unfairly treated, he is privileged to file a formal complaint with the president of the university who shall refer it promptly to the appropriate officer in the usual administrative channels for hearing and adjudication, personally or by committee appointed for the purpose by the administrative officer to whom the case is referred. The decision or recommendation for dealing with the case shall be filed with the president of the university. If the staff member concerned is not content with the decision thus reached, he is privileged to request the president to hear the case and to render a decision. If the staff member is still dissatisfied, he may appeal in writing from the decision of the president to the board of trustees, and the president shall present the appeal to the board at its next regular meeting. The board of trustees shall then determine whether it shall hear the case or refuse to take action upon it.

While this constitutes an excellent statement of the procedure for exhausting administrative channels, it contains no viable method for giving the staff member assistance in exhausting the channels or in providing for an impartial consideration of his complaint outside of administrative channels.

Statutes of the University of Illinois provide for election of a faculty advisory committee of nine members by the faculty of the university from its membership. This is a standing committee on which members serve three-year terms. Not more than two members from the same college can serve at the same time. The statutes state that "The functions of the committee shall be to provide for the orderly voicing of suggestions for the good of the university, for affording added recourse for the consideration of grievances, and for furnishing a channel for direct and concerted communication with administrative offices of the university, its colleges, schools, institutes, divisions, and other administrative units on matters of interest or concern to the academic staff or any member of it." This statute not only recognizes the need for an impartial body to assist a staff member, but it also recognizes that there may be general dissatisfaction on the part of many staff members about particular policies or the lack of policies. The committee is empowered to make suggestions to the administration of the university regarding such feelings.

Rules of the faculty advisory committee provide that a staff member may appeal to any member of the committee for help and assistance. It is not essential that a full-scale hearing be held every time a complaint comes to a committee member's attention. Informality, frankness, friendliness, free communication, and no publicity are keys to the successful settlement of many issues which could otherwise become local celebrated causes. A provision like that contained in many of the Indian agricultural university acts under which a staff member's complaint can be taken to the chancellor of the university for final decision is not very helpful. Since the chancellor is ordinarily the governor, the staff member is not likely to feel that he and the chief administrative officer of the university have equal status before such a tribunal. A few university acts provide that the chancellor can constitute an arbitration committee. This is somewhat better, though such a committee would not be expected to view the staff member's complaint as impartially as a committee elected by the academic council or senate.

We recommend a university statute providing for the election by the faculty of a grievance or arbitration committee. It should be a standing committee and its main function that of helping a staff member exhaust administrative channels for a remedy when he feels he is not being treated fairly. Emphasis should be placed on this role of the committee and its rules or bylaws should embody the concept that existing channels first be explored. A timid staff member who feels he has been wronged may be unwilling to approach even his own administrative superior, where the problem might be settled. A belligerent staff member may wish to make a public outcry, ask for political intervention, and go directly to the governing body without consulting with anyone in administration. We feel that a standing committee of sufficient size elected by the faculty on a rotating basis is better than ad hoc committees or small arbitration committees selected for specific causes. It can achieve more status and is more likely to be used.

15.8. APPLICATION OF CIVIL SERVICE

In a 1918 decision the Supreme Court of Illinois exempted the academic staff of the University of Illinois from the application of state civil service. The early laws relating to Massachusetts State College provided that "Employees of the college shall be exempt from civil service laws." The University of the Philippines Act states that "Professors and other regular instructors in the university shall be exempt as such from any civil service examination or regulation as a requisite to appointment." But the Peru National Universities Act provides that "Teaching in the state universities is a public career and the teachers shall enjoy the benefits which attach to the national magistrate and to the other civil servants." Likewise, members of the staff in government colleges in India have traditionally been civil servants subject to government promotion and salary scales.

With the establishment of the new agricultural universities and their separate boards of management, an attempt has been made to get away from civil service for the administrative and academic staff. There may be some benefits to the faculty through inclusion in a state civil service system as intimated in the Peru National Universities Act. If this can be done without impairing the right of the university to hire the best man for a job and to make assignments and promotions within the university strictly on the basis of merit and, further, if salary scales are not tied to government civil service scales, then this may not be objectionable. We feel, however, that the university act should state that the academic and administrative staff of the university shall not be subject to government civil service. The rapid turnover in positions, the inappropriateness of assignments which frequently occur, the seniority rule, and inability to attract or retain outstanding men through salary arrangements all argue against the use of civil service for the academic and administrative staff of a university. Special provisions may be necessary when new staff members come to the university from civil service positions in government. They may have certain rights which should be protected. The application of civil service to other employees is discussed in Chapter 16.

15.9. EMPLOYMENT OF RELATIVES

The Peru National Universities Act provides that "Husband and wife shall not both belong to the executive personnel of the university nor shall blood relatives within the fourth degree or relatives by marriage within the second degree." The statutes of Southern Illinois University provide that "no relative of a member of the board of trustees shall be considered for initial appointment to any position on the teaching or administrative staff but may be considered for reappointment when the initial appointment was antecedent to the board membership of a relative. The word relative shall be interpreted to mean father, husband, son, brother, grandfather, grandson, uncle, nephew, and corresponding feminine relationships." Statutes of the University of the Philippines provide that "It is the policy of the university to discourage nepotism in appointments to the faculty and administrative staff of the university except in cases where the interests of the university require otherwise and the board of regents so decides. This policy shall be observed and applied within the individual units of the university such as the colleges and schools."

Statutes of the University of Illinois provide that

It is the general policy of the university not to employ on its academic or administrative staff a person who is related within the third degree by blood or marriage to any other person employed on either of these staffs. The president is authorized to make exceptions when in his judgment the university may be prejudicially affected by such a policy. Exception shall not be made in any case, however, where one of the persons involved has authority and responsibility in the appointment or promotion of a relative within the third degree.

One can argue that if appointments are made strictly on the basis of merit the relationship of a staff member to any other staff member should not matter. Experience, however, must have proved otherwise, else we would not find provisions of the kind just quoted. Great hardship can result if such provisions are too strictly and rigidly stated and adhered to. On the other hand there must be enough certainty in the statement of a rule to prevent arbitrary determinations from being made. We believe a statute like that for the University of the Philippines is an appropriate one—with the further provision that rules and regulations should establish the particular degrees of relationship and the conditions under which relatives should not be employed and with a discretion on the part of the chief administrative officer to waive even these rules when, following the recommendations of an appropriate committee, he is convinced that undue hardship would be caused either the individuals or the university. Many instances can be cited, for example, of notable contributions to research which have been made by husband and wife, father and son, or brother and brother teams in the employ of a university.

15.10. GRADES OR RANK

There is great uniformity in the classification of the academic staff in universities throughout the world. Allowing for some variation in the terminology because of national language, there is even great uniformity in the naming of ranks. The notion, for example, of three professor grades—full professor, associate professor, and assistant professor—is well-nigh universal. A fourth rank commonly provided is that of instructor. Some of the Indian agricultural universities have just these four ranks—the term "lecturer" being frequently used to designate those who at other institutions would be at the instructor level. Another rank comparable to instructor and lecturer is research associate. This seems necessary to indicate that one has a research responsibility; the term "instructor" or "lecturer" does not properly denote this. The same may be said for extension.

An institution can do very well with four ranks—three professorial grades and instructor, with research and extension associate comparable to instructor. The designation of ranks should be in the university statutes. Members of the extension staff and others who would ordinarily not receive a rank designation should be accorded an appropriate rank. In many institutions this is accomplished by naming the position and then stating: " . . . with the rank of _____." We feel that fewer than four ranks do not permit sufficient flexibility and that too many ranks unduly complicate the salary, promotion and tenure structure, thus leading to unnecessary confusion. The Punjab Agricultural University Statutes, for example, make three classifications of teachers based on salary scales. We do not think this is good practice, though it may seem quite natural following a system where civil service prevailed for college faculty members. Cornell University lists six grades below instructor. Columbia University Statutes provide for sixteen grades including university professor, visiting professor, adjunct professor, research professor, preceptor, and curator.

We hold no brief for any particular number of ranks or for any particular method of designating them. We feel, however, that the statutes should recognize experience, responsibility, and educational achievement in establishing ranks and should embody the following ideas: (1) A sufficient number of ranks to give flexibility should be established, with salary scales arranged so that the top salary in one rank is somewhat higher than the lowest salary in the next higher rank. (2) The name for a rank should be as comprehensive as possible and inclusive of the kind of activity the staff member will perform. The term "professor," for example, is understood to cover any kind of activity, either research, teaching, or extension. The names for ranks below professor need to be somewhat more definitive. (3) If it is felt desirable to designate several kinds of assistants and associates, as many universities do, the statutes should state which ones are equivalent. These categories will not necessarily represent different grades as far as salary and status are concerned but are simply used to designate the kind of work in which a staff member is engaged. Extension, teaching, and research associates, for example, designate diffierent jobs but presumably would be at the same level. Statutes of the University of the Philippines clarify this by stating that a research fellow is the same as an instructor and that a professoral lecturer is equivalent to an associate professor.

Some ranks bear an honorary connotation—university professor, for example, is reserved for outstanding scholars and scientists; distinguished professor bears the same meaning; visiting professor generally assumes an outstanding member of the staff of another university. The term "adjunct professor" bears a similar connotation in that the invitee is worthy of joining another on the staff of the inviting university in a joint endeavor.

More important than the establishment of ranks themselves are the determinants for movement from one to the other. These cannot be adequately expressed in the university statutes but should be considered by the academic council and, to the extent feasible, expressed in internal rules and regulations of the university. The real determinant is appraisal by one's peers and administrative superiors. We would make only one comment in this regard— namely, that the degree requirement can be so strictly adhered to that good men are sometimes held back, both with respect to salary and movement to the next higher rank.

15.11. SALARY AND PROMOTION

Salary scales for the academic staff of public institutions may be determined by a general law, administratively at the state level (in case civil service applies), by the governing body (this is a usual provision), internally by the administration of the university, or not at all. In this latter case, salary ranges come to be understood within the institution and may even be expressed in budget information and other pronouncements without ever being formally adopted. We do not believe salary scales should be established either by the university act or university statutes. More flexibility is needed. Internally it is helpful if there are scales which come to be understood and which can be modified with the times. These should be established by the administration, approved by the board, and expressed in a business office procedure manual and in other places where their publication will serve to inform staff members and others who need to know university policy. Statutes of the Universidad Agraria in Peru state that the basic pay of the academic staff shall be fixed by the university council (its governing body) for each rank. Since one-third of the university council is students, this gives students a strong voice in determining faculty salaries. Most universities would not regard this as desirable—nor do we. Rules should make it possible to establish a beginning salary above the minimum for the grade. As competition for staff members increases, it will more and more be necessary to adjust salaries so that good men can be attracted. There should be some flexibility even when salary scales are fixed by law, by civil service scales, or by the board.

A staff member's salary cannot legally be reduced during the contract period of his service. Support for this principle can be found in a decision of the Supreme Court of Alabama holding that the trustees of the university could not reduce the salary of a tutor during the two years for which he was employed under contract. In some institutions salaries of administrative officials are fixed by adding a "responsibility allowance" to their regular academic salary. The salary of a new employee should be recommended by the appointing officer, approved through university channels, and finally approved by the governing body.

In the absence of a salary scale containing automatic annual increments, what should be the basis for making annual increments? These can be roughly divided into merit and nonmerit —the latter based on such factors as cost of living and years of service, the former on quality of performance. Statutes of the Universidad Agraria at La Molina, Peru, recognize two kinds of increments. They are called bonuses. One is an ordinary bonus based on the same factors described above under nonmerit increases, the other an extraordinary bonus to be based on excellence of performance. A standard procedure in many universities is to divide the amount available for increasing staff salaries into two parts—one for "across-the-board" increases, the other for merit increases. These would correspond to the ordinary and extraordinary bonuses described in the La Molina statutes. Other terminology can be found to express these two major kinds of salary increases. We believe both should be recognized in a university statute, thus insuring that consideration be given to merit increases during budget-making time.

Statutes of the University of the Philippines provide that in determining promotions, careful consideration shall be given to "the teaching ability of the candidate, his research competence and productivity, scholarly performance, dedication to service, positive evidence of educational interests, and marked academic growth, moral integrity, and good personal character and conduct." Regulations of the appointments and promotions committee of the University of Ibadan provide for "accelerated promotion," which means promotion to the next grade before reaching the top salary scale from the grade from which the staff member is promoted. "Ordinary promotion" means the staff member reaches the top of the salary scale before he moves to the next grade. Under the scheme at the University of Ibadan, recommendations for promotion are made by the department head and are then considered by an appointments and promotions committee. A staff member who is not recommended by a department head may state his own case before the committee in writing. A similar procedure is followed at the University of Nigeria. There it is done by the council of deans for the academic staff and by an appointed committee for the nonacademic staff. Statutes of the University of Agricultural Sciences in Mysore state that there shall be a careful evaluation made yearly by administrative officers.

Opinions vary about the use of the committee process for making determinations about promotions and salary increases. One theory is that these are determinations which should be made by an administrative officer under the assumption that he has the means of becoming well informed before making decisions. Furthermore, he has the privilege of calling into conference other administrators who are in position to judge the work of the staff member. For example, in considering the promotion of a staff member who has a joint research and teaching appointment, his department head, the dean of his college, the director of research, and the director of resident instruction should confer. We believe that the university statutes should go no further than establishing the principle that promotion should be made on merit and that procedures should be established by the university administration following recommendations from the academic council. Promotion to a higher rank requires that there be an open position in the higher rank or that an additional position be created. We do not believe that a system under which college or university councils determine promotions by secret ballot is acceptable. The whole process should be more frank and open. It is more difficult to be arbitrary when the academic staff knows how the process works. Committees to advise administrators on matters of promotion and salary are helpful, and we suggest their use, but we do not suggest they be given the power to make the final determinations.

15.12. RETIREMENT OR PENSION PLANS

A variety of schemes exists for providing retirement benefits to university staff members. In some of the American states there is a universities retirement system applying to all academic and nonacademic staff of all state universities. This is true, for example, in Illinois. Some of the Indian agricultural universities have by provisions in their university acts been brought under a government provident fund established in 1925. The legislature of the Philippines has provided a government service insurance system which covers staff members of the University of the Philippines. Some Indian universities have a provident fund which utilizes the postal savings system and postal savings bank of India as the vehicle for depositing funds and making other arrangements. Many university acts in different parts of the world empower the governing body to establish a pension or retirement plan sometimes referred to as a superannuation plan. Many American universities participate in providing retirement and other benefits through a plan under which policies are issued by a large private organization known as the Teacher's Insurance and Annuity Association. Under such an arrangement the staff member can take his policy with him from one institution to another and remain covered.

Problems sometimes arise for individuals who have been under a state or government system and then come under a different university system. Sometimes their total period of service in both agencies can be counted toward retirement in the agency where they were employed at the time of retirement; sometimes such periods cannot be added. The opposite is also possible—that is, qualification under both systems with retirement pay considerably in excess of that which would be available under only one plan. This points to the necessity for a university act which is carefully drafted with respect to retirement in order that duplicate benefits will be avoided on the one hand and hardship avoided on the other. The problem is simplified when all employees in the state, including university staff members, belong to one plan. But the government plan may not be suitable for the university. If there is a general university plan applying to all universities and public educational institutions in the state, fair treatment will be assured to those who transfer from one institution to another within the state.

American court decisions have held that a university does not have the right to establish a retirement or pension plan unless it is so authorized; otherwise, funds cannot be used for such a purpose. Hence, the university act should either authorize the university to establish a retirement or pension plan or should bring it under the provisions of an existing plan which is appropriate for staff members of the university. In some institutions, provision is made for a gratuity to members of the nonacademic staff whose earnings fall below a stated amount. They are not asked to contribute to a plan but are entitled to payments based on years of service when their service is terminated.

There are many important features of a retirement plan in which staff members have a vital interest. Some of these are:

Period for vesting—that is, after how many years will the staff member be entitled to withdraw not only his own but the institution's contribution in case his services at the university are terminated. Also there is the converse question when an employee comes to the university—can the university request a transfer to it on behalf of the employee of any former employer's contributions made during his previous employment?

Percentage of salary deducted for contribution to the plan and percentage contributed by the university.

Age of retirement. This varies considerably and depends somewhat upon employment conditions in the country. Mandatory retirement ages vary from as low as fifty-five in some of the Indian states to as high as seventy years at La Molina and the University of the Philippines, for example. Nearly all acts have a provision for retirement prior to the mandatory age on approval of the university. Many points of view exist about a desirable retirement age. No matter how high it is set, there will always be some staff members with a high capacity to teach and think long after the mandatory age is reached. The lower age in some countries is no doubt a concession to the pressure for positions in government service and universities.

Who participates? Temporary employees, employees below a specific salary level, and nonacademic employees covered by a state plan may be excluded.

When does participation commence? There is sometimes an employment probation period. Coverage may be made retroactive after the probationary period.

How will disability payments be handled?

How will retirement payments be made? By lump sum? By annuity payment? By a combination?

Will there be annuity payments for surviving spouses?

Can the staff member borrow on his retirement?

Will there be death or burial benefits?

Will it be possible to convert some of the earnings in the individual's account to government securities or post office cash certificates as is possible in some of the Indian agricultural university plans?

Can a portion of the deposit be used to purchase life insurance? These are some of the items that ought to be considered and settled in the plan which is evolved. Staff members should be supplied with a handbook telling them about the system and its benefits, and annually they should receive a statement showing their account with the system. Staff members of the Indian universities participating in the government postal saving system each have individual pass books. These not only show the status of their account but can be used to designate beneficiaries. We do not believe all this detail belongs in university statutes. The statutes should fix a retirement age, prescribe requirements for coming under the retirement system, and then provide that other details of the plan shall be prescribed by rules and regulations. Establishment of a good system will require the careful thought of more than one university administrative officer and a considerable amount of committee activity. The academic council should make recommendations regarding the system and should maintain a standing committee on the retirement and pension plan. Further discussion of retirement and pension plans is contained in Chapter 5.

15.13. INSURANCE—MEDICAL SERVICE

Though workmen's compensation acts may not apply to the university at all and are not likely to apply to the academic staff, they sometimes do apply to the academic staff. In an interesting Ohio Supreme Court case it was held that the vice-president of Ohio Northern University was in the employment of the university when he died as the result of a pinprick from a rose handed to him by a member of the high school graduating class where he was making the commencement address. His widow was allowed compensation. If workmen's compensation does apply to the university, this should be recognized in the university act and authorization made for any additional insurance deemed necessary by the governing body.

University statutes should state the conditions under which university staff members shall be insured. The development of a health and accident insurance plan should by statute be made the responsibility of the chief financial officer working in cooperation with appropriate administrative officials and faculty bodies. The statutes should permit group life insurance premiums to be paid directly by the staff member by withholding from his salary or by deduction from his contribution to the retirement system. Many institutions may not be in position to establish a group life insurance program, but the right should exist. The governing body may wish to establish by statute the proportion of the cost of health, accident, hospitalization, or group life insurance to be paid by the university. Some American institutions are now paying the entire cost of health insurance premiums. This is not usual, however.

In some institutions free medical service is supplied to a staff member and his family. This is particularly important in universities established away from cities and in locations where medical services are not available. Regulations should cover such questions as coverage when the staff member is on leave, his status when he cannot pass the necessary physical examinations but is permitted to remain on the staff of the university, and the nature and extent of coverage for the staff member's family.

15.14. HOUSING AND PERQUISITES

The university act should leave with the governing body the discretion of determining if housing or other perquisites are to be provided as a part of the remuneration of staff members. It is particularly important that the governing body have this right when the university is established away from the city and the only housing available is that provided by the institution. The university act should empower the governing body to provide for housing and other amenities which it may deem necessary. Establishment of a school for children of staff members, providing recreational facilities, medical service, and transportation—even subsidizing the establishment of a shopping center—might all be considered quite important in attracting staff to a location.

Many institutions in the developing countries which formerly relied on large numbers of expatriate staff members are confronted with the problem of eliminating from the perquisites for staff many expensive items provided to induce the expatriates to remain at the institution. Such things as passage for the staff member and all his family to the home country, outfit allowances, children's allowances, baggage allowances, advances for the purchase of motor vehicles, and subsistence allowances while traveling are examples. There should be no question about the right of the governing body to eliminate such extras on recommendation of the chief administrative officer. Such action would not affect existing contracts.

Some institutions supply utilities free to staff members occupying university housing; some charge for such services. Regardless of how problems of this kind are handled, the policy should be clear and firm so that there will be no inequity between the total salary and benefits received by staff members of equal ability and doing similar work, some of whom live in university housing and some of whom do not. The charter of Yale University contained this interesting passage:

All the lands and ratable estate belonging to the said college, not exceeding the yearly value of 500 pounds sterling lying in this government, and the persons, families, and estates of the president and professors lying and being in the town of New Haven, and the persons of the tutors, students, and such and so many of the servants of said college as give their constant attendance on the business of it, shall be freed and exempted from all rates, taxes, military service, working at highways, and other such like duties and services.

Harking back to an earlier chapter, we would again reiterate that when the university is so located that it must provide certain amenities to obtain staff, it should be entitled to the same tax exemption on property used for housing and other purposes as on that used strictly for educational purposes.

15.15. LEAVE—VACATIONS

There are many kinds of leave—regular, special, sick, sabbatical, annual, ordinary, casual, military, study, and maternity. These are all designations which may be found in university acts and statutes. The statutes of Punjab Agricultural University provide that "The vice-chancellor shall have power to grant leave of any kind to all officers, teachers, and other employees of the university." They further provide that deans and directors may grant leave to staff members serving under them if no substitutes are required. The statutes of Andhra Pradesh Agricultural University provide that leave cannot be claimed as a right and that the sanctioning authority may in its discretion, when the interests of the university require, refuse or revoke leave of any description. A few institutions provide that the chief administrative officer shall grant all leaves no matter how short and that staff members shall sign in and out in a book to be maintained for the purpose. This smacks of the army, and we do not recommend it! Rules on conditions of service of the University of Ife in Nigeria provide that "The academic board shall have power upon production of a medical certificate to grant sick leave to a member of the staff on full pay up to a maximum of six months. In case of application for the extension of sick leave beyond six months, the question of duration of stipend shall be considered upon individual merits."

The university act should authorize the establishment of university policies on leave regardless of type. University statutes should then designate the major kinds of leaves to be recognized and the conditions under which a staff member qualifies. Also, they should state who has authority to grant the leave and through whom application shall be channeled. The statutes should establish the period of ordinary leave for all staff members on full pay, indicate the extent if any to which it is cumulative, and provide that the time for taking ordinary leave shall be approved by the staff member's immediate administrative superior. The maximum amount of sick leave should be expressed in the statute but the conditions for granting it should be left to university regulation. Similar provisions should be included on maternity leave. The definition of casual leave and the level at which it should be approved are matters which should be left to university regulation and not expressed in the statutes. There should be a general provision giving the university administration the right to institute other kinds of leaves which might not have been expressed in the act or statute or contemplated at the time they were drafted.

Some institutions have special provisions imposing penalities for absence without leave. We do not feel this is proper. If a staff member is absent without good reason, this would be a factor in determining whether or not his contract should be renewed or whether he should receive promotion or a salary increase or enjoy other benefits which he might if he were more punctual and conscientious. In all rules having to do with leave, it should be clear whether the staff member is on full pay, no pay, or partial pay during the leave period. An early law of the University of Arkansas provided that "No person shall be entitled to any salary when on leave of absence except when on university business." This seems to overlook ordinary or annual leave when it is expected the staff member will be on salary. Technically it might be argued that he is on university business because it is a business of the university to give this leave. However, we do not recommend any such general statement. Salary is important to staff members and the conditions under which it is to be withheld, either in part or in whole, should be expressly stated for each particular situation.

Ordinarily, leave periods of any kind do not terminate the staff member's rights in a university retirement or insurance plan, and this time in service continues to accumulate while on leave. This should be expressly stated in the university statutes so that there is no doubt about it. Statutes of the University of the Philippines run to several pages of minute detail on the various kinds of leaves and on all the conditions surrounding them, but these provisions are well stated and constitute an excellent set of rules and regulations for the application of leave. We do not think, however, that a statement on leaves should be in the statutes, where it is difficult to make changes.

Another question which should be settled in the rules and regulations regarding leave is the right of the faculty member to accept employment while on leave. Military service leaves are usually in a special category. Some university statutes—those of the University of the Philippines, for example—provide that the staff member shall be entitled to his salary while absent on call under the National Defense Act. For those who are called to service, there may be national policies preserving certain rights in the civilian positions held by them. This would condition the right of the university to make provisions regarding salary, extension of leave, preservation of retirement rights, and other privileges of the staff member.

Vacation leave is ordinarily longer for the academic than for the nonacademic staff. When service is for the academic year, the staff member is off-duty during the period between terms. This is a part of his contract, either express or implied, and would not be covered under a statement about leave policy. Many university statutes specifically designate those days during the academic year which are holidays for both students and staff. Such a designation is wise, particularly in countries that have a large number of religious or other holidays, all of which would be excuses for no work on the part of students and staff. By naming the principal ones and stating that they are holidays, there is a presumption at least that the others are work days. Whether or not the staff is excused from duty during the longer vacation periods that accompany some holidays in some parts of the world—a Christmas holiday, for example—is a policy question which should be settled in the rules and regulations of the university. Though some institutions have formulas for determining the amount of a staff member's leave, it is generally established that when a staff member's contract requires twelve months of service he will be entitled to one month of vacation leave. Contracts of employment should incorporate by reference statutory provisions and university rules and regulations concerning leave. As a matter of policy the staff member should be entitled to extra pay if he works for the university at times during which his services are not required by his contract. Some institutions have rules permitting this but limiting the time for such extra employment to less than the vacation or leave period so that the staff member will, in fact, have some vacation.

15.16. SABBATICAL AND STUDY LEAVE

Terminology knows no barriers. While "sabbatical" stems from the biblical reference to sabbath and one day's rest in seven, it has come to mean for professors in universities one year's leave in seven —or six, or five, or some other period, but it is still sabbatical leave. Regulations of the University of Ife in Nigeria provide for a study leave of absence after nine terms of service. Ordinarily such leaves are not granted as a matter of right but are approved when the applicant meets the conditions specified in the statutes or regulations. While on such leave the staff member is expected to pursue studies or engage in activities which will benefit both him and the university. Generally a report of his activities is required when he returns. Many institutions require the staff member to remain in the service of the university for some minimum period of time after sabbatical leave. Some institutions do not grant such leaves to ranks below assistant professor. It is customary to pay the salary of the staff member while he is on sabbatical leave, though some institutions pay only a portion of the salary if the leave extends beyond one school term. The Punjab Agricultural University, however, provides that a teacher holding a permanent post in the university may after five years of service be granted leave on full pay for a period of two years and in special cases for three years with three-quarters of his pay for the third year. This is under a proviso that he spend the entire period in study or research at a university or other institution or in any approved manner outside of India and provided further that he execute a bond to serve the university for a period of five years after his return. This requirement is common in Indian agricultural universities.

Indian agricultural universities have encouraged training abroad to the Ph.D. level to upgrade their staff. Many contracts under which American universities aid and advise foreign universities provide for "participant training." Though this may serve the same purpose as study or sabbatical leave, it is regarded as special training for the good of the institution. Major costs are paid from nonuniversity funds. The staff member is regarded as still in the service of the institution though studying abroad. Also, his university continues to pay his salary or a portion of it.

We believe that sabbatical or study leave should be provided by university statutes together with a statement in the statutes of the conditions under which it is to be granted. Further details can be left to rules and regulations. The importance of the statutory provision is pointed up by a West Virginia Supreme Court case holding that a staff member on sabbatical leave was entitled to her salray. It had been withheld by the state auditor on the theory that the state college did not have the right to pay her salary while on leave. The court found that the legislature had specifically provided for sabbatical leaves in all state institutions and that payment of her salary was proper.

We recommend that there be a provision in the university act empowering the governing body to grant leaves of various kinds with or without pay. The university statute on sabbatical leave should contain provisions on the following: (1) the academic ranks entitled to such leave, (2) the period of service required before granting a leave, (3) the limitation, if any, on the number of leaves to which a staff member is entitled, (4) payment of salary on leave, whether full salary or partial salary and the conditions under which each apply, (5) the conditions other than rank and period of service which must be met to qualify for a leave and who shall determine if these conditions exist (normally this is left to officers of administration, but the conditions themselves should be recommended by the academic council; also, a committee of the academic council on sabbatical leaves may pass judgment on candidates and make recommendations to administrative officers), (6) requirements regarding reports by staff members after leave is terminated,

(7) duration of the leave, (8) obligation of the staff member to remain with the university for a stated period of time following his leave and provisions, if any, on giving bond in this regard, and (9) right to engage in any remunerative activity while on sabbatical leave.

15.17. TRAVEL POLICIES

The early law relating to Michigan State College (now Michigan State University) provided that "The board shall have power to expend the funds appropriated for the support of the college in paying the expenses of the president, secretary, professors, or other employees of the college in attending meetings at which in their judgment it is desirable that the college should be represented; in inspecting the buildings, equipment, and work of other institutions; and also in accompanying students on tours of inspection to such objects of interest as are germane to their work in college." Statutes of the University of the Philippines provide that "The president may in his discretion authorize any college or school of the university to spend from its appropriation for traveling expenses of personnel such amount as may be necessary for travel within the country for purposes of research, observation, or study." Punjab Agricultural University Statutes provide that "The employees of the university shall be entitled to travelling and halting allowances as prescribed by the Punjab government for its own employees until such time as the board prescribes its own rate." Statutes of the University of Agricultural Sciences of Mysore contain many details on the amount of compensation for various modes of travel, persons competent to authorize travel, and the purposes for which travel can be undertaken. They provide that when the vice-chancellor undertakes travel, he shall post a copy of his tour program on the university bulletin board. University of Illinois Rules of Organization and Procedure provide that "The university shall reimburse for actual and necessary expense of travel on university business for which proper approval has been obtained." This provision then refers the reader to *The Business Policy and Procedure Manual* where he can find the regulations concerning travel, including convention travel.

We believe the university act should empower the board to pay travel expenses of staff members under policies to be developed within the university and recommended by the chief administrative officer. This will remove all doubt about the inclusion of an item for travel in the university budget. The university statutes should then include a provision similar to the one which has been placed in the rules concerning university organization and procedure of the University of Illinois. Some Indian agricultural university statutes require approval by the vice-chancellor for out-of-state travel and approval by the governing body for travel out of the country. We believe this is a good provision to add to the statutes. Other details should be included in a business office procedure manual or in the rules and regulations of the chief financial officer of the university. Many items concerning travel should be under constant review. Alterations will be required depending on changes in cost of transportation, availability of motor vehicles, policies regarding the use of personal automobiles, and expansion of the university's programs and activities. Many universities in the developing countries will still have to wrestle with the liberal travel policies which were established to provide home leave for expatriate staff and members of their families. If the policy is well imbedded, a statutory provision may be necessary to convince members of the staff that a change has been made, but it is still a policy issue and if the university must rely on expatriate staff it will need to continue some of the inducements which have traditionally been offered.

15.18. RESPONSIBILITIES

Academic freedom can exist only when there is academic responsibility. They complement each other. In "The Rights and Responsibilities of Universities and Their Faculties," a 1953 statement by the Association of American Universities, is this observation about the obligation of a university faculty member: "As in all acts of association, the professor accepts conventions which become morally binding. Above all, he owes his colleagues and the university complete candor and perfect integrity precluding any kind of clandestine or conspiratorial activities. He owes equal candor to the public. If he is called upon to answer for his convictions, it is his duty as a citizen to speak out. It is even more definitely his duty as a professor. Above all, a scholar must have integrity and independence." The charter of Yale University required all staff members to execute an oath for the faithful execution of their duties. Statutes of the University of Illinois provide that full-time staff members cannot receive additional compensation for university work outside the scope of their regular duties without prior approval of the president. The statutes of Southern Illinois University provide that "Each member of the university faculty and staff shall have the following responsibilities: to operate within the general framework of university policy and practice, to represent the university creditably on all occasions, continually to improve his training and experience so as to qualify for the higher ranks, classifications, and salaries."

As a matter of law, a staff member's responsibilities are determined by his contract with the university, but as a matter of moral obligation his responsibilities extend beyond express provisions in his contract or those incorporated by reference. Legally there may be implied duties arising out of custom and general understanding. Also, there may be legislative or university statutory provisions which impose duties not referred to in his contract. It is not difficult for a staff member to meet the legal requirements imposed upon him by contract and still be an ineffective, unproductive, and lethargic teacher or research worker. If he fails to qualify on these counts, his contract should not be continued, but it is unlikely that he can be discharged for breach of contract. A conscientious staff member will do many helpful things which are not expressed or implied in his contract. He will meet with students willingly, counsel with those who seek his advice, accept his share of responsibility in the advisory system of his college, give some of his time to committee activity and some to public service, will do his share of "menial" chores to get his own job done and help other staff members accomplish theirs. In short, he will look for ways to be useful rather than for ways to be anonymous and insulated from university life.

15.19. PRIVILEGES

Members of the staff of a university and their families should be permitted in many ways to enjoy the university environment and benefit from it. Some universities, for example, conduct organized athletic and recreational programs for staff members, permit family members to register in university classes, grant library privileges, make gymnasium facilities available, make special concessions for tickets to university events and make other provisions which add to the attractiveness of employment at the university. Playgrounds for children, picnic areas, and campus planning and beautification might also be mentioned as activities which increase the privileges of staff members. In a dry and arid climate it is a pleasure—and a privilege —to view a well-watered and blossoming flower bed.

There are privileges which might be regarded by some as more substantial. The statutes of Southern Illinois University, for example, in a section entitled "Rights and Privileges of Faculty and Staff," provide that

Each member of the university faculty and staff shall have the following rights and privileges: (a) to participate in the formulation of basic policy in his area of concern and to assist in the promotion of the university's general welfare, (b) to receive the benefits of a defined and equitable system of annual service, service loads, assignments, vacations, sick leave, leaves with and without pay, and sabbatical leaves, (c) to receive at the time of initial appointment a statement detailing the above rights and privileges as they have been approved by the board of trustees.

This harks back to contract; some of these items are rights rather than privileges and are detailed either in the contract or in university statutes. Most of them we have discussed.

There are some negative aspects. It has been held, for example, that staff members of the university are not in the position of legislators and hence entitled to immunity from suit. Some university acts prohibit staff members from being on the governing board. This is discussed in Chapter 4. We do not believe it is a good provision. The statutes of at least one Indian agricultural university provide that university staff members cannot belong to associations without permission of the vice-chancellor. We do not believe in this kind of surveillance on the part of the university administration. It is not a privilege of a staff member, however, to engage in subversive activity. Some university acts and many university statutes contain provisions on this subject. The right or privilege of engaging in activities outside the university and in being employed outside the university are discussed in sections which follow.

15.20. PART-TIME SERVICE

In many universities, particularly those in Latin America, a high percentage of the teaching is accomplished by staff members who have other jobs and who teach on a part-time basis. Statutes of the Universidad Agraria in Peru provide that

According to the time dedicated to their work, the teachers may be appointed for part-time, full-time, or exclusive dedication. Full-time teachers are those who dedicate themselves to teaching and research in the agricultural university during the normal working hours as fixed in the general bylaws. They may also exercise administrative activities in the university. Part-time teachers are those who dedicate to teaching and research the number of hours required by the plan of the course or courses in their charge.

The policy is to discourage part-time employment. It does not beget the proper relation of the staff with students in the university. Though some part-time staff members are no doubt good teachers, they are not available to participate in other activities so important to academic and student life in the university. Furthermore, it is likely to lead to a much higher turnover in teaching positions with less continuity where it is needed and with less likelihood that courses will be revised and kept up to date.

We believe the university statutes should provide that all academic personnel shall be employed full time except for part-time graduate assistants and except for special circumstances which may justify part-time teaching—the decision about such circumstances to be made by the proper administrative officer following recommendations from an appropriate committee or faculty body. The expression of this policy should not prevent teachers in charge of a course from bringing to the classroom men of experience to deliver lectures, engage in discussion with students, conduct demonstrations, or in other ways relate their experience to the theory of the course. One of the special circumstances which might justify a part-time staff member is the teaching of a course like veterinary jurisprudence which does not justify full-time service but for which no regular staff member is qualified. In a large university with many disciplines it might still be unnecessary to employ a part-time teacher since arrangements could be made with another college to receive assistance in such a course from a full-time member of its staff.

15.21. EMPLOYMENT OUTSIDE UNIVERSITY— CONSULTING

An American work of law states that "So long as he performs his full duty to the college or university by which he is employed and does not compete with it or act in opposition to its interests, a professor, instructor, or tutor may properly render services for another university, give public concerts, publish books, and take private pupils." [7] This statement could no doubt be broadened to include

------

[7] 14 *CJS* § 1358.

other outside activities of the professor and still represent good law in most countries unless there are specific legislative or statutory provisions curtailing a university staff member's right to engage in outside activities. The statutes of Columbia University provide: "No officer of instruction shall be employed in any occupation which interferes with the thorough, efficient, and earnest performance of the duties of his office." Statutes of the Universidad Agraria in Peru establish three categories for teachers: part-time, full-time, and exclusive dedication. They provide further that "Teachers of exclusive dedication are those who spend all their time in teaching and research in the agricultural university. They are not permitted to pursue any other activity, public or private." This is the only institution we found which makes the interesting distinction between full-time and exclusive dedication. The Peru National Universities Act imposes some obligation regarding outside work on all teachers in a negative fashion by providing that they "Shall not be able to excuse nonfulfillment of university duties because they have other public obligations to attend to."

West Pakistan Agricultural University Statutes provide that "Except as specifically provided, no university employee shall engage directly or indirectly without the prior permission of the appointing authority in writing, in any trade, business, or occupation on his own account which may in the opinion of the appointing authority interfere with the due performance by him of the duties of his office." Punjab Agricultural University Statutes contain a similar provision but go even further in discouraging the teacher from outside activity by providing that a portion of his earnings over a stipulated amount shall be divided with the university and that all of his earnings over a higher stipulated amount shall be credited into the funds of the university. Statutes at the University of Illinois provide that "No person employed by the university shall have any interest incompatible with those of the university."

A variation of the problem raised by outside occupations of staff members is that which arises when a professional member of the staff engages in his profession for remuneration. Statutes of the University of the Philippines provide that "Permission to engage in private practice of the profession of faculty members may be granted only if such private practice may enhance their usefulness to the university or improve their efficiency. The privilege of private practice when granted shall be for a definite period of one year, renewable at the discretion of the president for one-year periods and under such conditions as may be prescribed by him regarding the nature of the work, the time of the performance, and other circumstances." The Statutes of Columbia University provide that when an officer of instruction is acting in a consulting capacity he shall not use the official title of the university or of any of its parts or refer to his professional connection with the university in rendering opinions or making certifications without the approval of the trustees.

We do not believe staff members should be prevented from carrying on any outside work or from consulting or engaging in their profession for remuneration, provided adequate safeguards are established in the university statutes. Provisions like those for the University of the Philippines, in our opinion, go too far and provide for too much surveillance on the part of the university. There may be good reason for creating a category of "exclusive dedication" for professors in Latin-American institutions as at La Molina, for example. We are not disposed to argue with the policy in that case. Generally we feel that a university statute permitting outside employment by members of its staff should provide that:

1. It not be incompatible with their responsibility to the university.

2. It be accomplished outside of university hours.

3. No university equipment be used.

4. No university personnel, either academic or nonacademic, be utilized when they are on university time.

5. The office of the professor or staff member not become a business office for his outside activity.

6. The amount of time and energy spent on the outside activity not be so extensive as to impair his ability to perform for the university.

We do not believe that formal approval is desirable, but we do feel the department head is entitled to know that a staff member is engaging in outside work or professional activity. Statutes of the University of Illinois provide that "Staff members may carry on some business or professional activity of an income-producing character . . . the head of the department of which the employee is a member should know and approve of these activities outside the university." We believe this is a wise provision. In case questions are raised by the department head or for that matter by a higher administrative official who knows of the activities of a staff member and a controversy arises between the staff member and the university administration, the usual channels for airing grievances and disputes over terms of employment exist.

15.22. HOLDING POLITICAL OFFICE

The 1780 Constitution of the Commonwealth of Massachusetts provided that the president, professors, and instructors of Harvard College were disqualified from holding seats in the legislature. In 1877 a constitutional amendment removed this disqualification. The Florida Board of Control, a body governing all state universities in Florida, adopted a rule compelling the resignation of any employee seeking public office. A law professor from the university became a candidate for an elective judgeship but did not resign. Shortly after filing as a candidate in the primary election he was called into the president's office and dismissed. The Supreme Court of Florida upheld his dismissal on the grounds that this was a reasonable regulation. Statutes of the West Pakistan Agricultural University provide that faculty members cannot contest or hold a local political office or a seat in the legislature. Statutes of the University of the Philippines provide that persons holding political office are not eligible for appointment to the faculty and that if a staff member is elected to any political office he must yield his position in the university. There is a further interesting proviso: "No person who has been defeated as a candidate for any political office in an election shall be eligible for appointment or reinstatement as a regular member of the faculty within a year after the election." This seems to imply that some taint persists for that long.

What provisions should there be, if any, in university statutes regarding the holding of political office? We believe there should be none. If the question arising from political activity has to do with communications by the staff member, his viewpoints, what he advocates, teaches, writes, and the like, then the principles and procedures for academic freedom established in the university should be sufficient. If he gets "out of bounds" he may be discharged or subjected to some lesser penalty. If holding a particular office would in any way militate against the best interests of the university, the problem is taken care of by the statutory provision that any outside activity should not conflict with the ability of the staff member to discharge his responsibilities for or be incompatible with the interests of the university. If the question has to do with extra compensation derived from holding the political office, this is taken care of by university statutes and internal regulations on salary and outside employment, and the principles applicable should be no different. If the question has to do with distribution of the staff member's time, this likewise is taken care of by a statutory provision that the staff member shall devote full time to his responsibilities in the university and shall engage in no outside activities which will impair his full and conscientious performance for the institution.

If, for example, a staff member is elected to the state legislature and is required to spend several months annually or biennially at the state or regional capitol away from teaching and research duties at the university, there is an obvious impairment and the university has its remedy. It does not have to rely on the fact that the activities are political in nature. If, on the other hand, the staff member is elected to a local body such as a city council, park board, or school board, or is appointed or elected to a state, regional, or national body advisory to an agency of government, it is quite possible for him to discharge these duties and still render full service to the university. In many cases such outside activity will enhance his value to the university through broadening and deepening his experience and concept of his own discipline. If campaigning for an office requires so much time away from the university that a staff member cannot perform his functions, the university has a remedy. Furthermore, a conscientious staff member would recognize this and would ask for a leave of absence.

15.23. EXCHANGE, VISITING, AND DISTINGUISHED PROFESSORS

Statutes of the University of Illinois provide that

On the recommendation of the head or the chairman of a department and with the approval of the dean, president, and board of trustees, a professor, associate professor, or assistant professor may be permitted for a period of one year or one semester to exchange his position with a professor of approximately equal rank in another university provided the arrangement does not involve substantial increase in the cost of instruction. The professor with whom the exchange is made shall during his period of service in this university be subject to the rules governing appointments and conditions of service applicable to regular members of the faculty.

Perhaps the right to approve such exchanges is implied. However, we feel that a statutory provision similar to that in force at the University of Illinois is desirable. There should be a further expression in rules and regulations of the preservation of rights and privileges of the staff member going to another university. It would be desirable to continue his retirement and insurance benefits as though he had not taken an assignment as a visiting professor.

Statutes of the University of the Philippines provide that "On the proposal of the dean or director, the president may recommend to the board the appointment of visiting professors who shall serve some special purpose for a limited period." This statute also provides that the university may send visiting professors to other public institutions. We do not believe the statutes should limit the kind of institution with which exchanges are to be made or to which a visiting professor may be sent. This should be left to the judgment of university administrative officers acting on the recommendation of appropriate faculties.

Many institutions create special positions for professors of distinction, either their own or others who may be invited to the institution. For example, the bylaws of Cornell University contain the following provision: "There may be elected to the rank of professor-at-large those individuals who have achieved outstanding international distinction in the humanities, the natural or social sciences, or the learned professions or have achieved such distinction and have demonstrated broad intellectual interest through their activity in such fields as public affairs, literature, or the creative arts. Professors-at-large shall be elected by the board upon the recommendation of the president for a definite term of not to exceed six years." It is further specified that professors-at-large need not be in residence and shall not be required to perform regular duties for the university. They are to receive such stipends and other perquisites as may be agreed upon at the time of their election.

Some universities have established institutes of advanced research or entities with a similar name, the purpose of which is to enable distinguished scholars in the university to devote full time for some specified period on projects or investigations which have received only a portion of their time due to other university obligations. The selection of professors for this distinction as well as the selection of outside professors to be designated distinguished professors and given special privileges should be made only on recommendation of the academic council, and the statutes should so provide. Statutes at the University of Illinois contain two other provisions which we feel are desirable. One creates a fund enabling the university to invite scholars of eminence to give public lectures; the other authorizes the president of the university to extend the privilege of working without charge in laboratories and libraries of the university to members of the faculties of other colleges or universities, providing such faculty members are recognized as authorities in their fields and come with written credentials from the faculties of their own institutions or from their governments.

15.24. RIGHTS OF RETIRED STAFF MEMBERS

Sometimes retired staff members exercise privileges which are embarrassing to their successors. This is particularly true if the retired staff member was an administrative officer and feels that he must appear at frequent intervals to make certain the unit he administered is not falling to pieces. But many staff members are still capable of rendering productive service and are conscious of the role they should accept as retired staff members. Some university statutes recognize their possibilities through special provisions. Statutes of the University of Illinois, for example, provide that a retired staff member may be supplied with office and laboratory space and with research assistants on a year-to-year basis. He is required to make annual reports. As long as these continue to show progress in his work, this agreement can be continued. These statutes further provide that "With the approval of the department head or chairman and the dean of the graduate college and of the president, a retired faculty member may offer conferences with graduate students in his line of work if he had offered graduate courses before his retirement. Retired faculty members who were members of a senate prior to retirement can continue as members of that senate with full floor privileges. Retired faculty members may participate in meetings of their college or school faculties but shall have no vote." Many university statutes provide for the re-employment of a retired faculty member under one-year contracts.

We believe that the university statutes should also provide for a continuation during retirement of certain privileges enjoyed by the retired staff member prior to retirement. These would include the kinds of things previously discussed—library privileges, health service, use of gymnasia and athletic facilities, enrollment in university courses, special concessions for attending university events, and others.

CHAPTER – 16

Nonacademic Staff—
Employment and
Conditions of Service

In an Indian agricultural university workshop convened to discuss mutual problems, one of the principle agenda items dealt with the simplification of office procedure and the delegation of authority to and training of ministerial staff. Among the problems listed were delays caused by cumbersome filing systems, inability to delegate authority effectively so that academic staff members could be relieved of routine, and lack of proper training of clerks and office secretaries. At about the same time this workshop was being held, the College of Veterinary Medicine at the University of Illinois felt it necessary to circulate a memorandum on the duties of animal caretakers. This memorandum pointed to the necessity for extreme care in feeding, watering, and management so that experimental work would not be impaired and other animals and human beings needlessly exposed to infection from animals in communicable disease experiments. This is just an intimation of the myriad ways in which the functioning of the ministerial or nonacademic staff can materially affect the work of a university.

Many nonacademic staff members are highly trained and hold positions of great responsibility in the university. This all points to more consideration than has ordinarily been given to their role in the institution and their status as employees. Many large universities in the developing countries still relegate the hiring and management of the nonacademic staff to some full-time university administrative officer as a sideline. In Chapter 9 we discuss the appointment and functions of a personnel officer for the ministerial or nonacademic staff. In the *Resource Book*[1] there is discussion of a nonacademic program for a university including suggestions about the training of nonacademic or ministerial staff. In the sec-

---

[1] Hannah, *Resource Book*, ch. 23.

tions which follow in this chapter is a discussion of those items which should be based on university statutes or internal regulations. Provisions on nonacademic employees do not apply to officers and other members of the administrative staff.

16.1. METHOD OF EMPLOYMENT—CIVIL SERVICE

Unless general civil service rules are applicable to a university, it is free to develop its own program for hiring nonacademic or ministerial personnel and determining their conditions of service. With respect to the applicability of civil service there appear to be three possibilities (1) The university is included in a general civil service act or is subject to specified provisions in the act. This situation pertains to many universities in the developing countries. (2) There is a special university civil service law applicable to the nonacademic employees of all state educational institutions. The state of Illinois, for example, has such a law. It specifically exempts administrative and academic employees of universities. (3) Civil service laws do not apply. Sometimes this is a debatable issue. It was put to rest for Massachusetts State College by a law which provided that "Employees of the college shall be exempt from civil service laws." In California it was settled by a state supreme court decision holding that the state personnel board does not determine employment policies of the board of regents since the latter are given full power by the California constitution to hire all employees.

Though exempt from civil service requirements, a university may be guided by them. Statutes of the University of the Philippines provide that "The civil service law as well as the rules and regulations issued by competent authority pursuant thereto, such as the prohibition against nepotism, shall be taken into account in addition to whatever measures the board of regents may adopt in connection with appointments to the administrative staff." These statutes further provide that "All administrative officers, clerks, and other employees shall be appointed by the board of regents on the recommendation of the president, provided, however, that an employee who is on the nonteaching staff shall be appointed by the president alone in case the salary of his position does not exceed 3,000 pesos per annum and for which funds are available in the budget." A similar provision applies to laborers and other helpers and employees working under the director of the physical plant. Statutes of the University of Agricultural Sciences in Mysore provide that

The administrative officer shall be responsible for the recruitment and employment of all service personnel below the rank of officers and of ranks and salary scales approved by the board and for the maintenance of the service and leave records of all such personnel. The university shall employ such service personnel as from time to time are needed to carry on the activities of the university. The scale of pay of service personnel and the duties, qualifications, and conditions of service for them shall be determined by the board and published as regulations.

These statutes are representative of situations prevailing in most universities except where civil service requirements apply.

Rules of Organization and Procedure of the University of Illinois provide that

All employment of nonacademic staff members is controlled by the law and the rules governing the university civil service system of Illinois. These include provisions for employment on merit through a system of examinations, the establishment of job classifications, the assignment of all positions to such classifications, and the establishment of appropriate salary ranges for each classification. The employment of all new members of the staff and any changes in status of present members are processed through the office of nonacademic personnel.

Statutes of the University of Illinois provide for a director of nonacademic personnel and state that he "is responsible under the executive authority of the president for the administration of policy and rules relating to compensation and working conditions of nonacademic employees as adopted by the board of trustees and the merit board of the university civil service system of Illinois and for the performance of such other duties as may be assigned to him by the president." This statutory provision then refers to the fact that policies and rules regarding nonacademic personnel are contained in a publication entitled *Policy and Rules Relating to Compensation and Working Conditions of Nonacademic Employees.*

Statutes of the Orissa University of Agriculture and Technology provide for a selection committee for nonacademic staff and empower the chief administrative officer to appoint members of the nonacademic staff. West Pakistan Agricultural University Statutes provide that appointments can be made by the vice-chancellor and that in all cases they shall be filled by promotion if possible. If initial recruitment is necessary, it is to be accomplished through advertising under provisions contained in the university ordinances. These statutes also provide that no person less than eighteen or more than thirty-five years of age shall be appointed through initial recruitment.

We recommend that university statutes provide for an office of nonacademic personnel and for a competent appointee to head it. In the beginning this might be a part-time position, but it should be recognized from the outset as a separate and important function. If there is a civil service act covering nonacademic employees of the university, this fact should be stated in the statutes with a reference to the source of rules and regulations covering employees in the university under the system. If there is no civil service, the statutes should authorize the university administration to develop the rules and conditions of employment and publish them in an appropriate manual. If union labor is involved, the university should be empowered to deal with the unions in effecting contracts. Also, there should be individual contracts of employment with each full-time nonacademic staff member, incorporating by reference provisions applicable to him in university statutes and regulations and in civil service rules. The contract should contain any additional provisions or conditions not covered through incorporation by reference.

16.2. SALARY AND PROMOTION—GRADES AND CLASSIFICATION—QUALIFICATIONS

Though most university acts provide that the governing body has the power to fix salaries for all employees, this may be conditioned by the application of civil service and by the unionization of university employees. This qualification of the right was recognized in the laws relating to the University of Wisconsin by a provision which stated: "The board of regents is empowered and directed to fix and establish the salaries of the janitors of the university so that the same shall be equivalent and equal to the salaries paid the janitors at the state capitol and shall conform to the salary schedule for janitors established by the civil service commission." This law also mentions another factor which many universities have felt compelled to consider—the local wage scale. Basic salaries, salary increases, and promotions are all keyed to the classification system. If civil service applies, the university is bound by its classifications; if it does not apply, then one of the functions of the office of nonacademic personnel is to establish such a classification and have it approved as part of the university's rules and regulations.

Even though there is a civil service system and grades have been established for employees, there may still be variation in the freedom which exists to make salary changes. At the University of Illinois, for example, employees may fall into one of three general groups: "open range," implying some freedom in making increases; "prevailing rate group," in which rates are determined from local rates; and "negotiated rate group," in which rates and salaries are determined through collective bargaining with the appropriate union.

We believe that the nonacademic or service employees of a university have responsibilities which differ sufficiently from those of similar employees in other government agencies to justify either a separate civil service system or variations in a general civil service system permitting the universities more flexibility in employing, discharging, and promoting. Many nonacademic jobs are more than routine and can be adequately discharged only by dedicated and able people. The temperament of academic staff members and the nature of youth argue strongly for nonacademic staff members with more than an average understanding of human nature. This simply suggests that appropriate administrative personnel and committees of the university should have a hand in determining qualifications, establishing grades and classifications, and rules for promotion. An intimation that universities should be concerned is evidenced by provisions such as one in the Punjab Agricultural University Statutes which states that "The establishment of grades, even by the board of the university, shall not affect the inherent right of the university to revise the sanctioned emoluments of any post at any time without adversely affecting an employee of the university already holding such a post." These statutes also state that "The appointing authority may sanction a higher start than the minimum of the grade on first employment or make advance increments if it deems fit." Orissa statutes provide that although rates of remuneration and conditions of service are subject to government rules, they shall be decided in agreement with the university and the university may submit proposals in this respect to government.

16.3. LEAVES, VACATIONS, AND ABSENCE

Statutes of the University of the Philippines provide that "Vacation leave of fifteen days and sick leave of fifteen days may be granted to officers and employees of the university at such times during the calendar year as may be approved by the president. Both leaves shall be cumulative and any part thereof which may not be taken within the calendar year in which it is earned may be carried over to succeeding years." Maternity leaves are also provided. Military service leave is granted to all employees with pay during the leave period when the service is required. Statutes of the Punjab Agricultural University provide that the vice-chancellor shall have the power to grant leave of any kind to all officers, teachers, and other employees of the university. According to the leave rules applicable to the Punjab government service, the registrar is authorized to grant leave to the lower salary ranks of nonacademic personnel. Other officers are empowered to grant leave to similar personnel working under them. The West Pakistan Agricultural University grants leaves under the terms of a university leave ordinance of considerable length and detail.

We recommend that the university act contain a provision empowering the governing body to establish such leaves as it deems appropriate for all personnel following recommendations of the chief administrative officer. Statutes should be developed differentiating in leave policies between academic and nonacademic staff, specifying the major types of leaves and the conditions under which staff members become entitled. Maternity, military, and sick leaves, for example, should be designated. Conditions under which leave is cumulative, when leave is with pay and when it is without pay, and the relation, if any, of the university's leave policy to a general state law should be specified. Other details should be left to regulations. Included would be specific excuses for leave such as funerals and family illness; requirements for certifying illness and the necessity of sick leave; preservation of leave rights when personnel are transfered within the university; application of a federal right-to-return-to-work law, if there is one; and rights and procedures when absences are unexcused, a leave is overstayed, or a job is abandoned.

There may be legal problems involved in paying staff members while on leave depending on the type of leave and the reason for granting it. In some cases in which a staff member is undergoing discharge proceedings and has been relieved of his work but is to be paid to the end of his contract term, auditors have raised objections on the ground that the university is not authorized to pay an individual unless service is being rendered. Ordinary leave has come to be accepted as part of an employee's contract and no question about continued payment is likely to be raised. Whether or not absence or failure to return following a leave are sufficient causes for discharge is not only a question of fact but a question which may be conditioned by the application of civil service rules.

16.4. LIABILITY—WORKMEN'S COMPENSATION

A general discussion of the tort liability of universities is contained in Chapter 3. The employment of nonacademic personnel calls special attention to this subject since many of the activities in which they engage are hazardous, semi-hazardous, or at least more likely to produce injuries on the job than the activities of the academic staff. In many jurisdictions, workmen's compensation or employer's liability laws apply to the nonacademic staff of universities. In a few instances they may apply to the academic staff. This is discussed in Chapters 3 and 15. In some American states the workmen's compensation law specifically excludes academic and administrative staff members of the university but includes nonacademic. Some compensation acts vary in coverage depending on the type of work being performed—even for the same employer. Decisions by the courts regarding coverage have not been consistent because in some instances the court has looked at the general occupation of the employer while in others it has looked at the specific job being performed by the employee.

With respect to an employer's liability or workmen's compensation act, the university may be covered expressly, it may be covered by implication, it may be covered only through its own election, or it may not be covered at all. This is a matter to be determined. Massachusetts law, for example, states that the act applies specifically to laborers, workmen, and mechanics but that it is optional with regard to other university employees. In American court cases it has been held that a state workmen's compensation act covered a student nurse who injured her back in the performance of duties, a county agricultural agent who suffered a stroke as a result of his work, a clerk who fell on the ice going to lunch, a woman employee who fell on a drive going to work, an elderly man injured by a group of boisterous boys while on his way to sign a payroll, a clerk who inadvertently shot himself while playing with the revolver of a campus policeman, and a football player who was admittedly in college to play football and was being payed enough to convince the court that this was his main occupation.

If a university is automatically covered by a state workmen's compensation or employer's liability law, then its main function in regard to nonacademic personnel is to see that the law is properly and thoroughly administered within the university. The director of nonacademic personnel or of university insurance would be the logical administrator of such a program. If the university is not automatically covered, we recommend a provision in the university statutes requiring that adequate coverage be provided through university regulations, either by election to come under a general law or through an insurance program maintained by the university. This is the kind of problem on which a university legal counsel can render valuable assistance. Rules and regulations should be developed and published.

16.5. PENSION AND INSURANCE PLANS

As a matter of policy we believe the same pension, retirement, and insurance benefits should apply to all personnel in the university. Some universities establish a gratuity for nonacademic employees whose earnings fall below a stipulated amount per month. Under this plan gratuities can be paid based on years of service of the employee. In case the employee dies before leaving the service of the institution, a death benefit can be paid to his survivors. For such employees no deductions from salary are required. Perhaps this is realistic and perhaps it is needed, but we still feel it would be better for all university employees to belong to a contributory system and receive salaries or wages which will permit them to make the necessary contribution. University retirement and pension plans are discussed in Chapter 15.

Even though, like the University of the Philippines, a university may participate in a government service insurance system, there may be gaps in the system which a university program could fill. University statutes should require adoption of a plan and its inclusion in the business office procedure manual. The plan should include both academic and nonacademic staff and should give protection to the pensionary rights of those who may be transferred from other government agencies or educational institutions or who are transferred to a new system. In a situation in which such transfers were made at the University of Washington, some of the university's previous contributions were left over after establishing all employees under the new system. In a suit to determine the right to this excess, the court held that it belonged to the employees. Provisions should be particularly clear on disability and accident cases and should require the development of a comprehensive safety program as a complement to the insurance plan.

16.6. PERQUISITES

Due to the location of the university or to particular units of it at which nonacademic personnel may be employed, it may be essential to supply housing, utilities, and schooling for their children—perhaps even certain concessions on travel. If these are to be supplied, it should be under a statutory authority to do so and under rules and salary arrangements which make it equitable when compared with the salary and perquisites of other nonacademic personnel. Individual contracts should state exactly what perquisites are included. A schedule of the values placed on such perquisites should be maintained by the chief financial officer. If a bonus or extra salary allowance is paid, the conditions permitting such payments and the amount allowable should be expressed in a schedule maintained by the chief financial officer.

16.7. EMPLOYMENT OF RELATIVES

A university policy on nepotism and desirable provisions in a university statute are discussed in Chapter 15. The same policy should apply to nonacademic employees as applies to academic employees, but if nonacademic employees come under the provisions of a general or a university civil service act, the provisions in such an act will control. Sometimes civil service laws contain no provisions on the employment of relatives. It is assumed, therefore, that there are no restrictions, in which case the university might not be able legally to impose a nepotism rule on nonacademic employees. Even so, it may be possible to avoid situations in which an employee is under the direct supervision of a close relative. University departments and employing units even under a civil service system are entitled to some choice among candidates offered for the position.

16.8. DISCHARGE AND SUSPENSION—CAUSE AND PROCEDURE

While the right to discharge a member of the academic staff is likely to be conditioned by his tenure status and application of the rules of academic freedom, the discharge of a member of the non-academic staff may be conditioned by the application of civil service rules and provisions in a union contract. The right to suspend, to issue reprimands, to withhold promotion, to withhold salary increments, or to demote are likewise subject to provisions which may be contained in the civil service law or in a union contract. In no instance, however, is a civil service law likely to deprive a university of its right to discharge; nor is a university expected to bargain away this right in a union contract. Hence, some substantive and procedural conditions must be stated. University statutes should contain a provision stating that nonacademic members of the staff may be discharged for good cause but that they shall first have the right to be informed and be heard, thus giving assurance of due process. Rules and regulations should then be developed which complement provisions in a civil service act if such is applicable.

The university may or may not have to deal with union contracts. As unions grow in strength and coverage and as universities grow and employ a greater diversity of both skilled and unskilled service personnel, there is an increased likelihood that bargaining with unions will be necessary. The university should strive to protect its right to discharge those who are not suitable. If protective rules and regulations are unduly onerous, it may be impossible for the university to employ and retain the kind of nonacademic personnel it needs. Certainly it should be protected by a provision for a probationary period of appropriate length, perhaps six months, following which an employee can be dismissed or separated without cause. A competent director of nonacademic personnel can be extremely helpful in preserving the rights of the university and of the employee and in affording effective liaison with labor unions and a state civil service commission.

16.9. DISPUTES AND GRIEVANCES

Disputes and grievances may be individual or collective. In either case the university should have a method of dealing with them. One of the functions of the director of nonacademic personnel is to take the lead in establishing procedures under which individuals can be heard. There should be a committee of the employee's own peers to hear his complaints and give him help in presenting them through administrative channels. The director of nonacademic personnel should be involved. If a union contract exists, there will be grievance procedures and a grievance committee in the union to act on the employee's behalf. The university administration should recognize the importance of good relations with nonacademic personnel and should assist the director in the establishment of policies which will reduce the number of complaints and grievances and which encourage all employing units in the university to discuss conditions of service with their employees so that understandings can be arrived at before grievances are magnified. It is helpful if each major employing unit, whether it be a college or department, designates some member of the academic staff with the temperament and the ability to deal with nonacademic employees to represent it on an informal basis in maintaining good relations and helping individual employees with problems arising out of their employment.

16.10. PRIVILEGES

Some universities provide free medical care including maternity care for nonacademic employees and their families. This would be particularly appropriate if the university is located where medical facilities are not available. If the university maintains an elementary school for the children of staff members, it should be available to the children of nonacademic staff on an equal basis. Many members of the nonacademic staff will be capable of further education in the university. Some institutions permit registration in courses at reduced or no tuition. The privilege of using the university library and athletic and recreational facilities should be extended to the nonacademic staff. In many institutions in the developing countries there may be wide social gaps between different categories of nonacademic personnel—the office secretaries, clerks, and stenographers, for example, and the daily laborers who dig around the flower beds or clean out the dairy barn. Some differentiation in conditions of service and privileges may be necessary, but on the other hand, in all the developing countries there are strong voices urging that menial labor is not degrading and advocating what has come to be known as the "dirty hands doctrine." What better place is there to put these noble sentiments into practice than in a university devoted to public service and to the solution of the country's problems of development?

CHAPTER – 17

Student Affairs

_____

Are universities structured and administered in such a way that a "living community of students" cannot be formed? This was the thesis of Roger Ebert, a discerning student at the University of Illinois, in an editorial in the student newspaper. He went on to remark, "One of the great errors which has been made by the philosophers of modern university administration is the decision that things can be done to students to make them be something. All I ask is that the university allow meaningful student life on the campus by ceasing to enforce and administer time-consuming meaningless substitutes."[1] Another student from the same university, in a paper delivered at a national fraternity convention, took a slightly different view.

Our institutions of higher learning are moving away from the argument that students are too immature to take part in the academic governing process. In general, student civil rights are not abrogated. Freedom of social mobility consonant with dignity, good taste, and regard for the rights of others is respected both on the campus and off. Many universities have made great progress towards encouraging activities and responsibilities similar to those imposed by society itself. What students want and need are more responsibilities akin to those in the "outside world" and more voice in their own government with the right attitude in respect to legitimate demands. I believe that college students will continue to be entrusted with greater freedoms.[2]

Aristotle said that youth "would always rather do noble deeds than useful ones. Their lives are regulated more by moral feeling than by reasoning. All their mistakes are in the direction of doing things excessively and vehemently. They overdo everything. They love too much, hate too much, and the same with everything else."

The lack of dialogue between students and university administration is an old complaint—and a valid one. But universities do try

_____

[1] Roger Ebert, "Testimony," editorial in _The Daily Illini_, November 11, 1964, p. 5.

[2] Richard G. Anderson, "Student Freedom and Responsibility." This paper was delivered by Anderson, a junior in civil engineering, University of Illinois, at the National Convention of Omicron Delta Kappa, Purdue University, April 22, 1966.

to do something about the problem. There is no lack of laws, statutes, and regulations compelling the university to do things *for* students—as well as *to* students. Unfortunately, many of the basic provisions were drafted by people who could not conceive of such a thing as a responsible community of students or who were confronted with a problem and sought to solve it through stringent requirements and prohibitions. No one would argue with the proposition that students ought to employ their minds and bodies usefully, but it is doubtful if this happy situation can be created by a law such as that enacted by the Illinois legislature, which states: "No student shall at any time be allowed to remain in or about the university in idleness or without full mental or industrial occupation."

The establishment of such offices as dean of student welfare, dean of students, or vice-president for student affairs indicates that universities do have some concern about student life and the student "community." The newer universities and many of the older universities which formerly admitted only male students are now confronted with the problems—and the opportunities—which stem from coeducation. Universities have no easy task developing and implementing a philosophy which satisfies the desire of parents for continued parental care on the part of the university and the desire of students for escape from bondage. The *in loco parentis* theory is still viable though it is difficult to see how it and many of the rules and regulations of a university can apply with equal justice to a particularly immature 18-year-old and a married 25-year-old with a family of his own who has returned to complete his education. And there are all sorts of gradations and combinations between these extremes—if, indeed, they be the extremes.

Some of the things which can be provided through university acts and statutes are discussed in the sections which follow.[3]

17.1. STUDENT RIGHTS—CODES AND REGULATIONS

An American work of law states that "The relation of a student to the college or university which he is attending is a contractual one and the terms of the contract are to be interpreted according to their natural meaning. Within the limitations imposed by applicable charter and statutory provisions, the governing body of a

---

[3] For a further discussion of university responsibilities and services for students, see Hannah, *Resource Book,* pp. 231-242.

university has a wide discretion . . . ." [4] But in an exhaustive report on student governance made by a special committee at the University of Illinois it is stated that "During the past half-century the broad legal powers of university officials have been narrowing and are now in a period of considerable change. Few modern courts would construe the relationship between the student and the public college solely as one of contract in which the student agrees to abide by whatever rules are stated at the time of his entrance." In this same report it is further stated that

The power of the university necessitates concern for the rights of students. The statutes of the University of Illinois clearly fix final authority in the hands of the board of trustees except where the board has delegated such authority to the president of the university or to others. While ultimate power cannot be placed in any administrative office or student or faculty organization, it may be delegated and may be exercised with more or less concern for the desires and needs of students. The necessary centralization of power makes the responsiveness of authority to students' concerns crucial in developing criteria for analysis of rules and regulations . . . the student's participation in the community of scholarship and education extends beyond the lecture hall and the laboratory. His social and political activities are part of the environment of university life, affected by and affecting the academic. The uses to which the university puts its power in the form of rules and the implementation of authority is thus a means of shaping that community.

What are the legal bases for determining student rights? Before answering this we should remind ourselves that students are citizens entitled to the constitutional and legislative guarantees which apply to all citizens. These cannot be impaired by university acts, statutes, or internal regulations. In reality the question becomes that of determining how far the university need go in imposing regulations and procedures to create and preserve a particular kind of academic environment. To achieve this objective and perform effectively *in loco parentis,* institutions may in their zeal invade rights which would otherwise be protected and deny natural justice or due process. A study of the internal working rules of any university discloses that those *in statu pupillari* are charged with a higher degree of conformity than the academics, though both may be dealt with in paternalistic fashion.

In some instances, particularly in the Latin-American countries, there are general legislative provisions controlling certain activities

---

[4] 14 *CJS* § 1358.

of and guaranteeing certain rights to students and student organizations. The Peru National Universities Act, for example, provides that "The statutes of the university shall set forth the rights and obligations of the students and the sanctions deriving from noncompliance with the obligations." The act states that student attendance of classes is obligatory and if the student's absences exceed 30 per cent he shall not be permitted to take the final examination. Here is a requirement at the legislative level which is ordinarily not even included in a university statute but which is determined by the professor teaching the course. The act also specifies how student delegates are elected for participation in university administration and states that such delegates are not denied the right to belong to a student federation. It further states that "The rights of the students to form associations in harmony with the goals of the university shall be recognized."

Some legislatures in the American states have passed laws outlawing and forbidding the use of university buildings by student organizations which are regarded as subversive or un-American. Ordinarily, however, one does not expect the legislature or the university act itself to express particular rules and prohibitions. Rather, it should contain the authority for proper university officers and entities to develop needed rules and regulations. The decree establishing the Rural University of Minas Gerais in Brazil provides for a general assistance directorate—this is the agency in the university dealing with students. Among its functions are those of planning services for students; promoting the integration of student and professor into the university community by means of cultural and recreational activities; orientation of students; and the administration of dormitories, dining halls, and a university social center. With allowance for variation from one institution to another—and the variation is greater between institutions than between countries—university acts authorize the governing body to do the following:

1. Appoint a dean of students or dean of student welfare and specify that his functions shall be as prescribed in university statutes.[5]

2. Provide for the disciplining of students.

3. Provide housing rules.

----

[5] The functions of a dean of student welfare are discussed in Chapter 9.

4. Establish the academic standards which apply to students.
5. Institute scholarships, fellowships, and student loan programs.
6. Establish fees and tuition.
7. Grant degrees.

With respect to all these subjects, authority is delegated by the board to the administration of the university. Sometimes there are further statutory provisions; more often there are not. With few exceptions, most of which occur in Latin-American universities,[6] the rules, regulations, and procedures which affect students are not expressed in university statutes, though the statutes contain either expressly or by implication an authorization for the development of internal rules by university officers and authorities. University statutes are certainly not the appropriate medium for detailing essential rules and regulations applying to students. However, the statutes should insure a basic framework within the university which will beget proper consideration of student rights and which will give the dean of student affairs the status his position deserves. In many institutions, functions which should logically fall in his jurisdiction are parceled out among other officers of the university with the result that the student suffers. Likewise, the dean of students is sometimes considered as a lower echelon officer and is not included as a member of the academic council or of important university committees having to do with the rights and welfare of students. The statutes can be used to correct these situations.

Though there is some evidence of change in the attitude American courts have taken toward university student rights, many early cases indicate a prejudice in favor of the institution. In 1913, the Supreme Court of Kentucky upheld a regulation of Berea College prohibiting students from eating in public eating houses. The court said, "For the purposes of this case, the school, its officers, and students are a legal entity, as much so as any family and like a father may direct his children, those in charge of boarding

---

[6] Statutes of the Universidad Agraria in Peru state that students have the obligation to attend classes, to pay tuition and fees punctually, to vote in all appropriate elections, to attend public functions of the university and of their college, to observe the proper behavior befitting a university student, to carry with them their university identification and present it when asked to do so, and to do anything else required by the bylaws. These same statutes give students the right to petition, either individually or collectively.

schools are well within their rights and powers when they direct their students what to eat and where they may get it, where they may go, and what forms of amusement they are forbidden." In an 1891 Illinois Supreme Court decision it was held that the University of Illinois could enforce a rule compelling students to attend a nonsectarian chapel service. In 1917, during World War I, the court upheld expulsion by Columbia University of a student who declared in a speech made outside the university that there would be a draft revolution during the war. The court upheld the expulsion on the grounds that he was morally unfit and that the university would be injured by his continued presence.

Many factors in American university life have produced changes in theories about student rights and the relationship of student and university. Segregation cases in the American federal courts and more effective student organization and expression of views have contributed to these changes. The record shows that students have not always been denied redress. The courts will allow mandamus to compel conferring of a degree which a student has earned but which is withheld without cause, in bad faith, or through failure to perform some ministerial act. They have held, likewise, that the action of mandamus lies to compel issuance of a transcript of the student's record—even though the student might have been expelled for disciplinary reasons. In a few instances the courts have followed the contract theory and have allowed specific performance to compel the university to perform. Courts have also recognized the confidential nature of many student records maintained by the university and have protected students in the use of these records.[7] Likewise, the courts have held that a public institution can be compelled to admit a student who meets its requirements and has followed the prescribed procedures.[8]

How do principles of academic freedom apply to students? In its report on student governance at the University of Illinois a special committee said,

A large and vibrant university drawing on a diversity of groups and nations is more than likely to be the scene of vigorous, stimulating, and often spectacular controversy. If the atmosphere of learning and intellectual challenge is present, it is quite likely to develop viewpoints which oppose accepted or authoritative opinion in many areas of politi-

----

[7] See Chapter 9, section 16 for a discussion of university records.

[8] A discussion of the right to admission is contained in Chapter 12.

cal action. This is the inevitable and necessary consequence of searching analysis, free flow of ideas, and access to expression and is the sign that the intellectual process is at work.

In "Toward a Standard for Student Academic Freedom," [9] Professor Phillip Monypenny states:

Students should not suffer penalties for the expression of their own viewpoint nor for refusing to accept the assumptions of their instructors nor for going beyond the classroom assignment to make an argument or test an assertion. They can properly be held to account for knowing the official viewpoint of the classroom, the particular selection of data which is there offered, and the necessary logical consequences of that viewpoint and data, but knowing or asserting other or more is certainly not to be penalized. If it is, student academic freedom suffers and academic freedom does not exist.

Many of the problems with which American universities are now confronted stem from a deeper student interest in social and political concerns. This is not new in Latin-American universities. There the right to political action by students is well recognized. But in all universities there must be some restraint in order that the educational process can continue and that some semblance of order can be maintained in the university community. Pressures sometimes induce university administrators to adopt constrictive institutional sanctions which are simply reiterations of civil sanctions already in existence, when a better approach would have been to establish a free speech area—as some universities have done.

We feel that the following are of sufficient importance to students to justify a university statutory provision under which the university guarantees:

Freedom of speech

Freedom of assembly

Freedom to organize for any lawful purpose

The right to petition

The right to publish

The right to pursue personal religious beliefs

We do not believe any of these guarantees should be compromised by hampering rules and regulations which may seem trivial but which in effect interfere with these rights. The excessive, un-

---

[9] Phillip Monypenny, "Toward a Standard for Student Academic Freedom," *Law and Contemporary Problems*, XXVIII (Duke Univ., 1963), p. 625.

lawful, or detrimental employment of any of these rights can be covered in a properly drafted statute on cause for student dismissal, reprimand, or the imposing of other penalties. Certainly the university has a right to enforce reasonable rules and regulations on the use of buildings and premises, timing of events, prior warning when security may be needed, cleanliness, sanitation, and other matters—as long as such regulations or rules are not in fact guises for prohibiting a legitimate activity.

There must be insurance through internal rules and their enforcement that students who are qualified will not be denied equal use of university facilities, admission to courses, and services of the university. Academic freedom for students does not mean that they can dictate the content of courses or the method of instruction. Individual teachers must have a high discretion in handling their courses and in making decisions about a student's standing in the course. Academic freedom for students should not mean that they can in any way threaten the right of the instructor to make these kinds of decisions. The University of the Philippines Statutes recognize that students should participate in controversial activities and that this is one way to train leaders of thought and action for the country. The statutes then contain rather extensive provisions on rights and limitations.

Who should formulate the rules and regulations applying to students? What role should students play in the process? Are different rules and regulations implied for postgraduate students? How should rules be codified, published, and distributed? These are all important questions which should be satisfactorily answered within the university. The rule-making process is not one in which it will be expected the governing body will engage, though the university act should give the board authority to establish rules and regulations for students with the provision that this authority may be delegated. University statutes should provide that the dean of student welfare be responsible for development of the general rules and regulations applying to students with approval by the chief administrative officer. The statutes should further provide for faculty participation in this process and for receiving recommendations from student government. It should provide also that rules pertaining to particular activities such as those necessary for the registrar, controller, director of physical plant, or the individual colleges be developed by them and published subject to approval by the chief administrative officer. This will give the latter an opportunity to have them reviewed by the dean of student welfare, the university legal counsel, or by anyone else who he believes can offer useful advice about their efficacy and application to students.

It is particularly important that the university and its colleges publish rules on academic standing. Since there is no question about the right of an institution to dismiss a student for failure to meet academic standards, these standards should be established and understood. Frequently the rules which govern students stem from a number of sources, are not kept up-to-date, and in case of legal controversy cannot be "pinpointed" with respect to their origin, exact wording (there may be more than one version), or authenticity. They may exist as directives from the chief administrative officer or other officers of administration, in the minutes of the governing body, sometimes by action of the legislature, or as rules formulated by the dean of student welfare subject to whatever committee activity or advisory assistance he might have had. The graduate school and professional schools at the university should be consulted because many of the rules which apply to undergraduate students are not applicable to graduate or professional students. Though in a large university it may be necessary to have several separate publications covering particular kinds of rules and regulations, all those affecting students generally should be published under the direction of the dean of student welfare in one publication in which the subject matter is logically organized and codified, clearly stated, and thoroughly indexed.

17.2. DISCIPLINARY MEASURES

Though university acts generally give the governing board authority to establish disciplinary procedures for students, it is either expressly stated or implied that rules of procedure shall be developed and administered by the faculty and administration of the university under provisions expressed in the university statutes. There is great diversity in such statutes with respect to both detail and substance. Some, like those of the University of the Philippines, run to several pages and include rules and regulations which are normally left to internal determination by appropriate authorities and officers. Some empower the chief administrative officer to develop the rules and procedures for disciplinary action, some place this authority with the academic council, some vest the individual college faculties with a high degree of authority but provide that no student can be dismissed or expelled without a faculty vote (Harvard University, for example). A few statutes provide for a disciplinary procedure, establish a disciplinary committee (sometimes more than one committee where there are professional and graduate colleges), give the student a right to a fair hearing with representation if he desires, and provide for appeal to a higher body within the university or directly to the governing board. Most statutes, however, do not contain the elements which would insure due process. If this is provided it is generally a matter of university regulation. Many times it does not exist.

In early decisions by American courts it was held that in effect a student had no right to due process if it were not provided by the university act, statutes, or regulations. Later and better decisions indicate that the right exists by implication if not by express provision. Though universities have a wide latitude in determining the cause for dismissal or other disciplinary action, in no case has a court upheld dismissal when no reason was stated. Courts have held such action to be arbitrary and capricious. Likewise, a student's rights are violated when a dismissal action stems from malice. With respect to cause, it has been held that a breach of conduct may justify dismissal without being in violation of any specific rule or regulation. The University of the Philippines Statutes, which list several rules the infraction of which will lead to discipline, state that the specification of these rules shall not be construed to exclude other offenses or breaches which might lead to disciplinary action. The University of Ibadan Act states that lack of diligence may be treated as misconduct for purposes of disciplining students.

As we have mentioned earlier, there is no question about the right of an institution to dismiss a student who fails to meet academic standards. There are generally provisions, however, that a student may petition for readmission after a lapse of time. Some institutions—Harvard University, for example—distinguish between dismissal and expulsion, the latter representing the highest academic censure and constituting a final separation from the university.

What procedural safeguards should exist for a student subjected by university rules to dismissal, suspension, or other serious penalty? Professor Sol Jacobsen in an article entitled "Student and Faculty Due Process," [10] states that "Considerations of fundamental fairness point to the following elements as a bare minimum":

1. Service of written charges and a clear and concise statement of the supporting evidence,
2. A reasonable opportunity to answer the charges in writing,
3. A trial before an impartial tribunal,
4. The right of examining and cross-examining witnesses and of producing witnesses and other evidence in his own behalf,
5. Representation by "counsel" or other friend in court,
6. A right of appeal to an authority higher than the trial court.

(In his article Professor Jacobsen used the term "court" to designate the university hearing tribunal.)

The statement in a 1958 decision of the Supreme Court of Michigan that "Courts do not interfere with administrative management of colleges and universities except when there has been an abuse of discretion" does not conflict with the following statement in a decision by a United States Federal Court of Appeals:

In the disciplining of college students there are no considerations of immediate danger to the public or of peril to the national security which should prevent the board from exercising at least the fundamental principles of fairness by giving the accused students notice of the charges and an opportunity to be heard in their own defense. Indeed, the example set by the board in failing to do so, if not corrected by the courts, can well break the spirit of the expelled students and of others familiar with the injustice and do inestimable harm to their education.

The judge goes on to quote with approval Professor Warren A. Seavey of the Harvard Law School: "It is shocking that the officials of a state educational institution which can function properly only if our freedoms are preserved should not understand the elementary principles of fair play. It is equally shocking to find that a court supports them in denying to a student the protection given to a pickpocket." [11] This statement by Professor Seavey was a criticism of an Illinois Appellate Court which held that the University of Illinois could, without informing a student of the cause until she

---

[10] Sol Jacobsen, "Student and Faculty Due Process," *AAUP Bulletin*, LII (June 1966), 6. 201.

[11] Warren A. Seavey, "Dismissal of Students: Due Process," *Harvard Law Review*, 70 (June 1957), p. 1406.

appeared with her attorney before the discipline committee, discharge her without supplying prior notice of the charges, providing for a formal hearing, or giving her an opportunity to confront or examine adverse witnesses. Whether private institutions, particularly those receiving large amounts of government financial aid, owe students less consideration than public institutions in dismissal cases is an open question. American courts have given some intimation that due process is still implied.

A definition of "cause" is not nearly so important as provision for due process or fundamental justice. In its report on student governance at the University of Illinois, a special committee stated that "We should remember that in relation to students, the university acts from a position of strength and the student from one of relative weakness. It is this consideration, for example, which leads us to emphasize the need for procedures which will insure that disciplinary actions follow due process and are based on standards which insure 'fair play' to the accused." The University of the Philippines recognizes this disparity by providing that the dean of a college shall appoint one professor as guidance counselor whose job it is to take the side of any student facing disciplinary action. Such a provision plus sensible handling in college deans' offices and by the dean of student welfare can solve many problems to the advantage of both the student and the institution and spare students and staff the stress and strain of disciplinary proceedings.

In summary, we recommend that the university statutes and appropriate university regulations establish a guarantee of due process for students subject to serious charges which might lead to dismissal, that students be provided with assistance in meeting the charges and furthering their own rights, that the procedures for appeal be clearly delineated, and that the final appeal body be the governing body of the institution. There should be provision for involvement of the academic council in the appointment of an appropriate committee or committees to hold initial hearings, provision for student representation on such committees, and some latitude in meting out punishment so that there may be alternatives to expulsion, dismissal, or suspension. Denial of credit in a course or of the right to participate in particular extracurricular activities, suspension of social privileges, probation, and reprimand are all devices which universities employ.

17.3. STUDENT GOVERNMENT—STUDENT UNIONS

In most universities there is an organization of students which acts to represent the student body. The nature of this organization, its authority, and its objectives vary considerably in different parts of the world and between institutions. In Latin-American universities, where students have a constitutional right to participate in university governance, the impact of a student organization or student union is much greater than it is likely to be in an American or African university where student government bodies play only an advisory role. Within a university there may be a delegation of some authority to engage in self-government—to housing groups, clubs, and other associations, for example, which are permitted and expected to develop their own rules and procedures, subject to general university rules or requirements.

Statutes of the Orissa University of Agriculture and Technology provide that "The Dean of Student Welfare shall control and for this purpose formulate rules for extracurricular activities including . . . student unions. . . ." The Peru National Universities Act provides: "The right of the students to form associations in harmony with the goals of the university shall be recognized." The statutes of Southern Illinois University provide for a student council and state that it "shall be the official organization designated to represent the students in matters pertaining to student welfare, student activities, student participation in university affairs, student participation in university planning and administration, and student opinion." These statutes further provide that the student council shall be composed of members elected from year to year by the student body and that it shall choose its own officers. Statutes of the Mysore University of Agricultural Sciences provide that "There may exist within the university, as an official authority of the university, an organization of the student body known as the student association." Provision is then made for submission of a proposed constitution and bylaws for the association to the dean of student welfare for eventual approval by the academic council. It is also provided that the academic council may recommend to the governing body dissolution of the student association when such action is deemed to be in the best interests of the university. Statutes of the University of the Philippines provide that "There shall be a student union which shall take charge of the cultural and social programs and activities of the student body at university level . . . the student union shall take the place of the university student council which is hereby abolished." Following this statement are detailed provisions about officers, rights, duties, election of members, offenses by the student union and other student organizations, and a number of matters which should not be a part of the university statutes.

We believe that university statutes should provide for a student organization or association to be the official voice of the students in bringing matters before the university administration. The statutes should not contain details but should provide that such an organization represent all students and that procedures be used which will insure fairness in election to the body and selection of its officers. If the student organization exists by virtue of law as in the Latin-American countries, then such a statute would be unnecessary. The university should not be given the right to make arbitrary judgments about recognition of student organizations, but it should be given the right to make judgments based on fact and to withdraw recognition or deny student membership in an organization when, after a statement of cause and an appropriate hearing and determination, the organization is found to be inimical to the welfare of the university. Many times student organizations are in fact dominated by nonstudent members and are not entitled to the status of a university student organization. On the other hand, the students themselves should be free to belong to any organization permitted by the laws of the country.

One of the problems with student government is the lack of communication which so frequently exists between its leaders and the university administration. This gap can be partially closed by providing for faculty advisers or counselors to organizations. When the right people are chosen, this can be very helpful. When the wrong people are chosen, students feel they are under surveillance and the intimidation may be so real as to prevent anything constructive coming to the university from student organizations. This is a matter which cannot be regulated by statute or internal rules; it depends on the philosophy and personalities of those who are in charge of university affairs. Ideally, a free flow of communications should exist between student government and other student bodies and those elements of the university concerned with their activities. There is no substitute for personal acquaintance and frequent informal discussions.

17.4. PARTICIPATION IN UNIVERSITY GOVERNMENT

In the Latin-American countries student participation in university government is insured by legislation and in some cases by constitutional provisions. In the Universidad Agraria in Peru, for example, one-third of the assembly, the university council, and all the college councils must be student members. Both the National Universities Act and university statutes contain provisions on elections and the duty of students to serve on these bodies. Conversely, the university acts in India contain no provisions on student representation in university government or administration and very few provisions are contained in statutes. Statutes of the Orissa University of Agriculture and Technology provide that "Student discipline boards appointed by the academic council may co-opt one student of the university unless the academic council directs otherwise." Other Indian agricultural university statutes studied did not make even this slight concession in the direction of student representation. The University of Nigeria Statutes go somewhat further by providing that two students shall be elected to the board of student welfare and that students shall serve on committees responsible for formulating regulations for hostel management and occupancy.

Most universities in the world would not subscribe to a policy which places students in the position of control on any university authority or committee. A majority of universities are likely to take an opposite view and deny to students rightful representation on university authorities and committees which affect their welfare directly and materially. The committee which studied student governance at the University of Illinois made this cogent statement:

Students bring one very important thing to the process of student governance and to university policy-making—themselves. Because they do participate in the operation of rules, regulations, and policies, even as passive subordinates, they have an understanding of how things work that no other part of the campus has. Theirs is the foot that the shoe pinches. The differences in age, status, and perspective which divide faculty and administration from the student are wide and often prevent anyone but the student from adequately finding and expressing his interests and needs.

We believe university statutes should provide for student representation on specified university bodies or permanent committees that are close to their interests and should further provide that they may have representation on other bodies or committees on approval of the chief administrative officer or academic council. The details of such representation should be left to internal regulations but should be primarily the responsibility of the student governing body. Furthermore, there should be provision that students be represented on ad hoc committees which consider matters important to them— the selection committee for a dean of students, for example. Such participation by students should be provided also at the college and departmental level with respect to committees or bodies on which they may appropriately serve. Students who serve on committees should have the same rights and privileges as other committee members. Decisions about the committees on which students should serve should be reached by the chief administrative officer and the academic council or the dean of a college or a department head after an appropriate joint committee of students and faculty have considered the matter and made recommendations.

17.5. STUDENT ORGANIZATIONS AND CLUBS

What control should a university exercise over student organizations, societies and fraternities, clubs, or other entities created by students? Statutes of the University of the Philippines provide that a group is not a student organization unless 50 per cent or more of its members and its principal officers are students. Provincial, sectional, and regional organizations are prohibited. A distinction is made between university student organizations and college student organizations, the former being under the supervision of the dean of student affairs. A committee on student extracurricular activities under the control and supervision of the dean of students is responsible for consideration of general policies and regulations governing the affairs of student organizations. One or more faculty advisers are required to be chosen by the organization and approved by the dean of student affairs. Constitutions for all student organizations must be approved by the dean of student affairs. Most of the Indian agricultural university acts give the dean of student welfare the right to control student organizations. Statutes of the Orissa University of Agriculture and Technology provide that the university controller shall act as treasurer of all student organization funds. The University of Illinois has a similar requirement. In many American universities, student organizations come under the jurisdiction of the dean of students and there is a requirement that their funds be in the custody of the controller or chief financial officer.

The Supreme Court of the United States in 1915 upheld a statute of the state of Mississippi prohibiting secret societies in state colleges and universities. Forty years later a federal district court in New York cited this Mississippi decision in upholding a resolution of the board of trustees of the State University of New York which barred social organizations in any of the units of the state university from being affiliated with national organizations and prohibited any campus organization from operating under any rule which barred students because of race, color, religion, creed, national origin, or other artificial criteria. But in 1882, the Supreme Court of Indiana held invalid a rule of the trustees of Purdue University which disqualified for admission any member of a Greek letter fraternity. In that case the court pointed out that admission to a public institution is one thing and the government and control of students after they are admitted is another. The court stated that a student who seeks admission impliedly promises to submit to the rules of the university and that the invocation of the above rule was, in a sense, prejudging the student's future actions. But the court also said, "It is clearly within the power of the trustees to absolutely prohibit any connection between the Greek fraternities and the university."

The philosophy of the university should be one of encouragement to student organizations and not one of repression. The object of a university should be to permit free association for any legitimate purpose but to prohibit the recognition or continued functioning of organizations which, either in terms of their policy or activities, are violative of the law or of fundamental policies of the university. For example, the board of trustees of the University of Illinois approved a policy on student organization membership, purpose, and program which states: "In order to receive and maintain university recognition, student organizations shall select members on an individual basis without restrictions based on race, religion, or national origin. An organization's purposes and programs shall not be in conflict with the university's established policy of nondiscrimination." There are, however, provisos in the official interpretation of this policy which permit the organization of religious groups and groups representing a national culture. Initial determination of compliance rests with the dean of student welfare. The policy statement quoted contains no restrictions about purpose or objective of student organizations except that they shall not conflict with the university's established policy of nondiscrimination.

We believe the above represents a proper approach and that without inventing onerous rules and requirements with respect to reporting, listing members, and other things which would bespeak an undesirable surveillance, the dean of student welfare or his counterpart should be empowered to make a first judgment on whether or not a student organization meets the university policy. Rules should provide that new organizations submit a petition to the dean of students containing a statement of their purpose, the names of their officers and original organizers, and a general description of their contemplated membership and activities. A requirement that the funds of all student organizations be maintained by the university business officer in a special account we do not feel is restrictive; it simply helps induce better business practices, insures the safety of the money, and still permits the organization to use it. We feel that it is appropriate also to require a faculty adviser of the students' choice for any student organization.

17.6. RESIDENCE REQUIREMENTS

There is a general assumption that the official residence of a student is that of his parents. This overlooks the fact that some students do not have parents, some are of legal age and no longer live at home, and others are married, living at the university with their families and that this is their residence. So far as local law is concerned, the test of residence may be the right to vote or the liability to pay taxes. Universities are interested in the residence of a student primarily because there are usually higher tuition fees and different admission standards for nonresidents. Hence, if a student who originally came from another state or region can establish the university community as his legal residence, he will be entitled to a lower tuition fee and perhaps to some other advantages which nonresidents do not have.

While the governing body can legally require the payment of higher fees by nonresidents and can adopt reasonable rules for determining residence, it cannot adopt rules which in effect result in unequal treatment of persons in the same class or category. The trustees of Idaho State College, for example, adopted a rule that "Any person who is properly classified as a nonresident student retains that status throughout continuous regular-term attendance at any institution of higher learning in Idaho." The Supreme Court of Idaho struck down this rule on behalf of a 25-year-old, self-supporting student who was a nonresident from the state of Vermont at the time he registered but who acquired residence after one year in Idaho. In an Ohio decision, the Supreme Court held that "citizen" of a city or state may for purposes of determining tuition to a university be construed the same as "resident." In the particular case the court held that the child of an alien residing in the city of Cincinnati was entitled to free tuition in the University of Cincinnati under a rule so providing.

If the university intends to make any distinction in any way between resident and nonresident students it should define residence in university statutes and authorize the chief administrative officer to develop rules and procedures for determining residence in accordance with the definition. The definition should accord with the general law of the country, state, or region. At least it should not require a longer period or impose conditions more difficult to meet. Likewise, the rules should be reasonable and should not contain procedural or ministerial features which make it difficult to qualify.

17.7. FEES AND TUITION

University acts generally authorize the governing body to fix fees and tuition. In some instances the law provides that tuition shall be free to residents of the state or region. The purpose of such a provision is to encourage attendance by qualified students with limited means. The trend, however, is toward making a charge for tuition and establishing a variety of fees. The University of the Philippines Act, for example, provides that "The board of regents has the power to fix the tuition fees required of students as well as matriculation fees, graduation fees, and fees for laboratory courses and all special fees and to remit the same in special cases." The Jawaharlal Nehru Agricultural University Act authorizes the governing body to establish fees for any purpose by university statute. The Peru National Universities Act authorizes the universities to charge tuition either by the particular course taken or by the entire course of study or curriculum. Statutes of Columbia University provide that "The fees to be paid by students in the several schools and colleges of the university shall be such in amount and in effect on such dates as the trustees shall from time to time fix and determine." Punjab Agricultural University Statutes classify fees in several categories: "admission, tuition, medical, examination, university registration, social and recreational, and any other prescribed from time to time." The statutes further provide that "The amount chargeable under each category at various levels of academic pursuit as well as terms of payment and the provisions of penalties for nonpayment shall be approved by the board upon the recommendations of the academic council, the finance committee, and the vice-chancellor."

Questions regarding the legality of fee and tuition charges have been before the American courts many times. Unless the governing body is expressly prohibited by statute from charging tuition to residents of the state, it has this right by implication, and in those cases where it is expressly provided that tuition shall be free, the courts have held that the governing body is not prevented from assessing fees for reasonable purposes. There has been some difference of opinion in the courts about items covered by tuition. The Kansas Supreme Court, for example, held that tuition included the right to use the library and that the board of regents was therefore prohibited from assessing a special library fee. On the other hand, the Supreme Court of Wisconsin held that the board could legally charge an incidental fee for heat and light. The right to charge higher tuition for nonresidents and the right to provide free tuition to particular classes of students based on a reasonable distinction have been upheld by the courts. When a student's application for admission is approved, there is an implied contractual obligation to pay the fees and tuition provided in any official university publication. Courts have held, however, that there is nothing to prevent the university and a student from making a different contract.

The right to a refund of tuition and fees becomes an important question when a student does not finish the term. American courts have held that even if university regulations do not provide for partial refund depending on the length of the term remaining when a student leaves the university, the student is entitled to a refund. However, university statutes or regulations providing that there shall be no refund of tuition or fees when a student is suspended, expelled, or withdraws without cause will be upheld.

The university act should provide that reasonable fees, tuition, and other necessary student charges may be established by the board on recommendation of the chief administrative officer. The act should require that fees, tuition, and other charges be published in the university register or other official publication. It should also provide that refunds shall be allowed under provisions to be established in the university statutes. The statutes should specify the kinds of fees and charges which can be made, but the amounts to be assessed and the details regarding their payment and refund should be in university regulations.

17.8. LOANS AND SCHOLARSHIPS

Almost without exception, acts creating the American land-grant colleges and universities provided for some system of free scholarships within the state. These were based on various criteria, geographical and otherwise, but in all cases the purpose was the same: to provide encouragement for able students who might not otherwise be able to attend. However, need was not the only criterion. In many states there were provisions for competitive examinations at the county or school district level, and even in those cases where a more arbitrary system of selection was provided, there was generally some conditioning language about "diligence and proficiency." More important are American court decisions holding that while it is proper to provide for such free legislative scholarships generally referred to as "tuition scholarships," they must not be provided to classes of recipients selected in an arbitrary manner or by an official who has a discretion to select those whom he chooses. Courts have held that children of deceased war veterans is not an arbitrary classification and that in all cases where there is provision for competition and examination, the scholarship program will be upheld.

The University of the Philippines Act provides that "The board shall have the power to provide fellowships and scholarships and to award the same to students giving special evidence of merit." The decree creating the Rural University of Minas Gerais in Brazil gives the university council authority to award scholarships. The Peru National Universities Act provides that

The state shall create scholarships in the national universities consisting of periodic payments sufficient to take care of the vital necessities of students of modest economic condition. The distribution of the scholarships among the universities will be done by the interuniversity council, keeping in mind the regional, social, and economic characteristics and necessities and merits of the applicants. The students who are awarded this type of scholarship are obligated to give service to the state for at least two years in the manner and under the conditions which the state or the interuniversity council shall set forth in each case.

This is more comprehensive than provisions generally found, im-

plies more aid for the student, and contains an additional feature—
one exacting a period of service from the recipient following graduation. Many of the American acts providing for county scholarships to the university designate all or a portion of these scholarships as agricultural and stipulate that they may be awarded only
to a student who enrolls in an agricultural course at the university.
This is one way higher education in agriculture can be encouraged
in a developing country.

With respect to scholarships other than those provided by the
legislature, it is customary for university statutes to empower
the governing body of the university to determine the conditions
under which they are granted. The statutes of Columbia University, for example, provide that "The university council shall have
the power to determine the conditions upon which fellowships and
university scholarships shall be awarded, to appoint all fellows and
university scholars, and to make rules for their government subject
to such restrictions as may be prescribed by the statutes or by the
terms upon which the several fellowships and university scholarships are established." Statutes of the University of the Philippines classify the various kinds of scholarships and give the president of the university the ultimate authority to grant or deny
them. However, appropriate faculty bodies are involved in recommending recipients. One category includes valedictorians and
salutatorians from public and private high schools and vocational
schools. Punjab Agricultural University Statutes provide that the
academic council shall propose the rules to the governing body
before the award of scholarships, fellowships, and other distinctions. The Andhra Pradesh Agricultural University Statutes lodge
this function with the dean of student affairs but provide that proposals shall originate in appropriate faculty boards. Statutes of the
Mysore University of Agricultural Sciences require the university
to establish and maintain a scholarship fund into which all money
for scholarships shall be deposited and from which scholarships
shall be paid. The statutes of several universities contain a similar
provision.

Whether or not "tuition scholarships" are to be created is a
question of legislative policy. We believe that agriculture in the
developing countries needs a boost of this kind. If such scholarships are provided, we believe they should be distributed geographically, that the recipients should be determined by competi-

tive examinations conducted under the auspices of the university, and that provisions should be made for granting additional scholarships to geographical or political subdivisions of the state or region when other such units fail to meet their quota. We recommend also that the university act provide for maintenance of a scholarship fund by the chief financial officer of the university and that all monies for this purpose from all sources, whether public or private, be placed in this fund. The act should provide that the use of this money for payment of scholarships and fellowships will be as provided in university statutes. The statutes, in turn, should establish the system under which appropriate committees of the various faculties in the university will be involved in recommending candidates. The graduate faculty should be involved in awarding fellowships. This implies cooperation between the dean of student welfare, the deans of the colleges, and the committees established to make recommendations. It implies also that the chief financial officer in cooperation with the dean of student welfare should publish and keep up to date essential information about available fellowships and scholarships, the legal conditions under which they can be granted, their duration, and the amount of financial help provided by them.

The university act should authorize the establishment of a student loan fund to be maintained by the chief financial officer and used in accordance with provisions in the university statutes. University statutes should then establish a system similar to that for awarding scholarships under which rules for making loans will be developed and administered. The statutes themselves should contain certain major policy provisions having to do with interest on such loans, time and period of payment, amount to be extended to any one student, and the general conditions under which a loan may be made. Many institutions have a scholarship and loan board on which college representatives, appropriate university officers, and some students serve. The chief financial officer, the dean of student welfare, and registrar or director of admissions are generally included. As with scholarships, we believe that loans are not to be determined wholly through administrative action, but that appropriate faculties should be involved. If general university funds are to be used in establishing a student loan fund, there should be statutory authorization. Final judgment about acceptance of gifts for student loans must be made by the governing body on recommendation of the chief administrative officer. Some offers may be accompanied by conditions which are unacceptable to the university. This applies likewise to trusts and other beneficences creating fellowships and scholarships.

17.9. STUDENT EMPLOYMENT—WORK PROGRAMS

An early law relating to the University of California provided that "A system of moderate manual labor must be established in connection with the agricultural college upon its agricultural and ornamental grounds for practical education in agriculture and landscape gardening." The original act establishing Michigan State College provided that the board in consultation with the faculty should establish rules about the number of hours students should devote to manual labor and to study, but with the proviso that a minimum of three hours per day be devoted to labor and that no student be excused except for sickness or infirmity. The agricultural acts in Punjab, Andhra Pradesh, and Orissa in India all provide that the dean of student welfare shall make arrangements for the employment of students in accordance with plans to be approved by the vice-chancellor. The Udaipur University Statutes contain a similar provision but require consultations with the director of the experiment station and the director of the extension service. Statutes of the University of the Philippines provide that "The president or the business executive on his behalf may appoint students as laborers or assistants, assign them to the various units, and grant them compensation commensurate with the nature and scope of their work. The working hours, academic load, and compensation of such students shall be in accordance with the rules of the university." Statutes of the University of Illinois provide that "All student employees are to be paid on the basis of the classification and scale of wages of student assistants approved by the president of the university." Schedules of wages and other procedure on student employment are contained in *The Business Policy and Procedure Manual.*

A student work program may be designed to accomplish some or all of three main objectives: (1) to give the student experience and the feel of working with his hands, (2) to accomplish needed work for the university, and (3) to permit the student to earn a portion of his university expenses. We believe these objectives should be reflected in a university act which provides for student employment and which places with the administration of the university the responsibility for developing such a program. University statutes should make the dean of student welfare responsible for overall features of student employment in the university but should provide for the involvement of college deans and the heads of other units which are affected. Student representation should be provided on the university body having to do with the student employment program. The emphasis to be placed on a student work program and the extent to which such a program can be successfully carried out will vary from one country to another depending on background and culture and on the pressure for jobs by people at the nonacademic staff level. There are many positions in the university, however, which can be filled by qualified students which could not be filled by most people who are employed at the service level.

Until a high percentage of students can come from a rural setting in which they have lived and worked through the period of their secondary education, a program providing experience and an opportunity to use agricultural tools will be important. Eventually it would be hoped that the main objective of a student employment program would be to enable students to earn and defray a portion of their college expenses.

Depending on the ability of the student and the number of hours he works, some reduction may be necessary in the amount of academic work he carries. Statutes of the Mysore University of Agricultural Sciences provide that "An enrolled student shall not engage in work for the university or outside the university for or without compensation when such work is found by the director of student welfare to interfere seriously with the quality of the student's classwork." This is a good provision with the following qualifications: the determination should be made by the dean of the student's college, not by the dean of student welfare; and, if the student needs the income, it should be possible for him to take a reduced academic schedule.

17.10. STUDENT HOUSING

University regulations controlling where students shall live and how they shall live frequently create issues between students and the institution. Such issues are complicated by the diversity of age and maturity of students and the difficulty of framing regulations which are equally appropriate for all students. Added to this is an economic urge on the part of those universities which have engaged in extensive housing programs for students; they naturally desire full occupancy, the achievement of which may entail a requirement that students live in university housing unless they can qualify under certain approved exceptions, such as local residence of the family or being married and having a family. American courts have upheld university regulations requiring residence in housing provided by the university. Some universities in the developing countries have been established in areas where the only housing available is that provided by the university. Obviously there is no problem in these institutions. Problems arise when private housing is available and when residential social clubs or fraternities have been established at an institution. Further complications arise when the institution is coeducational. There is a feeling that greater care must be exercised by the university in determining where women students shall be housed.

All of the Indian agricultural universities, either through their acts or statutes, require that students live in university hostels unless they get permission from the dean of student welfare to live elsewhere. Some acts or statutes provide exceptions, such as residence in a private dormitory approved by the university, in their own homes (if married), with their parents, or in the home of a guardian. University of the Philippines Statutes and those of many other institutions require the dean of student welfare or of student affairs to make determinations about the suitability of nonuniversity housing and to maintain lists of approved housing.

American courts have held that a student does not occupy the position of a tenant or lodger in university hostels or dormitories and hence is subject to rules and regulations which the institution may prescribe about his conduct as an occupant. In controversies which have arisen, it has been held that universities have a wide latitude in determining what is reasonable and what rules are needed. Obviously this is a touchy area, and unless the university has an internal organization which involves consultations with students and student groups and which attempts to consider feelings, needs, and desires of students in formulating such rules and regulations, it is "in for trouble."

We believe the university act should authorize the governing body to provide student housing and regulate its use. University statutes should then establish the structure through which rules and regulations are developed and through which policy decisions are reached about applications for and assignment of housing and compulsory residence in university housing. We believe these functions should center in the dean of student welfare but that regulations should provide for a housing committee composed of appropriate university officers and representatives of the academic council and student governing body. Under appropriate rules and regulations, student housing bodies should be represented in initial determinations about housing rules and regulations and should be enabled to make recommendations which can move quickly through channels to the housing committee and the dean of student welfare. There should be authorization to develop rules for nonuniversity housing and for surveillance of such housing by the dean of student welfare. In a large institution the assignment of space, the inspection of nonuniversity housing, and the handling of required forms and details is a heavy responsibility. A housing division in the office of the dean of student welfare is implied.

A part of the whole program should be the positive one of increasing the cultural and social opportunities of students through housing. The presence of a diversity of students, including foreign students and women, should be viewed as an opportunity and a challenge, not as a problem. This is an area in which gaps in communication can create misunderstanding and hostility. Qualified counselors, hostel wardens, hostel masters, or by whatever name they might be known, are needed, not only to supervise but to serve as sympathetic listeners and advocates for needed change.

Students in fraternities and privately organized houses provide their own governance, sometimes with, sometimes without, a resident counselor. If the size of the institution and the numbers of such fraternities, clubs, or private organizations justify, the dean of student welfare should appoint an assistant who can become familiar with and understand the special problems of such groups. If the university owns the property in which the club or fraternity lives, its responsibility and rights will be greater.

17.11. FOOD SERVICE

Though university acts seldom mention food service as a function of a university, it is implied. Many institutions are so located that there could not be any food service unless the university provided it. It is sometimes mentioned in university statutes. Those of the Andhra Pradesh Agricultural University provide that "The Dean of Student Affairs shall organize messing arrangements for students." Statutes of the Mysore University of Agricultural Sciences state that "The university shall provide and operate for enrolled students of the university such cafeterias and other facilities as may be deemed by the board to be in the best interests of the university. Regulations on the subject shall be prepared and adopted jointly by the aforesaid committee and council and shall provide for participation by the student association." The committee referred to is one on student quarters, cafeterias, and other accommodations to be appointed by the vice-chancellor. The statute also provides that the regulations shall be administered by the director of student welfare or by someone designated by him.

We do not believe the university act need contain any provision on food service. We do believe the statutes should contain a provision similar to that in the Mysore statutes. In many universities, food service is complicated by the presence of different religious groups for some of whom particular foods are not permitted or are permitted only on certain days. In some institutions students are given a wide discretion in running their own food service, generally with sad results from the standpoint of health, sanitation, economy, and a well-balanced diet. We believe the statutes should make certain that the responsibility for an adequate and safe food service is that of the university and that if it is delegated to the dean of student welfare, he be empowered to employ such assistance as is necessary to insure good food service. The serving of meals offers opportunities for cultural and social development, particularly if the institution is coeducational. These opportunities should not be overlooked. They logically fall in the domain of the dean of student welfare.

17.12. HEALTH SERVICE

University acts are generally silent about provisions for health service for students, but like food service, this is a function which must be implied. Virtually all universities require some kind of health examination before admitting students, and some require periodic examinations to determine if any communicable disease exists. In American court cases the right of the university to require compulsory vaccination has been upheld. Some institutions have statutory provisions, though many times the organization of the health service is left to internal arrangements in the office of the dean of student welfare. Statutes of the University of the Philippines provide for a university health service administered by a director serving under the president of the university.

There should be a university statute requiring the establishment of a health service and placing it under the dean of student welfare. The statute should authorize the health service to conduct medical and physical examinations of students and staff, to be responsible for environmental health in the university, and to maintain an infirmary. If the university has a faculty of medicine, this responsibility may be discharged by the medical college. The statutes should require the development and publication of rules and regulations on the services to be performed and the rights and obligations of students and staff members and their dependents. If the university maintains a health and accident insurance program for students and staff, the role which the health service plays in administering this program should be stipulated in the statutes.

Rules and regulations should be developed regarding use of hospital records. Controversies frequently arise over the right of the university to make these records available to insurance companies and to others without the consent of the student or staff member. Decisions by courts in the United States indicate that in the absence of specific agreement or of some different established policy, medical and hospital records are the exclusive possession of the hospital or medical institution but their contents are the property of the patient and that the latter must be allowed a reasonable right of inspection.

The statutes providing for the establishment of a health service should also provide that there be an advisory board composed of appropriate university administrative officers, representatives from the faculty, and representatives from the student government organization.

17.13. ATHLETICS AND PHYSICAL EDUCATION

In many American universities the management of competitive athletics is a major enterprise. This is not likely to be true in universities in the developing countries. Nevertheless, competitive athletics is an important part of the life of any university, and the interest and zeal of students bear no relation to gate receipts.

There are at least three major segments of a university's athletic and physical education program. One has to do with the management of competitive athletics; another, with intramural sports and athletics for all students; and another, with the formalized program in physical education and the offering of courses for the general student body and for professional physical education majors. The latter, being an educational function, should be under the jurisdiction of a departmental or college faculty, depending on the size of the program.

Competitive athletics may be handled in various ways. The University of the Philippines Statutes establish a university athletic association and vest its affairs in a board composed of specified university officers, faculty and student representatives, and one representative from the university alumni association. The function of the board of athletic affairs is to lay down broad athletic policies and administer the financial aspects of the university's athletic activities. In some American universities, athletic associations have been established as separate corporate entities subject to control, however, by the chief administrative officer and the governing body of the university. Because of the resources which they frequently command and their ability to exert influence, these separate corporate entities are sometimes regarded by faculties as inimical to the educational processes of the university. Without arguing the pros and cons of this contention, we recommend that competitive athletics be closely integrated with the university, that separate corporate entities be avoided, and that the program be held to its proper relation with the objectives and resources of the institution. University statutes should establish such a policy.

We believe that intramural sports are so important to all students that they should be recognized in the university act and that the act should authorize the dean of student welfare, in cooperation with appropriate university officials and student and faculty representatives, to develop an intramural program and make facilities available for both students and staff for games and sports. The academic council should take the lead in establishing university policy regarding required courses in physical education for all students. Recommendations from the college faculties should be required in establishing the latter. In many institutions the university health service is responsible for courses in physical and mental health, sex hygiene, and environmental health. This, too, is a matter which should receive consideration by the academic council before a program is established. It is quite easy to create overlapping jurisdictions in the areas of health, physical education, and athletics. The chief administrative officer should seek the best counsel available and should ask for advice from appropriate university bodies or special committees in formulating regulations which will result in an effective and integrated program. Faculty interest in the university's athletic program is generally sufficient to cause appointment by the academic council of a standing committee on athletics.

17.14. MILITARY TRAINING

The Morrill Act of 1862, which was the impetus for establishment of the American land-grant universities, provided that proceeds from sale of the land should go "to the endowment, support, and maintenance of at least one college where the leading object shall be, without excluding other scientific and classical studies *and including military tactics,* to teach such branches of learning as are related to agriculture and the mechanic arts." It has been ruled that this language requires institutions to offer instruction in military science but does not make it compulsory for students. Some state laws do, however, make it compulsory. In some cases the governing body of the university made it so. In recent years there has been a retreat from the mandatory requirement.

With respect to universities in the developing countries, we believe the university act should authorize but not require the universities to participate in any national cadet corps or officer-training program provided in the country. On advice from the faculty and administration of the university, the governing body can decide if the university should engage in such a program and can adopt an appropriate statute. We believe that, if adopted, the program should be voluntary. University statutes should definitely state whether it is or is not. If it is compulsory, then rules should be developed providing for exceptions—those who are physically unfit or who have had previous military training, for example. If conscientous objection is recognized in the country as a legitimate excuse from military service, it should apply likewise to a cadet training program in the university with the same kind of proof being required to establish a student as a conscientous objector.

If military training is offered, we recommend the creation of two kinds of bodies to help achieve proper liaison and coordination with the military unit in the university. One is a military affairs committee or a committee by a similar name composed of appropriate university administrative officers, representatives of the faculty, and representatives from the student government association. The other body should be a committee of the academic council to deal with educational policy and with course and curricular matters as affected by military training. The head of the military unit should serve on this committee ex officio. He should also serve on the military affiairs committee. We realize that whether or not a university offers a military training program and whether or not such program is compulsory may depend on national policies and law.

17.15. COUNSELING AND GUIDANCE

Three kinds of student counseling and guidance can be identified in universities: academic, psychological, and general. Academic and some general counseling are accomplished at the college faculty level, though the larger universities may provide central services having a direct bearing on the academic progress of students—writing and reading clinics, for example. Professional psychological and testing services as well as some counseling and guidance on general or personal matters are maintained at the university level, generally in the office of the dean of student welfare. Several of the Indian agricultural university acts provide that "The dean of student welfare shall direct a program of student counseling." Others make the same provision in their university statutes. In addition, the Punjab Agricultural University Act provides that "The dean of a college or the director of a school shall supervise the registration and progress of the students in the college or the school." This recognizes and places the responsibility for academic counseling in the college.

Statutes of the University of Illinois establish a student counseling service, and the general rules concerning university organization and procedure provide that it "shall conduct programs of professional psychological services to students and in behalf of students regarding their vocational, educational, and emotional or personality problems. It shall serve as a consulting and referral agency for other university administrative officers and staff members concerned with students' academic and personal problems. It shall provide diagnostic tests and perform the other functions commonly associated with psychological counseling." It is further provided that the director of the student counseling service shall be responsible to the academic vice-president rather than to the dean of students.

It is obvious that without some coordination of counseling, guidance, and advisement activities, there can be duplication, overlapping, gaps, and nonprofessional advice on matters which should have been referred to a psychological or testing center. Statutes of the University of the Philippines provide that "There shall be a coordinator of counseling and guidance services to be appointed by the Board of Regents on the recommendation of the president after consultation with the dean of students." Among his duties are those of coordinating and supervising the counseling and testing services of the university, participation in policy-making activities concerning student welfare and interest, maintenance and development of an occupational information library, submission of annual reports, and performance of such other duties as may be required. It is not likely that a small university can afford a fully staffed psychological counseling center, but it should have one professionally trained person on the staff from the beginning to serve at least part time in performing professional counseling functions.

The most important contact with students is at the college level where they are doing their academic work and where they feel some sense of identification. An approach to be recommended is one in which college faculty members participate in an advisement program, each faculty member becoming familiar with and developing an interest in the academic career of an appropriate number of advisees assigned to him by the college dean's office. Some planning and formalized rules are necessary if such a system is to work. If it is overformalized it will lose the values which can arise from voluntary cooperation between the faculty member and his advisees. On the other hand, if the adviser's signature is required before a student's course work can be approved for the next term, there must be some requirements.

We believe that the university act should provide for counseling and guidance services, that professional psychological counseling and testing should be provided through the office of the dean of student welfare, and that colleges should be required to establish an advisory program for students. Coordination of activities can then be achieved by the dean of students. The success of the program will depend on the information reaching college offices and faculty advisers, the services available, and the feeling of students about the services offered. A conscientious faculty adviser interested in the welfare of a student is reluctant to refer a student to any segment of the university unless he knows something about it and believes it is interested in helping students. Some faculty members make good student advisers; others prefer not to be bothered. There must be some discretion in the college office in assigning advisers and in determining the number of students to be assigned to any particular one. Within limits, also, students should be permitted to choose their advisers, particularly after they have established their major academic interest. If an advisement program is thoughtfully planned and administered, some staff members will have a heavy advisement responsibility; others will have none. We believe the university statutes should provide that teaching and research loads of the academic staff be reduced in accordance with their advisement and counseling responsibilities. Such a statute would strengthen the hand of department heads in recommending such adjustments and would provide a firmer base to the staff member in asking for an adjustment.

17.16. PLACEMENT

In many countries there is an assumption that university placement services are not necessary. This assumption stems understandably from the fact that a high percentage of the graduates from universities in developing countries enter the professions or government service. But as universities broaden the scope of their educational offerings and as a developing economy produces an increased need for educated manpower in business, industry, and agriculture, the need for contacts with prospective employers and for student guidance about future employment will increase. Many of the Indian agricultural university acts provide that one of the duties of the dean of student welfare shall be to assist in the placement of graduates of the university. The Udaipur University Statutes require that the dean "explore the possibilities of finding suitable employment for students and arrange their interviews with prospective employers." The general rules concerning university organization and procedure of the University of Illinois provide for a university coordinating placement office and for a placement coordinating council. The office functions under the dean of students. It operates under policies and procedures adopted by the coordinating council. These provisions recognize that many contacts are made and much placement activity of an informal nature is carried on at the college level. There is a need for coordinating this activity with the functions of a central university placement service. We believe the university act should establish a placement service for graduates of the university to be under the jurisdiction of the dean of student welfare. Provisions should be made for a university placement council with representation from the various colleges so that there can be coordination of activity in placement work.

17.17. STUDENT PUBLICATIONS

None of the university acts or statutes which we reviewed contained any policy statements about student publications. Yet, in many universities, there are student newspapers, either daily or weekly, and a number of professional or college-oriented publications produced by students. Sometimes there is a student humor magazine. We believe there should be a university statute guaranteeing students the right to produce a student newspaper or other publications free from surveillance by the university. There should be provision for a university publications council to advise regarding the business aspects of the venture and to give some guidance regarding the laws of libel and what might be considered good taste in certain touchy areas. The statutes should make it clear that such a council does not have authority to control or censor. It should be composed of appropriate members of the university administrative staff, faculty representatives, and representatives from the students.

If there is a faculty of journalism in the university, it should be in position to help improve the quality of student publications. In some large American universities, a separate corporate entity has been created for student publications, particularly for a student newspaper. The relation of the university to such a separate entity in the tort field is discussed in Chapter 3. The main purpose of the university statutes should be to prevent either the administration of the university or the governing body from taking hasty action which could sterilize the value to be gained from a free expression of student opinion. There is no question about the right of the university to suspend a student publication if it believes adequate grounds exist. But the university should desire a free student press and then live with the headaches and insight it produces. A censored and intimidated paper may cause no trouble but will produce no insight.

In a study of control of student publications in American universities, the author states: "The student at this time of life charges forth with the pure lance of ideal to battle the ugly world of compromise. This is the ever-renewing educational combat which does much to improve society and remove some areas of blight." [12] As more universities develop radio and television programs and more students become involved with these programs, there will be need for additional university statutory structuring of the activity and protection of the rights of expression of those involved.

17.18. CULTURAL AND SOCIAL ACTIVITIES

An atmosphere of culture and a desirable social climate cannot be created by provisions in a university act or in the university statutes, but they can both be augmented by programs established because of requirements which may be contained in the statutes or in the rules of the university. We believe that university statutes should impose upon the institution the duty of establishing a "center" for students, to be under the joint jurisdiction and management of students and the dean of student welfare. Such a center could do a number of things, including:

1. Sponsoring social and cultural events.
2. Providing lounges with books, magazines, games, radio, and television.
3. Providing committee rooms for student meetings.
4. Maintaining a mimeograph service for students.
5. Establishing a book and student supply salesroom.
6. Making tour arrangements for students.
7. Helping students arrange travel to foreign countries.

----

[12] Vernon W. Smith, *Case Histories in the Control of Student Publications.* This paper was written by Smith, a graduate student in journalism at Syracuse University, for delivery by William T. Birch at the 1963 annual meeting of the National Association of University Attorneys.

8. Implementing a student exchange program.

9. Providing a food service in the center.

Such a center, if managed with skill, enthusiasm, and imagination, could come to mean much to students and faculty alike. In many American universities, part of these functions are performed by a student union. Campus religious foundations also do some of the things suggested. We believe the university should accept responsibility and capitalize on the opportunities which would flow from a thoroughgoing program of the kind suggested. Such a program need not interfere with the activities of other campus groups. Through proper coordination and relationships, the tempo of their activities should be increased, not diminished.

17.19. ALUMNI AFFAIRS

Agricultural university acts in Punjab, Andhra Pradesh, and Orissa all provide that the dean of student welfare shall organize and maintain contact with the alumni of the university. The Peru National Universities Act provides that "The university shall promulgate formation of an alumni association and shall maintain a permanent link with its graduates by means of the association." Statutes of the Mysore University of Agricultural Sciences provide that "There may exist within but not as an official authority of the university an organization to be known as the Mysore Agricultural University Alumni Association. University degree holders and former students who have spent not less than one year of training in the university shall establish such an association under the guidance of the vice-chancellor. Active membership in the association shall be automatic for all graduates and all former students who have spent not less than a year in the university." The statutes of Cornell University provide that "There shall be a general alumni secretary who shall be a member of the university staff elected by the board upon recommendation by the president after consultation with the board of directors of the Cornell Alumni Association. He shall have charge of the alumni office and shall administer all appropriations made by the university for the operations of the alumni office and of the Cornell alumni association."

We believe a provision similar to that in the Mysore statutes should be included in the university statutes. A provision like that contained in the Cornell statutes for an alumni secretary is desirable when justified by growth of the institution. This does, however, raise a policy question: the alumni association, if financially able, might wish to select, hire, and direct the activities of its secretary. In the beginning, the secretary's functions could be discharged by another university officer—the registrar, for example. Once established, the alumni association should be free of university surveillance. An active and independent association can do many things for a university, such as: provide scholarships; inform prospective students about the institution; act as a source of information about the university, particularly to rural people; make donations for research and other work; and help the university through a system of advisory committees. As we have noted earlier, many university acts require that one or more alumni members serve on the governing body. Unless the act provides otherwise, the alumni association could constitute the medium for selecting these members. The Mysore statutes include a definition of those qualified to be alumni. This should be included in a university statute. Data on qualification for membership in the alumni association can be made available by the registrar, since he maintains a list of registered graduates of the university and has other records from which periods of attendance at the university can be ascertained.

Though a statutory statement of purpose is not essential, it would be helpful in giving guidance to the association and to university officials concerned with its affairs. The Mysore statutes contain a good statement: "The purpose of the alumni association shall be to encourage the university and its various activities, to assist in promoting its growth, and to help strengthen the university's capacity to render effective service to the agriculture of Mysore State and to the nation."

CHAPTER – 18

A Pattern for a University Act and University Statutes

This chapter is in substance a recapitulation and pulling-together of recommendations (with alternatives) made throughout the book. They are presented in the form which a legislative act might take and are divided into articles, sections, subsections, and sub-subsections. Sections are numbered consecutively throughout. The university statutory provisions are included under appropriate articles and sections of the act in order that all the material on a particular subject may be read together. If we recommend no legislative or statutory provision on a particular subject, there will be no reference to the act or statutes in the particular section or subsection. The numbering of sections and subsections in a proposal to the legislature would have to be altered somewhat because in this pattern there are some sections and subsections for which only act or statutory provisions are proposed.

We feel this is a desirable format for a university act and statutes. If the statutes are keyed to the university act, it will be easier to determine the legislative provisions on which they are based, to review the whole matter about which they are concerned, and to make additions to and revisions of the statutes. We have used directive language in phrasing some provisions but, with respect to others, have simply indicated what might be converted into such language. There is no dearth of competent legal assistance in any developing country for formulating proper terminology.

Following most section headings and some subsection headings are references by chapter and section to the portion of the book in which the subject matter is discussed.

TABLE OF CONTENTS OF ARTICLES AND SECTIONS
Article I Preliminary
Sections
    1. Short Title

93. The Rights of Students
94. Admissions
95. Student Government
96. Student Organizations
97. Loans and Scholarships
98. Discipline and Dismissal
99. Housing
100. Services
101. Military Training
102. Student Labor
103. Placement Services
104. Examinations
105. The Alumni

Article XI Statutes and Regulations
Sections
106. Statutes—Purposes
107. Statutes—Matter To Be Covered
108. Statutes—How Made
109. Regulations—Purpose and How Made

Article XII Supplemental Provisions
Sections
110. Annual Reports
111. Filling Vacancies
112. Delegation of Authority
113. Staff of Transferred Agencies
114. Students of Transferred Institutions
115. Advisory Committees
116. University Records
117. Patents and Copyrights
118. Removal of Difficulties
119. Interpretation
120. Planning for Development
121. Validation of Proceedings
122. Separability

TITLE OF ACT
This is a full legislative designation of the law.

ENACTING CLAUSE

This is language which indicates that it is the will of the legislative body that the material which follows shall become law. Such clauses frequently commence with the language "be it enacted."

ARTICLE I   PRELIMINARY

Section 1. Short Title

Act   This is a shorter and more convenient name for the law provided as a part of the act. It makes a shorter name official and thus prevents the likelihood that other short, unofficial names will be used. A typical short title is "Punjab University Act."

Statutes   A shorter and more convenient name for the statutes should be included, such as "Punjab University Statutes."

Section 2. Effective Date   (3.5)

Act   This section should simply state when the university act is to become effective.

Statutes   This section should state when the university statutes will become effective.

Section 3. Definitions   (3.7)

Act   Two kinds of terms need definition: those subject to more than one meaning, and those which recur throughout the act and which can be shortened for reference purposes. By so stating, for example, it is possible to use "act," "statute," "university," "board," and "chief administrative officer," with no doubt about the meaning of the terms. Each act should be studied for terms requiring definition.

Statutes   Likewise, when the statutes are formulated, they should be studied and necessary definitions included in a beginning section. There should be no inconsistency with terms defined in the act.

ARTICLE II   THE UNIVERSITY

Section 4. Name   (3.3)

Act   This should express the official name for the institution and should, in addition, contain a clause stating that the official name of the university shall not be used by any other institution or by any other individual or agency for any purpose without the consent of the university.

Statutes Repeat the name as designated in the act for identification purposes, and provide for a shorter designation if desired, or for a name in another language.

Section 5. Incorporation (3.1)

Act This should consist of a short and clear-cut statement making the university a corporate entity and empowering it to sue and be sued by its official name. A phrase such as "constituted a body corporate" provides the proper legal connotation.

Section 6. Location (3.4)

Act If determination of location is to be made by law, it should be expressed. If the location is to be left to the determination of some other body, this should be clearly expressed with language giving the necessary authority. This section should also authorize the governing body to establish branches or units of the university at other locations.

Statutes If and when the governing body establishes units or branches of the university at other locations, there should be a statutory provision designating such location.

Section 7. Jurisdiction (3.6)

Act This section should be worded so that it creates both a right and an obligation on the part of the university to serve the whole state or region. Whether or not it should have exclusive jurisdiction to carry on all research or all extension work is a policy question. If the legislature desires it to have these exclusive rights, there should be such a statement in this section.

Section 8. Purpose (3.2)

Act The statement of purpose should commit the university to a philosophy of liberal education and of service to agriculture and the rural economy of the state or region, and assure an integrated program of teaching, research, and extension.

Statutes The purpose of the university is important. It cannot be stated too many times. The statutes should repeat and amplify the purpose as expressed in the law. However, the statutes cannot alter the purpose as expressed in the act.

Section 9. Powers (3.12, 3.15-16)

Act The following powers should be provided and may be

listed in subsections in the following manner. The university shall have the power:

(a) Of eminent domain.

(b) To sue and be sued.

(c) To enter into and enforce contracts.

(d) To acquire, hold, and otherwise deal with movable and immovable property.

(e) To erect, equip, and maintain all buildings necessary, suitable, and convenient for the objects of the university, including the maintenance of ancillary facilities for employees and students.

(f) To accept gifts, legacies, and donations.

(g) To establish trusts and act as trustee.

(h) To employ and act through agents.

(i) To invest monies by way of endowment or in other ways and to change or vary such investments.

(j) To borrow money and pledge the security of the university.

(k) To cooperate with other universities and authorities and become a member of any association of universities or colleges.

(l) To create separate corporations, foundations, or other entities for the accomplishment of university functions.

(m) To provide for instruction, research, and extension in all areas of knowledge comprehended by the university.

(n) To create necessary academic, administrative, and other posts.

(o) To hold examinations and grant degrees.

(p) To grant honorary degrees.

(q) To establish and collect fees and other charges.

(r) To institute fellowships, scholarships, and other forms of awards and assistance.

(s) To perform any other function necessary to achieve the purpose of the university.

Statutes None. (The powers of the university must be derived from the legislature. They cannot be created by university statutes. Elsewhere in the act there will be statutory provisions implementing certain of the powers expressed in this section.)

Section 10. Constituent Colleges (3.11)

Act This section should provide that any college which becomes a part of the university, whether located on the main campus or at a separate geographical location, shall be a constituent college and hence an integral part of the university. The division of authority and administration of the constituent college between the authorities in the university and in the college shall be provided by statute.

Statutes A statutory provision could officially "record" inclusion of the constituent college. Since the statutes will be concerned with administration and the functioning of university authorities, pertinent provisions will be included under subsequent sections of the statutes dealing with these subjects.

Section 11. Affiliation

Act This section should provide that another institution can be affiliated with the university only after approval by both the academic council and the governing body of the university. This section should also provide that disaffiliation can be achieved in the same manner.

Statutes A provision could recognize any action taken under this section of the act.

Section 12. Relation to Government Agencies (3.8)

Act This section should provide that the university shall not be an agency of state government. It shall not be required to carry on regulatory programs or assist any government agency in the discharge of functions which are not educational in nature. The section should also empower the university to enter into memoranda of understanding or agreement with government agencies at all levels to effectuate plans which will achieve the purposes of the university, to make an appropriate division of responsibility between the university and such agencies, and to allow for participation by the university in programs which any such agencies may offer.

Statutes Formal agreements reached with other agencies may be expressed in the statutes.

Section 13. Transfer of Government Agencies (3.10-11)

Act If other colleges, government research agencies, or extension agencies are to be transferred to the university, this section should express the conditions under which they are to be transferred and the time by which the transfer is to be accomplished.

Section 14. Tax Exemption (3.13)

Act This section should clarify the position of the university with regard to both state or regional and local taxes. If there is to be exemption from all taxes with respect to all activities and functions of the university and regardless of the nature of property owned by it or the use to which such property is put, this should be clearly stated. If there are to be differentiations, with certain taxes applying to the university and certain others not, this should also be clearly expressed. This will depend, of course, on national or state policy regarding the taxation of public entities. If the university is to be empowered to make contractual arrangements for supporting police, fire, and other local services in lieu of taxes, this authority should also be contained in this section of the act.

Section 15. Liability (3.14)

Act This section should state that the university shall enjoy such immunity from tort liability as other public agencies enjoy. Furthermore, it should empower the governing body to maintain such liability insurance as in its judgment is needed to adequately protect the institution. If there is a state workmen's compensation law in effect which does not exclude university employees, then this section should state that university employees shall be included under it.

Section 16. Inspections (3.8)

Act This section should provide that the legislature may through an appropriate committee and with adequate advance notice inspect the university and make recommendations for the improvement of its administration.

ARTICLE III OFFICERS OF THE UNIVERSITY

Section 17. Chancellor (3.8)

Act (a) Normally the position of chancellor is honorary. Usually the post is filled by the governor of the state or region. If such a position is desired, this subsection of the act should state that the governor or such other official as may be designated shall be the chancellor and that the position is honorary.

(b) This subsection should empower the chancellor to preside at convocations and to exercise any other powers provided by the university act.

Section 18. Pro-Chancellor (9, Introduction)

Act (a) This position, also, is normally honorary and is frequently bestowed upon a cabinet member such as the minister of agriculture. If this is to be done, this subsection should state that the pro-chancellor of the university shall be the designated officer and that his position shall be honorary.

(b) This subsection should state that the pro-chancellor shall, when requested by the chancellor, perform in the chancellor's place and that he shall have such other powers and duties as may be specified by the act or delegated to him by the chancellor.

Section 19. Chief Administrative Officer—Appointment and Conditions of Service (6)

Act (a) Appointment (5.1, 6.1)

This subsection should state that the chief administrative officer shall be appointed by the governing body to serve at its pleasure. It should provide also that when the position is to be filled, nominations shall be made to the governing body by a committee appointed by the academic council following procedures to be established by university statutes for involving members of the academic staff in the consideration of a nominee for the position. If there is reason for the first chief administrative officer to be appointed by government or by the chancellor, such a provision should be included in the subsection.

Statutes The statutes should authorize the academic council to appoint a representative university committee composed both of council members and nonmembers to consider nominees for the position of chief administrative officer. They should provide that the chairman of this committee meet with the committee of the governing body considering nominees, so that liaison can be preserved, and that in due course the committee thus appointed shall inform the governing body of its choice or choices. If there are several choices, they should be ranked in order of preference. The statutes should make it clear that nominations from such a committee are not binding on the governing body but are suggestive only.

(b) Conditions of Service (6, generally)

(1) Term of Office (6.2)

Act   It should be provided that the chief administrative officer serve at the pleasure of the governing body. If the legislature feels that a definite term is desirable, then this section should specify a term of preferably four or five years with the right of reappointment to succeeding terms.

(2) Salary and Perquisites (6.4)

Act   The chief administrative officer's salary should be fixed by the governing body and should not be varied to his disadvantage after appointment. It should also be stated that he shall be entitled to such perquisites as may be determined by the governing body. A written contract should be required.

(3) Residence (6.4)

Act   It should be provided that the chief administrative officer shall reside in the university community.

Statutes If the governing body builds and furnishes a home for the chief administrative officer, there should probably be a statutory provision requiring that he reside in the home provided.

Section 20. Chief Administrative Officer—Removal, Vacancy, Leave, and Resignation (6)

Act (a) Vacancy (6.5)

The governing body should be empowered through university statutes to designate the officer to become acting chief administrative officer in case of vacancy. Also, the governing body should be required to initiate immediately the appointment process for selecting a new chief administrative officer.

Statutes A provision in the statute should designate the university officer to become acting chief administrative officer immediately if a vacancy occurs.

(b) Leave (6.8)

Act It should be provided that the chief administrative officer receive annual or other leave as determined by the governing body and that during sick leave the chief administrative officer shall have the right to designate another university officer to act for him.

Statutes None, unless the governing body wishes to formalize a policy regarding leave for the chief administrative officer.

(c) Removal from Office (6.6)

Act It should be provided that the governing body may remove or suspend the chief administrative officer at its pleasure. However, it should be provided that suspension is with pay and that removal is effective only after a reasonable period of notice, such period being specified in this provision.

(d) Resignation (6.7)

Act The chief administrative officer should be given the right to resign through a communication addressed to the governing body, the resignation to become effective when accepted by the governing body or at the end of a period which should be specified in this subsection.

(e) Temporary Disability (6.9)

Act This subsection should state that when the chief administrative officer informs the governing body of a temporary disability or the governing body determines that he is temporarily disabled for performing his functions, the governing body shall designate an officer of the university to fill the position during the period of disability.

Section 21. Chief Administrative Officer—
Powers and Duties (7, generally)
(a) General Direction and
Control of University Affairs (7.1, 7.8-9)

Act This subsection should provide that the chief administrative officer is in charge of all educational and business operations of the university, that he should carry out the general policies laid down by the governing body, and that all officers, staff members, and employees shall be responsible to him and shall work under his direction.

(b) Presentation of the University
Budget (7.3)

Act This provision should make the chief administrative officer responsible for presentation of the budget and accounts to the governing body and for the financial affairs of the university.

(c) Appointments   (7.4)

Act Though appointment procedures should be specified in university statutes, this subsection of the act should state that no appointments shall be made by the governing body except upon recommendation of the chief administrative officer. This subsection should also authorize the chief administrative officer to make temporary and emergency appointments subject to confirmation by the governing body and also should empower the governing body through the formulation of a proper university statute to authorize the chief administrative officer to make appointments below specified ranks or salary scales without approval of the governing body.

Statutes None. (The statutory provision referred to above should appear in Article VIII on appointment of the academic staff.)

(d) Salaries   (7.4)

Act This subsection should provide that the chief administrative officer shall prepare and submit for approval of the governing body a system of salary scales throughout the university, and that all recommendations for appointment made to the governing body by the chief administrative officer be accompanied by a recommended salary for the nominee.

(e) Discharge and Suspension   (7.5)

Act The chief administrative officer should be authorized to suspend or otherwise punish staff members for causes stated, through procedures to be provided in university statutes, and with approval of the governing body to discharge staff members.

(f) Construction of University Facilities   (7.7)

Act This subsection should state that the chief administrative officer shall be responsible for presenting recommendations and plans for construction of new buildings to the governing body and that he shall be responsible for the construction of new buildings through appropriate university agencies.

(g) The Custody and Use of University Property   (7.6)

Act This should provide that the chief administrative officer be responsible for the custody and use of all university property for the purpose of the university, and that additional provisions regarding the use of property shall be contained in university statutes.

(h) Delegation of Authority (7.12)

Act There should be a provision that the chief administrative officer may, with approval of the governing body, delegate to other officers of the university duties and functions which he would otherwise be legally required to perform.

(i) Administrative Committees (7.11)

Act The chief administrative officer should be authorized to appoint an advisory committee or a council of deans and other university officers. Also, he should be authorized to appoint such standing or ad hoc committees as he deems necessary in the performance of his functions.

(j) Membership in Academic Bodies (7.10)

Act The chief administrative officer should be designated as presiding officer of the academic council and made a member of all faculties of the university. He should also be empowered to convene the academic council.

(k) Reports and Communications (7.1, 7.13)

Act The chief administrative officer should be required to submit an annual report on the functioning of the university to the governing body. He should also be required to carry on a program of public information about the university and its activities.

(1) Discipline (7.14, 17.2)

Act The chief administrative officer should be charged with the duty of maintaining discipline throughout the university. It should be stated that disciplinary procedures shall be as contained in the university statutes.

Statutes None. (Disciplinary procedures are outlined in Article X on students.)

(m) Security of the University (7.15)

Act The chief administrative officer should be made responsible for maintaining order and for preserving the security of university property, members of the staff, students, and other persons rightfully within the confines of the university.

(n) Emergency Powers (7.17)

Act The chief administrative officer should be empowered to act when in his judgment an emergency exists and to report his actions as soon as possible for confirmation by the governing body.

(o) Other Powers and Duties

Act This should specify that the chief administrative officer shall have such additional powers and duties as may be provided in this act or in the university statutes.

Section 22. Vice Chief Administrative Officer (9.1)

Act (a) The governing body should be authorized on recommendation from the chief administrative officer to create such vice-positions to the chief administrative officer as are needed.

(b) The powers, duties, and conditions of service of such officers shall be as specified in the university statutes.

(c) Appointments to such positions shall be made by the governing body on recommendation of the chief administrative officer following nominations to him from a selection committee appointed by him.

Statutes Until a vice-position is recommended, there will be no statutory provisions. Assuming that most institutions will either provide from the beginning or will soon need a vice-position in charge of academic affairs, the following statutory provisions are recommended:

(a) Vice-Position for academic affairs (9.1, 9.4)

(1) This should state that his term of service shall be for some definite period, such as two years, subject to reappointment and that his salary and emoluments shall be as approved by the governing body on recommendation of the chief administrative officer.

(2) He should discharge the responsibilities of the chief administrative officer with respect to academic affairs in the university and should perform such other functions and have such other duties as may be delegated to him by the chief administrative officer.

Section 23. Appointment of Other Officers

Act This section should provide that all officers provided for in subsequent sections of this article shall be appointed by the governing body on recommendation of the chief administrative officer following nominations presented to the chief administrative officer by a selection committee appointed by him; that there shall be a right to reappointment on recommendation of the chief administrative officer and approval by the governing body; and that salary and conditions of service shall be as recommended by the chief administrative officer and approved by the governing body.

Section 24. Deans of Colleges (9.2)

Act (a) It should be provided that there shall be a dean for each college, including the graduate college.

(b) The dean should be charged with responsibility for the faithful observance of the statutes and regulations relating to the faculty of the college and for the organization and conduct of the teaching, research, and extension work in the departments comprising the college. He should have such additional powers and responsibilities as are designated in the university statutes.

Statutes (a) This subsection should provide that appointment shall be for a specified term with the right to reappointment on recommendation of the chief administrative officer and approval by the governing body.

(b) Powers and duties may be listed as follows:

(1) Organize the teaching, research, and extension work of the college.

(2) Formulate college policies.

(3) Preside at meetings of the faculty.

(4) Supervise the registration and progress of students.

(5) Prepare and submit the budget of the college.

(6) Allocate office space and the educational use of buildings assigned to the college.

(7) Serve as the official medium of communications with other authorities of the university, with students, and with the public.

(8) Represent the college in conferences.

(9) Grant leaves and authorize travel.

(10) Procure necessary equipment and supplies.

(11) Exercise necessary jurisdiction over land assigned to the college for research and experimental work.

(12) Submit annual and other reports to the chief administrative officer.

(13) Perform such other powers and duties as may be specified in the act or university statutes, or delegated to him by the chief administrative officer.

(14) The dean of the graduate college shall, in addition to discharging the above powers and duties, cooperate with department heads in the colleges in determining the programs and progress of postgraduate students.

Section 25. Director of Research (9.5, 13.2)

Act (a) This subsection should provide that there be a director of research for the university.

(b) He should be responsible for the coordination and development of research throughout the university and should have such additional functions as are specified in the university statutes or assigned to him by the chief administrative officer.

Statutes He should have powers and duties which may be listed as follows:

(a) Make recommendations to the chief administrative officer regarding the research budget.

(b) Assist in the search for research personnel.

(c) Disseminate information about research policies and procedures.

(d) Encourage and assist in the publication of research results.

(e) Help implement cross-disciplinary research.

(f) Maintain statistical and other services for research workers.

(g) Be administratively in charge of substations and separate research facilities in cooperation with colleges and departments concerned.

(h) Represent the chief administrative officer in consultations having to do with grants and contracts for research.

(i) Make recommendations regarding the allocation and use of land and other research resources of the university.

(j) Make evaluations of the university's research efforts.

(k) Consult with the deans on appointments, promotions, and salaries of the research staff.

(l) Make an annual report and other required reports to the chief administrative officer.

(m) Perform such other duties as may be prescribed by the university statutes or chief administrative officer.

Section 26. Director of Extension (9.6, 14.2)

Act (a) This subsection should provide that there shall be a director of university extension.

(b) This subsection should provide that the director of extension shall have the responsibility for development of the total extension program of the university, including the training of extension workers, and that he shall have such additional functions as may be prescribed in the act or statutes or by the chief administrative officer.

Statutes (Some institutions require that the director of extension have a background in technical agriculture. If this is desired, it may be provided in a separate subsection.)

Powers and duties of the director of extension may be expressed as follows:

(a) Be responsible for all extension activity within the university.

(b) Coordinate the university's extension effort with government extension programs.

(c) Prepare and submit the extension budget.

(d) Supervise the field activities of the university extension staff.

(e) Develop visual aids and other extension teaching materials.

(f) Plan and execute an information publication program.

(g) Cooperate with the director of research and with college deans and department heads so that research information can be made available for extension purposes.

(h) Conduct special training schools for government agricultural officers.

(i) Plan and hold field days and events at the university for farmers and special-interest groups.

(j) Cooperate with the deans of colleges in the development of extension education courses.

(k) Maintain good relationships with farmer groups and outside agricultural agencies.

(l) Counsel with the deans of colleges on the appointment and promotion of extension personnel.

(m) Submit annual and other reports required by the chief administrative officer.

(n) Perform such other functions as may be required by the university statutes or the chief administrative officer.

Section 27. Chief Financial and Business Officer (8.1, 9.7)

Act (a) This subsection should provide that there shall be a chief financial and business officer for the university.

(b) This subsection should provide that he shall be responsible for all the business and financial affairs of the university and that he shall perform such functions and have such duties as may be prescribed in the act or statutes and by the chief administrative officer.

Statutes The powers and duties of the chief financial and business officer may be stated as follows:

(a) Prepare the university budget.

(b) Maintain university funds and accounts, and make reports to the chief administrative officer and governing body with respect to such funds and accounts.

(c) Account for the use of tuition and student fees.

(d) Receive and account for the use of grants from all sources.

(e) Manage the investments of the university.

(f) Arrange for the deposit and safekeeping of university funds.

(g) Establish purchasing procedures.

(h) Establish disbursing and accounting procedures.

(i) Arrange for internal audits.

(j) Provide for the keeping of student organization funds.

(k) Maintain a payroll and pay the staff, making such deductions from the payroll as are authorized by staff members.

(l) Develop procedures for the payment of travel expenses.

(m) Maintain necessary insurance.

(n) Manage the university pension or retirement fund.

(o) Develop a health and accident insurance plan for the staff.

(p) Maintain student loan and scholarship funds.

(q) Make annual and other reports as may be required on the financial status of the university.

(r) Perform such other functions as may be prescribed by the university statutes or chief administrative officer.

Section 28. Registrar (9.11)

Act (a) This subsection should provide that there shall be a registrar for the university.

(b) This should provide that the registrar shall be responsible for administering the university's admission program, registering students, maintaining student records, and performing such other functions as may be designated in the university act or statutes or by the chief administrative officer.

Statutes The powers and duties specified in the statutes may be as follows:

(a) Admission of students.

(b) Administration of entrance examination.

(c) Registration of students.

(d) Maintenance of student records.

(e) Assessment and collection of tuition and student fees.

(f) Publication of catalogs, registers, timetables, course descriptions, admission information, and other essential materials.

(g) Maintenance of records of registered graduates.

(h) Preparation of the university examination schedules.

(i) Publication of the university calendar.

(j) Service as secretary of the academic council unless the academic council provides otherwise.

(k) Preparation of such reports as may be required by the chief administrative officer.

(l) Performance of such other functions as may be prescribed by university statutes or the chief administrative officer.

Section 29. Dean of Student Welfare (9.10)

Act (a) This should provide that there shall be a dean of student welfare.

(b) This subsection should state that the dean of student welfare shall be concerned with, and shall discharge on behalf of the chief administrative officer, his responsibilities regarding the extracurricular activities of students and that he shall perform such other functions as may be prescribed in the act or statutes or by the chief administrative officer.

Statutes His powers and duties may be expressed as follows:

(a) Make arrangements for the housing of students.

(b) Direct a program of student counseling.

(c) Arrange for student employment.

(d) Foster and supervise the activities of student organizations.

(e) Assist in the placement of graduates.

(f) Organize and maintain contact with the alumni organization of the university.

(g) Supervise food services for students.

(h) Supervise health services for the university.

(i) In cooperation with the chief financial and business officer, supervise the loan and scholarship program for students.

(j) Cooperate with appropriate university officials in fostering an intramural athletic program.

(k) Perform such other functions as may be specified in the university statutes or by the chief administrative officer.

Section 30. Librarian (9.9)

Act (a) This should provide for the appointment of a university librarian.

(b) His functions should be to administer the university library and the branch libraries in colleges and schools, divisions and departments, and to perform such other duties as may be prescribed in the act and statutes and that are assigned to him by the chief administrative officer.

Statutes His powers and duties may be stated as follows:

(a) Be in charge of and administer professional library training in the university.

(b) Serve as chairman of the university library committee.

(c) Prepare and present the budget for the library and all branch libraries.

(d) Recommend the appointment of librarians and other library personnel in accordance with university appointment procedures.

(e) Manage the library so that it is of maximum use to staff and students.

(f) Within budgetary limitations, cooperate with staff members in the procurement of needed books.

(g) Make an annual report to the chief administrative officer on the condition of the library.

(h) Perform such other functions as may be prescribed by university statutes or the chief administrative officer.

Section 31. Director of Physical Plant (9.8)

Act (a) This should provide for appointment of a physical plant director.

(b) The physical plant director should be charged with the duty of maintaining buildings, grounds, and service facilities, supervising construction, and discharging such other functions as may be prescribed by the act, statutes, or the chief administrative officer.

Statutes His powers and duties may be stated as follows:

(a) Supervise construction.

(b) Maintain utility services.

(c) Maintain the roads, fences, and lands of the university.

(d) Landscape and care for the university grounds.

(e) Maintain fire and police protection.

(f) Maintain university security.

(g) Cooperate with the chief financial officer in the preparation of the building budget of the university.

(h) Cooperate with appropriate university officers in the allotment of space and buildings.

(i) Supervise and provide maintenance for university vehicles.

(j) Provide for waste disposal and for a sanitary system.

(k) Manage telephone, mail, and messenger service.

(l) Operate a central store for university office supplies.

(m) Maintain an inventory of university property.

(n) Cooperate with the dean of student welfare in managing food services.

(o) Perform such other functions as may be prescribed in the university statutes or by the chief administrative officer.

Section 32. Personnel Officer (9.14)

Act (a) This should provide for a personnel officer.

(b) The personnel officer should be responsible for the administration of policy and rules relating to the employment, compensation, and working conditions of nonacademic employees and should discharge such additional functions as may be prescribed in acts, statutes, or by the chief administrative officer.

Statutes His powers and duties may be stated as follows:

(a) Promote the recruitment of nonacademic staff.

(b) Select members of the nonacademic staff through competition and examination.

(c) Establish training courses.

(d) Provide for orientation of new employees and help them adjust to their work.

(e) Review and administer plans for job classifications.

(f) Study salaries and promotions and make recommendations to university administrative officials.

(g) Prepare appointment forms and papers.

(h) Maintain registers of skilled workers and other job applicants.

(i) Provide for physical and mental examination of employees.

(j) Handle cases of discharge, transfer, and other personnel problems.

(k) Act as liaison for the university with employee unions or other employee groups.

(l) Perform such additional functions as may be prescribed in university statutes or by the chief administrative officer.

Section 33. Other Officers (9.15)

Act This should provide that with the approval of the governing body the chief administrative officer may appoint such additional officers as are needed. (For suggestions regarding other officers which may, in time, be needed by the university, see Chapter 9, Sections 12, 13, & 15.)

ARTICLE IV AUTHORITIES OF THE UNIVERSITY

Section 34. Designation of Authorities

Act The following shall be authorities of the university:

(a) The governing body.

(b) The academic council.

(c) The faculty boards or committees of colleges, schools, and departments.

(d) Such other authorities as may be established by the governing body and included in the university statutes.

Section 35. The Governing Body—Composition and Organization (4, generally)

Act (a) Constitution of the Governing
Body (4.1-3)
If the recommendations in Chapter 4 are followed, this
section could be worded as follows:
The governing body shall consist of thirteen members as
follows:

(1) The minister or secretary of agriculture, ex officio.

(2) The minister or secretary of either finance or education, ex officio.

(3) The chief administrative officer of the university.

(4) Two registered graduates of the institution (one
woman and one man to be selected by the registered
graduates or alumni organization. Two men may be
selected until there are women graduates).

(5) Two members of the faculty to be elected by the
academic council.

(6) Two progressive farmers, two professional educators, and two members representing business and industry, labor and the professions, none of whom shall be
members of government, to be appointed by the chancellor or governor. Nonresidents of the state or country
shall not be disqualified for membership on the governing body.

Act (b) Term of Office (4.4)
The following provisions may be made:

(1) Ex officio members and the chief administrative officer shall serve during the period of their tenure.

(2) The registered graduates shall serve for six years
with terms staggered so that one is appointed every three
years.

(3) The members of the faculty shall serve for six years
with terms staggered so that one is appointed every
three years.

(4) Terms of the six members appointed by the governor or chancellor shall be six years with terms staggered
so that two members are appointed every two years.

(5) In all cases above where staggered terms are provided, the electing or appointing authority shall designate the individuals who initially shall serve shorter
terms than six years.

Act (c) Removal from Office   (4.4)

It should be provided that the governing body may remove any of its members in categories (2), (3), or (4) of subsection (b) above for just cause, provided:

(1) The member is informed of the cause and is given adequate notice.

(2) The member is afforded a hearing before the governing body if he so requests, with a right to be represented by counsel.

(3) The governing body does not take action until after a hearing or if there is no hearing until at least one meeting following the meeting in which the recommendation of removal is made.

(4) An absolute three-fourths of the governing body votes in favor of removal.

(5) That if the action involves any of the members appointed by the governor, his concurrence shall be required.

Act (d) Officers of the Governing Body   (4.6-7)

(1) Chairman. This should provide that the chairman be elected by the governing body from among its non-governmental members for a designated term with the right to be reelected. (If there is a strong feeling that the chief administrative officer should be chairman of the governing body, this provision would, of course, need to be varied. For a discussion of the pros and cons on chairmanship by the chief administrative officer, see Chapter 7, Section 2.)

(2) Secretary. This should provide that, upon recommendation of the chief administrative officer and approval of the governing body, some university officer serve as secretary of the governing body. The secretary shall not have a vote and shall serve at the pleasure of the governing body. His duties shall be as specified by rules of the governing body.

(3) Treasurer. This should provide that the treasurer be appointed by the governing body to serve at its pleasure and to perform such functions as may be specified in rules of the governing body. It should provide that the treasurer not be an officer or a member of the university

or of the governing body itself. The governing body should provide that the treasurer be adequately bonded. (4) Other Officers. This should provide that the governing body may appoint such additional officers as it deems necessary.

Act (e) Meetings (4.5)

(1) This should provide that regular meetings of the governing body shall be held not less than four times annually and that at least half of such meetings shall be on the campus of the university.

(2) This should provide that special meetings may be called by the chairman or by any three members of the governing body, provided that at least ten days' notice is given and that the notice contains a statement of items to be considered at the meeting.

(3) The chairman should preside at all meetings of the governing body or, if he is unable to preside, should designate another member of the governing body to act in his place. Failing this, the board may appoint a chairman for the meeting.

(4) Meetings of the governing body should be conducted according to the rules established and published by it.

(5) The secretary, in cooperation with the chief administrative officer, should prepare an agenda in advance of meetings and supply all governing body members with such agenda together with supporting information and materials. He should be required to keep an accurate record of all meetings and mail copies to each member of the governing body.

(6) A quorum for ordinary business should consist of a majority of the total membership of the governing body.

(7) Discharge of the chief administrative officer and action on other important matters as designated by rules of the governing body should require the concurrence of three-fourths of the total membership of the governing body.

(8) Minutes of the governing body should be open to public inspection during regular business hours.

(9) Except when in the opinion of the governing body

it should meet in closed session, all meetings should be open to the public.

Act (f) Committees (4.8)

This should provide that the governing body may appoint an executive committee and such other committees, standing or otherwise, as it deems necessary. The executive committee shall consist of the chairman and two members selected by him. It shall have authority to act for the governing body on all routine matters, reporting such action to the governing body. It shall have authority to act for the governing body on any matter in an emergency subject to confirmation of the governing body at its next meeting.

Act (g) Expenses (4.10)

This should provide that members of the governing body shall receive no pay for their services but are entitled to actual expenses incurred in discharging their functions as governing body members. Procedures for claiming expenses should be designated in rules of the governing body.

Act (h) Conflicts of Interests (4.9)

This should provide that except for the chief administrative officer and faculty members, no member of the governing body shall hold any office under the authority of the governing body nor be directly or indirectly interested in any contract made by the governing body.

Section 36. The Governing Body—Powers and Duties (5, generally)

Act (a) General Control and Responsibility (5, Introduction)

Provision should be made that the governing body shall be responsible for the policies and programs of the university and shall be responsible to the legislature for the achievement of the purposes expressed for the university.

(b) Appointment of Chief Administrative Officer (5.1)

This subsection should provide that the governing body shall appoint the chief administrative officer of the university in the manner provided and under the terms and conditions expressed in this act and in the statutes.

(c) University Statutes (5.2)

This should provide that the governing body shall provide for the formulation and adoption of university statutes through procedures contained in this act and in the university statutes.

(d) Appointment of Staff   (5.3)

This subsection should state that subject to provisions contained in the act and in the university statutes the governing body shall have the right to approve appointments and approve the salary and conditions of service of all staff members.

(e) Finance and Budget   (5.4)

It should be provided here that the governing body shall be responsible for the finances of the university and for approval of the university budget. In connection with budget and finance the governing body may be given the following authority:

(1) To appoint a treasurer and require that he be bonded.

(2) To select a depository for university funds.

(3) To fix tuition, fees, and hostel or dormitory rentals.

(4) To decide on the acceptance of specific gifts and grants to the university.

(5) To invest the funds of the university.

(6) To collect, disburse, and account for funds.

(7) To borrow for university construction without being subject to any debt limit set for other state agencies.

(8) To issue bonds and give appropriate security.

(9) To provide for the auditing of university accounts.

(10) To publish the budget in such manner and in such detail as it deems appropriate.

(f) Control, Use, and Disposition of Property   (5.5)

This should state that the governing body has authority to hold, control, and administer property and to acquire and dispose of property or rights in property to the extent necessary to achieve the purposes of the university, and that it may hold title to property in trust on behalf of the state to achieve the purposes of the university.

(g) Contracts   (5.5)

It should be provided that the governing body shall have exclusive authority to enter into contracts necessary in carrying on the business of the university, but that through procedures to be developed and stated in university regulations it may provide for delegation of authority for receiving bids and for general procedures to be employed in purchasing and procurement.

(h) Student Housing   (17.10)
The governing body should be authorized to provide student housing, regulate its use, and make rental charges.

(i) Security   (5.5)
The governing body should be responsible for the security of the university.

(j) Removal of Staff Members   (5.6)
The governing body should have authority to remove staff members for adequate cause and under procedures which afford due process or fundamental fairness, the procedures to be expressed in university statutes.

(k) New Units   (5.7)
The governing body should be given the right to establish new units of instruction including postgraduate instruction or new units and branches of the university under procedures provided in the university act and statutes.

(l) Courses of Study and Curricula   (5.8)
It should be provided that the governing body has authority to approve courses of study and curricula on recommendation from the academic council and the chief administrative officer.

(m) Degrees and Diplomas   (5.8)
This should provide that the governing body has authority to grant degrees and diplomas on recommendation from the academic council.

(n) Retirement Plan   (5.9)
The governing body should be empowered to establish retirement, pension, and insurance plans for all university employees and to establish health and accident insurance plans for students.

(o) Admission to the University   (5.10)
Subject to provisions in the university act and statutes, the governing body should have authority to establish admission standards for the university and to prescribe the procedures for admission in university statutes and regulations.

(p) University Calendar   (5.11)
The governing body should be empowered to establish the

academic year, the divisions of the academic year, and the university calendar, subject to procedures prescribed in the act, statutes, and university regulations.

(q) Ancillary Services

The governing body should have authority to establish such ancillary services as are needed for employees and students. This would include, but not be limited to, health, recreational, and school facilities.

(r) Additional Authority

It should be provided that the governing body shall have such other powers and duties as may be prescribed in the university act and statutes and such other powers and duties as may be reasonably implied or necessary for the achievement of the purposes of the university.

Section 37. The Academic Council—Composition and Organization (11.1)

Act (a) This should provide that there shall be an academic council to be constituted as follows:

(1) The chief administrative officer who shall serve as its chairman.

(2) All professors in the university.

(3) All deans and department heads.

(4) Directors of research, extension, and instruction.

(5) Such others as may be provided for in the university statutes.

(b) The registrar shall act as secretary of the academic council unless it elects another secretary.

Statutes (a) In addition to the members of the academic council designated by the act, the following should be members:

(1) Administrative officers of the university, but they shall not have a vote.

(2) Such additional members of the academic staff as the academic council itself may determine to be elected or appointed under provisions established by it.

(b) The secretary of the academic council should be required to maintain records and minutes, prepare and mail out agenda and supporting materials to members prior to meetings, and perform such other functions as the academic council may determine.

(c) The academic council should be empowered to adopt rules of organization and procedure and should establish regular meeting dates.

(d) The academic council should appoint such committees, standing and otherwise, as it deems necessary. Members of the academic staff who are not members of the academic council may be included as members of such committees. While serving, such committee members shall have the privileges of members of the academic council including the right to vote.

(e) Emeritus professors should be given the right to continue as members of the academic council but without the right to vote.

(f) It should be provided that special meetings may be called by the chief administrative officer or on the request of 10 per cent of the members of the council.

(g) It should be provided that a quorum for carrying on business shall consist of a majority of the members of the academic council unless a different number is specified by the council in its rules.

Section 38. The Academic Council—Powers
and Duties (11.1; 12, generally)

Act This should provide that the academic council shall be concerned with academic and educational affairs in the university and shall have such powers and duties as are specified in the university statutes.

Statutes This section should state that the powers and duties of the academic council may be as follows:

(a) To approve admission requirements.

(b) To determine courses of study and curricula.

(c) To approve the university calendar.

(d) To establish the requirements for all degrees.

(e) To determine what degrees shall be conferred.

(f) To approve those on whom degrees are to be conferred.

(g) To establish procedures in student disciplinary cases.

(h) To determine academic standards.

(i) To develop policies for the awarding of fellowships, scholarships, medals, prizes, and other honors.

(j) To recommend policies for the libraries and library services.

(k) To approve the establishment of new educational units.

(l) To approve general policies regarding research and extension.

(m) To approve the conferring of honorary degrees.

(n) To propose, consider, and approve university statutes and amendments to statutes as provided in the university act and statutes.

(o) To consider and act upon other matters involving educational policy or the academic activity of the university.

Section 39. College Faculties—Composition and Organization (11.2)

Act This section should state that the composition and organization of college faculties shall be such as are provided in the university statutes.

Statutes (a) It may be provided that the membership on college faculties shall be as follows:

(1) The dean of the college who shall serve as chairman of the faculty.

(2) The chief administrative officer.

(3) The directors of research and extension for the university.

(4) Associate and assistant deans of the college.

(5) All members of the teaching, research, and extension staff of the college, except that the college faculty by its own action may limit the membership of lower ranks.

(6) By agreement between the appropriate deans, a representative of a group, department, or any other university activity which participates in the program of the college.

(b) There should be provision for an executive committee of the college faculty elected by the faculty. The number of members, their terms of service, and the committee's general functions should be determined by the faculty. The dean of the college should be designated its chairman.

(c) There should be a provision that the faculty shall

elect a secretary and appoint such committees as it deems necessary.

(d) The faculty should be empowered to develop its own rules and procedure including a schedule of regular meetings and the requirements for calling special meetings.

(e) Emeritus members of the faculty should be given the right to attend meetings and participate in discussion without vote.

Section 40. College Faculties—
Powers and Duties (11.2)

Act This should provide that college faculties shall have such powers and duties as are prescribed in the university statutes and regulations.

Statutes This should state that the college faculties may have the following powers and duties:

(a) To determine entrance requirements for courses of study in the college.

(b) To recommend courses of study to be pursued for degrees.

(c) To recommend candidates for degrees.

(d) To approve courses to be offered in the college.

(e) To make recommendations regarding the orientation, counseling, advisement, and placement programs of the college.

(f) To establish educational standards for the college.

(g) To make recommendations regarding the establishment or disestablishment of departments or other educational units of the college.

(h) To make recommendations to the academic council regarding university educational policy in matters affecting the college.

(i) To consider, initiate, or make recommendations to the academic council regarding university statutes affecting the college.

(j) To engage in any other activities which will improve the intellectual and social atmosphere of the college.

Section 41. Graduate College Faculty—
Composition and Organization (10.5)

Act This should provide that the composition and organization of the graduate college faculty shall be as provided in university statutes.

Statutes (a) This should provide that the faculty of the graduate college shall consist of the following:

(1) The chief administrative officer of the university.

(2) The dean of the graduate college.

(3) The university director of research and university director of extension.

(4) The deans of colleges or directors of schools and institutes.

(5) The full professors of the university.

(6) Such other members of the academic staff as the executive committee of the graduate college may approve for giving graduate instruction and supervision.

(b) This subsection should provide for the constitution of an executive committee with the dean of the graduate college serving as its chairman. Other members should be elected by the faculty of the graduate college under regulations to be developed by the faculty.

Section 42. Graduate College Faculty— Powers and Duties

Act This section should state that to the extent applicable the powers and duties of the faculty of the graduate college shall be as expressed in the university statutes for college faculties.

Statutes None, unless the governing body gives the graduate college faculty additional powers and duties.

Section 43. Department Faculties   (11.2, 11.4)

Act This section should provide that the faculty of each department shall be an authority of the university. Its composition, powers, and duties shall be as prescribed in university statutes and regulations.

Statutes (a) Provision should be made that the faculty of a department shall consist of its full-time teaching, research, and extension staff and such other members as may be included by action of the departmental faculty. The head of the department shall be a member and chairman. The dean and associate and assistant deans of the college shall be members also.

(b) Under this subsection, the departmental faculty should be empowered to determine its own rules and procedures and elect its own officers. It may appoint such committees as are deemed necessary.

(c) This subsection should provide that the departmental faculty shall have those powers and duties expressed in these statutes for a college faculty which are applicable to the department and which are not inconsistent with the superior authority of the college faculty. It shall have such additional powers and duties as may be determined by regulations of the college faculty.

Section 44. Other Authorities (11.4)

Statutes This should provide that there may be such additional authorities as are approved by the governing body on recommendation of the academic council.

ARTICLE V   EDUCATIONAL UNITS OF THE UNIVERSITY

Section 45. Establishment of Units (10.1-2)

Act (a) This should state that there shall be a college of agriculture, a college of veterinary science, a college of basic arts and sciences, and such additional colleges as may be established by the governing body on recommendation of the academic council.

(b) Existing colleges may be included as constituent colleges in accordance with provisions of the act, with such additional administrative arrangements as may be approved by the governing body.

(c) It should be provided that there shall be such departments within colleges and such institutes, branches, or other units of the university as shall be established by the governing body on recommendation of the academic council following recommendations to the academic council from any college faculty involved.

Statutes None, until the governing body establishes additional units.

Section 46. The College (10.3)

Act It should be stated that the college is a major educational and administrative grouping of disciplines within the university. The college should comprise those departments or divisions which are best served by their inclusion within it. Its academic affairs shall be governed by its faculty, and it shall be administratively in the charge of a dean. Its responsibility includes teaching, research, extension, and public service.

Section 47. The Graduate College (10.5)

Act This section should state that there shall be a graduate college when established as provided in this act. It shall be in charge of all graduate instruction in the university.

Section 48. The Department (10.4)

Act (a) A statement should be included here that the department is a basic unit of administration carrying on an integrated program of teaching, research, and extension in a particular field of knowledge. It should have the fullest measure of autonomy consistent with the maintenance of college and university educational policies and correct academic and administrative relations with other divisions of the university.

(b) The department shall be administered by a head who shall be appointed as provided in Section 76. He shall be responsible for the functioning of his department and for the integration of the teaching, research, and extension work of the department, and shall have such other powers and duties as are designated in the act and university statutes or delegated to him by the dean of the college.

Statutes The powers and duties of a department head may be listed as follows:

(a) Be responsible for organization and conduct of work of the department.

(b) Cause the formulation and execution of departmental policies.

(c) Be responsible for the general supervision of the work of students in the department.

(d) Supervise jointly with the dean of the graduate college the postgraduate instruction which is undertaken in his department.

(e) Prepare and submit the departmental budget.

(f) Supervise departmental funds and property.

(g) Supervise the use of departmental space and land areas.

(h) Cooperate actively with the director of extension, the director of research, and the dean of the graduate college.

(i) Make appointments to the staff of the department through procedures specified in Article VIII.

(j) Submit annual and other reports to the dean of the college.

(k) Perform such other powers and duties as may be specified in the university statutes or delegated to him by the dean of the college.

Section 49. Other Units (10.6-7)

Act It should be provided that when other units are established as provided in this act and in the university statutes, they shall be defined in the statutes.

ARTICLE VI RESEARCH AND EXTENSION

Section 50. Responsibility for Research (13.3)

Act This section should state that the university shall engage in research both fundamental and applied in all the disciplines existing in the university and that budgetary allowance shall be made for research work.

Section 51. Scope of University Research (13.1, 13.4)

Act (a) This should state that the university shall have authority to engage in research in all areas but that its particular responsibility will be to engage in that research which will aid agricultural development and the betterment of the rural population.

(b) This should provide that the university may establish experiment stations at different locations in the state or region to further facilitate its research effort.

Statutes This section should encourage the publication of research results through bulletins, scholarly journals, and other means.

Section 52. Cooperation with Other Research Agencies (13.3, 13.5)

Act It shall have authority to cooperate with other research agencies, both state and national, in the development of its program.

Section 53. Research Advisory Committee (13.3)

Act This section should state that there shall be a committee advisory to the director of research and constituted as provided in the university statutes.

Statutes This section should provide that the research advisory committee shall be composed as follows:

(a) The director of research who shall serve as chairman.

(b) The director of university extension.

(c) The dean of the graduate college.

(d) The deans of colleges.

(e) Two members of the staff to be appointed by the chief administrative officer.

(f) Two prominent farmers or agriculturalists to be appointed by the chief administrative officer.

(g) Two government officials concerned with research, to be appointed by government.

Section 54. Responsibility for Extension (14.3)

Act This section should provide that there shall be a university extension service responsible for making educational resources of the university available to farmers and other qualified persons who are not students in residence. Particular emphasis in the university extension program should be on agriculture and home science. The education of personnel to engage in extension work shall be a prime responsibility of the university. Budgetary allowances shall be made for extension work.

Section 55. Scope of University Extension (14.1)

Act This should state that the extension program of the university shall involve all appropriate disciplines and educational units of the university. The extension program shall be available to rural people throughout the state under a program to be developed by the university and coordinated with existing national or state extension organizations.

Section 56. Cooperation with Other Extension Agencies (14.4)

Act This section should provide that in planning and conducting its extension program the university shall cooperate with other extension agencies, both state and national, and that it shall make its facilities available for training extension workers for such other agencies.

Section 57. Extension Personnel (14.3)

Act (a) Provision should be made that all subject matter extension specialists shall be members of their departmental and college faculties and shall be responsible to their department head for the educational content of their program. They shall be responsible to the director of university extension with respect to travel and administrative and programming aspects of their work.

(b) All other extension personnel shall be responsible to the director of university extension and shall be recommended by him for appointment under provisions contained in the university act and statutes. Such extension personnel shall be accorded an appropriate academic rank in the university.

Section 58. The Extension Advisory Committee (14.3)

Act This section should provide that there shall be a committee advisory to the university director of extension. Its composition shall be as provided in the university statutes.

Statutes The composition of the extension advisory committee may be as follows:

(a) The director of extension who shall serve as chairman.

(b) The director of university research.

(c) The deans of colleges.

(d) The head of home science of the university.

(e) Two staff members to be appointed by the chief administrative officer.

(f) Two prominent farmers or agriculturalists to be appointed by the chief administrative officer.

(g) Two government officials concerned with extension, to be appointed by government.

ARTICLE VII   UNIVERSITY FUNDS, FINANCE, AND BUSINESS OPERATIONS

(If there are government regulations applicable to the university in the exercise of any of the functions prescribed in the following sections, and adherence to these regulations would unduly hamper the university, the act should except it from their application.)

Section 59. Finance Committee (5.4, 8.3)

Act This section should provide that there shall be a university finance committee whose constitution, powers, and duties shall be as prescribed in the university statutes.

Statutes (a) Constitution. The finance committee may be constituted in the following manner:

(1) The chief financial officer of the university, who shall serve as secretary of the committee.

(2) Two members of the governing body to be selected by the governing body, one of whom (a nongovernmental member) shall serve as chairman.

(3) A representative from the state department of finance to be designated by the department.

(4) The chief administrative officer, who shall have the right to meet with the committee at his pleasure.

(b) Functions of the Committee

The committee shall be advisory to the governing body and perform the following functions:

(1) Consider the university budget and make recommendations to the governing body concerning it.

(2) Study additional sources of income for the university and make recommendations to the governing body regarding them.

(3) Make recommendations regarding the financial management and relationship of the university to such ancillary agencies as may exist.

(4) Make recommendations to the governing body regarding long-term building and capital improvement programs.

(5) Study and make recommendations regarding other university financial matters which it regards as important.

Section 60. University Funds (8.2)

Act This section should provide that there shall be a general fund and such additional funds as may be established by regulation.

Section 61. University Budget (7.3, 8.4)

Act This should provide that the chief financial officer shall prepare and the chief administrative officer shall submit to the governing body for its consideration and approval the annual budget of the university.

Statutes (a) It should be provided that in the preparation of the budget the chief financial officer shall confer with the finance committee and with any university-wide committee or committee of the academic council which has to do with finance or budget.

(b) The university budget should be developed to show amounts needed for teaching, research, and extension and for the separate units of the university down to and including departments.

(c) Each educational unit designated in the budget should be allowed to prepare its portion of the budget under such instructions as may be issued by the chief financial officer and to submit such budget to the next higher authority by the dates designated.

Section 62. University Contracts (5.5, 8.14)

Statutes (a) This should provide that contracts involving more than an amount of money to be stated in regulations must be approved by the governing body.

(b) This should state that certain contracts can be let only on the basis of advertisement and bids as designated by regulations to be contained in the business office procedure manual.

Section 63. Tuition and Fees (8.6, 17.7)

Statutes (a) This subsection should state that tuition and fees shall be assessed and collected under procedures to be mutually agreed upon by the registrar and the chief financial officer.

(b) This should provide that a schedule of tuition and fees shall be prepared by the chief financial officer acting on the advice of appropriate university officers and committees after approval of the chief administrative officer. Such schedules shall be submitted to the governing body for its approval.

(c) This should provide that refunds can be made as established by regulation.

(d) If the tuition schedule requires nonresidents to pay higher tuition than residents, a provision should be included providing that a student who is of legal age or is married and maintains a residence at the university for one year shall be considered a resident of the state or region for tuition purposes.

Section 64. Gifts and Grants (8.8-10)

Statutes (a) Provision should be made that when gifts are offered to the university, the chief administrative officer shall designate the staff member to negotiate with the prospective donor, and, if he deems it advisable, shall appoint a committee to consider the proposed gift. The university legal officer shall be consulted regarding the wording of the gift instrument.

(b) It should be stated that when objects of art are offered to the university, the chief administrative officer shall appoint an appropriate committee to advise him regarding their acceptance.

Section 65. Investments (8.11)

Act (a) This should provide that the governing body has authority to establish a separate corporate entity for the acceptance and management of gifts and investments.

(b) The governing body should be authorized to invest funds of the university in an employees' credit union.

Section 66. Deposits (8.12)

Act This should provide that university funds must be deposited and that they shall be deposited by the treasurer of the university in the depository selected by the governing body.

Section 67. Insurance (8.20)

Act This should empower the governing body to authorize the chief financial officer to procure insurance of any kind which is deemed by the governing body to be necessary.

Section 68. Pension Plans (5.9, 15.12)

Statutes The following provisions may be included in the statutes:

(a) All regular employees of the university whether academic or nonacademic shall be members of the university pension or retirement system, when qualified under provisions in these statutes.

(b) Temporary employees and other employees during a probationary period shall not be members of the retirement or pension system. When temporary employees become regularly employed and when new personnel serve beyond the probationary period, they shall become members of the retirement or pension system, their membership to commence on the date of first employment.

(c) The age for retirement shall be that established by general law. If there is no general law or if a different age is desired, then the retirement age should be expressed in this subsection.

(d) The rights and obligations of participants in the retirement plan shall be as specified in university regulations.

(e) A separate fund for the retirement or pension plan shall be maintained by the chief financial officer unless the funds are managed in some different manner to be approved by the governing body.

(f) There should be authorization to supplement the pension plan with a staff group insurance program.

Section 69. Travel Expenses (8.18)

Act This should state that the governing body may establish policies, rules, and regulations on payment for travel by employees of the university when on university business.

Statutes (a) This should provide that all employees shall be reimbursed for actual and necessary expense of travel on university business when approved by their immediate administrative superior.

(b) Necessary rules, procedures, and forms should be developed by the chief financial officer and published in a business office procedure manual.

(c) Provisions for travel should be made in the budgets of all units of the university, and the travel expenses of employees should ordinarily be paid from the budget of their unit unless, upon approval of the appropriate university administrative officer, they are to be paid from the budget of another unit.

(d) A provision should be made that payment of travel expense of the academic staff to one convention annually may be included in rules and regulations made by the chief financial officer upon recommendation from the academic council. Travel to such conventions shall be approved in advance by the department head or other appropriate administrative official.

Section 70. Auditing (8.17)

Statutes This should provide that the chief financial officer of the university shall establish a system of internal auditing and determine the rules and regulations under which the auditing is to be accomplished.

Section 71. Student Organization Funds (8.19)

Statutes This should provide that the chief financial officer shall maintain a fund for all student organizations to be managed as a service for such organizations and without authority to exercise surveillance over the use of such deposits by student organizations.

ARTICLE VIII THE ACADEMIC STAFF

Section 72. Academic Freedom and Responsibility (15.5)

Act This should provide that principles of academic freedom shall be recognized throughout the university.

Statutes This should state that it is a policy of the university to maintain and encourage full freedom within the law of inquiry, discourse, teaching, research, and publication, and to protect any member of the academic staff against influences from within or without the university which would restrict him in the exercise of these freedoms in his area of scholarly interest. In his role as a citizen, a faculty member may exercise the same freedoms as other citizens without institutional censorship or discipline. He should be mindful that accuracy, forthrightness, and dignity befit his association with the university and his position as a man of learning, and that the public may judge his profession and the university by his conduct and utterances.

Section 73. Qualifications (15.2)

Act (a) The act should provide that color, religion, sex, nationality, or other factors which have no bearing on the staff member's ability to perform shall not be a bar to appointment.

(b) This should state that members of the academic staff shall not be required to be citizens of the state or country.

(c) This should provide that additional qualifications for positions in the university based on experience, past performance, and educational achievement may be established upon recommendation of the academic council.

Statutes This section should provide that the following factors shall be considered in making appointments:

(a) Physical ability to perform the job.

(b) Resident and extension teaching ability and performance.

(c) Research ability and achievement.

(d) General usefulness or promise thereof to the university.

Section 74. Academic Ranks (15.10)

Act This should provide that there shall be such academic ranks as shall be provided in the university statutes.

Statutes It is suggested that the following provisions be included:

(a) Professor, associate professor, assistant professor, instructor, and such additional categories as may be approved by the academic council shall be recognized as academic ranks in the university.

(b) Distinctions between the ranks shall be in terms of educational attainment, experience, salary, duties, and responsibility.

(c) Appropriate academic ranks shall be accorded extension personnel and such officers and other administrative employees as may be recommended for such ranks by the chief administrative officer and approved by the academic council.

(d) The academic council may recommend creation of one or more honorary rank designations.

Section 75. Integration of Educational Functions (2.12, 13.7)

Act (a) This should state that, where appropriate, teaching, research, and extension shall be recognized as coordinate functions in all educational units of the university.

(b) This should state that staff members' contracts shall reflect their responsibility for these functions, and combined responsibilities shall be encouraged, particularly the combination of teaching and research in staff appointments.

Section 76. Method of Appointment   (5.3; 15, Introduction, 1-2)

Act This should provide that appointments to the staff of the university shall be made strictly on the basis of merit and that in all cases an appropriate selection committee shall have made recommendations. Appointments shall be made by the governing body on recommendation of the chief administrative officer. All appointments shall be made by written contract. Procedures for making appointments shall be as specified in the university statutes and in university regulations.

Statutes (a) It should be provided that the following procedures shall be followed in making appointments to the academic staff of the university and in the appointment of department heads:

(1) A selection committee of three to five members shall be appointed by the administrative officer under whom the prospective employee is to serve. This committee shall include some membership from the unit in which the prospective employee is to serve, some from the college in which he will serve, and some from other appropriate units of the university. The committee shall engage in such activities as it feels will disclose the best candidates for the position and, following its activity, shall make recommendations to the immediate administrative officer.

(2) The committee and the immediate administrative officer shall discuss the recommendations of the committee and, if the recommendations are acceptable, the committee shall be discharged. Otherwise it shall continue its activities and report again to the officer.

(3) The immediate administrative officer shall select one nominee and forward his name through administrative channels for approval of the chief administrative officer and submission to the governing body for appointment.

(4) The governing body shall either approve or disapprove. If it disapproves, the chief administrative officer will be notified. He then will notify the immediate administrative officer, and the selection process described above will again be followed.

(b) The secretary of the governing body shall immediately notify nominees of their appointment and shall send them two copies of the contract, one to be signed and returned to the secretary.

(c) Annually the secretary shall mail renewal contracts to members of the academic staff who are continuing in the service of the university.

(d) Appointments below the grade of instructor or at salaries less than _____ may be made by the chief administrative officer and reported to the governing body for subsequent approval.

(e) Appointments of an urgent nature may be made by the chief administrative officer and reported to the governing body for its confirmation.

Section 77. Terms and Conditions of Service   (5.9; 15, generally)

Act (a) This subsection should state that salary and other conditions of service shall be as determined by university statutes, regulations, and the hiring officer, and shall be included in the contract either expressly or by reference. Such conditions of service are subject to approval by the governing body.

(b) This should provide that all academic staff members of the university shall be entitled to participate in any pension or retirement plan which may be provided under provisions to be contained in these statutes and university regulations.

Statutes The following provisions should be included:

(a) The term of employment and specific conditions of service shall be explicitly stated by the nominating officer.

(b) Members of the academic staff shall not be subject to government civil service. (If this provision is inapplicable, it should be omitted.)

(c) Members of the academic staff may resign as provided in regulations of the university and in the contract of the staff member.

(d) Promotions and salary increases shall be made on the basis of merit under procedures established by the chief administrative officer, following recommendations from the academic council.

(e) Members of the staff and their families shall be entitled to the services of the university health service as provided in regulations.

(f) Members of the academic staff and their families shall be entitled to library and other privileges as provided by university regulations.

(g) If elementary schools are not available for the children of members of the staff, the university shall either provide such schooling or shall defray a portion of the expense for such schooling as provided in regulations.

Section 78. Tenure (15.4)

Act This section should provide that the principle of indefinite tenure shall be recognized, such tenure to be attained under provisions to be included in the university statutes.

Statutes The following provisions should be included:

(a) Appointment as professor or associate professor shall be for an indefinite term.

(b) Full-time academic staff members below the rank of associate professor shall be appointed for definite terms under a six-year probationary period, following which, providing a one-year notice of discharge has not been given, they shall acquire indefinite tenure in the rank which they hold at that time.

(c) These rules shall apply to the academic staff members of institutions which become constituent units of the university as though such staff members had been serving on the staff of the university.

(d) Officers of the university and members of the administrative staff shall be appointed for definite terms and shall not achieve indefinite tenure. However, if they are accorded an academic rank they shall have the tenure that accompanies the rank.

Section 79. Discharge and Suspension (7.5, 15.6)

Statutes The following provisions may be included:

(a) In all cases, discharge, suspension, and official reprimand shall issue from the chief administrative officer.

(b) Before charges are prepared, the chief administrative officer shall attempt to settle the matter by conciliation.

(c) Before charges are delivered to a staff member, the

chief administrative officer shall confer with an advisory committee of the faculty.

(1) The advisory committee of the faculty referred to above shall be elected at large by members of the faculty under procedures to be developed by the academic council.

(2) The functions of the committee shall be to hear grievances of staff members and make recommendations, to confer with the chief administrative officer in cases which might involve dismissal or suspension, and to make recommendations to the chief administrative officer for the good of the university.

(d) If, following a conference with the faculty advisory committee, the chief administrative officer still wishes to take action to discharge, he shall deliver to the staff member an adequate statement of charges which shall also inform the staff member about relevant information regarding laws and statutes applicable, procedures to be followed, his rights, and the time by which a reply to the charges shall be made.

(e) The staff member shall be entitled to a hearing before a standing committee of the academic council, one of the functions of which shall be to constitute a hearing body in cases involving possible dismissal or suspension.

(f) The staff member shall have the right to be represented by legal counsel and also by some member of the academic staff if he so chooses.

(g) The staff member shall be permitted to call witnesses and produce such evidence or material as he deems desirable in his defense. Following the hearing, the committee shall recommend to the chief administrative officer either that the matter be dropped or that the staff member be removed. An adequate record of the hearing shall be kept. It shall accompany the recommendation of the committee to the chief administrative officer.

(h) The chief administrative officer shall consider the recommendation of the committee but shall not be bound by it. If he decides that no further action need be taken, the matter shall be dropped. If he decides that the staff member should be discharged, he shall notify the staff member following which the staff member shall have the right within a time to be specified in regulations to appeal to the governing body.

(i) If the staff member appeals to the governing body, he shall have the right to be represented by counsel, to call witnesses, and to produce other evidence in his favor. The record of the hearing before the faculty committee of the academic council shall be made available to him, and other procedures shall be followed to make his adversary position as nearly as possible equal to that of the chief administrative officer. Following this hearing, the governing body shall either confirm the action recommended by the chief administrative officer or shall dismiss the case.

(j) Unless suspended, the staff member shall, during the pendency of the charge and proceedings, continue the performance of his duties.

(k) Suspension shall be regarded as an emergency action and may be used by the chief administrative officer, after consultation with the faculty advisory committee, when he feels the situation is serious and such action is necessary. During the period of suspension the staff member shall continue to receive his salary. Official reprimand may be made by the chief administrative officer after he has:

(1) Conferred with the staff member.

(2) Conferred with the faculty advisory committee.

Section 80. Leaves

Statutes (a) This should provide that all members of the academic staff whose appointment requires a rendering of services for a calendar year shall be entitled to one month annual leave at such time as is mutually agreed upon between the staff member and his immediate administrative superior.

(b) This should provide that annual leave shall not be cumulative.

(c) This should provide that sick and maternity leave shall be granted as provided in regulations approved by the chief administrative officer.

(d) There should be provision for the granting of sabbatical or study leave under the following conditions:

(1) Such leave may be granted after a continuous period of service of six years in the professorial ranks, for study, travel, or other activities which will improve the staff members' ability to serve the university.

(2) Such leave shall be with full pay when granted for one academic year or for a shorter period.

(3) Leaves for longer than one year may be granted, but the total salary paid during such period shall not exceed that for one year of service.

(4) There shall be no limit on the number of such leaves that may be granted a staff member, provided he meets the requirements specified in this section.

(5) A staff member desiring leave shall petition his immediate administrative superior at least one term in advance of the time the leave is to commence and shall state his study, travel, or other educational plans during such leave period.

(6) Leave shall not be granted unless the staff member agrees to remain in the service of the university for one full year following the termination of such leave.

(7) At the conclusion of such leave a report of activities shall be made to the staff member's administrative superior.

(8) While on such leave the staff member shall not engage in any remunerative activity without prior approval of his immediate administrative superior and the chief administrative officer of the university.

(e) It should be stated that such other leaves may be granted as are approved by the chief administrative officer and the governing body and specified in regulations of the university.

Section 81. Employment of Relatives (15.9)

Statutes (a) This should state that it is the policy of the university to discourage nepotism in appointments to the faculty and administrative staff of the university, except in cases where the interest of the university requires otherwise.

(b) This should provide for the promulgation of regulations which specify the degrees of relationship to which this policy applies and which establish a discretion in the chief administrative officer to waive these rules when undue hardship would result to the university or the individual. (c) It should be provided that exceptions to the above rule shall not be made in any case, however, where one of the persons involved has authority and responsibility in the appointment or promotion of the other.

Section 82. Grievances

Statutes (a) If the staff member has a grievance or complaint, it is expected that he will first attempt to resolve it with his immediate administrative superior.

(b) If a staff member's grievance or complaint is not handled to his satisfaction by his immediate administrative superior, he shall have the right to proceed through regular administrative channels and, if necessary, confer with the chief administrative officer.

(c) If a staff member has exhausted administrative channels or for some reason feels that he should not attempt to do so, he may appeal to the whole committee or to any member of the faculty advisory committee established under Section 79. The action of the committee or of any one or more of its members shall be advisory, but it shall have authority to contact university officers or personnel involved regarding the grievance or complaint and make suggestions to them. When it deems such to be in the best interest of the staff member and the university, the faculty advisory committee shall submit a formal report and recommendations to the appropriate administrative official of the university.

**Section 83. Outside Employment and
Part-time Services** (15.20, 15.21)

Statutes (a) This should provide that all academic personnel shall be employed full-time with the exception of part-time graduate assistants and except for special circumstances which may justify part-time service.

(b) It should be stated that employment less than full-time shall be approved by the chief administrative officer following recommendation from the immediate administrative superior of the staff member.

(c) This should provide that staff members may engage in some professional activity or remunerative employment outside their service for the university provided that:

(1) Such activity is not incompatible with their responsibility to the university.

(2) It is accomplished outside university hours.

(3) No university equipment is used.

(4) No university personnel either academic or nonacademic are utilized while they are on university time.

(5) The office of the staff member shall not become a business office for the outside activity.

(6) The amount of time and energy spent on the outside activity shall not be so extensive as to impair his ability to perform for the university.

(7) Such outside activity is reported to the staff member's department head or immediate administrative superior.

Section 84. Retired Staff Members (15.24)

Statutes The following provisions should be included:

(a) Retired staff members may be supplied by their departments on a year-to-year basis with office and laboratory space and with research assistance to continue their research and investigations. An annual report of accomplishments shall be made to the department head.

(b) With the approval of the department head and the dean of the graduate college, a retired faculty member may offer consultations with graduate students in his line of work.

(c) Retired faculty members may continue as members of the academic council and of their college faculty with full floor privileges but without the right to vote.

(d) Library and other privileges shall be available to retired faculty members on the same basis as they are for active faculty members.

(e) Retired faculty members may be employed on a year-to-year basis for teaching, research, or other service to the university.

Section 85. Exchange and Visiting Professors (15.23)

Statutes The following provisions should be included:

(a) Members of the academic staff may serve as exchange or visiting professors in other institutions without impairment of any rights or privileges as members of the staff of the university. Such rights and privileges shall be outlined in regulations.

(b) Exchange or visiting academic staff members in this university shall during their period of service be subject to the conditions of service applicable to regular members of the faculty.

(c) Distinguished professorships and similar honorary positions may be created on recommendation of the academic council and approval of the chief administrative officer.

ARTICLE IX THE NONACADEMIC STAFF

Section 86. Civil Service (16.1)

Act This section should state that the nonacademic employees of the university are subject to a state, university, or other civil service act. (If no such act is applicable to the nonacademic employees of the university, then this section should be omitted.)

Section 87. Office of Nonacademic Personnel (16.1)

Statutes This should state that there shall be a university office of nonacademic personnel in the charge of a personnel officer who shall perform such functions and duties as are prescribed in the university act and as may be delegated to him by the chief administrative officer. All nonacademic personnel shall be hired through this office under regulations to be developed by the personnel officer and approved by the chief administrative officer.

Section 88. Terms and Conditions of
Employment (16, generally)

Statutes The following provisions should be made:

(a) Basic conditions of employment shall be as determined by the department head or other university employing officer and the nonacademic personnel officer. Regulations shall be developed and published.

(b) Basic salaries, salary increases, and promotions shall be determined by provisions in a classification system to be developed and approved by the chief administrative officer. If civil service is applicable, the classification system provided by it shall be used.

(c) Nonacademic personnel shall be entitled to such

leaves, vacations, and absences as are approved in regulations.

(d) Nonacademic personnel shall participate in the retirement or pension plan according to rules and regulations developed under the plan.

(e) Nonacademic personnel shall be entitled to those services supplied to academic personnel, such as schooling for their children, university health service, and others.

Section 89. Discharge (16.8)

Statutes (a) Members of the nonacademic staff may be discharged for good reason.

(b) In all cases, the employee shall be informed of the cause of discharge and be given an opportunity to be heard. He may be represented by counsel if he desires. Procedures shall be developed and published as regulations. If civil service applies, the university shall adhere to the rules of civil service regarding discharge. If the staff member belongs to a union, the nonacademic personnel officer shall have authority to confer with the grievance committee of the union.

Section 90. Grievances (16.9)

Statutes This should provide that the director of nonacademic personnel shall establish grievance procedures involving grievance committees composed of nonacademic staff members and incorporating the principles of due process when any penalty is recommended against the nonacademic member.

Section 91. Employment of Relatives (16.7)

Statutes This should provide that, unless altered by civil service rules, nonacademic employees shall be subject to the same rules on nepotism that govern the employment of academic personnel.

Section 92. Workmen's Compensation (16.4)

Statutes In case there is a state workmen's compensation act applicable to the university this section should state that claims under it and other procedures shall be handled by the personnel officer. If a state workmen's compensation act is not applicable, then this section should authorize the university to provide adequate liability insurance coverage and to have claims under such policies handled by the nonacademic personnel officer through procedures to be adopted by him.

ARTICLE X THE STUDENTS

Section 93. The Rights of Students (17.1, 17.17)

Act The act should provide that in all relations with students the following rights of students shall be respected, subject to such reasonable rules and regulations as are necessary to insure the proper functioning of the university:

(a) Freedom of speech.

(b) Freedom of assembly.

(c) Freedom to organize for any lawful purpose.

(d) The right to petition.

(e) The right to publish.

(f) The right to pursue personal religious beliefs.

Statutes This should provide that students shall have a right to produce a student newspaper or other publications free from the surveillance of the university. There should be a university publications board or council appointed by the chief administrative officer and consisting of both students and faculty members to advise all student publications regarding the business aspects of the venture and to give guidance regarding the laws of libel.

Section 94. Admissions (5.10, 12.2, 17.6)

Act (a) This should state that admission shall not be denied any qualified student because of race, color, religion, sex, national origin, caste, or any other personal factor not related to the individual's capacity to perform.

(b) This should state that nonresidents of the state and foreign students may be admitted subject only to such limitations on numbers as may be imposed by the governing body following recommendations from the academic council and chief administrative officer.

(c) This should state that no student shall be denied admission because of age.

(d) It should be provided that other qualifications for admission shall be approved by the academic council and expressed in regulations of the university. In the development of such qualifications, college faculties shall have the right to recommend to the academic council secondary school requirements and academic achievement levels essential for admission to the college.

Statutes This section should state that the registrar, acting on recommendation from college faculties and the academic council, shall allow transfer credit for acceptable work done by students at other institutions. Proficiency examinations may be used to establish credit for transfer students.

Section 95. Student Government (17.3-4)

Act This should provide that there may exist within the university, without excluding other student organizations, a student governing body which shall be the official medium for conveying student recommendations and opinion to the administration of the university regarding all activities of the university affecting students.

Statutes (a) This should provide that the administration of the university shall cooperate with the official student government body and shall invite it to appoint representatives to various university committees as determined by the academic council.

(b) The chief administrative officer should be required to appoint student representatives to ad hoc committees which are charged with consideration of matters important to students.

(c) This should state that the student government body shall be constituted so as to be representative of the total student body. Rules regarding its organization and functioning shall be developed by students and shall be subject to approval by the chief administrative officer.

Section 96. Student Organizations (17.5)

Statutes (a) This should state that the university shall encourage the organization of student groups for any legitimate purpose.

(b) Student organizations should be required to meet organizational standards recommended by the academic council and approved by the dean of student welfare and the chief administrative officer.

(c) It should be provided that one or more faculty advisers of the students' choice shall serve each student organization.

Section 97. Loans and Scholarships (17.8)

Statutes (a) This should provide that the academic council shall determine the conditions upon which fellowships and scholarships shall be awarded.

(b) This should state that faculties of the individual colleges and of the graduate college shall make recommendations to the academic council regarding the awarding of scholarships and fellowships.

(c) Provisions should be made that the funds for such scholarships shall be managed by the chief financial officer and shall be disbursed under rules and regulations to be developed jointly by him and an appropriate committee of the academic council. Determinations regarding the awarding of scholarships and fellowships to individual recipients shall be made initially in the colleges concerned.

(d) This should authorize the establishment of a student loan fund to be maintained by the chief financial officer and to be used in accordance with regulations to be established.

Section 98. Discipline and Dismissal (17.2)

Statutes The following provisions should be made:

(a) In all cases of dismissal, students shall be entitled to due process or fundamental justice. This shall include the right to a hearing, to be represented, and to be informed of the charges.

(b) There shall be a student disciplinary committee appointed by the academic council. It shall constitute the initial hearing body in all discipline cases.

(c) When a student is subject to discipline, the dean of student welfare should confer with him to see if it is possible to defer action and have the student engage in some remedial activity. If this is not possible, the student shall be referred to the discipline committee.

(d) There shall be student representation on the committee on student discipline of the academic council, to be selected by the student governing body. Such representation shall not constitute more than one-third of the membership of the committee.

(e) Proceedings of the committee shall be conducted in such manner as to protect the position of the student.

(f) The student shall be provided with an adviser to counsel him in his appearance before the disciplinary committee.

(g) Procedures for an appeal to the governing body of the university shall be specified in university regulations.

(h) Appropriate punishment less than dismissal shall be provided for in regulations and shall be commensurate with the degree of seriousness of the student's actions.

(i) Nothing in this section shall interfere with the right to dismiss or to impose conditions to be met because of academic performance.

Section 99. Housing

Statutes (a) The dean of student welfare shall have surveillance over the housing of students, both university and private, and shall develop such rules and regulations as are necessary to insure adequate standards of health and social activity in housing units. He shall cooperate with the chief financial officer in collecting rental payments.

(b) Students shall live either in housing provided by the university or in private housing approved by the dean of student welfare.

(c) The dean of student welfare shall encourage the organization of student housing groups.

Section 100. Services   **(17.11-13, 17.15, 17.18)**

Statutes (a) This should state that the responsibility for an adequate and safe food service for students rests with the university and that the dean of student welfare should supervise the functioning of such cafeterias and other eating facilities as may be deemed to be in the best interest of the university.

(b) This should require the university to establish a health service and place it under the supervision of the dean of student welfare. It should be authorized to conduct medical and physical examinations of students and university employees, be responsible for environmental health of the university, and have authority to compel vaccination when such is deemed necessary by the health service and approved by the chief administrative officer. Rules and regulations regarding the health service should be developed and published.

(c) This should provide that competitive athletics shall be

handled under rules and procedures to be approved by the academic council and recommended to the governing body for its approval by the chief administrative officer. A university athletic committee should be established, with both faculty and student representation. Intramural athletics and the participation of all students in healthful sports shall be encouraged by the dean of student welfare working in cooperation with appropriate university officers and staff members.

(d) It should be provided that the following counseling and guidance services shall be made available to students:

(1) The dean of student welfare shall provide general counseling and guidance including psychological counseling and the maintenance of a testing center.

(2) Each college shall establish an advisory system under which students are assigned a faculty adviser. The advisement load of faculty members shall be taken into consideration in the assignment of teaching, research, and other work.

(3) There shall be established an all-university committee on counseling and guidance under the chairmanship of the dean of student welfare. Additional membership shall consist of two faculty members appointed by the academic council, two students selected by the official student government body, and two members of the academic staff to be appointed by the chief administrative officer. Also, the chief administrative officer may appoint to the committee to serve ex officio but without vote such officers as he deems will be helpful to the work of the committee.

(e) This should provide that the dean of student welfare shall foster the establishment of a student center and maintain supervision over it jointly with a committee of students to be selected by the official governing body. The following kinds of services shall be offered in the student center:

(1) Arranging for social and cultural events.

(2) Providing for lounges and a rest area with books, magazines, games, radio, and television.

(3) Providing committee rooms for student meetings.

(4) Maintaining a mimeograph service for students.

(5) Establishing a book and student supplies sales room.

(6) Making tour arrangements for students.

(7) Giving information on travel to foreign countries.

(8) Implementing a student exchange program.

(9) Providing snack bar services.

Section 101. Military Training

Act This should authorize the university to participate in any national cadet corps or officer-training program provided in the country.

Statutes (a) (If the law under which the university establishes a cadet corps program gives the university discretion as to whether it is voluntary or not, this section of the statutes should state which it is.)

(b) (If it is a compulsory program, this section should state that students may be exempted according to rules which shall be developed.)

(c) This should state that there shall be a military affairs committee appointed by the chief administrative officer and advisory to him. Its membership shall include appropriate university administrative officers, representatives of the faculty, representatives of the student government association, and the head of the cadet training unit.

(d) This subsection should provide that the academic council shall appoint a committee to deal with educational policy, course, and curricular matters involved with the military training program and its integration with other programs of the university. The head of the cadet training unit shall serve on this committee ex officio but without vote.

Section 102. Student Labor   **(17.9)**

Act This should provide that there shall be a student work program for the purpose of:

(1) Giving students work experience.

(2) Permitting students to earn a portion of their university expenses.

(3) Accomplishing needed work for the university.

Statutes (a) The dean of student welfare in cooperation with appropriate university officers and deans of colleges shall be responsible for instituting and supervising a student employment and work program.

(b) The chief administrative officer shall appoint a committee advisory to the dean of student welfare on the student employment program. It shall consist of student and faculty representatives and such officers serving ex officio and without vote as the chief administrative officer deems will be helpful to the work of the committee.

(c) Provision should be made for the colleges to adjust and reduce a student's academic schedule when he carries a heavy work load.

Section 103. Placement Services (17.16)

Act This should provide that the university shall establish a placement service for graduates to be under the supervision of the dean of student welfare.

Statutes This should provide that there shall be a university placement council under the chairmanship of the dean of student welfare. Its membership shall include the deans of colleges or their representatives and two students to be selected by the official student governing body. The chief administrative officer may appoint such officers as he deems will be helpful to the work of the council to serve ex officio and without vote.

Section 104. Examinations (12.6)

Act (If the external examination system is to be abolished and the university is to establish an internal examination system, the act should so provide in this section. If the policy is to gradually replace an external examination system with another, this section of the act should provide that the university shall gradually establish an internal system of examination for all levels of academic pursuit, with the examinations to be conducted within each course by the instructor of the course.)

Statutes (a) It may be provided that the instructors shall assign a grade to each student completing a course and shall report the grade to the dean of the college.

(b) In order that examinations and grading procedures may be improved, each college shall make a continuing study of grading patterns and methods of examination used by instructors. Based on such studies, recommendations shall be made from time to time regarding methods of examinations and grading.

(c) College offices shall maintain such grade records and shall transmit such records to the registrar as are required by him.

Section 105. The Alumni

Act (a) This should provide that the chief administrative officer in cooperation with the dean of student welfare should foster the organization of an alumni association, the purpose of which would be to encourage the university and its various activities, to assist in promoting university growth, and to strengthen the university's capacity to render service to the people of the state and nation. The alumni association shall not constitute an authority of the university.

(b) This should state that qualifications for membership in the alumni association should be determined by regulation following recommendation from the academic council.

(c) This should provide that until the alumni association is organized and chooses to elect some other person as secretary, an officer of the university to be designated by the chief administrative officer shall serve as secretary.

(d) Provision should be made that the alumni association shall organize, elect its own officers, and establish its own rules of procedure.

(e) The alumni association shall select registered graduates for membership on the governing body, as provided in Section 35(a)(4).

ARTICLE XI   STATUTES AND REGULATIONS

Section 106. Statutes—Purposes   (1.6)

Act This should state that the purposes of university statutes are to:

(a) Further implement the application of the university act.

(b) Provide necessary procedures and make lines of authority clear.

(c) Cover all matters of concern to the university which are not adequately expressed in the act or which are not expressed at all in the act and on which there should be firm policies and clear procedures.

Section 107. Statutes—Matter to Be Covered (1.1)

Act (a) This subsection should provide that judgment should be exercised in determining the line between statutes and university regulations so that the statutes will not be unnecessarily detailed and so that they will not deal with matters of lesser importance which should be left to regulations.

(b) This should state that the matter to be covered by statutes should be determined by the authorities, university bodies, officers, and faculty members who are concerned in the process of formulating statutes.

(c) This should state that in all cases where the act indicates that further provisions shall be made by university statutes, such provisions shall be made.

(d) It should be provided that the format for statutes shall follow as nearly as possible that of the university act in order that:

(1) The legislative basis for statutes can be more easily determined.

(2) All of the legislative and university statutory material on a particular subject will appear in the same article and if possible in the same section of the act and statutes.

Section 108. Statutes—How Made (5.2)

Act This section should provide that the authority to make, repeal, or amend university statutes rests with the governing body subject to the following provisions:

(a) All proposals involving educational policy or academic matters shall follow regular academic channels, finally coming to the academic council for its action. Proposals originating with the governing body itself having to do with academic matters or educational policy should likewise be first submitted to the academic council. With respect to recommendations coming to the governing body from the academic council involving such matters, the governing body shall either approve or disapprove. If it disapproves, the matter shall be returned to the academic council through the chief administrative officer with an explanation of the governing body's reasoning. The academic council can then again take action in the light of the governing body's objections or can let the matter rest. If desired by the academic council, a joint committee for reconsideration of the proposal may be formed between the academic council and the governing body.

(b) Any appropriate university authority or officer shall have the right to propose statutes or statutory changes.

(c) All proposals which do not involve academic matters or educational policy shall go through regular administrative channels and finally be submitted to the governing body by the chief administrative officer with his recommendations.

(d) The university statutes shall be published and made available to members of the faculty and to anyone else upon request.

(e) If either the governing body or the academic council feels that it is essential to formulate a definition of academic matters and of matters involving educational policy, a joint committee of the academic council and the governing body shall be appointed by the chairman of the governing body to formulate such definitions for approval by the academic council and the governing body. The chief administrative officer shall be included as a member of such committee and may be designated as chairman.

Section 109. Regulations—Purpose and How Made (1.1)

Act (a) This subsection should provide that the purpose of university regulations shall be to augment the university act and statutes by supplying those details and procedural requirements which are not appropriate for the act or statutes. They shall include administrative pronouncements on matters of lesser importance than those included in the act and university statutes.

(b) This should provide that the various officers, authorities, and entities of the university shall develop such regulations as are needed to accomplish their work and to inform the staff and students of the university and other interested parties. Where practicable, these regulations shall be codified so that they can be more readily comprehended and amended. Each authority or body of the university shall develop its own internal operating rules.

Statutes None, unless the governing body wishes to further delineate the regulation-making power and procedure.

ARTICLE XII SUPPLEMENTAL PROVISIONS

Section 110. Annual Reports (7.13)

Act (a) This should provide that the chief administrative officer shall make an annual report to the governing body on the condition, progress, and needs of the university. He shall make such additional reports on particular subjects as the governing body may require.

(b) This should state that officers of the university, deans of colleges, and heads of separate educational units shall submit annual reports on their progress and accomplishments to the chief administrative officer, as required by him.

(c) The chief administrative officer should be empowered to require such additional reports as he deems necessary.

Section 111. Filling Vacancies

Act This should provide that all vacancies except those involving ex officio members on any authority or body of the university should be filled as soon as possible by the person or entity who appointed, elected, or otherwise designated the member whose place has become vacant.

Section 112. Delegation of Authority

Act Provision should be made that:

(a) Authority may be delegated under provisions contained in the university act and statutes.

(b) Any university officer may provide for reasonable delegation of his authority by securing from his administrative superior approval of the general plan of delegation.

Section 113. Staff of Transferred Agencies (3.10)

Act This section should provide that the academic, administrative, and nonacademic staff of agencies or institutions transferred to the university to become constituent parts of it shall become provisional employees of the university. While in such status, they shall be subject to the same conditions of service and other provisions as regular employees of the university, insofar as this does not impair their contractual rights as expressed in any agreement with the transferred agency. Their right to continued tenure, however, following one year of service in such provisional status shall be determined by provisions in the university act and statutes regarding appointments and tenure.

Section 114. Students of Transferred Institutions (3.10)

Act This should provide that when a college or other educational institution becomes a constituent part of the university, its students shall be permitted to continue substantially the same program they were pursuing before the transfer and shall be entitled to a degree from the university following satisfactory completion of the course or curriculum which they were pursuing.

Section 115. Advisory Committees (7.11)

Act This should provide that the chief administrative officer of the university may recommend to the governing body the appointment of consultative committees of interested citizens to advise the colleges, schools, departments, or other divisions of the university. He may also recommend the appointment of a university-wide consultative or advisory committee.

Section 116. University Records (9.16)

Act (a) This should provide that all records which are required to be kept or which are necessary to the discharge of the functions of any office of the university shall be available for inspection by the public under such regulations as may be established by the university, but that health and other records which are determined to be highly confidential may under university regulations be withheld from public inspection.

(b) Students shall be entitled to a copy of their academic record upon request and may be entitled to additional copies under regulations to be developed by the registrar.

Section 117. Patents and Copyrights (13.8)

Act This should provide that the governing body shall develop a policy on patents and copyrights of discoveries or work produced by employees and students of the university and that such shall be expressed in the university statutes.

(a) This should provide that all patentable discoveries growing out of service for the university by either students or staff shall belong to the university and shall be assigned to it. Those made outside the university on the individual's own time are not subject to the university's patent policy. (b) Provision should be made that the chief administrative officer of the university shall appoint a patent committee. The dean of the graduate college, director of university research, and university legal counsel shall be ex officio members of the committee. This committee shall consider patentable discoveries and:

(1) Decide what disposition to make of the discovery in case they consider it to be patentable.

(2) Determine the equity of the staff member or student in the invention and what proportion of the royalties, if any, he should receive.

(c) This should state that the right to copyright a work or to assign it to a publisher normally belongs to the author, but that when a member of the staff is specifically commissioned by the university or one of its departments to prepare a manuscript, such material and all rights to it shall belong to the university. Details regarding administration of the copyright policy shall be handled by the committee on patents. It shall also determine what equity if any the author should have in royalties which may be derived from the copyrighted material.

Section 118. Removal of Difficulties (3.17)

Act (a) This should provide that if any difficulties arise as a result of provisions in the act or statutes, in carrying out the purpose of the act, or in giving effect to any provisions of the act, state government may publish an order removing the difficulty.

(b) This should state that any order published as above shall not be questioned in any court of law on the ground that a difficulty requiring such action did not exist.

Section 119. Interpretation (3.18)

Act This should provide that the university act shall be liberally construed to enable the university to achieve its objectives.

Section 120. Planning for Development

Act This should provide that the chief administrative officer shall appoint an appropriate committee consisting of university officers designated by him, representatives of the academic council, representatives of the student governing body, and interested citizen members from outside the university to make a continued study of future needs of the university and the lines along which it is felt it should develop. Such a committee should be advisory to the governing body, but should report to it through the chief administrative officer.

Section 121. Validation of Proceedings

Act This should provide that the proceedings of any authority or body of the university shall not be invalidated because any unauthorized person was present at a meeting or because there were unfilled positions or vacancies, so long as quorum requirements are met.

Section 122. Separability   (3.18)

Act This should state that in case any part of this act is determined to be invalid or unenforceable, the remainder of the act shall not be affected.

APPENDIX I

Glossary

Academic council. The paramount academic body of a university. It may be called "senate" or by other terms. It includes some ex officio members, professors, and sometimes lower ranks or elected members.

Academic freedom. The right to pursue truth. This right is implied whether or not expressed in the legislation creating a university. Sometimes it is defined in university statutes. The principle should be recognized though adequate definition is difficult.

Academic rank. A designation within a scheme designed to make proper distinctions between staff members in a university based on academic achievement and responsibility and to some extent on experience and ability. Most systems provide for at least three ranks; some for four or five; some for more. Reasonable requirements for moving from one to another and reasonable gradations of salary are to be desired.

Academic staff. In the broad sense, those employed by the university to teach and engage in research or extension work, as distinguished from the administrative staff and officers of the university, and from the nonacademic or service staff.

Act. See *University act.*

Affiliation. The relation of an independent college to a university under which the latter prescribes the syllabuses for courses, conducts examinations, and confers degrees.

Agriculture. In a broad sense, this includes not only farming and livestock production of all kinds but also homemaking, rural social organization, and those industries and businesses engaged in processing, supply, marketing, and other pursuits closely related to production.

Assembly. See *University assembly.*

Authority. A university entity created by act or university statute. Usual ones are the governing body, the academic council, and college faculty councils, boards, or committees.

Board. The governing body. However, the term may be used in connection with other university entities.

Board of studies. The professors and usually some other elected and ex officio members of a college faculty. It deals with college courses and curricula. When used, it generally supplants the college council or a courses and curricula committee.

Bursar. The term may be used to denote the chief financial officer but is oftentimes used to denote an administrative officer under the comptroller whose particular duty is the receipt and disbursement of funds.

Cadet Corps. The student military training component of a university. It is known by various names; in the book the term "cadet corps" or "national cadet corps" is used. This may be a program simply providing the benefits of military training to the student body or it may be a program leading to a reserve commission.

Chancellor. This is usually an honorary title conferred on the governor, premier, or other chief officer of government in the state, country, or province. Sometimes the position is purely honorary; in other situations some duties and powers are included. In India, for example, the chancellor presides at convocations, may be empowered to name the vice-chancellor, has certain rights with respect to the adoption of the university statutes, and may cause inquiries to be made into affairs of the university.

Chief administrative officer. The administrative and educational head of a university. Used in this book in place of president, vice-chancellor, rector, or other terms.

Chief financial officer. The officer in charge of university business operations. Other terms are "comptroller" and "business officer."

College. A large, semi-independent educational and administrative unit of a university containing those departments related to a broad subject matter area. It prepares and recommends candidates for degrees. It may exist apart from a university as an independent institution.

Community development. A term used in some countries, India, for example, to denote the overall extension program being carried on by government. Such a program will include health, literacy, local government, and other things besides agriculture and home economics.

Comptroller. Sometimes spelled "controller," it refers to the chief financial officer of the university. He may be referred to as the chief business officer or a vice-president, or administrative officer in charge of business and finance.

Congregation. The whole faculty body of a university. Sometimes it means a meeting of the university senate.

Consortium. A formal and structured organization of universities to achieve specified common objectives. Membership is voluntary, and member universities retain their autonomy.

Constituent college. A college which is an integral administrative and educational unit of a university regardless of physical location.

Convocation. An assembly of the graduates of an institution; a university function at which degrees are conferred.

Co-opted. Elected or appointed to membership in a body by the body.

Council. See *Academic council.* A term which may be applied also to a college faculty group, an elected student body, an administrative group advisory to the chief administrative officer, or other university units which may be created.

Court. The name used in some institutions for a large governing body from which is usually selected an executive group to manage the affairs of the institution. Some boards of control or boards of management may also be large and actually carry on functions through a smaller executive group. The court may be composed of a variety of people, some from within the university, some from government, and others from private life.

Dean. The chief educational and administrative officer of a college. The term may be used to designate a vice-position to the chief administrative office or the officer in charge of student welfare.

Decree. The verdict and opinion of a court. A government order.

Department. A major academic unit in a college with an administrative head. The department is responsible for teaching, research, and extension in its subject matter area.

Director of extension. In the book this generally refers to the university administrative officer in charge of the extension program for the university. In proper context it may mean the director of the government's program.

Director of research. The name applied throughout this book to the administrative officer in charge of the overall research operation of a university.

Due process. A term stemming from phraseology in the American Constitution. The concept exists in all legal systems, but under different names. As applied to university personnel it means the right to be informed, to have a fair hearing, to employ and be represented by counsel, to introduce testimony, and to appeal to a final authority.

Eminent domain. The right of governmental units and public agencies to acquire necessary land by condemnation.

Examination. This term is used in the book to denote not only the final examination at the end of the course or at the end of an academic year, but also the testing and quizzing which an instructor may do during the course.

Ex officio. Membership on a body by virtue of an office. It implies full membership rights unless expressly conditioned.

Experiment station. A term properly used to denote an establishment for carrying on research and experimentation either of a particular or general nature and at a particular location. In the American land-grant universities the term is used to denote the whole research operation in agriculture carried on by the colleges of agriculture with aid from the federal government and other sources.

Extension. The term used to denote the adult education program carried on, usually by government, for the benefit of rural people. In American parlance the term usually means the extension program in agriculture and home economics carried on by the land-grant universities. This should more properly be called agricultural extension, because the universities themselves engage in a program of extension that includes other areas besides agriculture and home economics. In the book an attempt has been made to use modifiers which will let the reader know what kind of extension is being discussed.

Extension education. A term which, depending on context, may denote the education, ordinarily at university level, of extension workers; the training and education of all extension workers; or the extension program carried out to rural people.

Extension specialist. This term generally refers to one who provides information in usable form and conducts meetings with extension workers, farmers, and others in a particular subject for which he is qualified. Specialists may be on the staff of the university; in some cases they may be at some intermediate level in the national extension scheme. Some may also be at the governmental level. They may be referred to sometimes as "subject matter specialists."

Extension worker. This term usually refers to one who is working with rural people, either in agriculture or home science. Extension agent, village level worker, field worker, and other terms may be used.

Extramural course. A regular university course taught away from the campus or for persons not otherwise enrolled in the university.

Faculty. The academic staff of the university and of its units: college, school, department, division. It includes all who are engaged in teaching, research, and extension, though membership may be limited by definition.

Government. In its less comprehensive usage, the administrative branch as under the British parliamentary system—generally meaning the council of ministers or ministers and secretariat.

Gratuity. An annuity based on years of service and paid to those whose salaries fall below the minimum required for contribution to a pension plan.

Home science. A term to denote education primarily for women in all the fields comprehended by the terms "home economics," "home science," "domestic science," and others.

Hostel. A student dormitory or an accommodation for food and lodging together with some recreational facilities and, hopefully, some planned social program.

Incorporation by reference. Language in a contract or other instrument which makes the language of some other instrument a part of it.

Institute. A unit created in the university to emphasize an area of service or educational activity and generally including several disciplines. It may be either in a college or responsible directly to the chief administrative officer.

Land-grant. A term which has significance only because it has come to be recognized as applying to those institutions formed under the Morrill Act, those institutions receiving initially a grant of land from the federal government and pledged to carry on an educational program which would include agriculture, the mechanic arts, and some of the liberal arts, and whose doors, with support from the state, would be open to the sons and daughters of the working classes giving them access to the higher educational opportunity previously available only to those who could attend the more expensive private schools. The land thus granted was sold and the income used to further the required objectives. Many American universities which are not land-grant universities by this definition nevertheless carry on programs which include public service and a heavy commitment to research, similar to those of the land-grant institutions.

Mandamus. A legal action or writ to compel a public officer to perform his duty.

Nepotism. The employment of close relatives by the same employing unit. Many universities define the degree of relationship and prohibit or restrict such employment.

Ordinance. A government decree or order. The legislation of any public body.

Participant training. A term used to describe the special study and training leave of university staff members who come to American universities with financial assistance under contracts with the United States Agency for International Development.

Perquisite. Consideration other than salary or wages for services performed under contract.

Physical plant director. A term used in American universities, and to some extent in other universities, denoting the administrative officer of a university responsible for grounds, maintenance, repair, upkeep, and frequently for new construction.

Principal. Sometimes used to denote the administrative head of a college, faculty, or other university unit and sometimes to denote the administrative head of a university. For the most part, the word "dean" has come to supplant it.

Pro-Chancellor. A vice position to the chancellor. It is generally honorary and may be bestowed upon a Minister of Education or Agriculture.

Proclamation. An administrative pronouncement by an officer of government empowered to deal with the subject of the proclamation.

Provident fund. A name sometimes applied to a pension or retirement fund.

Provisional body. A group which may be appointed by government to serve in the place of the governing body of a university before the latter is appointed and functioning.

Quorum. The number of members of an authority or other body required to be present at a meeting so that business can be legally transacted.

Recorder. A term sometimes used to denote the officer whose primary duty is the maintenance of student records.

Rector. The term used in Latin-American and several other countries for the chief administrative officer of the university.

Registrar. The university officer having to do with admissions, carrying out the admissions policy, receiving new students, and publishing registers, catalogs, and other information having to do with the educational program. He maintains student records and may be assigned other duties in the university.

Regulations. See *University regulations.*

Rules. The duly accepted meeting procedure and guides for any authority or deliberative body.

Sabbatical leave. A leave granted on full or partial pay to members of the academic staff. It is for the purpose of engaging in scholarly work and can be granted only once in seven years—more or less.

Senate. The chief academic body of a university, generally composed of professors and sometimes of associate and assistant professors and certain administrative officers. There may also be elected members. It deals largely with academic affairs in which its voice is normally quite strong.

Separability clause. A section of an act which states that in case any portion of the act is held to be invalid, such finding shall not affect the remainder of the act.

Statutes. See *University statutes.*

Student union. An organization of students, sometimes federated, which in some countries (Latin America) is the student government organization and in other countries an organization and center for social, cultural, and nonacademic affairs.

Study leave. See *Sabbatical leave.* This may also apply to special leave for study and would not count as sabbatical leave.

Syllabus. Detailed outline of the subject matter in a course. When the external examination system is used, such outlines are published officially by the university.

Syndicate. A large and heterogeneous governing body for a university which generally operates with a smaller executive group.

Tenure. The right of a staff member to continue his employment. Sometimes used to mean "permanent tenure" or an indefinite term.

Tort. A civil wrong for which there is a legal remedy. Negligence is usually the basis.

Trustees. See *Board.* May also refer to those who manage property given to the university in trust.

Union. See *Student union.*

University act. The basic law of the country, state, or province creating the university and making it a corporate entity. The act specifies the general powers and duties of the university and enables it to operate as an independent educational entity.

University assembly. See *Congregation.*

University council. In some institutions this is the governing body. It may have student representation as well as faculty and outside members. In some institutions it is a pseudo-executive group operating at the administrative level and in some ways superior to the university senate, though not normally in academic matters. However, in most institutions it is an academic body comparable to a university senate.

University regulations. These generally refer to internal rules of the university developed in some detail to provide guidance to students, faculty members, and others in using and being a part of the university.

University statutes. These generally refer to the internal laws of the university, made in accordance with and under provisions of the university act; adopted by the governing body of the university; and when participated in, with respect to academic matters, by the faculty of the university, approved by the chief administrative officer and forwarded to the board for its action.

Vice-Chancellor. This is the term applied, particularly in India and several Asian countries, to the chief administrative officer of the university.

Workmen's Compensation Act. A law requiring payment to workmen for injuries received by them in the course of employment. Insurance, a schedule of recovery limits for specified kinds of injuries, and removal of defenses which employers might make if sued are involved.

APPENDIX II

References

Allen, H. R. *Open Door to Learning*. Urbana: University of Illinois Press, 1963. 193 pp. This book, written as a summary and commentary on papers delivered in connection with the centennial of the American land-grant colleges and universities, evaluates their present educational programs and offers suggestions for future expansion and broadening of educational offerings.

Ashby, Sir Eric. "A Contribution to the Dialogue on African Universities," *University Quarterly* (December, 1965), pp. 70-89. This article discusses the pros and cons of the adoption by African universities of various basic concepts and practices of United Kingdom universities.

Brookings Institution, The. *Development of the Emerging Countries—An Agenda for Research*. Washington, D. C., 1962. 239 pp. The papers collected in this publication suggest research which would increase American understanding of the economics, politics, sociology, and psychology of development in the developing countries.

Chambers, M. M. *The Colleges and the Courts, 1936-40*. New York: The Carnegie Foundation for the Advancement of Teaching, 1941. 126 pp.

———. *The Colleges and the Courts 1941-45*. New York: The Carnegie Foundation for the Advancement of Teaching, 1946. 156 pp.

———. *The Colleges and the Courts 1946-50*. New York: Columbia University Press, 1952. 202 pp.

———. *The Colleges and the Courts Since 1950*. Danville, Ill.: The Interstate Printers & Publishers, Inc., 1964. 415 pp. These four volumes plus the publication by Edward C. Elliott and M. M. Chambers, *The Colleges and the Courts*, contain a succinct, well-organized discussion of nearly two thousand decisions of the higher state and federal courts which affect higher education in the United States dating from the early nineteenth century. The authors found Mr. Chambers' writings highly useful in the preparation of the *Legal Base* book. His volumes contain a wealth of information particularly for American universities, but many of the principles can also be applied to problems which arise in universities in the developing countries.

Committee on Agricultural Universities. *Progress Report.* 1962. 477 pp. This report is a compilation of materials including Indian university acts and statutes and drafts of proposed acts and statutes collected by the committee as it counseled persons interested in establishing agricultural universities and worked on the preparation of a model Indian agricultural university act.

———. "First Draft—Model Act for Agricultural Universities in India." (Mimeographed.) 1966. 41 pp. This is the first draft of recommended provisions for an Indian agricultural university act.

Corpus Juris Secundum. Brooklyn, N. Y.: American Law Book Co. This is an American encyclopedia of law.

Duke University School of Law. "Symposium on Academic Freedom," *Law and Contemporary Problems,* XXVIII (summer, 1963), 429-671. This is a collection of twelve scholarly articles on both student and faculty academic freedom in the United States, Latin America, and the United Kingdom.

Eddy, Edward Danforth, Jr. *Colleges for Our Land and Time.* New York: Harper & Brothers, 1957. 328 pp. Dr. Eddy has related the story of the land-grant movement from its beginnings to the present, including the development of the philosophy and program of these institutions.

Elliott, Edward C., and M. M. Chambers. *The Colleges and the Courts.* New York: The Carnegie Foundation for the Advancement of Teaching, 1936. 563 pp. See statement under Chambers, above.

———. *Charters and Basic Laws of Selected American Universities and Colleges.* New York: The Carnegie Foundation for the Advancement of Teaching, 1934. 640 pp. The authors collected and synopsized the charters and basic laws of fifty-one American universities, colleges, and technical schools.

Hannah, H. W. *Resource Book for Rural Universities in the De-*

veloping Countries. Urbana: University of Illinois Press, 1966. 375 pp. This is the senior author's first book about university organization and growth in the developing countries. It deals with establishment, internal structure, and functioning.

Hart, Henry C. *Campus India.* East Lansing: Michigan State University Press, 1961. 217 pp. This is a critical analysis of the early years of the programs instituted by American agencies and universities to assist India in developing higher educational institutions with a commitment of service to the people.

Hughes, Raymond M. *A Manual for Trustees of Colleges and Universities.* Ames: Iowa State College Press, 1951. 178 pp. This book is designed to be an aid to members of university and college governing bodies in the performance of their complex jobs as policy makers.

Jacobson, Sol. "Student and Faculty Due Process: A Study in Contrasts at the City University of New York," *American Association of University Professors Bulletin,* LII, No. 2 (June, 1966), 196-204. This article makes a detailed analysis of the City University's bylaws and shows that while staff members' rights seem to be adequately protected, there is a lack of due process for students.

Liming, O. N. A collection of papers on problems involved in the organization and functioning of Indian agricultural universities. 1965. 132 pp. These papers offer pertinent suggestions and guidelines for the creation and administration of agricultural universities in India

McVey, Frank L., and Raymond M. Hughes. *Problems of College and University Administration.* Ames: Iowa State College Press, 1952. 320 pp. The presidents of two universities have combined their experience and ideas to present a book for use as a guide by university and college administrators.

National Association of College and University Attorneys. *Annual Conference Reports,* 1962 to 1965. Each report is a collection of the papers given at the annual meeting on selected legal problems encountered by American colleges and universities.

National Association of Directors of Agricultural Schools. *Agricultural Education, Investigation and Extension in Mexico—A Preliminary Study.* Monterrey: Publications Department of Monterrey Institute of Technology, 1964. 268 pp. This is the report of a commission which conducted a study of Mexican agricultural education, research, and extension, and incoporated its findings and conclusions into a plan for future development.

Palmer, Archie M. *University Patent Policies and Practices.* Washington, D. C.: National Research Council of the National Academy of Sciences. 1952. 229 pp. This publication is a synopsis of the findings in a survey of patent policies, practices, and procedures in universities, colleges, technological institutes, and professional schools in the United States and Canada.

Scofield, Herbert T. *Final Report on Academic Affairs, North Carolina Contract—AID Peru.* 1965. 25 pp. Dr. Scofield analyzes the progress which the Universidad Agraria at La Molina has made in academic affairs since its inception in 1960.

Smith, Vernon W. *Case Histories in the Control of Student Publications.* 1963. 41 pp. This paper is a compilation of American court cases concerning the control of campus publications in an effort to establish what is being done in campus press control.

United States Code Annotated. St. Paul, Minn., and Brooklyn, N. Y.: West Publishing Co. and Edward Thompson Co. This is an annotated edition of the Code of the Laws of the United States with yearly supplements.

University of Illinois. *Code on Undergraduate Student Affairs.* Urbana: University of Illinois, 1963. 41 pp. This code includes all regulations governing the extracurricular affairs of undergraduate students and their organizations.

———. *Regulations Applying to All Undergraduate Students.* Urbana: University of Illinois, 1965. 30 pp. These are regulations concerning the academic activities of students such as registration, discipline, grades, and scholastic requirements.

University of the Punjab. *Calendar of the University of the Punjab for the Year 1963-64.* Lahore: University of the Punjab, 1963. 294 pp. This is a compilation of the acts, statutes, and regulations of the university.

Weidner, Edward W. *The World Role of Universities.* New York: McGraw-Hill Book Co., Inc., 1962. 366 pp. This publication is based on a study of the international exchange programs of American universities and attempts to indicate the role which universities can play in developing greater understanding among the world's peoples.

West Pakistan Agricultural University. *The Calendar of the West Pakistan Agricultural University, Lyallpur, for the Year 1963-64.* Lyallpur: West Pakistan Agricultural University, 1963. 101 pp. This publication includes the charter, statutes, and ordinances of the university; and examination and degree requirements.

Woodburne, Lloyd S. *Faculty Personnel Policies in Higher Education.* New York: Harper & Brothers, 1950. 201 pp. The author presents an analytical discussion of faculty personnel policies and practices in forty-six American universities and colleges.

APPENDIX III

---

*Institutions from Which Legislation
and Statutes Were Procured*

1. Ahmadu Bello University, Zaria, Northern Nigeria.
   Ahmadu Bello University Law, 1962
2. Andhra Pradesh Agricultural University, Hyderabad, Andhra Pradesh, India.
   Andhra Pradesh Agricultural University Act, 1963
   First Statutes of the Andhra Pradesh Agricultural University (as amended to January 27, 1966)
3. Ataturk University, Erzurum, Turkey.
   Ataturk University Law, 1957
   Ataturk University Act (the 1964 proposed draft)
4. Catholic University of Chile, Santiago, Chile.
   General Statutes of the Catholic University of Chile, 1938
5. Columbia University in the City of New York, New York, U.S.A.
   Charters and Statutes of Columbia University (as amended to February 7, 1966)
6. Cornell University, Ithaca, New York, U.S.A.
   Charter of Cornell University (as amended to July 1, 1962)
   Bylaws of Cornell University (as amended to October 9, 1965)
7. East Pakistan Agricultural University, Mymensingh, East Pakistan.
   East Pakistan Agricultural University Ordinance, 1961
8. Haile Selassie I University, Addis Ababa, Ethiopia.
   Charter for Haile Selassie I University
9. Harvard University, Cambridge, Massachusetts, U.S.A.
   Massachusetts Constitution and Laws providing for Harvard University
   Statutes of Harvard University (as amended to June 11, 1964)

10. Iowa State University, Ames, Iowa, U.S.A.
    Laws of Iowa providing for the Agricultural College, 1858
11. Jawaharlal Nehru Agricultural University, Jabalpur, Madhya Pradesh, India.
    Jawaharlal Nehru Agricultural University Act, 1963
    Jawaharlal Nehru Agricultural University Statutes, 1964
12. Mysore University of Agricultural Sciences, Hebbal, Mysore, India.
    University of Agricultural Sciences Act, 1963
    University of Agricultural Sciences Statutes, 1964
13. Orissa University of Agriculture and Technology, Bhubaneswar, Orissa, India.
    Orissa University of Agriculture and Technology Act, 1965
    Statutes of the Orissa University of Agriculture and Technology, 1963
14. Punjab Agricultural University, Ludhiana, Punjab, India.
    Punjab Agricultural University Act, 1961, and Statutes framed thereunder
15. Purdue University, Lafayette, Indiana, U.S.A.
    Indiana Statutes providing for Purdue University
    The University Code
16. Rural University of Minas Gerais, Viscosa, Brazil
    Law Establishing the Rural University of Minas Gerais, 1958
    Organization of the Rural University of the State of Minas Gerais Decree, 1964
17. Southern Illinois University, Carbondale, Illinois, U.S.A.
    Bylaws and Statutes of the Board of Trustees of Southern Illinois University, 1964
18. Texas A. & M. University, College Station, Texas, U.S.A.
    Civil Statutes of Texas providing for Texas A. & M. University
19. Universidad Agraria at LaMolina, Lima, Peru.
    Peru National Universities Act, 1964
    Universidad Agraria Statutes, 1963
20. University of Concepción, Concepción, Chile.
    Statutes of the University of Concepción (as amended to May 6, 1960)
21. University of Ibadan, Ibadan, Western Nigeria.
    University of Ibadan Act, 1962

22. University of Ife, Ibadan, Western Nigeria.
    University of Ife (Provisional Council) Law, 1961
23. University of Illinois, Urbana, Illinois, U.S.A.
    Illinois Revised Statutes providing for the University of Illinois
    University of Illinois Statutes, 1957 (as amended to 1966)
    General Rules concerning University Organization and Procedure, 1958
24. University of Lagos, Lagos, Nigeria.
    University of Lagos Act, 1962
25. University of Nigeria, Nsukka, Eastern Nigeria.
    University of Nigeria Law, 1961
26. University of the Philippines, Quezon City, Philippines.
    Revised Code of the University of the Philippines
27. University of Udaipur, Udaipur, Rajasthan, India.
    Udaipur University Act, 1962 (as amended by the Rajasthan Agricultural University Amendment Act, 1963, and the Udaipur University Amendment Act, 1964)
28. Uttar Pradesh Agricultural University, Pantnagar, Uttar Pradesh, India.
    Uttar Pradesh Agricultural University Act, 1958
    Uttar Pradesh Agricultural University Statutes
29. West Pakistan Agricultural University, Lyallpur, West Pakistan.
    West Pakistan Agricultural University Ordinance, 1961

APPENDIX IV

Chart on Sources of Authority

This chart is an attempt to illustrate graphically how authority
for the accomplishment of selected university functions is divided
among entities of the university, i.e. the authorities, officers, and
other administrative personnel. Across the top of the chart is a
listing of all the university entities. University functions are listed
down the left-hand side. The authority which an entity may exercise is classified under four headings:

1. Initiates the action
2. Entitled to consider and advise
3. Must approve prior to final authority
4. Final authority

The numbers are used as code designations in the chart for each
of the types of authority.

We acknowledge that the governing body is the final authority
for all university functions, but where it normally delegates its
authority to another entity, we will consider that entity as having
the final authority.

The allocation of functions and authority differs somewhat from
university to university. Nevertheless, a fairly consistent pattern is
evident. We realize that opinions will differ about how some of
these functions are or should be allocated.

CHART ON SOURCES OF AUTHORITY

Entities Involved in the Exercise of the Legal Functions of a University

STATUTES, FINANCE, AND PROPERTY

Functions	Government	Governing Body	Academic Council	Faculties	Selection Committee	Chief Administrative Officer	Deans	Department Heads	Chief Financial Officer	Registrar	Director of Instruction	Director of Research	Director of Extension	Physical Plant Director	Dean of Students	Personnel Officer	Librarian	Manager of Univ. Press	Treasurer	Legal Officer	Others
Formulation and adoption of university statutes	1,4	1,2,3		1,2		1,2	1,2	1,2	1	1	1	1	1	1	1	1	1	1		1,2	
Acquisition of property		1,4				2			2					2						2	
Construction of property		1,4				1,2			2					2							
Management of property		1,4				2								2							
Custody, use, and maintenance of property						4	2	2	2			2	2	3							
Letting contracts		1,4				2			2					1,2						2	
Approving contracts		4				2			2					1,2						2	
Procurement						4	1,2	1,2	2	1,2		1,2	1,2	1,3	1,2	1,2	1,2	1,2			
Supervision of buildings and grounds		4				4	2	2			2	2	2	3	2	2	2	2			

Function											
Allocation of land and facilities for research	4	2	2	1,3	2						
Maintaining security	4	1,3	2								
Purchase and distribution of books	4	1,2	1,2	2	1,2	1,2	1,3	1,2			
Securing university finances	4	3	1,2	2	2						
Formulation of budget	4	3	2	2	1,2	2	2	2	2	2	2
Acceptance of gifts	4	1,3	2	2	2	2[a]					
Administration of gifts	4	2	2	2[a]							
Fixing tuition and fees	4	1,3	2	1,2	2						
Collecting tuition and fees	4	1,2	1,2								
Borrowing funds	4	1,2	1,2	2							
Disbursing	4	1,3	2								
Investing	4	2	1,2	2							
Depositing	4	1,2									
Purchasing	4	1	1	3	1	1	1	1	1	1	2
Accounting	4	3	1,2	2							
Internal auditing	4	1,3									
Authorizing payroll deductions	4	1,3									

KEY: 1. Initiates action   2. Entitled to consider and advise   3. Must approve prior to final authority   4. Final authority
[a] Staff Member Concerned

CHART ON SOURCES OF AUTHORITY (Continued)

Entities Involved in the Exercise of the Legal Functions of a University

Functions	Government	Governing Body	Academic Council	Faculties	Selection Committee	Chief Administrative Officer	Deans	Department Heads	Chief Financial Officer	Registrar	Director of Instruction	Director of Research	Director of Extension	Physical Plant Director	Dean of Students	Personnel Officer	Librarian	Manager of Univ. Press	Treasurer	Legal Officer	Others
STAFF																					
Selection of chief administrative officer	1,4				2																
Removal of chief administrative officer	1,4																				
Establishing appointment qualifications for academic staff	4		1,3	1,2																	
Appointment of officers	4				2	1,3															
Appointment of academic staff	4				2	3	1,2	1,2													
Appointment of nonacademic staff	4					4	2		2	2		2	2	2	2	1,3	2	2			
Removal of staff	4					1,3	1,2	1,2								1,2				2	2[b]

Punishment and censure of staff			1,4	1,2	1,2	1,2	2[b]
Formulation of salary scales	4	2	1,3	2	2		
Establishing staff fringe benefits	4	2	1,3	2			2[b]
Settling employment disputes	4	2	4	2	2	2	2[b]
Acting upon grievances	4	2	4	2	2	2	2[b]
Establishing grades or ranks	4	1,3	1,2				
Establishing tenure policy	4	1,3	1,2				
Establishing part-time service policy	4	2	1,3				
Establishing political office policy	4	2	1,3				
Establishing leave policy	4	2	1,3				
Granting leave	4		3	1,2	1,2	1,2	
Establishing travel policy	4	2	1,3				

KEY: 1. Initiates action 2. Entitled to consider and advise 3. Must approve prior to final authority 4. Final authority
[b] Faculty Committee

CHART ON SOURCES OF AUTHORITY (Continued)
Entities Involved in the Exercise of the Legal Functions of a University

Functions \ Entities	Government	Governing Body	Academic Council	Faculties	Selection Committee	Chief Administrative Officer	Deans	Department Heads	Chief Financial Officer	Registrar	Director of Instruction	Director of Research	Director of Extension	Physical Plant Director	Dean of Students	Personnel Officer	Librarian	Manager of Univ. Press	Treasurer	Legal Officer	Others
ACADEMIC MATTERS																					
Establishing new units	4		1,3	2		1,2															
Establishing new branches	4		1,3	2		1,2															
Establishing institutional standards			1,4	2		1,2															
Establishing admission standards			1,4	2		1,2				2											
Formulating university calendar	4		1,3	2		1,2															
Formulating periods of instruction	4		1,3	2		1,2															
Prescribing courses of study			1,4	3		1,2															
Prescribing methods of instruction			1,4	3		1,2															

Function							
Prescribing syllabi	1,4	3	1,2				
Prescribing examinations and grading system	1,4	3	1,2				
Establishing degree qualifications	1,4	3	1,2				
Certifying for degrees	4	1,3					
Granting degrees	4		1,2				
Establishing patent policies	4	2	3	2		1,3	2
Publishing extension materials		3				1,4	
Organizing and planning research	4	2		2		1,3	
Supervising research programs				1,2	1,2	4	
Organizing and planning extension	4	2		2		1,3	
Supervising off-campus extension programs				1,2	1,2	4	
Administering extramural and correspondence courses				1,2	1,2	4	

KEY: 1. Initiates action   2. Entitled to consider and advise   3. Must approve prior to final authority   4. Final authority

CHART ON SOURCES OF AUTHORITY (Continued)
Entities Involved in the Exercise of the Legal Functions of a University

Functions / Entities	Government	Governing Body	Academic Council	Faculties	Selection Committee	Chief Administrative Officer	Deans	Department Heads	Chief Financial Officer	Registrar	Director of Instruction	Director of Research	Director of Extension	Physical Plant Director	Dean of Students	Personnel Officer	Librarian	Manager of Univ. Press	Treasurer	Legal Officer	Others
Establishing policy on consulting			2	2		4		1,2				2	2								
Establishing physical and military training		4	3	2		1,2															
Supervising libraries							2	2			2	2	2				4				
Formulating annual reports						1,4															
STUDENT AFFAIRS																					
Supervising student organizations									2						1,4						
Supervising student employment															1,4						
Supervising food services									2					2	1,4						
Supervising health services															1,4						

Supervising student housing							2	1,4	
Establishing loan and scholarship programs	4		3	2	2	2		1,3	
Maintaining student discipline	3	2	4	2				1,3	
Supervising alumni affairs								1,4	
Establishing student rights	2	2	4					1,3	2

KEY: 1. Initiates action 2. Entitled to consider and advise 3. Must approve prior to final authority 4. Final authority

APPENDIX V

_____

A Note on Temporary Provisions[1]

Many of the problems facing new or reorganized universities in the developing countries are those which arise while a university is in its infancy and which are normally outgrown as the university matures. This, however, does not make the difficulties any less critical at the time they occur. They may prove particularly embarrassing if no ready solution is available. Many of these problems can be met and solved by temporarily distributing some powers and duties among officers and authorities in a manner different from that provided in the university act.

These temporary problems can be divided into two categories; those arising during the period between the decision to establish a new university and the date it opens its doors; and those arising after the university is officially open but before it becomes a complete functioning unit.

During the first phase, several important tasks must be undertaken with dispatch. The university act must be formulated and guided through the legislature. Following this, the first statutes must be drafted and approved. Then such basic steps as the appointment of key officers and members of the staff; obtaining initial resources; setting up the physical plant; and providing for admission policies, courses, and curricula must be accomplished. Since a full university structure does not exist, these matters cannot yet be handled in the manner provided in the act and statutes.

During the second phase, other tasks must be undertaken— appointments to complete the staff; appointment of the remaining officers; the institution of research and extension projects (even

---

[1] The suggestions contained in this appendix apply to universities before they commence functioning and during the initial "build-up" years. They will not have any importance for many readers, hence their inclusion in the appendixes.

though all officers and advisory committees are not yet functioning); distribution of funds (without the benefit of an established procedure and a full staff); additions to and deletions from the curriculum to conform to the available staff members; securing more funds, equipment, and supplies as needed; and the direction of teaching programs when departments are yet to be organized or are not yet fully staffed. During this period the board members, vice-chancellor, and most officers will have been selected, but not all of them will as yet be fully conversant with their positions and the accompanying responsibilities and duties.

The experience of existing institutions in regard to temporary provisions is rather sparse. Some governments have constituted a development advisory board and appointed a temporary administrator to act in the interim between the adoption of the university act and the selection of the permanent board and chief administrative officer, and have clothed them with extraordinary powers. This is good as far as it goes, but the fact that the board and chief administrative officer are in existence and acting does not mean that the university is fully functioning. Further temporary provisions are needed to assist the key officers and authorities in expediting the operation of the university after it opens its doors.

Granted that a redistribution of powers at the outset is a necessary policy, the questions arising from it are many. What redistribution of powers should be made? How long should such temporary provisions remain in effect? Who will be vested with the power to determine when the temporary provisions shall cease to be in effect—the chancellor, the legislature, the vice-chancellor, the board, or a combination of these?

Following is an outline of the subject matter which might be included in a set of temporary provisions. These provisions are divided into two parts: those necessary for the establishment of the university after the passage of the act and prior to the appointment of the first board and first vice-chancellor (these will vary depending on whether the university is being started anew or is being constituted from an existing institution or institutions); and those concerned with the period after the appointment of the first board and first vice-chancellor and prior to the time when the university is fully functioning.

After passage of the act and prior to the appointment of the board and first vice-chancellor, the initial step is the appointment of a development advisory board. This board will function essentially as a board of control prior to the time when the first board can be constituted. Its membership should include government officials, both state and federal, contract team members, USAID specialists, prominent educators, persons interested in the development of the university, and a temporary administrator. Government officials who will be closely associated with the development of the university need to be included to provide liaison with the government. These will include finance officers, officers from the public works department (or its counterpart) and from the Department of Agriculture. The contract team members should be the chiefs of party from the AID contract teams. USAID specialists will perhaps be the Food and Agricultural Officer and the Chief Educational Advisor. Persons interested in the development of universities may be recruited from the foundations and educational agencies already established in the country. The purpose of a development advisory board is to do all things requisite and necessary for the establishment of the university. This covers a wide area. Any action taken by this board should have the same force and effect as if it had been taken by a regularly constituted board.

The first task of the board is to recommend a candidate for appointment by the governor as temporary administrator if such has not already been done. Major problems which must be faced are the initial financing of the institution and construction of the campus and outlying buildings if the university does not take over existing campuses. The drafting of the first statutes as provided by the university act is another major task. It should be done jointly by the temporary administrator and the board.

Starting with the selection of key officers and deans of the various colleges to be constituted, staff members must be recruited at the same time the university physical structure is being developed. The more quickly these people are selected, the more quickly they can begin to function. The development advisory board also needs the power to establish the following:

Initial courses and curricula.

Departmental organization.

The allocation of subjects to each department.

Academic ranks.

Pay scales.

Qualifications for staff positions.

An initial admissions policy.

An outline of educational, business, and administrative functions within the university.

The initial university calendar showing vacation periods, division of the academic year, and essential dates and procedures.

A grading system including the method of examination and certification for degrees.

A loan scholarship scheme so that students from low income families may be admitted to the university.

The major function of the temporary administrator will be to work closely with the development advisory board, making suggestions when suggestions are needed and carrying out those duties assigned to him by the board. He will be particularly concerned with the establishment of an internal structure and the adoption of the initial university statutes. His powers need to complement those of the development advisory board in such manner that the greatest amount of progress can be achieved.

After the appointment of the first board and the first vice-chancellor, a redistribution of power needs to occur. It is at this point that universities begin to operate in conformity with the provisions of the university act and internal statutes. However, in most cases the university is not able for some time to implement fully all provisions of its act and statutes. Actually, during this stage in a university's development, the chief administrative officer—if he has a strong hand—often tends to disregard university legal provisions to the extent necessary to achieve needed results. This procedure cannot be faulted too strongly when it affords the only means of making progress. However, a problem arises when a university's chief administrative officer is not able or willing to forge ahead on his own. Other university authorities and officers, for example, may demand an inordinate amount of time to consider and pass upon various problems as outlined in the checks and balances system of the university act and statutes—a procedure which may result in unnecessary delay and in the university being unable to take all the essential initial steps.

The Jawaharlal Nehru Agricultural University Act contains a temporary provision entitled "Extraordinary Powers of the First Vice-Chancellor." It states:

The first vice-chancellor shall, for a period of one year from the date of his appointment or for such shorter period as may be determined by the chancellor, have the following powers: namely, a) With the previous approval of the chancellor to make additional statutes to provide for any matter not provided for by the first statutes, b) With the previous approval of the chancellor to constitute provisional authorities and bodies and on their recommendations to make rules providing for the conduct of the work of the university, c) Subject to the control of the chancellor, to make such financial arrangements and to incur such expediture as to enable this act or any part thereof to be brought into operation, d) With the sanction of the chancellor to make such appointments as may be necessary to enable this act or any part thereof to be brought into operation, e) With the previous sanction of the chancellor to appoint committees as he may think fit, to discharge such of his functions as he may direct, and f) Generally to exercise all or any of the powers conferred on the board by this act or the statutes.

This provision is also included in substantially this language in a model act for agricultural universities in India, developed by a special committee appointed by the government of India.

Another example of temporary provisions applicable after the university has begun to function is one entitled "Temporary Arrangement" in the Udaipur University Act. It states: "At any time after the passing of this Act and until such time as the authorities of the university are duly constituted any officer of the university can be appointed by the vice-chancellor with the prior approval of the chancellor to carry on the duties of any such authority. The vice-chancellor may make temporary appointments subject to the approval of the board at the next meeting following the making of such appointments."

Following are some suggestions for provisions to be included in a university act to govern the operation of the university after it has begun to operate but before it reaches the point of "smooth functioning":

1. Vice-Chancellor

   a) The first vice-chancellor should be appointed by the governor and should be chairman of the board. While normally the vice-chancellor is the administrative head only and should not be chairman of the governing body, there are reasons why in the beginning he should be allowed to do more than propose policy and participate in its making. He will be the experienced man in academic affairs and the board will be inexperienced. Many things will need to be decided and carried out quickly if the university is to "get off the ground."

At such stage of the university's development there is not
time for extended debate.

b) The vice-chancellor should be responsible for all academic matters. Those matters which normally fall within the
purview of the academic council and upon which the staff
are allowed full hearing should, in the beginning, be delegated to the vice-chancellor. The purpose of the academic
council is to allow staff participation in the deciding of
academic matters. The need for this is not pressing in the
beginning. The real need is to get a workable program established; later such program can be debated and amended by
the academic council during which time the operation of the
university will not be suspended awaiting its decisions. This
power of the vice-chancellor need not be suspended when
the academic council is first organized. Rather, his power in
this area should extend for some specified length of time.
The vice-chancellor can get help in this area from an advisory
committee composed of his deans and the directors of extension and research.

c) The vice-chancellor should have the power to perform
the functions of officers not yet appointed.

d) He should have an unrestricted power to appoint. At
this stage there is not time to go through a regular selection
process. Such appointments made by the vice-chancellor
should contain a provision that they are for a specified length
of time at the termination of which the contract may be
terminated through the procedures provided in the act and
statutes.

The vice-chancellor's powers in these areas need not be subject
to ratification by the chancellor. The appointment of the first vice-
chancellor will be made with the knowledge that he will hold these
powers for the first two or three years. If there was not faith in his
ability to handle them, he would not have been appointed. Thus,
approval by the chancellor of such things as the constitution of
provisional authorities and bodies, the making of additional statutes, the making of temporary financial arrangements, appointments, and the exercising of other powers is not necessary.

2. The Board

a) Initially, certain positions on the board cannot be filled—

those calling for registered graduates, faculty representatives or student representatives, for example. The board should be given full power to act without these members until such time as they can be regularly selected.

b) The board is the policy-making body. However, it may not be familiar with university policy problems when it is first constituted and might spend valuable time debating them when immediate action is necessary. For this reason, the vice-chancellor needs to be able to lend a strong guiding hand to the board, stronger than at any other time in the university's life. Any action will still be the board's action but it will be guided by decisions of the vice-chancellor as to need and urgency. Such arrangement goes against the principle of dividing policy-making and administration, but practically it is necessary if the young university is to establish itself in a minimum length of time as an effective educational and service institution.

3. Academic council

The purpose of the academic council is to provide staff participation, but staff participation should be postponed until such time as sufficient staff are available and the university can profit from a studied scrutiny of its academic policies and procedures. The responsibilities of the academic council should be handled by the vice-chancellor, who will later present his decisions for study and possible amendment. The subject matter falling in this area will concern such things as admission qualifications, courses and curricula, degree qualifications, and teaching procedures.

4. Colleges

a) The dean will exercise powers within his college as the vice-chancellor does within the university. Initially he will have to make decisions about academic matters. These matters will not be referred through departments until the departments are established and functioning.

b) College faculty bodies will not ordinarily become decision-making bodies until such time as the academic council becomes operative.

The period of time during which such temporary provisions should be in operation presents a real problem. Jawaharlal Nehru

Agricultural University vested the vice-chancellor with extraordinary powers for one year. However, the act was later amended and, with the approval of the legislature, the time was extended for an additional year. Perhaps this decision should lie with the governor rather than with the legislature since he is in position to view continuously the operation of the university and to judge the success of the vice-chancellor in bringing it to full fruition. To give this power to the board would tend to defeat the establishment of a close working relation between the board and the vice-chancellor. To give it to the vice-chancellor would put him in the position of determining when his own extraordinary powers should come to an end.

APPENDIX VI

The Agricultural Experiment Station at the University of Illinois

This statement was made by Dr. M. B. Russell, Director of the Station, to the staff of the College of Agriculture.

THE OVERALL PURPOSE OR OBJECTIVE OF THE AGRICULTURAL EXPERIMENT STATION

To increase our understanding of the phenomena and processes involved in the use of natural and human resources to meet man's needs for food, clothing, shelter, and for his intellectual and cultural growth. In the final analysis, society as a whole is our clientele.

OPERATIONAL OBJECTIVES OF THE AGRICULTURAL EXPERIMENT STATION

1. To keep the Station program responsive to changing needs of agriculture and alert to advances in research techniques and knowledge.

2. To encourage the intellectual and professional growth of the research staff.

3. To stimulate greater participation by Station staff in the intellectual activities of the University-wide scientific community and thereby to utilize more fully the experience and research competence of staff members in other colleges and to relate more fully the work of the Station to the central mission of the University.

4. To develop, on a selective basis, areas of research emphasis that are recognized as "centers of excellence."

5. To encourage innovation and originality and to develop a "can do" attitude with respect to new ideas.

6. To develop means of expanding and upgrading the graduate training aspects of the research program.

7. To create an intellectual environment that is stimulating, exciting, forward looking, and objectively critical, in which existing dogma is continuously challenged and in which innovation and change flourish.

8. To develop an international dimension to the research program.

9. To assist and encourage investigators to more clearly define and

conceptualize problems, to generate, state and test hypotheses, and to seek generalizations and principles of broad significance.

10. To stimulate and facilitate the cross flow of ideas, concepts, and people across departmental and disciplinary boundaries as a means of promoting interdisciplinary problem analysis and research.

11. To assist in broadening and increasing the level of support for research.

NEEDED CHANGES IN EMPHASIS IN THE PROGRAM OF THE STATION

1. An increase in work on social and cultural phenomena and problems of rural society.

2. Greater emphasis to the study of "non-traditional" uses of natural resources.

3. Increased attention to study of phenomena over a wider ecologic and geographic range; the development of an international comparative approach in agricultural research.

4. Greater emphasis on the study of basic phenomena coupled with less emphasis on empirical studies which yield results applicable only to single crops, single class of animals, or specific type of economic enterprise.

5. The transfer to other agencies of those studies consisting primarily of repetitive data collection which provide little opportunity for creativity and innovation.

ACTIVITIES DESIGNED TO ASSIST IN MEETING STATION OBJECTIVES

1. The use of *ad hoc* review committees for new project proposals.

2. Review of research programs in depth including the use of outside consultants.

3. The initiation of funded experiment station projects on foreign agricultural problems.

4. Organization of an interdisciplinary graduate program in cellular physiology, growth, and aging.

5. Support and encourage staff participation in research conferences and similar events.

6. (Omitted)

7. Provide support for research assistantships on a station-wide competitive basis.

8. Give emphasis to the purpose and substantive content of annual reports.

9. Provide funds to bring short-term visiting scientists to the campus.

10. Provide encouragement and funds for staff to work at other institutions to acquire new ideas and techniques.

11. Conversations have been held with department heads in other colleges of the University in an effort to stimulate participation in interdisciplinary research.

12. Provide professional assistance in meeting facilities needs.

13. Maintain a block of uncommitted funds to meet extra budgetary needs that arise during the year.

14. Develop long-range plans for major buildings and for land acquisition and prepare schedules, funding schemes, and decision-making strategy to implement the plans.

15. Make informal visits to various laboratories to learn of current research ideas and needs.

16. Establish and maintain contacts with various granting agencies and keep current information on sources of funds for research.

17. (Omitted)

18. Assist in organization of Center for Human Ecology, the Survey Research Center, and the Center for International Comparative Studies.

INDEX